CIB ASSOCIATESHIP SERIES

LAW RELATING TO BANKING SERVICES

Second Edition

Paul Raby

Series Editor: B Julian Beecham

C.I.B.=Chartered Institute of Bankers.

Pitman

To two of the best
'tears for souvenirs'

Pitman Publishing
128 Long Acre, London WC2E 9AN

A Division of Longman Group UK Limited

First published in 1990
Second edition published in Great Britain 1992

© Longman Group UK Ltd 1990, 1992

British Library Cataloguing in Publication Data
British Library Cataloguing in Publication Data for this title
can be obtained on application to the Publishers.

ISBN 0 273 03966 0

Typeset, printed and bound in Great Britain

Contents

Contents

Series Editor's Foreword

This book is one of the Pitman Publishing series of textbooks which are written to cover the post-Wilkinson syllabi of the four core subjects of the Associateship exams of the Chartered Institute of Bankers (CIB).

The author, Paul Raby, has taught, led revision courses in the pre-Wilkinson 'Law Relating to Banking' subject, and has examined the exam scripts as CIB assistant examiner for the subject for several years. He is a practising banker with 12 years of banking experience, and it shows in his practical approach to the new subject, 'Law Relating to Banking Services', in this book. His style is conversational, in plain English, with humorous titbits to make the subject interesting and readable.

The book starts with no fixed assumptions, and therefore people with no prior legal knowledge will be able to understand the subject. There are many cross-references in all chapters to enable you to achieve an overall picture of the complete syllabus from the book's 19 chapters, most of which contain past exam questions and full answers to assist you with your exam technique. Exam technique is also fully emphasised and explained in the Introduction. Knowing the exam technique, backed-up by a thorough study of this CIB-recommended book, will help you do well under the stress of exam conditions.

There is a comprehensive table of the major relevant legal cases at the front of the book to help you to locate quickly information you need.

I believe that this book, and the series as a whole, will help you establish a well-grounded understanding of the required knowledge and exam technique which will help you do your best in the exams you take.

Good luck!

B. Julian Beecham FCIB
Cardiff

Acknowledgements

I acknowledge that all mistakes, errors and omissions in the text of this publication are my own. However, I would like to express my gratitude to the Chartered Institute of Bankers for their support throughout and for allowing me to use the examination papers and examiners' reports, and in particular to Andrew Laidlaw, Chief Examiner Law Relating to Banking Services, for his assistance and for never refusing to offer his help and guidance whenever requested.

Naturally a project such as this text is never completed by the one person quoted on the cover and I could never have finished on time (almost) without the support, encouragement and love given as generously as ever by my wife during what has been a very difficult time.

Finally, I would like to thank Bolton Wanderers for giving me the relaxation needed and most importantly an excuse to spend some time with someone very special.

Table of cases

Table of statutes

Introduction

Firstly, let me welcome you to this publication and thank you for allowing me to lead you through the Law Relating to Banking Services syllabus in the Banking Diploma of the Chartered Institute of Bankers. I will try to keep you interested and awake, but most importantly, I will try to prepare you for the exam and leave you in a position to pass. The law relating to your job is one of the most important areas of study that you as bankers will undertake. It tells you why you don't accept that cheque crossed 'account payee' into Mr Smith's account and why you cannot give out the balance of Mrs Jones' account over the telephone. Unfortunately it will not tell you why you did not get that promotion, but then again who will?

Each chapter of the book will begin with the syllabus requirements for that topic, underlining the fact that the book is written with the sole aim of preparing you for the exam, and will finish with a fact sheet on that same topic. The fact sheets should be particularly useful at revision time. They cover the most salient points in the chapter and ignore the points that are there as introductory or background material. Also, there will be a selection of longer 'essay type', problem solving questions. Each category of question will have its own answer. It is *essential* that you attempt to answer the questions before you look at the answers. I recommend that you look at the question, read the relevant section of the book involved and then have a break. The whole point of including the question section is that you test your understanding and powers of recall, not whether or not you can copy sections out of the book. Oh, I nearly forgot, in between the syllabus requirement and the fact sheet there will be a lucid and detailed reconstruction of the subject matter of the syllabus. The subject matter will be arranged in a way that (I hope) will be easy to follow with many memory joggers or mnemonics. Unfortunately I cannot make the subject matter any less difficult or the syllabus any shorter, but I can promise that if you do subscribe to my recommendations you will have a good chance, a very good chance, of passing.

I firmly believe that there are two main reasons for candidates failing this exam:

1 *Lack of knowledge*: there is nothing I can do here other than provide you with a text-book which gives you all the information you need to pass; the rest is up to you.
2 *Poor technique*: this I can solve. One question I am constantly asked by students on revision courses is 'How do I pass Law Relating to Banking?', and they are quite stunned when I reply 'you pray', or to be more accurate UPRAY, which is a mnemonic made up as follows:

Underline – the key words and question words. For example if the question refers to registered land then underline *registered*, so that you do not spend half an hour waffling about *unregistered* land. Question words such as *how* and *why* should also be underlined so that you realise that there are two separate questions here and that you do not solely discuss the *how* and never mention *why*.

Principle – state the area of law which the question is discussing. Sometimes the best way to do this is by repeating the question in your own words, for example: 'this question is probing the area of a bank's duty to its customers and the protection available to the paying bank should it be accused of conversion'.

Relate – here the candidate should relate the facts stated in the question to the law in that area. This relation should be backed by authorities, quoting relevant law, be it, for example, statute law (eg. s.60 Bills of Exchange Act 1882) or case law from a case where the facts were similar to those quoted in the question (eg. *Greenwood* v *Martins Bank*).

Answer – answer the question as set, not as you wish it had been set. It is important that where possible you come to a conclusion and if this is not possible you should tell the examiner why it is not.

You – must then check **A** against **U**, that is, check that you have answered the question. If you have answered the wrong question, or only part of the question, you will be able to correct the position there and then.

Note: This format is mainly designed for the problem solving type of question, eg, Advise the bank, what is the position of Albert? etc. For questions which merely ask for a list or a comparison, eg, What are the advantages and disadvantages of a floating charge? then it is sensible to omit the **P** and **R** sections above, but it is still essential to keep a format, and so remember the **U**, **A** and **Y**.

As I said earlier, the whole objective of this book is to prepare you for the exam, and one important factor in this is that you are aware of the format of the paper. The paper will be made up of three sections reflecting the structure of the syllabus. Each section will comprise three questions, the candidate needs to answer at least one question from each section and a total of five in all. Section A will consist of questions on Banking Law and the Customer and Types of Customer; Section B, Cheques, Payment Orders and Payment Systems and Section C, Types of Security.

  I have identified the two main reasons for failure above, and the Examiner has made many comments on these areas, some of which are quoted below:

  'May I emphasise that anyone studying the subject must follow the current syllabus.'

  'There is no objection to any particular style/type of answer so long as there is displayed a process of reasoning, with discussion of the relevant authorities, leading to conclusions of law which are applied to the facts.'

  'I think it would be misleading if an examination at this level encouraged students to go through their career thinking that every question must have a black and white conclusion.'

  'Assistant examiners commented on the appalling lack of basic knowledge.'

  '[candidates] hardly bothered to read the question or to apply their material to the facts given', . . . and so on . . .

Finally, in order to avoid the tiresome 'her/his' and 'he/she', I have used 'his' and 'he' as depicting both the sexes throughout this book. Anyway, here endeth the first lesson. I hope that you enjoy what is to come as much as I have enjoyed writing this book and teaching Law Relating to Banking Services. Good luck!

CHAPTER 1

The banker/customer relationship

Syllabus requirements
- To examine the bank's duty of care and duty to act on mandate (payment of cheques, constructive trustee).
- Duty of confidentiality, particularly in relation to banker's references, Data Protection Act (basic principles, guidelines and data subject rights) and Credit Reference Agencies.

■ Introduction

The nature of the relationship between the bank and its customers is an obvious place to start a book on the Law Relating to Banking. Many questions raise their head and need to be answered, such as:
- What is a bank?
- What is a customer?
- Why should we care?

The last question is perhaps the easiest one to answer; the usual reason is that the bank wants to know if a particular statute applies to a situation that it is in. For example, it is possible for an institution to collect a cheque for someone other than the true owner, yet still claim a form of statutory protection under s.4 Cheques Act 1957 (see Chapter 5). However, to do this the institution involved must be a bank and the other party a customer. So again the questions, what is a bank?' what is a customer?

■ What is a bank?

Unfortunately, this is a largely unanswered question, and it reminds me very much of the search for the missing link. There are bits of evidence here and there but not one concrete definitive item that says 'this is what a bank is'. In the past one has had to rely on definitions such as s.2 Bills of Exchange Act 1882 'a body of persons . . . who carry on the business of banking'. Thankfully, things have improved lately, although not by a great amount. 'What is a bank?' needed to be answered in *United Dominions Trust* v *Kirkwood* (1966), as Kirkwood claimed that a loan to him was unenforceable as United Dominions Trust (UDT) should have been registered as a moneylender under the Moneylenders Act 1906. However, UDT claimed that as a bank it was not compelled to register. Hence the whole crux of the case was whether or not UDT was a bank. In considering whether or not UDT was a bank, the Court of Appeal felt that a bank should:

(i) accept money from and collect cheques for their customers, placing them to their customers' accounts,

✓(ii) honour cheques or orders drawn on them by their customers, when presented for payment,

✓(iii) keep current accounts (or something of that nature) and record debits and credits in them.

In coming to their decision the court also took into consideration the fact that UDT was recognised as a bank within the banking community.

The irony of this case was that UDT did not satisfy all of the criteria above, but after placing a high emphasis on UDT's reputation the Court of Appeal, by a majority, decided that it was a bank.

Surely, you may think, we will find an all embracing definition of a bank in the Banking Act 1979, as amended by the Banking Act 1987. Alas, no. The main aim of the Act was to licence and supervise deposit taking and as such all the definitions referred to in the Act apply only to this one function. However, it does tell us that for an institution to use the name **'Bank'** or **'Banker'** the institution must have a fully paid up equity base of five million pounds, and provide an extensive range of services or a specialist service. There are also a number of other restrictions such as the prudent running of the business and the competence of senior management and directors.

So it can be seen that not one all embracing definition of a bank exists, but that a definition must be sought from applying the facts in each particular case and that perhaps the most important factor is the reputation that the institution holds within the financial community.

■ What is a customer?

Again, unfortunately, there is no single definition of a customer. However, there does seem to be a split between the customer as an account holder and the customer as a user of bank services. In *Great Western Railway* v *London and County Banking Corporation* (1901), it was decided that the mere cashing of cheques over the counter did not mean that the bank had acted for a customer. It was decided in *Barclays Bank* v *Okenhare* (1966), that the opening of an account, even without a deposit, was sufficient. This latter case effectively overruled the decision in *Ladbroke* v *Todd* (1914), which stated that a deposit was necessary. In *Commissioners of Taxation* v *English, Scottish and Australian Bank* (1920), it was decided that the duration of the relationship was not relevant.

Thus the position of the customer as an account holder does not appear to be well established. However, in *Woods* v *Martins Bank* (1959), it was held that the bank owed a duty to a non account holder, to whom it gave inaccurate investment advice, the non account holder being accepted by the courts as a customer.

■ Characteristics of the banker/customer relationship

Debtor/creditor

The main basis of the banker/customer relationship is one of debtor and creditor. In *Foley* v *Hill* (1848), it was decided that where a customer's account was in credit then the bank was in effect the customer's debtor, that is to say that the bank owed the money to the customer. This interpretation, whilst at first glance seemingly unimportant, has meant that banks have been free to deal with their customers' deposits as they have wished (either to lend them or invest them elsewhere). There is one major difference between banker/customer and the normal debtor/creditor relationship, in that normally the debtor (the person owing the money) must seek out the creditor (the person to whom the money is owed) and repay him, but in the banker/customer relationship the creditor (the customer – if in credit) must seek out the debtor (the bank) if he should want his money back. This obviously makes sense otherwise the bank would be forever chasing its customers asking them to take their money back and not to leave it in the bank!

The importance of the *Foley* v *Hill* decision can be appreciated when compared with the alternatives. For example, (i) if the bank would have been adjudged to be holding the funds as an agent of the customer then the bank would need to account to the customer for its action and would not be able to make a profit from the transaction without first informing the customer. (ii) If the bank would have been deemed to be the trustee of the customer's funds then it would be bound by instructions given to it by the customer. (iii) If the bank were held to be the bailee (safe keeper) of the customer's monies then it would not be able to use them at all.

Thus, we see that in relation to the account the relationship between the bank and its customers is that of debtor and creditor. However accounts are not the only service that banks offer to customers and debtor/creditor is not the only relationship that occurs. The relationship can also be that of:

Principal/agent

For example, in the buying and selling of shares or the collection of cheques. Here the bank is acting as the customer's agent, enabling the customer to achieve his desired end result. The bank acquires all the duties and responsibilities of an agent and as such owes a duty of care and must not take a secret profit (for example, the stockbrokers' and bank commissions must be clearly quoted on the sale contract).

Bailor/bailee

This relationship exists in the bank's safe deposit or safe custody services. It has been widely accepted that the courts expect a very high standard of care from a bank when acting as bailee. The bank is not liable for loss, theft or fire damage provided the bank's negligence did not lead to the event. There have been many recent occurrences of loss from safe deposit boxes, some not involving banks. The trend appears to be out of court settlements for undisclosed sums. The banks do not wish to know the contents of the deposit boxes and advise the depositors to arrange their own insurance for items deposited.

Trustee/beneficiary

The most obvious example of this is the bank's trust company funds. However it is also important, in this connection, to read the section on the bank as 'constructive trustee' (see later in this chapter).

As well as the different categories of relationships between the bank and its customer, it is also important to realise the **implied** duties of each party. Once again we refer to case law and in particular to *Joachimson* v *Swiss Bank Corporation* (1921), which clearly stated the **implied** terms of the relationship (for the effect of **express terms** see later in this chapter). As you can imagine from the date of the case it has been severely tested by further cases or statute since, which in some circumstances have modified the terms even further. If there were such a thing as a league table of cases and statutes, then this would probably be at number 3 or 4. When I studied Law Relating to Banking it took four weeks before the textbook arrived and we had to rely on dictation from the lecturer. The first topic we covered was banker/customer and when we discussed the *Joachimson* case I thought that the lecturer must have personally known the parties involved as I thought he had said Joe Atkinson and not Joachimson! I doubt that I will ever forget the name of the case or the importance it holds in the Law Relating to Banking syllabus. The duties and rights of the bank and the customer are as follows:

■ Duties of the bank (rights of the customer)

1. To comply with the customer's mandate. It is important to realise that this duty not only refers to the original mandate completed when the customer opened the account but also various other documents which are interpreted as mandates, including standing orders, direct debits and cheques (for detailed discussion on each of these, see subsequent chapters). However, students must realise that when a bank pays a cheque bearing a forged signature or pays an incorrect amount on a standing order, the bank is in fact acting in breach of its mandate with its customer, and as such leaves itself open to litigation.

2. To inform the customer as soon as it becomes aware of forgery of the customer's signature.

3. To receive money and collect bills (cheques) for its customer's account.

4. To allow the customer to draw his money at the account holding branch and during bank hours. As mentioned in *Foley* v *Hill* (above), the bank is effectively the customer's debtor and this duty is merely the ability of the customer to demand repayment of his debt. *Joachimson* actually refers to a written order, although it was never decided whether or not this was actually necessary.

However, the bank's duty to repay is not absolute but conditional, subject to the following three requirements:

(a) The instruction must be in an unambiguous form, and correctly drawn. If the instruction (be it a cheque or a withdrawal form) is ambiguous, then the bank need not pay as it could possibly be exposed to undue risk, as per *London Joint Stock Bank* v *Macmillan & Arthur* (1918). Examples can include a disagreement between the amount in words and figures although the bank may pay the amount in words; see s.9 Bills of Exchange Act 1882, but need not do so).

(b) Payment must be made in accordance with the mandate, this can mean the mandate completed by the customer when the account was opened (eg, no forgeries of signature, correct number of signatories — two out of three signatures etc.) or in accordance with the cheque as a mandate itself (eg, payee not fraudulently inserted or the amount fraudulently inserted), and no legal bar to payment (eg, insolvency of customer, or customer countermanding).

(c) There must be sufficient funds. Here the things to consider include:

    (i) Whether the balance is made up of cleared funds. The bank has the right to refuse payment against uncleared effects unless it has agreed expressly or impliedly to allow the customer to draw against the uncleared sums: *A.L. Underwood* v *Bank of Liverpool & Martins* (1924).

(ii) If an overdraft facility has been agreed, then the available balance includes the limit on the overdraft.

(iii) If there is an overdrawn balance on another account then the bank can refuse to pay, but if there is a credit balance at another branch the bank can still refuse to pay (see 'combination', later).

(iv) If funds have been paid in to meet a particular cheque (earmarking) then that cheque must be met and payment cannot be refused on grounds of the account being overdrawn: *Barclays Bank* v *Quistclose Investments Ltd* (1970) (see 'appropriation', later).

(v) A recent consideration has been the writing of cheques supported by a cheque card; here the bank has a contractual duty to meet the cheque despite any insufficiency of funds, providing it is drawn in accordance with cheque card rules.

5. The bank promises not to cease to do business with the customer except after giving [No NOTICE TO MRS.] reasonable notice. What is 'reasonable' will vary from account to account, depending on the circumstances and complexity of the account; obviously a greater length of notice will be required for an average business account than an average personal account. In *Prosperity* v *Lloyds Bank* (1923), it was held that a month's notice was not adequate to allow the company to make alternative banking arrangements.

6. The bank undertakes to provide the customer with either a passbook or regular statements. However, in *Tai Hing Cotton* v *Liu Chong Hing Bank Ltd* (1986), it was held that a customer does not have a duty to inspect his statements. Under the Consumer Credit Act 1974 the bank must supply a statement to each party to a joint account unless specifically stated otherwise. [NEVER ADDRESSED TO MRS.]

7. The bank has a duty to keep its customers' dealings confidential but this is not an absolute duty. (For exceptions, see *Tournier* v *National Provincial Bank* (1924), later in this chapter).

8. The bank has a duty of care in its dealings with its customers. There has been much case law in this area and examples of breaches of this duty of care have included improper investment advice *Woods* v *Martins Bank* (1959), and a lack of advice on the completion of a guarantee in favour of the bank *Lloyds* v *Bundy* (1975), although the *Tai Hing* case mentioned above also stated that the details of the *Bundy* case were very unusual and unlikely to be repeated. Section 13 Supply of Goods and Services Act 1982, states that in a contract for the supply of a service the supplier (the bank) has a duty to carry out the service with reasonable care and skill. This will take the form of an implied term. The most common occurrence of the bank's duty of care is in the collection and payment of cheques (see Chapter 10). However, the bank does not have a duty to advise as to the risks associated with one particular collection: *Redmond* v *Allied Irish Banks* (1987).

■ Duties of the customer (rights of the bank)

1. The customer has a duty to draw his cheque in such a way as not to facilitate fraud or mislead the bank: *London Joint Stock Bank* v *Macmillan & Arthur* (1918).

2. The customer must inform the bank as soon as he is aware of a forgery on his account: *Greenwood* v *Martins Bank* (1933). Failure to do so will result in the customer being estopped from denying the genuineness of the instrument.

3. The bank has rights of lien (right to retain), of combination (right to treat a number of accounts as if they were one) and of appropriation (right of placing a credit to a particular debt). For full discussion of each see Chapter two.

4. The bank has a right to make a reasonable commission or charge, in line with contemporary practice in the banking industry. Section 15(1) Supply of Goods and Services Act 1982, states that where there is no express determination of the consideration in return for the service, the party contracting with the supplier (the customer) will pay a 'reasonable' charge. Under s.15(2) what is reasonable will depend on the facts of each case.

■ The bank's duty of confidentiality

As mentioned earlier under *Joachimson*, the bank has a duty of confidentiality in its dealings with its customers. However, this duty is not absolute, that is to say, there are times when the bank can disclose information regarding its customers' accounts. Perhaps the most obvious is when it has its customers' express consent, for example, a letter from a business account customer requesting the bank to supply the customer's accountant with information of his account (eg, copy statements etc.). *Tournier* v *National Provincial Bank* (1924) dealt with the bank's duty of confidentiality when the customer had not given this express consent. The court concluded that there were four instances when the bank could disclose without this express consent:

(i) With the implied consent of the customer. It was decided that there are times when the customer by his own actions implies that he has given his consent for the bank to disclose information on his account. The main example within this category is status enquiries (also known as bankers; opinions). The customer, by giving the details of his account to the enquirer (for example, a credit card company or a supplier), has in fact intended that the enquirer write to the bank to obtain an indication of the credit-worthiness of the customer. A further example of the implied consent of the customer is that a guarantor has the right to know the extent of his liability under his guarantee, which is naturally the balance on the customer's account. It is important to note here that the bank must not disclose any other information (eg, returned items) or it would be breaking its duty of secrecy.

(ii) By compulsion of law. There are certain times when the bank, by its compulsion to comply with the law, must disclose information regarding its customers' accounts. There are many examples of this duty, one of the most recent being the Drug Trafficking Offences Act 1986. This legislation states that where the bank 'suspects' or knows that its customer is trafficking, has trafficked, or has benefited from trafficking in drugs, then the bank commits an offence if it retains or controls the proceeds or places them at the disposal of such a person (s.24). No offence is committed if the 'suspicion' or belief is communicated to the authorities as soon as possible. No such disclosure would be treated as a breach of the bank's duty of non-disclosure. Also in *Holtham and Another* v *Commissioner of Police* (1987), it was decided that 'suspicion is a state of surmise where proof is lacking. It is not to be confused with the provision of proof.' In a practical situation I have been approached by the police for disclosure, and the police have quoted the above statute. When asked why they suspected that the customer was trafficking in drugs, I was informed that they had found drugs on her person. Being a basically honest person I stated that they could have been planted on her; the police replied that the customer was naked at the time. Needless to say I felt that this was sufficient to make me suspicious too, and I disclosed the information the police requested.

The Prevention of Terrorism Act 1989 places similar duties on a bank, but obviously for transactions where a terrorist connection is suspected. Another example of disclosure by compulsion of law is taxation. Under the Taxes Management Act 1970 banks can be compelled to disclose interest paid, securities held and other information to the Inland Revenue. Also under the Bankers' Books Evidence Act 1879, a bank may be compelled to produce its books in legal proceedings to which it is a party. The Act has been extensively tested and we have the following position:

(a) Section 3 states that duly authenticated copies are totally acceptable.
(b) Section 9 (as amended by the Banking Act 1979) includes ledgers, day books, cash books, account books, used in the ordinary course of business of the bank, whether in writing, magnetic tape, microfilm or any other mechanical or electronic system (in an attempt, no doubt, to cover any future innovations). *Barker* v *Wilson* (1980) confirmed that micro-filmed records were included. However, in *Williams* v *Barclays Bank* (1987), it was decided that the bank was not compelled to produce copies of deposit slips and cheques as these were not covered under the statute.
(c) Section 6 states that even if the bank is not a party it may, in special circumstances, still be compelled to disclose. For example, where the proceeds of a fraud are passed through the bank account, then production of the statement relating to the account is essential. However, an order made under the Police and Criminal Evidence Act 1984 can compel the bank to produce **all** its records relevant to its customer including interview records and vouchers. In *Barclays Bank* v *Taylor* (1989), it was held that not only was the bank justified in releasing the information under the above Act, but would also be justified as disclosing 'in the public's interest' (see (iv) below).
(d) The authorities must have a reason for the information and cannot be on a 'fishing expedition' hoping that the information provided will be of benefit to the prosecution: *R* v *Nottingham Justices ex parte Lynn* (1984).
(e) Where the court action is against a wife the authorities can also seek disclosure of the husband's account: *R* v *Andover Justices ex parte Rhodes* (1980). This is obviously due to the possibility of the wife passing transactions through her husband's account to deceive. One can only assume that the same could be said of a wife's account should her husband be involved in proceedings.

However, should a bank be served with an order under the Police and Criminal Evidence Act (known as a 'PaCE order'), then the bank may have to surrender all relevant documentation including the correspondence file, if requested. It is for this reason that PACE orders are now very common, whereas orders under the Bankers' Books Evidence Act are relatively rare.

Other examples of disclosure under compulsion of law can include writs of sequestration (for example, recent industrial disputes and writs being made against the trade unions involved), garnishee orders (a garnishee order is a remedy open to a judgment creditor: the order nisi attaches money belonging to the judgment debtor – the customer, in the hands of a third party – the bank) and certain powers under the Companies Act, Financial Services Act, Insolvency Act and Criminal Justice Act (via the Serious Fraud Office).

(iii) Where disclosure is the bank's interest. The most obvious example in this category is where the bank is suing for the recovery of a debt. Naturally, in order to sue the bank must state the details of the debt (eg, amount, security, etc.). Another example is to protect the bank's reputation; in *Sunderland* v *Barclays Bank* (1938) it was held that the bank was justified in disclosing to the customer's husband that his wife was a gambler. This was because the husband was attacking the bank's reputation, as it had returned his wife's cheques and he disagreed with the bank's decision. A contributory factor in this case was that the customer had actually handed the telephone to her husband during the conversation with the bank regarding the returned items.

(iv) Where disclosure is in the public's interest. Again there is an obvious example here, and that is where the customer is trading with the enemy in a time of war: *Weld-Blundell* v *Stephens* (1920). Also where the bank *knows* that the account is being used for a criminal purpose then the bank should disclose, where it merely *suspects* then it should not. The problem here is the distinction between 'knowing' and 'suspecting' and one can only return to *Holtham and Another* v *Commissioner of Police* (1987) (above).

∎ Data Protection Act and the banks

The main aims of this Act were

● to give individuals the right to know what was stored on computer about them, enable them to obtain copies of the information and have it corrected, and obtain compensation if necessary. All institutions that use or process information on computers must register the fact with the Data Protection Registrar (referred to as the Registrar). There are four main exceptions to registration, and these are:

(a) calculating pay and pensions;
(b) keeping accounts or records or purchases and sales;
(c) mailing lists; and
(d) preparing the text of documents (eg, word processors).

An individual may apply to the holder of the computer based information for a copy of the information held on him; this will ususaly be subject to a nominal charge. If the information held is incorrect then the customer can apply to the Registrar or the courts to have the incorrect information corrected or erased. If the courts see fit then the customer could also seek compensation. Naturally the customer would need to prove that he had suffered damage as a result of the incorrect information held. Users of computers are not, by this legislation, allowed to hold such personal information as opinions on race, sex, politics or religion. Also, only such details of a customer's physical and mental health should be stored as are relevant to the relationship between the bank and its customer. Thankfully for banks most information on customers is presently held in personal files or other paper based systems and customers are not able to insist on sight of these documents under the Data Protection Act. However, many banks are moving towards greater use of computer-based systems, releasing storage space and staff to be used in greater cost-effective, customer contact, marketing roles. Hence, it is important that as technological advancements are made, the banks keep in mind the reasons and possible remedies under the Data Protection Act.

● to ensure that information given is not abused. For example, if the bank decides to send a mail shot to its customers within a certain income band, with the view to selling mortgages, then this is acceptable. However, to disclose this information to its subsidiary in an attempt to sell these same people pension plans is not acceptable.

It is the disclosure of the information that is in breach of the Act, as is failure to inform the customer at the outset as to the reason for obtaining the information.

∎ Credit reference agencies

Under the Consumer Credit Act 1974 a credit reference agency is defined as 'a person carrying on a business comprising the furnishing of persons with information relevant to the financial standing of individuals, being information collected by the agency for that purpose'.

If a bank uses a credit reference agency in the assessment of lending or account opening decisions, then this fact must be disclosed to the customer. The customer then has the right to know the name and address of the agency used, to obtain a copy of the information registered against him, and if the information is incorrect, can have the information corrected or erased. Also, at the court's discretion, the customer can seek compensation if damage can be proved; for this purpose refusal of credit could be deemed damage.

■ Status enquiries (bankers' opinions)

Status enquiries (also known as bankers' opinions) are confidential enquiries from one bank to another. The enquiring bank will be doing so for its customer and the contents of the reply will be passed back to its customer. The enquiry will usually be on the credit-worthiness of the receiving bank's customer. The receiving bank owes a duty to both its own customer and to the enquirer. These duties are as follows:

Duty to customer

(i) **Confidentiality.** We have already discussed status enquiries in the context of the bank's ability to disclose details of its customer's account *Tournier* v *National Provincial* (1924). It is accepted that the customer gives his implied consent, knowing that by giving his bank details an enquiry will be made.

(ii) **Libel.** Banks are very careful in the replies they give, in order that they do not commit the tort of libel (written defamation of character). Replies such as 'respectable and trustworthy', or 'should prove good for your figure and purpose' are typical replies, in that they disclose no information at all regarding the customer's account. It is the interpretation given to the reply by the enquirer that is important and for this reason it makes a claim for libel unlikely.

Duty to enquirer

(i) **Negligence.** In *Hedley Byrne and Co Ltd* v *Heller and Partners Ltd* (1964), it was established that a bank has a duty of care to the enquirer when replying to status enquiries. However, in this case the bank had included a disclaimer of liability clause which protected it from prosecution. Since the introduction of the Unfair Contract Terms Act 1977 (see below), it has been a topic of discussion as to whether or not such a disclaimer would stand the test of reasonableness required by that act.

(ii) **Fraudulent misrepresentation.** In *Derry* v *Peek* (1889) it was held that a fraudulent misrepresentation is a reply given knowing it to be false or not caring whether it is false or not. Also, the intention must be that it be acted on and the recipient must act on it. However, s.6 Statute of Frauds Amendment Act 1828, states that liability for a fraudulent misrepresentation can attach only where the document is in writing and signed. Hence, banks do not sign status enquiry replies and always supply a disclaimer of liability.

In an Australian case, however, (which is not binding on English courts, but can be persuasive when courts are coming to their decision) it was held that a bank was guilty of fraudulent misrepresentation despite the reply not being signed and a disclaimer being present. The facts of this case are a little unusual in that the customer was over his overdraft limit and the bank knew that the customer was in financial difficulty yet still gave a favourable reply. The case was *Commercial Banking Co of Sydney* v *R H Brown* (1972) (if you can remember it was an Australian case then the name of the case should easily be recalled).

Banks will also attempt to avoid the liability incurred on credit reference agencies under Consumer Credit Act 1974 by specifically excluding the Act. If you examine your bank's status enquiry replies you will note at the foot of the reply 'the bank is not a credit reference agency under s.145(8) Consumer Credit Act 1974', or similar wording.

◢ Effect of express terms on the banker/customer relationship

There are many express terms which are now appearing in the relationship between the banker and his customer. One of the most obvious is the restriction on the signing instructions on the account; for example banks would usually expect on a joint account that either customer would have the power to sign cheques etc. However where the customers stress that they wish both signatures to be present then the bank is bound by this instruction, even if it is unable to trace the original mandate, as in *Catlin* v *Cyprus Finance Corporation (London) Ltd* (1982).

Where the bank attempts to alter the mandate between itself and its customer the bank must be able to prove that the customer has read the new condition or has otherwise agreed in writing to the alteration. In *Burnett* v *Westminster Bank Ltd* (1966), the bank inserted a new clause in a cheque book stating that cheques must be applied to the account expressed on the cheque. The customer had two accounts at different branches (say branch A and branch B) and altered the sort code on the magnetic strip from branch A to branch B, in ink; he later attempted to stop the cheque and informed branch B, the cheque (via the magnetic strip) being presented at branch A. According to the new instruction he should have informed branch A. The court held that the variation was not effective, but if the cheque book had been the first cheque book to be issued then it might have been effective.

In a Privy Council case (a Hong Kong case decided by the Privy Council, and hence indicating that English courts would react in a similar manner), *Tai Hing Cotton Mill Ltd* v *Liu Chong Hing Bank Ltd and others* (1985), it was held that the variation had to be 'brought home to the customer' and that a 'clear and unambiguous provision is needed'. In this case the bank failed to have the customer bound by a duty to check its statements and to inform the bank of any irregularities. The court reaffirmed that the customer has no duty to inspect his bank statements.

The Unfair Contract Terms Act 1977, states that any terms agreed must pass the test of 'reasonableness'. That is to say that if they are unreasonable, they are unemforceable. Examples of this legislation affecting banks could be disclaimers of liability (eg status enquiries) and express conditions; in fact is is possible that had the *Tai Hing* case not failed on the grounds that it did, it might well have failed the test of reasonableness under the Unfair Contract Terms Act. The aim of the Act (UCTA) is to protect the weaker party (customer?) when entering into a contract with a much stronger party (bank?).

The bank as a constructive trustee

The concept of constructive trusteeship arises where the bank knew or should have known that the money deposited with it was held on trust. It was held in *Re Gross (ex parte Kingston)* (1871) that an account styled 'police account' should have acted as notice that the funds were held on trust. If the bank has no notice (either actual or constructive) of the trust it will treat the monies as belonging absolutely to the customer: *Thomson* v *Clydesdale Bank* (1893). This is obviously of great benefit to banks, for otherwise banks would have to enquire about the origin of any funds paid into any account just in case it could be held on trust.

In *Barnes* v *Addy* (1874) a classification was made which created two types of constructive trust, these being:

(a) **'knowing assistance'** – the giving of knowing assistance to a dishonest trustee. This can include any act which assists the dishonest trustee (except the receipt of funds) and would usually include an act such as dishonesty, lack of integrity or morally reprehensible behaviour to such a degree that the bank might be said to have become a party to the dishonesty. In knowing assistance cases the bank's liability can include all losses to the trust fund caused by the dishonest trustee, regardless of whether or not the monies passed through the bank account.

(b) **'knowing receipt'** – the knowing receipt of and dealing with trust monies. Knowing receipt requires only the lack of integrity, and as such the bank's liability is reduced to monies which actually pass through the bank account.

In *Baden Delvaux & Lecuit* v *Société Générale S.A.* (1983) a number of problems were quoted in which the bank could be deemed to be at fault when faced with a constructive trustee (knowing assistance) situation:

(i) actual notice (where the bank is aware of the breach of trust);
(ii) shutting one's eyes to the obvious for fear of discovering unpleasant facts;
(iii) intentionally failing to make reasonable enquiries;
(iv) inferred notice, where the bank is aware of the facts, from which an honest and reasonable man could infer there had been a breach of trust, but the bank did not; and
(v) a failure to enquire in circumstances amounting to gross negligence or ordinary negligence.

It is possible for a bank to be guilty of knowing receipt, but innocent of knowing assistance (due to the lack of fraud or dishonesty): *Belmont Finance Corporation Ltd* v *Williams Furniture Ltd* (1980). Also in *Lipkin Gorman* v *Karnaple Ltd* (1986), it was stated that 'in knowing receipt cases fraud is irrelevant, the recipient will be liable if with want of probity (integrity) on his part he had actual or constructive notice that the payer was misapplying trust money. In knowing assistance the stranger to the trust must be proved to know of the fraudulent scheme of the trustee, or shut his eyes to the obvious, or to have wilfully and recklessly failed to make such enquiries as a reasonable and honest man would make'. This indicates the high standard of care expected of the banks and the importance of constructive notice and the fact that a lack of knowledge of the fraud will not protect the bank in knowing receipt cases.

Where a bank benefits from the receipt of funds (for example the repayment of an overdraft) the bank should enquire as to the origin of the funds and the lack of enquiry would make the bank liable under *Baden Delvaux*, above.

◼ Quistclose trusts

In *Barclays Bank* v *Quistclose Investments Ltd* (1970) it was held that where funds were paid in to be applied to a particular purpose then that purpose must be met and the funds were not available for combination (see Chapter two) with other (debit) accounts. The funds were held to be on trust for the purpose stated, in this case a dividend, and not available for general use by the company or their bankers. The purpose quoted could be vague, but still effective in creating a trust as per *Re Northern Developments (Holdings) Ltd* (unreported).

◼ Safe custody

As most of you will be aware, a common service offered to customers is that of safe custody, whereby the bank holds items in safe keeping for the customer, returning the items upon the customer's request. However, there are risks involved:

1. Conversion. This risk would occur when the bank releases the parcel without the customer's consent, as in *Langtry* v *Union Bank of England* (1896).
2. Negligence. If the item held is damaged or lost whilst in the bank's possession the bank will be liable if it has been negligent. It is important to realise that if there is no negligence there is no liability. The bank will normally try to limit its liability by a specific clause in the safe custody agreement. However, this must pass the test of reasonableness as stated in the Unfair Contract Terms Act 1977.

◼ Code of Banking Practice

Following much press comment and the publication of the Jack Report (Report on Banking Services produced by the Review Committee under the chairmanship of Professor R B Jack) the banks have now produced a Code of Banking Practice. At present the code is a voluntary code of conduct although it has been mooted that should the code be interpreted as insufficiently protective of the customer's interests, a statutory code will be introduced.

The main points of the code are:

● where a multifunctional card is offered to a customer, the customer can refuse to be issued with a Personal Identification Number (PIN) thus removing the ATM usage of the card.
● information cannot be passed to other members of the Bank's group of companies (eg an insurance subsidiary) if the customer's consent is not held or implied.
● customer's liability on stolen or fraudulently used plastic cards, including credit, charge, payment or ATM cards is to be limited to a maximum of £50. There is an exception to this rule where the misuse is due to the customer's negligence. As you will see later in the syllabus, negligence is very difficult to define. For example, to write your PIN on the card is obviously negligent, but the scrambled number written in your diary may be open to interpretation.
● customers will not incur charges if the only reason for being charged is a previous charge (eg an immediate charge taking an account overdrawn and for this reason *only* periodically being charged at the end of the month/quarter).

Some banks have taken the code one step further, for example TSB have undertaken that all customers will be informed in advance of a charge being debited to their account. Girobank already implement this practice. Barclays and National Westminster offer their customers a change in PINs.

◢ Banking Ombudsman

This is a free service offered to bank customers who find themselves in dispute with their banks. The scheme is actually financed by the banks themselves. The cost, in the region of one million pounds, is met by the 17 member banks. The customer must first of all complain to the bank and exhaust all normal channels before the Ombudsman will agree to accept the case. Awards up to £50,000 can be made. By far the greatest number of complaints involve ATMs in general and particularly 'phantom' withdrawals. Recently charges disputes have been increasingly common.

FACT SHEET

Banker/customer relationship

Introduction

1. What is a bank? s.2 Bills of Exchange Act 1882
   UDT v *Kirkwood*, 3 conditions plus 'reputation'
   Banking Acts 1979, 1987 restrictions

2. What is a customer?
   - account holder *GWR* v *London and County*, cashing of cheque insufficient
     Barclays v *Okenhare*, account holder no deposit necessary
     Commissioners of Tax v *English, Scot & Aust Banks*, duration irrelevant
   - other services *Woods* v *Martins*, negligent investment advice

3. Why is it important? Statutory protection (eg s.4 Cheques Act 1957)

Characteristics

(a) debtor/creditor *Foley* v *Hill* – importance and advantages to bank
(b) principal/agent – when and what is significant
(c) bailor/bailee – when and what duties owed (customer to arrange own insurance)
(d) trustee/beneficiary – when?

Implied terms

Joachimson v *Swiss Bank*

Duties of bank – (rights of customer)	especially compliance with mandate, duty to repay, notice of closure, confidentiality, duty of care.
Duties of customer – (rights of bank)	especially *London JSB* v *Macmillan & Arthur*, estoppel, lien, appropriation & combination.

Tournier v *Nat Pro*, disclosure without express consent
  (i) implied consent, status enquiries
  (ii) compulsion of law, Drug Trafficking Offenses Act, Bankers' Books Evidence Act
  (iii) banks interest, suing the customer
  (iv) public interest, trading with enemy

Data Protection Act

Only applies to information held on computer, registration, copies to be available, possible compensation. Duty to ensure information held is not abused.

Credit reference agencies

Customers' right to know, correction or removal & possible compensation.

Status enquiries

(i) duty to customer, confidentiality, libel

(ii) duty to enquirer, negligence, fraudulent misrepresentation

Effect of express terms

Catlin v *Cyprus Finance Corp.*, *Burnett* v *Westminster Bank*, *Tai Hing* and Unfair Contract Terms Act.

Bank as constructive trustee

Identifying monies on trust *Re gross, Thomson* v *Clydesdale) Barnes* v *Addy*, knowing assistance and knowing receipt (especially different extent of liability). *Lipkin Gorman Quistclose* trusts – funds applied to particular purpose.

Code of Banking Practice

Banking Ombudsman

This is one of the more basic areas of the syllabus and as such the questions tend to be relatively straightforward. For this reason a past examination question is not supplied but a question from the specimen examination paper produced by the Chartered Institute of Bankers, along with a brief 'sketch' answer is reproduced.

Question

A bank's current account application form asks for a number of personal and financial details. What legal principles govern the use and disclosure of this information by the bank?

Key words

legal principles   *use and disclosure*

Sketch answer

Bank has a duty to maintain confidentiality (*Joachimson* case), unless specific authority is held. Exceptions are detailed in *Tournier* case. Special emphasis should be placed on the recent increase in statute law concerning release of information, with bank being liable if it does not disclose in certain situations (Drug Trafficking Offences Act, Prevention of Terrorism Act, etc).

Other statutes could include Bankers' Books Evidence Act and Police and Criminal Evidence Act, advantages and disadvantages (to authorities and banks) of each.

Computer based information must be available for inspection: Data Protection Act. And must not be abused.

CHAPTER 2

Appropriation, combination and banker's lien

Syllabus requirements
- Appropriation (the rule in *Clayton's Case*).
- Rights of set-off and banker's lien.

▮ A. Appropriation

The customer's right of appropriation

Appropriation is the choice of applying a particular deposit to a particular debit. This is of relevance where the customer (the debtor) has more than one debt with the bank (the creditor). The first right of appropriation is the customer's; that is to say if a customer makes a deposit, then the first choice of where that credit is to be applied can be made by the customer: *Simson* v *Ingham* (1823).

   The appropriation should be made at the time of making the deposit. An important point to make here is that the customer can apply the credit to pay a cheque which has only recently been drawn and not yet been debited to the account. Hence, it is possible for a customer to have an overdrawn account, write a cheque, deposit funds to the account and demand that the cheque just written (or even about to be written) be paid when presented, despite taking his account into an overdrawn (or further overdrawn) state. The bank would have to act on the customer's instructions. This process is called 'earmarking'.

   Even if no specific appropriation has occurred it is still possible for the customer to do so by a course of dealings or other circumstances, eg deposit of exact amount of cheque, but a mere entry in his own books is not sufficient: *Manning* v *Westerne* (1707).

The bank's right of appropriation

If the customer does not appropriate then the next right of appropriation is the bank's. The bank will obviously wish to appropriate to its debts in such a way as is advantageous to itself. For example:

 (i) Appropriation can be made to a statute-barred debt, that is a debt which is not legally enforceable under the Limitation Act 1980.

 (ii) The credit can be placed to a debt in a sole name, clearing that debt, leaving the bank to enforce a debt in joint names.

(iii) Under the Insolvency Act 1986, in an insolvency (personal or corporate) the creditors (people owed money by the insolvent party) will be paid in order of priority. Hence, if a bank is concerned that the customer may be insolvent (or may become insolvent), it would be prudent to appropriate any credits received to a debt that ranks low on the list of priorities. This would leave the bank with an improved chance of receiving full payment. An example of such an action would be applying a credit received to an unsecured overdraft (which is at the bottom of the list of priorities) and not to a wages account (a preferential debt, near the top of the list). However, appropriation cannot be made to an illegal debt.

Current accounts and appropriation

As can be seen from the above it is important to realise that an overdrawn balance on an account is not merely one debit balance (as, say, a loan is) but it is a series of debit balances, represented by each individual debit item. For example:

CURRENT ACCOUNT J TURNER & A JOSEPHS

DATE	DEBIT	CREDIT	BALANCE
1 Jan	300		£300 DR
3 Jan	400		£700 DR
5 Jan	100		£800 DR

As can be seen, the £800 debit balance on the account on 5 January is made up of the three separate debit balances made on 3 and 5 January.

The default rule of appropriation

Where neither the debtor nor the creditor appropriates, then the default rule of appropriation will apply, known as the rule in *Clayton's Case* (*Devaynes* v *Noble*) (1816), which states that where no prior appropriation has taken place then the credits will be applied to the debits in strict chronological (date) order. The rule is out of particular importance to the bank when lending is on current account. Thus, if the account of J Turner & A Josephs (above) were to continue operating, as shown below, with a credit of £300 being made to the account on 10 January and neither the customer nor the bank appropriated the funds to a particular debt, then under *Clayton's Case* the credit would be applied to the oldest debt, being the £300 debited on 1 January.

DATE	DEBIT	CREDIT	BALANCE
10 Jan		300	£500 DR
12 Jan	200		£700 DR

Under normal circumstances this would be fine and of little consequence to the bank. However, if something should happen in between 5 and 10 January to cause any further debt to be unenforceable (say the death or insolvency of one of the parties or notice of second charge) then out of the total debt of £700 outstanding on 12 January only £500 would have been enforceable against the estate of the survivor (or solvent) party or against the original security.

How to overcome the effect of *Clayton's Case*

(a) As can be seen above, one of the effects of *Clayton's Case* is that if a party to an account dies or becomes insolvent then the bank could (if it allows the account to continue) be left with a debt unenforceable against the estate of the deceased or insolvent party. As the rule applies only to debits and credits within the same account, the simplest way of overcoming the rule is by opening a separate account on notice of death, insolvency etc. For example, on the above account, if a separate account had been opened on 9 January, the total debt of £800 would have been enforceable and the separate account would have a credit balance of £100.

(b) It is possible to defeat the operation of *Clayton's Case* by inserting a clause expressly excluding the rule. This is a typical clause in a bank's security forms and protects the bank from the rule operating against the bank should anything occur which could determine the liability of the guarantor (eg, death). The validity of such a clause was confirmed in *Westminster Bank* v *Cond* (1940).

Examples of *Clayton's Case* operating to the bank's disadvantage

(i) Failure to stop the account on notice of the death or insolvency of a joint account holder, or partner of a partnership account, will mean that subsequent credits will be applied to (and clear) the earliest debits to the account, for which the deceased or insolvent party is liable. Any other debits to the account will not be enforceable against that party. Hence, on an active current account it is possible that the liability of the party will soon be eroded and the possibility of the bank retrieving its funds could be seriously diminished (especially if that party is relatively wealthy and the remaining party not so).

(ii) Notice of subsequent charge. Where the bank has a legal charge (see Chapter 13) and receives notice of a subsequent charge, then any further borrowing will rank behind the interest of the second charge holder. This is obviously of great consequence to the bank where the borrowing is on overdraft. As seen above it is possible to view debits to an overdrawn account as separate advances. Hence, if a bank is lending on overdraft and receives notice of a subsequent charge it should stop the account and place all entries to a separate account to be maintained in credit or supported by additional security. Failure to do this may result in the whole of the debit balance ranking after the interest of the subsequent charge holder: *Deeley* v *Lloyds* (1912).

Rule operating in bank's favour

It is normal for the rule to operate to the bank's disadvantage, but there is one main example of the rule operating in the bank's favour. Where a bank takes a floating charge (see Chapter 18) and the company is insolvent at the time of the charge, or becomes insolvent at the time of giving the charge, and the company is wound up within 12 months, the charge is invalid except for new monies lent: s.245 Companies Act 1985. Naturally, in this instance *Clayton's Case* will act in the bank's favour with credits clearing the unsecured debt and new debits creating a new secured debt.

Exceptions to the rule

(a) **Trust monies.** If monies held on trust are mixed with the trustees' own funds, the operation of *Clayton's Case* would mean that the earliest entries would be extinguished first. This could be unfair to the beneficiaries of the trust monies, as their funds could be cleared and the remaining balance belong to the trustee. Hence, where trust monies and personal funds are mixed then the whole of the trust monies **must** be repaid to the trust fund first. This is known as the rule in *Hallet's Case (Re Hallet's Estate, Knatchbull* v *Hallett)* (1880).

(b) Contrary appropriation. As mentioned above, *Clayton's Case* applies only if neither the debtor (customer) nor the creditor (bank) appropriates. Thus, if either party does appropriate, expressly or impliedly, then this defeats the operation of the rule.

Appropriation and realisation of securities

When the bank has taken security for an advance and has then realised its security (for example on the customer's failure to maintain his loan repayments) it is free to appropriate the funds obtained to its own advantage (naturally the proceeds cannot exceed the total amount of the debt). Thus where a bank has a preferential debt and a non-preferential debt (as mentioned in 2(iii) above), and insufficient funds are received to clear the debt in full, the bank is free to apply the funds to the non-preferential debt, thereby leaving the preferential debt intact: *Re William Hall Contractors* (1967). This course of action could be beneficial to the bank as it could well improve the chances of receiving full recovery of the debt.

■ B. Combination of accounts (or banker's set-off)

Introduction

If a customer has more than one account with the bank (with the same branch or separate branches) there may be a time when the bank or the customer needs to know the net position, or if the accounts can be combined to obtain an overall picture (eg, when deciding to pay cheques or on receipt of notice of bankruptcy/winding up proceedings).

When can a bank combine accounts?

There have been numerous cases in this connection which have set the pattern for many years, the position can be illustrated as follows:

(i) The bank has a right to combine the balances on two current accounts held at different branches when returning cheques – one account in debit and one in credit: *Garnett* v *McKewan* (1872). In this case there was no overdraft agreement in existence. However, it was also stated that the bank did not have the duty to check the balance in the second current account when deciding to return cheques. It is thought that this rule would also apply to an overdrawn account and a credit deposit account.

(ii) The accounts must be of the same type (e.g. payable on demand) and as such a loan account, not in default, cannot be set-off against a credit balance. On the other hand overdrafts are automatically repayable on demand: *Williams & Glyn's Bank* v *Barnes* (1980). Also, if there is an implied or express agreement not to combine then this overrules the decision in *Garnett* v *McKewan*; see *Buckingham* v *London & Midland Bank Ltd* (1875); here the bank sought to combine a loan (which was not in default) and a credit current account. It was held that as there had been no default on the loan then the bank had no right of set-off. There is no right of combination on contingent liabilities, for example, performance bonds, indemnities or guarantees: *Jeffreys* v *Agra & Mastermans Bank* (1866).

(iii) The implied or express agreement is ended on insolvency: *National Westminster Bank* v *Halesowen Pressworks* (1972), or on the termination of the bank/customer relationship: *Joachimson* v *Swiss Bank Corporation*.

(iv) If there are numerous accounts, including a preferential debt (eg, wages account) upon insolvency of the customer the combination cannot be made in any other than a pro-rata basis (ie, the credit balances must be combined in proportion to the amounts outstanding on the debit acounts): *Re Unit 2 Windows* (1985). This must not be confused with the position in *Re William Hall Contractors* (1967), where a secured creditor used its right of *appropriation* under *Westminster Bank v Cond* (1940) to apply the funds from a realised security to a non-preferential debt, thus retaining the full extent of the preferential element.

(v) The accounts must be in the same right (eg, same name).

    (a) Thus, where the bank is aware either expressly or impliedly that funds are held on trust then the bank has no right to set-off, as in:

        1. *Barclays Bank v Quistclose Investments Ltd* (1970), where money placed in a company's account to meet a dividend was held to be 'in trust' and thus not available for set-off.

        2. *Re Gross (ex Parte Kingston)* (1871), where an account styled 'Benjamin L Gross, Police Account' was sufficient for the bank to be aware that the funds were held on trust.

    (b) A credit account in the sole name of one member of a joint debt account (this includes partnership accounts) can be combined with the joint debit current account only if a joint and several mandate (see chapter 14) has been taken in respect of the joint/partnership account. A joint credit account **cannot** be combined with a debit in the sole name of one of the parties.

    (c) In *Basna v Punjab National Bank* (1987) and *Bhogal v Punjab National Bank* (1987), it was held that a bank cannot set off a credit balance on one account against an overdraft on another on the suspicion that the accounts are held by nominees for the same beneficiary (this is known as 'equitable set-off'). In these two connected cases the court also held that for a claim of 'equitable set-off' to succeed there would need to be unquestionable documentary evidence. In *Uttanchandi v Central Bank of India* (1989) the need for undisputed evidence that the accounts are held beneficially for the same person was again stressed.

(vi) The bank still has the right of combination even if served with notice under the Drug Trafficking Offences Act 1986, with a restraining order. The combination of an overdrawn account and two credit deposit account was not deemed to be a disposal, but merely an internal accounting exercise: *Re K* (1989).

■ Mandatory set-off

(a) Under s.323 Insolvency Act 1986, when credit and debit accounts are held and the customer is declared insolvent, the bank **must** exercise set-off. This section is mandatory and overrules all implied or express agreements to the contrary: *National Westminster Bank v Halesowen Pressworks* (1972).

(b) The accounts do not need to be of the same type, which means that contrary to the common law right of combination, contingent liabilities can be set-off: *Re Charge Card Services Limited* (1986).

(c) Also, future debts are termed 'bankruptcy debts' (eg, a loan due for repayment in the future), and as such the bank is able to set-off these future debts: *Rolls Razor Limited v Cox* (1967).

(d) The ruling in respect of preferential debts is exactly the same as in (iv) above.

(e) The accounts to be set-off must still be in the same right as in (v) above, in that no set-off is available, for example, between a debit sole account and a credit joint account etc.

(f) Transactions accepted after the commencement of insolvency (date of order for individual insolvency, date of petition or resolution for corporate insolvency) are not available for set-off except for the period between date of petition and receipt of notice. This is due to credits being deemed as being held on trust for the trustee and debits being void (except on ratification or validation order).

(g) Mandatory set-off does not apply to a secured debt: *Re Norman Holding Co Ltd* (1990).

■ C. Banker's lien

Introduction

A lien is generally a creditor's 'right to retain' a debtor's property which has come into his hands, until the debt has been cleared. One important point to note is that the title to the property does not change, the debtor is still the owner. Examples of liens in everyday life include garages refusing to release cars until their bill has been paid or solicitors refusing to supply the title deeds of a recently purchased property to their client until they have been paid by him in full. This can also be of benefit to bankers, where a customer is unwilling, or unable, to clear a debt with a bank but the bank also has possession of an asset of the customer.

Characteristics of a banker's lien

(i) Normally a lien does not give the possessor of the asset a power to sell the property. However a banker's lien has been interpreted to be an 'implied pledge' and the bank has the additional power of sale, after reasonable notice, without the necessity for a court order.

(ii) Under *Brandao* v *Barnett* (1846), a banker's lien was stated to apply to 'all securities deposited with them as bankers by a customer, unless there be an express contract, or circumstances that show an implied contract, inconsistent with lien.' Thus, the item must be (a) deposited with the bank and (b) there must be no contrary intention. Items which have been covered under the banker's lien have included cheques, bills of exchange, insurance policies, share certificates and other negotiable instruments.

The banker's lien and cheques

Perhaps one of the most common examples of the occurrence of a banker's lien is the returning of a cheque to the collecting bank. If that bank is unable to debit his customer's account (in order to correct the initial entry) without overdrawing the account then the bank will be said to have a lien over the cheque and be able to enforce payment of the cheque (say, against the drawer) in its own name. Under s.27(3) Bills of Exchange Act 1882, anyone who holds a lien on a cheque is deemed to have given value and as such will be classed as a holder for value or holder in due course (see Chapter 10).

However to maintain its lien (right to retain) the bank must retain possession of the cheque; if it were to return the cheque to its cutomer (as per normal procedures for returned cheques) the bank would lose its lien as it no longer possessed the cheque: *Westminster Bank* v *Zang* (1966).

Items not covered by the banker's lien

(i) Where there is a contrary intention (either express or implied). This includes items held in safe deposit and safe custody and sale of shares where the bank is merely acting as agent, introducing the customer to the stockbroker, for the purposes of sale.

(ii) Where there is a prior legal interest, as in *Siebbe Gorman & Co Ltd* v *Barclays Bank* (1979), where the bank held a fixed legal charge over present and future book debts (see chapter 18).

(iii) Where there is no right of appropriation. As you have read the section on appropriation already, I do not intend to repeat all of the conditions. However, the main factor of importance here is that a lien cannot occur where the only debt outstanding is one which specifically states that the loan is payable over a period of time (eg, a term loan regulated by agreement under the Consumer Credit Act 1974), the one exception being if the loan is in default.

(iv) Where the bank is aware of the fact that the monies are held on trust or constructive trust (see chapter one).

FACT SHEET

Appropriation, combination and lien

Appropriation
(i) First right is customer's. Can be specific or implied but mere entry in own books not sufficient – *Simson* v *Ingham; Manning* v *Westerne. Earmarking.*
(ii) Second right is bank's. Bank applies to its advantage – statute barred, sole debts or non-preferentials. NB *Re William Hall Contractors.*
(iii) If no appropriation then default rule of appropriation (*Clayton's Case*) applies. Debits and credits applied in chronological (date) order. Special relevance to current accounts and death, insolvency of joint account holder, notice of subsequent charge, hardening period of floating charge.
(iv) How to overcome *Clayton's Case*: (a) stopping account and (b) special clause (*Westminster Bank* v *Cond*).
(v) Exceptions to *Clayton's Case*: (a) Rule in *Hallet's Case* (trust monies) (b) contrary appropriation.
(vi) Realisation of securities – *Re William Hall Contractors.*

Combination
(i) Why? Need to know net position – payment of cheque, notice of insolvency, customer in default. *Garnett* v *McKewan.*
(ii) Conditions
 (a) Must be of same type. There must be no implied or express agreement not to combine: *Buckingham* v *London & Midland Bank.*
 (b) Must be in same right (name), trust accounts (*Quistclose, Re Gross*), joint accounts (joint debit with sole credit only if joint & several, sole debit with joint credit never).
 (c) Equitable set-off needs documentary evidence (*Bhogal* v *Punjab National Bank*).
(iii) Implied or express agreement not to combine ends on termination of banker/customer relationship.
(iv) *Re Unit 2 Windows*: in insolvency combination must be on pro-rata basis – not as with appropriation.

(v) mandatory set-off. *Nat. West* v *Halesowen* overrules express or implied agreements. No need to be in same right, can combine contingent liabilities, future loans. Accounts must still be in same right (name). Preferential debts must be combined pro-rata.

Banker's lien

(i) Characteristics. Differences between bankers and other liens. Implied pledge, right of sale. *Brandao* v *Barnett*, securities deposited with bank and no contrary intention.

(ii) Cheques. S.27(3) Bills of Exchange Act, holder for value, in due course. Must retain possession of cheque (*Westminster Bank* v *Zang*).

(iii) Items not covered. Safe custody, safe deposit, prior legal interest, no right of appropriation, notice of trust or constructive trust.

Question

What is meant by 'the right of appropriation'? Giving examples, show how, in practice, this rule and the 'default rule of appropriation' (the rule in *Clayton's Case*) affect the banker. (20 marks)

Key words

meant by	*in practice*
the right of appropriation	*this rule*
examples	*default rule*
show	*affect the banker*

Answer

1. **General.** The right is initially that of the customer to insist that funds paid in go to whatever account he wishes, or to meet a particular cheque or debit item: *Simson* v *Ingham*; *Deeley* v *Lloyds Bank Ltd*; *Farley* v *Turner*. If the customer does not specify which account, the banker may do so: *Simson* v *Ingham*. He could even appropriate to a statute barred item: *Mills* v *Fowkes*. If the appropriation is made it is final: *Deeley* v *Lloyds Bank Ltd* (though the bank can afterwards combine accounts).

2. **Default rule.** If no positive appropriation is made by either party, the default rule is the rule in *Clayton's Case*. This is the rule applicable to banking accounts peculiarly, and is a presumption which can be displaced by contrary intention (*Westminster* v *Cond*): but this must be express (*Deeley* v *Lloyds Bank Ltd*) where the bank argued that the appropriation must have been to unsecured, not to secured debts, because they would not have wished to lose the security (the House of Lords disagreed). Candidates could give the facts of *Clayton's Case*.

   The rule is often significant for bankers. Six particular cases might be mentioned: (i) that already mentioned, where the customer appropriates to meet a particular cheque: the bank must obey; (ii) the effect of the rule on securities for particular debts which may be discharged if the original debt is: note the countering of this by an all monies, continuing security. But the no-tacking rule applies anyway, so need for caution when second mortgages learned of (*Deeley* v *Lloyds Bank Ltd*); (iii) if a joint account holder such as a partner dies, becomes bankrupt, retires etc. so that his liability is fixed, the debt may be reduced: (*Clayton's Case* itself; *Royal Bank of Scotland* v *Christie*); (iv) if a guarantee is determined the guarantor's liability is fixed, and the debt for which he is liable may become reduced, not if it is a 'whole liability' guarantee with limiting proviso; (v) the rule may be beneficial to bankers in the context of the 12 months' rule, where the passage of money through the account replaces 'old' debt with 'new' debt which is good consideration; (vi) the rule helps with the administration of wages accounts, enabling easy 'transfer out' of old debt by credit in each four months, for bookkeeping purposes (though in law separate wages accounts are not needed as the debt is still preferential).

   The default appropriation rule does not apply:

- between trustee and beneficiary: *Re Hallett's Estate*
- to separate accounts at the bank even if at the same branch: *Bradford Old Bank* v *Sutcliffe*
- to a stopped account: *Deeley* v *Lloyds Bank Ltd*
- if an express contrary appropriation: *Westminster Bank* v *Cond*
- to accounts other than running current accounts: *Cory Bros* v *Mecca Turkish SS (Owners)*.

Author's comment

This is a question that tends to achieve high marks for the well prepared candidate, those less well prepared will achieve either poor marks or avoid the question altogether. There is a temptation to think that the question is an opportunity to write all you know about *Clayton's Case*, and while this would result in a reasonable mark, better marks are available if the question is attacked in an organised manner. The natural starting place would be a brief discussion of the meaning of appropriation, moving on to discuss the order and the implications of neither party appropriating. The candidate should then discuss the incidents of the default rule working for and against the bank and concluding with instances of the rule not applying. All in all a question with many more than the maximum 20 marks available, but alas only available for the well prepared candidate with the remaining ones merely discussing their understanding of *Clayton's Case* and obtaining 3 or 4 marks.

CHAPTER 3

Main principles of Consumer Credit Act lending

Syllabus requirements
- Advertising, canvassing, credit brokerage, loan agreements, forms, exempt credit.
- Security and land secured agreements.
- Credit tokens, connected lender liability, overdrafts on current account.

▌Introduction

The main aim of the Consumer Credit Act 1974, as amended in 1985, was to protect consumers by introducing the concept of 'truth in lending'; for example all lending institutions regulated by the Act must inform borrowers of **all** charges connected with regulated lending (Total Charge for Credit) and the rate of interest must be calculated and quoted in a similar manner (see Annual Percentage Rate (APR) below). Customers can request quotations before deciding whether or not to borrow the money and must have sight of all other forms related to the advance (eg, security forms).

NB, the Act applies only to individuals, **limited company borrowing is not covered by the Act.**

The Act applies to lending transactions, unless exempt (see note below), in the areas of hire purchase, conditional sale, credit sale, personal loans, debt adjustment, debt counselling and debt collection. There had been many historical problems in these areas with particular complaints of inaccurate advertising, canvassing (also known as 'knocking'), borrowers being unaware of extortionate rates of interest and realisation of security. One would hope that the majority of such complaints were not levelled against the banks but, like all other lending institutions, banks were caught under the legislation. In many ways the Act has been viewed as a remarkable piece of legislation, and whatever views you may have on it, its complexity cannot be denied. It is due to this complexity that following its full implementation in 1985, many of the major banks had differing interpretations of its clauses. However, for the purpose of the examination an understanding of each individual section of the Act is not necessary, but merely an understanding of the main principles and how these relate to bank operations. As previously mentioned the Act applies only to personal borrowing and the main thrust of the Act is for smaller advances (up to and including £15,000).

When discussing the Act we shall first discuss how banks are permitted to seek business be it through advertising, canvassing or circulars. What should the banks do if a prospective customer should ask for a quotation, and if this is acceptable what details need to appear on the agreement, the additional details which are necessary if security is taken, and what extra procedures are required if the security is land. Next we will discuss the measures available to a bank should the borrower default. Finally, we will look at other sundry matters covered by the Act, such as credit brokerage and credit tokens.

▮ Advertising

Under the Act all forms of advertising are covered and include:

(i) Radio and television.

(ii) Displays of notices, goods, signs, posters, pictures and articles.

(iii) Distribution of samples, circulars, leaflets.

Each of the above is included in the conditions, unless it is made clear that the lending applies only to limited companies or exceeds £15,000. The advertisements fall into three categories, simple, intermediate and full. The difference in categories refers in reality to the amount of information that **must** be supplied, for example:

(a) Full advertisements must contain:

(i) The name and full postal address of the advertiser (unless the advertisement is fixed on a bank's premises).

(ii) The true cost; this has been interpreted to be the Annual Percentage Rate (APR) and is covered in greater detail later in this chapter.

(iii) Information on APR (eg, if interest can vary).

(iv) If security will be required, then this should be stated in the advertisement, and security includes compulsory life insurance.

(v) Frequency of payments.

(vi) If offer is restricted to a particular class or group of the public.

(b) Intermediate advertisements must contain:

(i) Name and address of lender.

(ii) Whether or not security is normally expected.

(iii) The APR and any information on it.

However, there is no compulsion to disclose frequency of repayments or any restrictions on the offer. Section 75 liability (see later) for debtor/creditor/supplier cannot be used as a marketing ploy.

Any advertisement which fails to adhere to the above restrictions or falls between them, or is misleading, could result in a fine or imprisonment (s.46), not only for the lender but also for the publisher or producer of the advertisement (s.47).

▮ Canvassing

Section 49(1) states that it is an offence to canvass debtor − creditor agreements (eg, a regulated agreement − see later in this chapter) off trade premises. Canvassing can be interpreted as oral representations soliciting the entry into the agreement (s.48), the emphasis is on **oral** and as such does not include postal canvassing or, rather surprisingly, telephone canvassing.

Trade premises are defined as the normal trade premises of the bank, whether of a permanent or temporary nature (eg, hospitality units at public relations events or temporary 'portakabin' type units), or the business premises of the customer. As personal customers obviously do not have business premises, this means that the only time when canvassing is permitted is on bank premises. For banks there are only three main exemptions to this rule:

(i) where the canvasser has been invited in writing, which must be signed by the customer;

(ii) where the canvassing is in respect **only** of an overdraft to an existing customer;

(iii) where the visit was not made with the intention of canvassing the credit facility, and the topic was first raised by the customer.

▮ Minors

Section 50 states that it is an offence for the bank to send to a **minor** any document which entices him to borrow money or to seek any further information or advice on borrowing money or otherwise obtaining credit. Section 50(1) states that it is a defence to prove that the sender had no cause to suspect that the recipient was in fact a minor, or if the canvassing letter is sent to a school or educational establishment, that the sender did not know or suspect it to be so. In all cases, however, it is an offence to send a credit token (this includes credit cards) to anybody unless in response to a request in writing.

▮ Quotations

Where a request is made for a 'quotation', a reply must be made in writing and must contain the amount of the advance plus the following (s.52):

(i) **Total charge for credit** (TCC), including:
- arrangement fees
- security fees
- legal fees
- disbursements
- interest chargeable

Where these items are 'front ended' (ie, charged at the time of granting the loan or on drawdown of the loan) then it must be stated if the items are actual or estimated.

(ii) **Interest rate.** The annual percentage rate (APR) must be quoted, although where the interest rate is to be linked to the base rate, and as such is variable, then it is permissible to state this fact in the quotation, quoting the lending rate as it currently stands.

▮ Regulated agreements

A regulated agreement is an agreement between an individual (the debtor) and any other person (the creditor) by which the creditor provides the debtor with credit (s.8). Credit includes a cash loan, and any other form of financial accommodation (s.9). The maximum advance subject to agreement is £15,000 and includes advances to individuals (individually or jointly), sole traders, partnerships, trustees, executors etc., but not limited companies. An agreement must contain the same information as in a quotation, (see above), the signature of the lender (bank), the signature of the borrower (customer) and a clause stating that the borrower has a period during which he can withdraw from the agreement (if applicable).

There are many types of agreements, including:

(a) Debtor-creditor agreement (s.13). This is an agreement by the creditor to supply monies to the debtor for any purpose he likes or some transaction involving a supplier, with whom the creditor does not have a business relationship. Also included in this section are refinancing transactions. This is the typical form of bank lending on personal loan or overdraft.

(b) Debtor-creditor-supplier agreement (s.12). This is an agreement where a pre-arranged business relationship exists between creditor and supplier, the creditor to supply finance to the debtor in order to enable that debtor to enter into a relationship with the supplier. A topical example of this form of credit is a store card or credit card.

(c) Restricted use agreement (s.11(1)). This is to be interpreted literally, in that the use of the funds is restricted, usually by the creditor providing the funds direct to the supplier for a specific purpose. It must not be confused with a debtor-creditor-supplier agreement which can be used for many purposes and not one specific purpose.

(d) Unrestricted use agreement (s.11(2)). This is where the creditor has a free choice as to how to spend the funds.

It is important to note at this stage that although an overdraft is subject to certain conditions under the Act (s.10) it is not subject to agreement. If this were not so then many every day repercussions would arise with, for example, each temporary and formal overdraft not being available to a customer until an agreement had been signed, and further complications arise if the Rule in *Clayton's Case* were to be applied and every debit to an overdrawn account be considered a new debt and thus subject to agreement (for a full discussion of *Clayton's Case* see Chapter 2). An important recent development is the Determination under s.74(1)(b), whereby a lender, by way of overdraft, falling within CCA criteria, must inform the customer, and subsequently confirm in writing: (i) the credit limit; (ii) the annual rate of interest and charges applicable; (iii) the procedure for terminating the agreement. Also, if any unauthorized overdraft has been outstanding for three months, the borrower must be informed of the last two above.

In conclusion:

1. A regulated agreement is totally unenforceable against a borrower when:

    (a) the debtor has not signed the agreement.
    (b) the agreement was not complete when signed, or was not in the correct form.
    (c) the agreement was cancellable and a copy of the agreement was not given to each borrower.

2. If the above are present, absence of any of the following will render the agreement only enforceable by court order (s.65):

    (a) a heading referring to the Act and stating that the agreement is regulated by the Consumer Credit Act 1974.
    (b) the name and address of both the borrower and lender.
    (c) the financial details (cash price, amount of advance, APR, and Total Charge for Credit). It is important to remember that the APR will be quoted as a percentage, whereas the TTC will be an actual amount (in pounds and pence). The TCC must state whether the figures are actuals (eg arrangement fees) or estimates (eg security disbursements).
    (d) security details and whether the security is direct (given by the borrower) or third party (given by someone other than the borrower).

Annual percentage rate (APR)

The APR must be quoted as mentioned above, on regulated agreements (s.20). However, it is important to have a basic understanding of its meaning. Basically the APR is meant to be a reflection of the true rate of interest and as such be a figure of comparison between one institution and another. The rate is based on the compounding of interest and thus it makes allowance for the reducing balance on the loan, as the repayment instalments are made, and is not purely an indication of the flat rate being charged on the loan (eg, personal loans must quote the APR, whether or not the flat rate is quoted). As a general rule the APR will be substantially higher than the flat rate, as the flat rate is applied on the whole of the original balance, whereas the APR takes into account the fact that each repayment reduces the outstanding balance.

The rate must include any fees incurred in the arrangement of the facility or the perfection of any security taken in connection with it. It is not necessary to have a knowledge of the actual calculation of the APR.

Executing agreements

After the format of the agreement has been checked (usually agreements are on bank standard form) it should be signed on behalf of the bank and then handed to the customer(s) to sign. Once signed a copy must be handed to each borrower (s.63). It is important to note that where the agreement is signed off bank premises then this would usually make the agreement 'cancellable'. Obvious examples of this occurrence are where only one party of a joint account attends for interview and the agreement is taken home or posted to the other party for signature, or where discussions are undertaken by phone and the agreement is posted out for signature. If the agreement is cancellable, s.64 of the Act states that a copy of the agreement must be sent within seven days of signature and/or a statutory Notice of Cancellation Rights advising the borrower(s) of the right to cancel. Cancellation must be in writing and received by the bank within five days of receipt of the notice or second agreement; this is known as the 'cooling-off period'.

The 'cooling-off' period commences the day after the receipt of this notice. The borrower has the right to receive his cancellation rights in writing and the agreement form itself. Examples of non-cancellable agreements include any agreement where the security is to be land (see following section), or a loan for the purchase of land or a bridging loan.

Where the persons giving the security (mortgagors or guarantors) differ from the borrowers (known as third-party security) then these parties must also receive a copy of the agreement and the security form. The security form, be it guarantee, indemnity or any other, must refer to the agreement and contain prominent warnings as to the liability being undertaken.

Exempt agreements

As previously mentioned, certain borrowing is exempt from the regulations of the Act; this could be because either the imposition of regulation would not be in the interests of the consumer or sufficient control already exists. Section 16 states that the Act does not apply where:

(i) the creditor is a local authority, building society, insurance company, friendly society or charity, and
(ii) either (a) the agreement is a debtor-creditor-supplier agreement for the purchase of land or the provision of land or is secured on land or (b) a debtor-creditor agreement secured on land or to enable the purchase of land.

Small agreements

Small agreements are transactions under £30, which are totally unsecured except for a guarantee or indemnity (s.17) and do not relate to consumer credit hire involving payment of over £30.

Modifying a regulated agreement

Where the terms of a regulated agreement have been altered then it is necessary to execute a modifying agreement. Examples could include the taking of addition security or, where the borrower is in default, the extension of the term or reduction in repayments. This can be of grave importance to banks as it is normal practice for banks to accept repayment proposals where their customers are in financial difficulties. Modifying agreements can be avoided if the alteration is made to the terms of the original agreement to accommodate the borrower and no direct benefit is gained by the bank, although this is difficult to quantify.

Land secured agreements (s.58)

As previously mentioned, any agreement referring to land as security is automatically non-cancellable. However, the situation is a little more complicated than that (of course). The borrower (or mortgagor of a third party security) must be given a 'consideration period', during which he must not be approached by the bank (s.61). This is effected by sending the borrower a copy of the agreement marked 'copy of proposed credit agreement containing notice of your right to withdraw. Do **not** sign or return this copy' along with a specimen of the legal charge form that he will be expected to sign. The theory behind the consideration period is to give the customers sufficient time to consider the seriousness of their actions and the possible repercussions should they default on the loan.

Not earlier than seven days after the commencement of the consideration period the bank should send the original agreement form (and specimen charge form) to be signed by the borrower and returned to the bank. The consideration period ends on receipt of the signed agreement or seven days after the agreement has been sent to the borrower. If the lender fails to comply with these conditions the agreement is unenforceable, except with a court order (s.65).

The above regulations do not apply if the borrower is purchasing the property.

Other security implications

As mentioned above any security to be taken should be stated on the agreement, as should any costs involved, along with a statement as to whether the costs are actual or estimated. Also, the borrower should be supplied with a copy of any security documentation referred to in the agreement. Although the Act does not state that any particular wording must be used in legal charge forms, it does prescribe a format for the wording of guarantees and indemnities (see Chapter 14). If the guarantee does not contain an indemnity clause it must contain a heading 'Guarantee subject to the Consumer Credit Act 1974'; if an indemnity clause is included the heading must read 'Guarantee and Indemnity subject to the Consumer Credit Act 1974'. There must be a reference in the form to the agreement and the form must also contain certain warnings such as 'Important – you should read this carefully' and in bold type '**you may have to pay instead**'. Many banks state these two items separately and at least one on the same section of the form where the guarantor signs, giving them extra prominence.

Also, where the advance is regulated and secured against residential property, it will be necessary, in every circumstance, to approach the courts for their consent prior to realising the security (for example entering into possession; for greater detail see Chapter 15).

∎ Ending the agreement

Customer in default

The contents of formal default letters have been agreed by the Act (s.88) and must specify:

(a) the nature of the breach, quoting the clause of the original agreement;

(b) the action necessary to remedy the breach;

(c) if the breach is not capable of remedy, the sum required as compensation.

The default notice must be in writing and legible and served on the borrower within seven days of default. The borrower should be told that if he cannot afford the sum stated in the default notice he can apply to the court for a 'time order' or if he is not sure what to do he should approach either a solicitor or Citizens Advice Bureau. If the bank is unaware of the customer's present address then serving the default notice on his last known address is sufficient.

If the borrowing is in joint names then a copy of the default notice must be served on both parties separately. In *Forward Trust PLC* v *Whymark* (1989), it was decided that where the borrower defaults on his repayments under a regulated consumer credit agreement, the lender is entitled to claim, and the court to give judgment for the whole amount outstanding, without first deducting any rebate allowable for early repayment. Once liability for the outstanding sum has been established however, it can be discharged by the borrower paying an amount which takes into account any rebate due to him.

Enforcement

An enforcement of the advance is subject to a period of notice (usually 30 days) served by either the borrower or the creditor. This is of specific advantage to banks where no specific breach has been committed, yet the bank still wishes to terminate the loan. An example could be the bankruptcy of the borrower.

Security implications

Where the advance is secured then a copy of the enforcement or default notices should be sent to the mortgagor or guarantor, marked 'surety's copy'. Also, where a regulated agreement is secured against land, the security is enforceable only with a court order or the mortgagor's consent.

Early settlement by borrower

The borrower is able to settle the advance at any time, without notice, by paying the full amount of the outstanding balance in cash (s.94), and the borrower is entitled to make a claim for a rebate of interest and charges levied, as per the original agreement. The borrower is also able to ask at any time for a settlement figure; no charge should be made for this service.

Death of borrower

Providing the debt is a fully secured regulated agreement, the executors or administrators may continue to make the repayments at the amount and regularity stated in the agreement. However, if the advance is not secured or only partially secured then the bank can apply to the courts to have the repayments increased.

∎ Other sundry considerations

Credit tokens

A credit t ken is an article issued by a company in the credit business which allows an individual either, on production of the article, to be supplied with cash, goods or services on credit, or, upon presentation of the token to a third party, to be supplied by that third party with cash, goods or services, the company paying the third party, with the individual paying the company in the future (s.14).

Obvious examples of credit tokens are store cards (which fall into the first definition – the individual being supplied with goods or services on credit), or, more relevant to banks, credit cards (which fall into the second definition with, for example, the customer obtaining petrol and the credit card company paying the garage and claiming the money from the customer at some future date).

Under s.51 it is an offence to issue a credit token unless requested to do so. Hence the previously seen mass distribution of unrequested credit cards or the automatic replacement of cheque guarantee cards with a credit card carrying a cheque guarantee facility is no longer seen. The mailing of cards on the review (either annual or otherwise) of the credit card facility on its expiry, is not subject to these regulations.

A credit token is subject to agreement, under the same rules as any other credit transaction, and upon signature of the credit token agreement a copy should be handed to the customer (s.85). If the issuer fails to adhere to these regulations the debt could be unenforceable and the issuer could be subject to a fine.

One of the main problems caused by credit tokens is their misuse. Under current legislation the card holder is liable for the lower of £50 or the credit limit (s.84), on the loss or theft of his card, although this limit is rarely imposed by banks unless the loss or theft is thought to be due in some way to the customer's negligence or actions. Naturally, the customer is not liable for any misuse after he has notified the company of its loss or theft. However, should the misuse occur with the consent of the customer then he will be liable for the full amount.

The Consumer Credit Act introduced a new concept into credit card transactions. Under the Act (s.75), a credit card company shares with the supplier of goods or services paid for with the use of the credit card, responsibility for any fault or failure of those goods or services. As mentioned overleaf, charge cards (where the debit comes direct from the customer's bank account) are thought by the majority of correspondents in this area to be exempt for s.75 liability, due to the exemptions under the Banking Act 1987 (s.89) for electronic transactions.

Credit brokerage

Credit brokerage is the act of introducing people seeking credit, desiring to purchase goods or services on credit, or seeking to purchase property and prepared to offer land as security, to establishments willing to offer such services. All persons acting as credit brokers must be registered (s.145) and as such the growing trend of estate agents referring clients to lending institutions for mortgage business in return for a fee or commission on insurance- related products, must also be registered. It is possible that where a lender enters into an agreement with a customer, following an introduction by an unlicensed broker, the agreement (and any security taken to support the lending) could be unenforceable unless decided otherwise by a court order stating that the transaction can be treated as if the broker was registered at the time. This is only so where the broker has subsequently obtained a licence.

In principle the regulations concerning the advertising and canvassing of credit brokerage are very similar to those relating to regulated agreements in that the advertisements must be accurate and must contain certain information, and canvassing off trade premises is prohibited.

Connected lender liability

This liability refers to a debtor-creditor-supplier agreement (see previous note under 'Agreements') and briefly states that where the supplier commits a breach of contract or misrepresentation (eg, supplying faulty or defective goods or services), then the creditor and supplier are jointly and severally liable (s.75), which literally means that both the supplier and the creditor are liable for the full extent of any amount involved. In these circumstances the creditor will be indemnified by the supplier stating that if the creditor has to pay then he can in turn claim that amount, plus any reasonable costs incurred, from the supplier.

Once again the intention here is to give maximum protection to the consumer (debtor), and in relation to banking the main connection is with credit cards (as you read earlier in this chapter), where the credit card company could be involved following the supply of faulty goods or poor service by the supplier. However, the purchase of goods by charge card (eg American Express) is not covered by s.75, as any 'credit' available must be repaid in one lump-sum repayment. Connected-lender liability does not attach to EFTPoS transactions, such as debit cards, since they are an electronic transfer of funds and as such are exempt under s.89 Banking Act 1987. In order to claim s.75 liability the cash price of the transaction must range from £100 to £30 000, although the damages incurred can exceed £30 000. Section 75 cannot be used as a marketing ploy.

Appropriation

You may recall that appropriation is the right of the bank, as a creditor, to place a credit to whichever debt it chooses, providing the customer, as debtor, has not already exercised his choice. If neither appropriate, then *Clayton's Case* (the default rule of appropriation) will apply.

Under the normal rule of appropriation (see chapter one) if the debtor (customer) does not appropriate, then the creditor (bank) can appropriate. However, where the customer has more than one regulated agreement and fails to appropriate then the bank must appropriate between the two in proportion.

Status enquiries

Section 145 states that recipients of enquiries must make their replies available for inspection and correction if necessary. Thankfully the Office of Fair Trading has decided that banks are not subject to the restrictions under s.145. Consequently banks now quote on all their replies that they are not a credit reference agency and therefore are not subject to such restrictions.

Joint accounts

Anything done to any one member of a joint account should be done to each member individually (s.185). For example, a default notice should be served on each member separately. Also, any action done by any member shall be binding on all of them, for example, the cancellation of the agreement.

Finally, under s.78 each member should be served with a separate regular statement. However, most banks exercise their rights to ask one member to forsake this right, so that the bank needs to issue only one statement to the person and at the address quoted in the account opening mandate.

Licensing

Before starting to trade in the business of consumer credit it is necessary to obtain the relevant licence. This includes banks, credit brokers, debt collectors or any one else undertaking one of the activities quoted in the Act. The licence is granted by the Director General of Fair Trading by direct application and licences are granted depending on the category in which the applicant falls:

Category A: Consumer credit business. Covers the lending of money, offering of credit and giving people time to pay for goods and services. The type of businesses requiring such a licence would include banks, credit card companies, finance houses and pawnbrokers.

Category B: Consumer hire business. Covers the hiring, leasing or renting of goods for more than three months. Businesses requiring such a licence would be TV, car, caravan hiring etc.

Category C: Credit brokerage. This covers the arranging of credit for others, and persons requiring such a licence would be mortgage and insurance brokers and retailers introducing clients to finance houses (such as motor dealers, furniture shops etc.).

Category D: Debt adjusting and debt counselling. This covers any persons who offer assistance with debt problems either by refinancing their debts or negotiating on their behalf, or by offering advice. Examples of persons requiring such a licence would include accountants, mortgage and insurance brokers, social advice agencies etc.

Category E: Debt collecting. Covers the collection of debts for others, so you do not require this licence merely to collect your own debts. Examples of businesses requiring this licence would include debt collectors and finance houses which discount the debts of others.

Category F: Credit reference agency. Covers persons collecting information on the creditworthiness of people with a view to passing this information onto others. Examples of persons requiring such a licence would be credit reference agencies and trade protection societies.

A licence is not required if the credit business undertaken is only with limited companies; or merely to enable customers to pay their bills at the end of the week or month or whatever period is agreed; or to accept someone else's credit cards; or where all transactions will exceed £15,000 or where all transactions are of £30 or less.

Once the decision has been made as to which licence is to be applied for the application form and relevant fee must be submitted to the Office of Fair Trading. Once the application has been received it will be analysed and the Office of Fair Trading must be satisfied that the applicants are fit to run the type of business applied for: (s.25). The application can be refused on the grounds that the applicant is not fit or that he has committed an offence involving fraud or dishonesty or that the name may be misleading or undesirable. However, the applicant will have a right of appeal to the Secretary of State for Trade: (s.41).

Once granted the licence will be valid for 15 years; the Consumer Credit (period of standard licence) Regulations 1975, as amended by The Consumer Credit (period of standard licence) (Amendment) Regulations 1979 and 1986. However, once granted the licence can be revoked, varied or suspended if the Office of Fair Trading should be satisfied that the licensee is no longer fit to hold the licence: ss. 31, 32 Consumer Credit Act 1974.

Finally, if an activity requiring a licence was undertaken without one, then the trader will be liable to a fine, imprisonment or both. Also the transaction would be unenforceable and thus cannot be enforced against the borrower: s.40 Consumer Credit Act 1974.

Credit reference agencies

If a credit reference agency has been used in the assessment of a customer or a lending proposition, then the customer has the right to the name and address of the agency used and can request a copy of the file held by that agency on him. If the entry is incorrect, the customer can insist on the entry being corrected.

FACT SHEET

Introduction

   (i) £15,000 or less
  (ii) corporate bodies excluded
 (iii) truth in lending

Seeking business
1. Advertising
   (i) all forms of advertising affected
  (ii) simple, intermediate & full
 (iii) penalties
2. Canvassing
   (i) oral representation – hence does not include mail or telephone
  (ii) off trade premises
 (iii) unless invited, or only regarding overdraft to existing customer, or topic first raised by customer.
3. Minors. Not covered by mail exception above.
4. Quotations. Reply must be in writing. Items to be included.

Accepting the business
1. Agreements
   (i) Different types: (a) debtor-creditor, (b) debtor-creditor-supplier, (c) restricted use, (d) unrestricted use
  (ii) items to be included, (and what if not included?)
2. Executing the agreement
   (i) signed by bank & then by customer
  (ii) copy to each borrower
 (iii) cancellable agreements, cooling off period
3. Exempt agreements
4. Small agreements
5. Modifying agreements

6. Land secured agreements
    (i) automatically non-cancellable
    (ii) consideration periods
    (iii) purchase loans
7. Security implications

Ending the agreement

1. Customer in default
2. Enforcement
3. Security implications
4. Early settlement
5. Death of borrower

Other sundry matters

1. Credit tokens
    (i) what is a credit token
    (ii) restrictions on marketing
2. Credit brokerage
    (i) definition
    (ii) restrictions
3. Connected lender liability
    (i) debtor-creditor-supplier agreements
    (ii) joint & several liability
    (iii) indemnity
4. Appropriation
    (i) normal situation
    (ii) where there are CCA regulated agreements
5. Status enquiries. Reason for rider on standard replies.
6. Joint accounts
    (i) notice of actions must be served on all parties
    (ii) action of one binds all
    (iii) duty and practice on statements
7. licensing
    (i) types of licence
    (ii) exceptions
    (iii) right of refusal and appeal
    (iv) duration and right to evoke, amend or suspend
    (v) penalty for trading without a licence
8. Credit reference agencies. Customer's right of access.

Question

(a) You are the manager of Downtown Branch and your clerk has brought to you a loan agreement for signature. Assuming that the agreement is regulated by the Consumer Credit Act 1974 and you are satisfied with the lending, list the details you would check and state why.

(12 marks)

(b) If the lending is to be secured against residential property what additional details should be present and what additional procedures should be followed?

(8 marks)

Total 20 marks

Key words

(a) assuming CCA and satisfied with lending list details, why
(b) secured residential property, additional details and additional procedures

Answer

(a) The underlying principle here is that if a regulated agreement is not complete and regular, then the borrowing relating to that agreement may be totally unenforceable against the borrower or enforceable only after a court order. The type of agreement referred to in the question is known as a debtor–creditor agreement (s.13 CCA) and as most banks produce standard agreement forms covering such transactions the manager should need to concentrate only on the details below:

   (i) An agreement is totally unenforceable against a borrower if:
   - the debtor has not signed the agreement
   - the agreement was not complete when signed, or was not in the correct form
   - the agreement was cancellable and a copy of the agreement was not given to each borrower.

   (ii) If the above are present, the absence of the following will render the agreement enforceable only by court order (s.65 CCA):

   - a heading referring to the CCA and stating that the agreement is regulated by the Consumer Credit Act 1974
   - the name and address of the borrower and lender
   - the financial details (cash price, amount of advance, APR and Total Charge for Credit). It is important to remember that the APR will be quoted as a percentage, whereas the Total Charge for Credit (TCC) will be an actual amount (in pounds and pence). Both will include interest, fees and charges linked directly to the loan. The TCC will state whether the figures are actuals (eg arrangement fees) or estimates (eg security disbursements).
   - security details and whether the security is direct or 'third party' (involving a party other than the borrower).

(b) If any security is to be taken then this must be mentioned in the agreement and the Total Charge for Credit must include any associated charges. Residential property is not an exception to this rule. However, further complications arise as follows:

   (i) A land-secured agreement is automatically non-cancellable (as opposed to most agreements signed off bank premises);
   (ii) The borrower, and mortgagor if the security is third party, must be given a consideration period (s.58). During this time that person or persons must not be approached by the bank. This is an attempt to give the borrower or mortgagor sufficient time to consider the implications of offering their home as security;
   (iii) The borrower/mortgagor must be supplied with a copy agreement and a specimen of the legal charge form that will have to be signed. It is from the date of receipt of these documents that the consideration period commences;
   (iv) Not less than seven days after the commencement of this period the bank must send the borrower the original agreement, and a further specimen charge form, the agreement to be signed by the borrower and returned to the bank. The consideration period ceases upon signature of the original agreement, or seven days after receipt of the original agreement, by the borrower for signature (s.61).

There are exceptions to these procedures (s.58(2)); eg if the property to be charged is being purchased, or if the advance is by bridging loan to purchase the property charged or any other property.

CHAPTER 4

The Financial Services Act 1986

Syllabus requirements

● Main principles (including licensing), investment advice, customer agreements, advertising, canvassing.

▌ Introduction

References in this chapter are to the Financial Services Act 1986, unless indicated otherwise.

Prior to the introduction of the Financial Services Act 1986 (FSA), the investment industry was regulated by mainly outdated legislation which was not designed to cope with the large diversification seen in the industry in the 1980s. The system was open to abuse and in 1982 a report was published by Professor Gower entitled 'Review of Investor Protection', as requested by the Secretary of State for Trade and Industry following a number of scandals involving the investment industry. The report recommended many alterations which were later incorporated into the new legislation.

The main aim of the FSA is to regulate the investment business by the specific prohibition of persons conducting investment business unless they are either authorised or exempted. The method of implementing this is by a controversial method of self-regulation supported by authorisation (or exception) and inspection by the authorities.

In essence the industry will be supervised by the Securities and Investment Board (SIB) and the board will have powers transferred to it by the Secretary of State for Trade and Industry. The SIB has authorised the establishment of five Self Regulating Organisations (SROs), and it is these SROs which will regulate and authorise their members to conduct investment business. It is also possible to be authorised directly by the SIB, or for the SIB to recognise certain professional bodies (for example the Law Society of England and Wales, Institute of Chartered Accountants in England and Wales and Royal Institution of Chartered Surveyors). Insurance companies, friendly societies and certain investment operations of persons resident in the European Community (EC) can be authorised.

As mentioned previously certain organisations are exempt from registration and these include the Bank of England, Lloyds (Insurance not Bank), Lloyds underwriting agents, listed money-market institutions subject to approval by the Treasury.

Although authorisation is made in respect of institutions and employers (eg, banks) the employers have a duty to ensure that their employees are fully trained and aware of the implications of the FSA. The authorities must have a complete list of all persons entitled to do investment business. The individual interviewers have a duty to 'know your customer' and offer 'best advice'; the interviewer must also keep written records of the interview and be able to produce these for inspection by an official of the appropriate SRO if required. Each institution has to make a choice as to the products in which it is going to deal. The choices are that they can either:

    (i) offer advice across the whole financial market and sell or arrange products of all
       companies (financial intermediary), or
   (ii) merely sell and advise on their own products (company representative).

It is not possible for one individual (or authorised body) to act in both roles but it is possible for two members (under separate authorisation, possibly with separate SROs) of the same group to act in either capacity.

    Finally, what would happen to organisations if they were to undertake investment business when not authorised, or if they should not comply with the conduct of business rules (or similar for SROs), or if they should not be in a position to reimburse a customer where such an action is expected? The answers to these questions are to be found later in the chapter, but briefly except for a few strictly limited exempt categories, it is a criminal offence to carry on investment business without authorisation. The penalty for doing so can include up to two years' imprisonment, and any contracts made in the course of unauthorised business will be invalid.

▌ Securities and Investment Board (SIB)

1. Format

The SIB is a limited company, limited by guarantee (see Chapter eight), to which the Secretary of State for Trade and Industry is able to transfer certain powers concerning regulations. Although the SIB is seen in many eyes as the main regulatory body, this is not so. The powers of the SIB are transferred by the Secretary of State and he has the right to revoke these powers should he not be satisfied with the functions and standards of the SIB. The members of the governing body of the SIB are appointed (and can also be removed) by joint agreement of the Secretary of State and the Governor of the Bank of England. The membership of the governing body will comprise individuals with experience of investment business (including regular users and professional persons) and other independent persons of experience relevant to their future functions within the SIB.

    Prior to transferring his powers, the Secretary of State will satisfy himself that the composition of the governing body is adequate; in particular he will ensure that the balance is right between the interests of persons carrying on investment business and the interests of the public. Transfer will not occur until the Secretary of State is satisfied that the level of investor protection is adequate but that there is also no unnecessary restriction of competition.

    There must be a satisfactory structure for complaints, monitoring of standards, recording of decisions and storage of such records.

2. Powers transferred to the SIB by the Secretary of State

The following powers are transferred by the Secretary of State to the SIB:

   (i) Concerning registration or withdrawal.
      (a) To recognise, or withdraw recognition of, an SRO.
      (b) To insist on a change of rules of an SRO
      (c) To recognise, or withdraw recognition of, a professional body.
      (d) To grant, or withdraw, direct recognition.
      (e) To withdraw registration from a person authorised in another member state of
         the EC.

(ii) Concerning regulation.
    (a) To set minimum standards for the rules of SROs and professional bodies.
    (b) To set rules on cooling-off periods, unsolicited calls, segregation of client's funds, compensation funds and indemnity insurance.
    (c) Prohibition of individuals.
    (d) Investigation of either authorised or unauthorised persons and prosecution of the offenders.

3. Powers not transferred
(a) To amend the exceptions to authorisation.
(b) To amend the rules for acceptance of EC member countries.
(c) Public issue of securities.

4. Powers retained by Secretary of State
(a) To remove or appoint members (jointly with Governor of Bank of England).
(b) Withdrawal of powers of SIB (subject to agreement of Parliament).
(c) To alter the rules of SIB.

∎ Self Regulatory Organisations (SROs) (s.14)

In essence, in order for a bank to be entitled to carry on investment business it must be affiliated to a Self Regulatory Organisation, which in turn must be authorised by the SIB. At present there are five SROs, each one covering a specific area of investment business.

1. The Association of Futures Brokers and Dealers (AFBD) covers those involved in financial and commodity futures and options and investment services incidental to that business.

2. The Securities Association (TSA) covers those dealing and broking in securities, international money market instruments, forward agreements and related futures and options and investment management and advice incidental to that business.

3. Financial Intermediaries, Managers and Brokers Regulatory Association (FIMBRA) covers independent intermediaries, investment managers and advisers dealing direct with the public.

4. Investment Management Regulatory Organisation (IMRO) covers investment managers and advisers including managers and trustees of collective investment schemes and in-house pension fund managers.

5. Life and Unit Trust Regulatory Organisation (LAUTRO) covers those involved in the marketing of life assurance and unit trust products either by themselves or through their sales forces. LAUTRO is unique among SROs in that its membership does not in itself mean that its members can operate in that business, and registration with another SRO (eg IMRO or FIMBRA) will be necessary.

For an SRO to be recognised by the SIB there are certain requirements to be satisfied:

(a) Its members must be 'fit and proper' persons, able to carry on the investment business regulated by the SRO. The governing body of the SRO must contain a fair balance between the interests of its members and the interests of investors. There must also be a fair and reasonable method of admission, expulsion and discipline of members with adequate provisions for appeal.

(b) There must be a level of investor protection that is at least equivalent to that of the SIB.

(c) The SRO must have powers to intervene in the affairs of its members. There must also be the power for the SRO to prevent the resignation of one of its members until a full investigation of that member has taken place. This is to prevent the resignation of a member which is deliberately intended to forestall an investigation into its dealings.

(d) The SRO must have sufficient resources and arrangements to effect adequate control and monitoring and compliance with its rules. Again, the standard expected is at least that of the SIB.

(e) There must be an adequate complaints procedure for both itself and its members.

(f) The SRO must appear to be able to promote and maintain a high standard of integrity and fair dealing and must co-operate with the Secretary of State or any other regulatory or supervisory authority.

∎ Others able to carry on investment business

1. Professional bodies (s.15)
The intention behind this is that the majority of members of professional bodies will carry on a very small amount of investment business when compared with both their normal business and the amount of investment business carried on by the persons requiring authorisation. Bearing this in mind, each professional body will limit the amount and type of business each of its members can undertake; the actual limit will be a matter of judgment for the professional body. There are two main conditions for the recognition of a professional body by the SIB; these are:

(i) that it regulates the practices of a profession that is not, wholly or mainly, in the investment business, and

(ii) it regulates the practice of a profession recognised for a statutory purpose or in the exercise of statutory powers.

Examples include the Law Society, Institute of Chartered Accountants and Royal Institution of Chartered Surveyors.

The rules for recognition are almost identical to the above rules for SROs, **plus** the two additional conditions mentioned as (i) and (ii) above.

2. By direct authorisation by the SIB (s.26)
One example of this is thought to be where an application to an SRO is outstanding but the applicant wishes to commence trading (eg, at the inception of the Act).

3. Authorisation as an insurance company under the Insurance Companies Act 1982, or as a friendly society under the Friendly Societies Act 1974.

4. Members of the European Community, either authorised by a member state or operating as a recognised collective investment scheme in a member state.

5. Exempt persons. A very small number of institutions are exempt from the legislation, these include the Bank of England, Lloyds, Lloyds underwriters, listed money market institutions, holders of public office, recognised investment exchanges and recognised clearing houses.

∎ What is meant by investments and investment business?

1. Schedule 1 to the Act defines investments as:
- (i) stocks and shares;
- (ii) debentures;
- (iii) government, local authority or other public authority securities;
- (iv) unit trusts;
- (v) options & futures;
- (vi) long-term insurance policies.

Important exceptions to the above list are bank accounts, land and other assets such as pieces of art, gold, antiques etc.

2. Schedule 1 also defines investment business as:
- (i) dealing in investments (buying & selling);
- (ii) arranging deals in investments;
- (iii) managing investments;
- (iv) advising on investments;
- (v) collective investment schemes (including acting as trustee of such schemes).

Exceptions include where the person involved is 'acting as principal' (ie, on his own behalf), transactions between members of the same company group structure, employees' share schemes and newspaper articles, even if explicit investment advice is given, providing the overall purpose of the whole publication is not to give such advice.

∎ Implications of non-authorised investment business

Any unauthorised person convicted of carrying on investment business whilst unauthorised (unless exempt) commits a criminal offence and as such faces a fine or imprisonment, or both. He will not be able to enforce any investment agreements he enters into and the 'investor' will be able to recover any money or other property paid or transferred by him and will also be eligible for compensation from the offender (for example, loss of interest on investment). Naturally, it would also be unlikely that the unauthorised person could ever obtain authorisation and as such this could have grave consequences for that individual firm or person.

There are two possible defences:

(i) The unauthorised person must prove that he took all reasonable precautions and exercised due care when committing the offence. An example may be that he sought legal advice and was advised that authorisation was not necessary.

(ii) He believed that authorisation was not necessary and that his ignorance was reasonable. An example of this could be a person authorised for one particular field of investment business who did not realise that the transaction in question fell outside his field of authorisation.

However the courts do have discretion to enforce agreements involving unauthorised persons where they consider it to be just and equitable to do so.

■ Conduct of business rules

In many ways the conduct of business rules of the SROs must reflect those of the SIB, as laid down under s.48 of the Act. The rules of the SIB can alter from time to time, in response to a particular deficiency or problem. It is this flexibility that is one of the reasons for the structure adopted, as opposed to direct statutory control which could take longer and be more complicated to amend.

Schedule 8 to the Act states three main objectives of the conduct of business rules:

(i) investment business should be conducted honestly and fairly;
(ii) those involved in the business should act capably, carefully, and to the best of their abilities, and
(iii) they should be fair to their customers, avoiding a conflict of interest.

The conduct of business rules consist of the following:

Business plan

Each authorised body will be authorised to conduct only business quoted within its business plan, submitted at the time of authorisation, or as later revised. A description of its activities (in very basic terms) will need to be featured on its stationery and business literature.

Complaints

A comprehensive record of written complaints must be kept and all complaints must be investigated impartially and competently. It is possible for the investigation of complaints to be undertaken by an outside party. All persons complaining must be informed of their rights to complain to the SIB or the relevant SRO.

Canvassing

A call, by telephone or personal visit, cannot be made at an unsociable hour unless the representative has been invited, or has arranged the visit previously (s.56). If the call is completely cold (ie, without appointment or invitation), then the representative must ask the customer if the call is convenient and acceptable and if not must end the discussion immediately. If the caller is a company representative (only entitled to sell products of his own company, see later note), then he must inform the customer of this at the commencement of the interview.

The Act also states that any business written as a result of a cold call (or unsolicited call) will not be valid, this also extends to any business written later as an indirect result of the cold call. However there are exceptions, namely:

(i) A call on a business or professional investor.
(ii) Where the call is following previous discussions and the client is well aware of the nature of the agreement, for example previous business written within 12 months of the call.
(iii) Unit trust and life assurance sales. However, customers will have a 14-day cooling-off period, running from the date of receipt of documentation relating to the sale.
(iv) The customer is on the premises of the caller when the call is made.

Know your customer

It is an important element of writing investment business that the interviewer ensures that the product arranged meets the customer's requirements, and that the interviewer ascertains the knowledge and expertise of the investor. The Act defines four types of investor:

(a) professional investor;
(b) business investor;
(c) experienced investor;
(d) ordinary individual investor.

The degree of knowledge assumed to be held by each type of investor decreases in the order of the above list. Each investor **must** be assumed to be an ordinary individual investor unless the person arranging the investment can prove otherwise. This also applies to persons who appear to be members of one of the other classifications.

There are many details which the investment arranger must gain from the customer. These include the customer's tax position, and ability to pay (ie, to ensure that the transaction does not place a burden on the customer which could mean that he will be unable to meet his other existing commitments). The arranger must ensure that the customer understands the risks involved in the transactions; for example if he is investing in unit trusts he must understand that the investment value can go down as well as up. It is important to note that there is a definite difference between an investor being told of the risks and his understanding them. The arranger must ensure that the investor **understands** the risks.

The exceptions to the 'know your customer' rule are:

(a) Where the customer is an experienced or professional investor, where it can be assumed that the investor should know the risks involved.
(b) Where the investor is an 'execution only customer', that is one who is unwilling to divulge all the relevant information or merely wishes to arrange the investment and not to take any advice on the transaction. Many banks would ask that such a customer sign stating that he does not wish to disclose all relevant information or that he does wish to be advised on the transaction.

Customer agreements

A customer agreement is the validation of investment business between the investor and the investment company. Full customer agreements are not necessary for business, professional and experienced investors as defined above (a mere terms-of-business letter is sufficient here) and an occasional customer (one with whom the investment firm reasonably believes it will be dealing only on a one-off basis) may be offered an 'occasional customer agreement'.

Thus, there are in essence three forms of agreements:

(i) Terms-of-business letter. This must state investment areas in which the investment firm can treat the investor as either a business, professional or experienced investor. If the transaction is to be executed on the customer's behalf then the best execution rule (see later) must apply.
(ii) Occasional customer agreement. This must state the advice given to the investor and any instructions given by the investor to the investment company. Particulars of the type of investment must be quoted on the agreement, and business cannot be

undertaken until the agreement has been received and agreed by the investor.

(iii) Full agreements. Here a full agreement is required, and business can commence only after the customer has received and signed it.

All agreements must include:

(a) details of the business;
(b) type of services offered;
(c) if single premium life policies or unit trusts are included, a warning must be included stating that the agreement cannot be cancelled other than with mutual agreement;
(d) where the investor is not a professional or business investor and agrees to a cold call, a warning should be included that the investor loses his right of cancellation under the standard unsolicited call rules mentioned above; and
(e) details of remuneration and commission.

Full agreements must additionally include:

(f) the aims of the investment, whether the customer wants capital growth or income or perhaps a combination of the two;
(g) a warning of the risks involved, especially if the funds are not readily realisable; and
(h) arrangements for the withdrawal of the deposit.

There are other items which need to be included but they are not of particular relevance to this syllabus.

There are two exceptions to the need for customer agreements:

(i) effecting an 'execution only' transaction, and
(ii) where the transaction involves unit trusts or long term life insurance.

Best Advice

Where a bank is acting as an investment firm, it must (bearing in mind the need to 'know your customer' as mentioned above) give its customer the best advice possible. In fact the duty extends beyond this to include the fact that the bank must record facts that have led the bank to believe that the advice it is giving is in fact the best for its customer, bearing in mind all of his personal circumstances (tax position, disposable income, capital, etc.). Also, the bank must give warnings as to any possible dangers, for example the fact that units in a unit trust can go down as well as up.

If the customer is not likely to benefit from the type of investments the bank offers, then no sale should be made.

If the transaction is an 'execution only' transaction then the best advice regulations do not apply.

Best execution

Where the transaction does not involve any request or offer of advice then the transaction must be undertaken as a 'best execution' transaction. Perhaps the most relevant example to everyday banking is the sale of shares via a stockbroker, where the sale has not been on the advice of the bank. The bank must obtain the most advantageous deal at the time, involving price, commission and charges.

Polarisation (s.48)

Under the Act, banks have to decide if they are to sell the whole range of investment products available on the market or only their own products. This choice is known as 'polarisation'. If the decision is made to sell across the board, the persons involved are known as **independent financial intermediaries**, whilst persons selling products from their own group's range are known as **company representatives**.

(a) Independent financial intermediaries

The emphasis here is on the word independent, and as such as effectively ended the previous practice of financial dealers arranging policies with the insurance company that paid the highest commission or with the company that offered the highest incentives such as reciprocal business. An independent intermediary must offer the product that is the best on the market for the investor. An independent intermediary can sell his company's products only when he can reasonably prove that his was in the best interests of the customer.

(b) Company representatives

A company representative can sell only his own company's products, or products from members of his employer's group or an associated company (see below). The fact that the interviewer is a company representative and not an independent intermediary must be disclosed at the start of the interview. Where a company representative has identitifed that the 'best advice' to a customer would be to arrange a product outside his product range, he must refer the customer to an independent intermediary. Companies must keep records of company representatives and the products upon which they can advise, plus the method of assessment, training, etc.

As previously stated, banks have to decide whether to be independent or to be tied to their own products. Originally only National Westminster Bank decided upon the independent route. Building societies faced a similar problem, except that many societies did not have their own products to sell. Many building societies therefore teamed up with insurance companies in respect of endowment mortgates (eg, Abbey National/Friends Provident); this in effect made Abbey National employees company representatives for Friends Provident, with Friends Provident being responsible for training, compliance, authorisation, etc.

Many banks have compromised, in that although their mainstream branch staff are company representatives, many banks also have a subsidiary that is an independent intermediary. This means that should an interviewer discover that a customer's requirements can be met only by a product outside his bank's product range, he could refer the customer to the bank's independent intermediary subsidiary, who could then offer independent advice and the bank would still receive any commission payable.

Client's money (s.55)

If a financial adviser should hold client's money, for whatever reason, then this money must be held separately from any of his own funds, the money being held on trust for the investor. Although this does not directly affect banks in their investment business, it does not affect them in their dealings with customers who themselves happen to be in the investment business. It is also possible that the bank could be subject to the constructive trustee legislation as discussed previously in Chapter one.

Compliance manual and compliance officer

Each establishment seeking to deal in the investment business must produce an FSA Compliance Manual, distributed to each of its outlets (branches). The manual must contain the steps taken to ensure successful compliance with the Act. The Bank must appoint a compliance officer who must be of a senior grade able to command an interview with senior management of the bank and having access to all necessary areas of operation.

■ Enforcement

The main thrust of enforcement will be by random spot check inspection of members by the appropriate SRO. On these inspections it is not necessary for the SRO inspector to identify himself (ie, he can act as if he is an investor). On such visits (ie, acting as an investor) it is envisaged that the inspector will be looking for acts of non-compliance, for example a company representative not disclosing his status and appearing to offer advice across the whole industry. Where the inspector is on an official visit he will be looking for other items of non-compliance, such as the failure to keep accurate records or the failure to hold a compliance manual.

The SRO will also have extensive powers to investigate complaints beyond the information provided by the investor or the member itself.

If a member is found guilty of a breach of compliance procedures, then it is possible for the authorisation of the firm, or of the individual, to be rescinded.

■ Advertising (s.57)

In general only authorised persons may produce advertisements seeking to encourage potential investors to enter into investment agreements. The advertisements must be accurate, concise and clear. The main restrictions are as follows:

  (i) An advertisement may state that the investment carries a 'cooling-off' period but cannot use this as a selling point and misleading the would-be investor (eg, no obligation).
 (ii) An advertisement must state that the advertiser is authorised by the SIB (or relevant SRO etc.)
(iii) If any past record quotations are used the timing and source must be stated.
 (iv) Any risks associated with the investment must be quoted (eg, unit trust prices can go down as well as up).

If advertisements do not conform with these regulations, then the advertiser can be liable to imprisonment, a fine or both. Also any investments undertaken as a direct consequence of such an advertisement will not be enforceable.

Certain advertisements are not subject to these restrictions and these include securities to be quoted on the Unlisted Securities Market.

FACT SHEET

Financial Services Act 1986

Supervisory structure

1. *SIB*
(a) Format – governing body, composition. (b) Powers. (c) Powers not transferred by the Secretary of State for Trade and Industry. (d) Powers of Secretary of State

2. *SROs*
(a) Types (LAUTRO, IMRO, AFBD, FIMBRA, TSA). (b) Members. (c) Investor protection. (d) Powers. (e) Resources. (f) Complaints procedures. (g) Standards.

3. *Others able to authorise investment business*
(a) Professional bodies (eg Law Society, RICS etc). (b Direct authorisation. (c) Insurance companies and friendly societies. (d) EC members. (e) Exempt persons.

4. *Definitions of investments and investment business*

(a) Investments – stocks & shares, debentures, government & local authority securities, unit trusts, options & futures.

(b) Investment business – dealing in investments, arranging deals in investments, managing and advising on investments.

(c) Exceptions – acting as principal, transactions within group members, employee share schemes, newspaper articles (details).

5. *Implications of non-authorised investment business*

Imprisonment, fine or both. Non-enforcement of transaction. Defences: reasonable care and reasonable ignorance.

6. *Conduct of business rules*

Aims: (i) honesty & fairness, (ii) capably, carefully and to best of ability, (iii) avoidance of conflict of interest.

(a) Business plan – authorisation only for items in business plan.

(b) Complaints – records & investigation. Complainants to be advised of rights.

(c) Canvassing – definition & restrictions. Exceptions: (i) call on business or professional investor, (ii) following previous discussions, (iii) unit trust and life assurance; note 14 day cooling-off period.

(d) **Know your customer** – types of investor, assumption that all investors are ordinary individual investors. Exact position of investor must be ascertained (eg, tax position, disposable income, capital etc). Investor must understand the nature of the risks involved. Exceptions: (i) experienced or professional investor (ii) 'execution only' customers.

(e) Customer agreements – three types: (i) terms of business letter, (ii) occasional customer agreement, (iii) full agreements. Contents and uses of each. Exceptions: (i) execution only, (ii) unit trusts and life assurance.

(f) **Best advice** – duty to advise the customer and record such advice. Warnings to be noted.

(g) Best execution – rules and examples.

(h) Polarisation – investment businesses may choose to operate:

    (i) as independent financial intermediaries, sell products across whole range not only their own, or

    (ii) as company representatives, can sell only their own products, must advise the investor of this fact. If product identified is outside his range he must refer investor to independent intermediary. Many banks have chosen company representative route with independent intermediary within group.

(i) Clients' money – this must be kept separate from own funds. Special relevance to banks with investment firms as customers, beware 'constructive trustee'.

(j) Compliance manual and compliance officer – manual to be produced and held in every branch. Compliance officer to have 'the ear' of senior management and right of entry.

Enforcement

Random spot checks by SRO inspector, (i) not identified, or (ii) identified. Investigation of complaints. Consequential removal of authorisation.

Advertising

Conditions, results of non-compliance with conditions. Exceptions.

Question

(a) Under the Financial Services Act 1986 two of the main Conduct of Business Rules are 'know your customer' and 'best advice'. Describe fully the implications of one of these two rules.

(12 marks)

(b) You are an interviewer at your branch and the discussion turns to investments. Describe what procedures you should now follow and why.

(8 marks)

Total 20 marks

Key words

(a) describe fully implications of ONE
(b) interviewer, investments, describe procedure

Answer

(a) The Conduct of Business Rules of the SRO with which the bank is registered must be in line with those of the SIB, which in turn can be varied in line with current practice or to overcome a certain problem or to prevent a certain happening recurring. At the time of writing, the SIB rules (upon which the rules of each SRO must be based) have been re-written but not yet published. So the answer below is based upon the original rules. The aims of the Conduct of Business Rules are:

●   fair and honest dealings in investment business
●   those involved in investment business to act carefully, capably and to the best of their capabilities
●   advisers should be fair to their customers, avoiding a conflict of interests

Failure to comply with the rules could result in the offender losing his registration (effectively being banned from conducting investment business), being fined or jailed or both.

1. 'know your customer'

The adviser, prior to giving advice, has a duty to obtain all relevant information regarding the investor, including his investment knowledge and experience. The FSA 1986 describes four levels of investor, ranging from an ordinary individual investor (who, it is assumed, is completely inexperienced with no knowledge) to a professional investor (where little, if any, advice is necessary). Every investor is presumed to be an ordinary individual investor unless proved otherwise. The information gleaned by the adviser should include: the investor's tax position; ability to pay without placing other existing commitments at risk; the customer's family position (dependent children, etc.); and possible capital gains tax/inheritance tax liability.

The adviser must also ensure that the customer *understands* the nature of the investment involved; for example, that the value of units in a unit trust can go down as well as up. Partly in order to comply with another rule (customer agreements) and partly to reduce the possibility of future repercussions, it has become common practice to record these details in written or computer-based records.

2. 'best advice'

Once the adviser has satisfied the rule described above, the adviser must then offer the investor the best advice available, bearing in mind: the information gained; and the adviser's position, i.e. is the adviser a company representative or an independent financial intermediary? If the adviser is a company representative, he can only offer products from his own company's range. The investor must be made aware of this at the start of the interview. On the other hand, an independent financial intermediary can offer suggestions from the whole range of available products. From a practical point of view at the time of writing, National Westminster Bank is the only major clearing bank to have chosen the independent financial intermediary category of adviser. Once the adviser has obtained the relevant information and has advised a specific product, he must be able to show why it was recommended. Inability to show this will be interpreted as failure to comply with the rule. If a company representative identifies that the best advice to a customer would be to take a product outside his company's range he must not make a sale, even if the product sold is the nearest one from his range to that needed by the customer. For this reason, most of the banks that have gone down the company representative route will have either a contact with a financial intermediary or a financial intermediary in its group of companies. If the transaction is an 'execution only' transaction then the best advice rules do not apply.

(b) The procedures that the interviewer should follow at this stage are basically to comply with the Conduct of Business Rules relevant to his SRO. Failure to do so could mean removal of registration with the SRO, a fine, imprisonment or both. The main rules that are relevant here are:

(i)   is the interviewer a company representative (ie able to deal only with products from his company's range)? If so, this must be disclosed immediately.

(ii)   know your customer; as discussed above the adviser must obtain basic facts from the investor.

(iii)   best advice; based upon the information gained in (ii) and upon the adviser's position (company representative or independent intermediary) the advice given to the investor must be the best advice possible.

(iv)   customer agreements; this is the compulsion placed upon the adviser to ensure that the investor is completely aware of the nature of the transaction and of the protections available. A full agreement will include the procedure for the withdrawal of the deposit, the details of the risks involved, and the procedure for cancellation if appropriate.

CHAPTER 5

Basic types of customers

Syllabus requirements
- The main legal considerations to which a banker must have regard when dealing with the following types of customer: individuals, sole traders, joint account holders, trustees, unincorporated associations.
- In particular, the following aspects: age (minors), account opening, death or mental incompetence of individual customers and termination of mandate including the effect of insolvency.

▌ Account opening procedures

Identification

As we will discuss in Chapter ten, one of the main considerations when opening an account for a prospective customer is whether or not the person in front of you is in fact the person he purports to be. The identification of the prospective customer is important to the banker because if the bank should be shown to be negligent in allowing an account to be opened by an imposter, the bank will lose its statutory protection against conversion given to it by s.4 Cheques Act 1957. An important point to note here is that if the account to be opened is a joint account then suitable identification must be sighted for all parties.

Historically, banks have relied upon a system of identification by taking up references from persons known to both the prospective customer and to the bank. If the referee is not known to the bank then a further reference will be taken on the referee, usually from the banker of the referee. However, this procedure proved to be cumbersome and resulted in delays in the account being opened (usually to the dissatisfaction of the customer) and many cases have arisen from the reference procedures; these are discussed fully in Chapter ten, and include *Ladbroke* v *Todd* (1914) and *Hampstead Guardians* v *Barclays Bank Ltd* (1923).

More recently banks have adopted a method of accepting 'suitable identification', with or without a supporting credit reference search. 'Suitable identification' has now been generally accepted as a driving licence or passport plus one other form of general identification. If none of these documents is available then the different banks appear to have differing levels of acceptability, including credit cards, cheque guarantee cards, building society/bank passbooks and employer's identification cards. In order to protect themselves further, banks not only insist on sighting suitable identification but will also note the identification in their records (for example, recording the driving licence number).

However, despite the variation in items as acceptable identification the position is that no bank will open an account unless satisfied as to the identification of the prospective customer.

The position can become more complicated where the person opening the account is a sole trader, trading under a name other than his own. Under the Business Names Act 1985, where a business is trading under a name other than that of the proprietors (eg, Fanfare

Carpets), the name of the proprietors must be quoted on all stationery (letter headings, invoices etc) and in a prominent position at the business address. If a bank should open an account for such a business without sight of the letter-heads it would almost certainly be guilty of negligence and lose the protection of s.4. Whether or not the mere sight (and normally retention of a copy) of a letter-head is sufficient (a letter head can be produced by any stationers without any corroborative documentation), is a matter of great discussion and will not be settled until case or statute law decides the matter. However, it is difficult to see what options the banks have, as little other documentation is available.

Another variation on this theme is an author writing under a 'nom de plume', where the standard practice is to ask for written confirmation from the publishers.

Bank mandate

Once the banker is satisfied with the identification of the customer the next step will be to complete the bank's mandate. The implied conditions of the banker/customer relationship were laid down in *Joachimson* v *Swiss Bank Corporation* (1921) and have been discussed fully in Chapter one. If the bank wishes to overcome any of the implied rights of the customer it must do so expressly, usually via the account opening mandate. The mandate is designed to protect the bank, usually by removing the customer's rights. However, the mandate is governed by the Unfair Contract Terms Act 1977, and each clause must pass the 'reasonableness' test laid down in the Act. In *Tai Hing Cotton Mill Ltd* v *Liu Chong Hing Bank Ltd* (1985) the Privy Council held that the addition of an express term stating that the customer must check his statements and report any discrepancies to the bank should have been 'brought home' to the customer; failure to do so meant that the express term was not enforceable.

Clauses contained within the mandate include:

(a) A request from the customer(s) to open the account.
(b) A statement that the mandate remains effective unless cancelled in writing.
(c) if a joint account is opened the mandate will also contain:
    (i) Signing details − how many signatures are required on cheques, direct debits etc. In *Husband* v *Davis* (1851) it was held that unless express contradiction is present (for example, in the mandate) all payment instruments must be signed by **all** parties to the account. Therefore the mandate will always enclose an either/or clause which needs to be deleted and signed by the account holders, leaving the bank with an express instruction as to the number of signatories required.
    (ii) Joint and several liability − if this clause were not included then each party would be jointly liable only (discussed fully in Chapter fourteen). If a party to a joint debt who is only jointly liable dies, his liability automatically ceases and the debt cannot be enforced against the estate of the deceased party.
    (iii) Survivorship clause − this enables the bank, upon the death of one party to the account, to continue the account and accept instructions from, or pay away credit balances to, the surviving party or parties to the account.
    (iv) Under the Consumer Credit Act 1974, each party to a joint account should each be forwarded a statement on the account. Many banks ask one party to sign away this right, thus saving costs by sending only one statement per account.
(d) If an agent is to be allowed access to the account (discussed fully in Chapter six) the mandate will state precisely the powers of the agent. For example, will the agent be permitted only to draw cheques or to draw money from the account also? This is

typically known as a third party mandate. Other powers could include borrowing in the principal's (account holder's) name or withdrawing items from safe custody or pledging items as security.

∎ Specific types of account holders

Minors

(a) Minors, generally

A minor is someone aged under eighteen: s.1 Family Law Reform Act 1969 and, due to his age, he has limited contractual capacity. Basically, only contracts for 'necessaries' are enforceable against the minor. In *Nash* v *Inman* (1908) a contract for 11 expensive waistcoats was found unenforceable as the clothes were not 'necessaries'. The results of the 'necessaries' test depend wholly upon the minor's circumstances and will vary from individual to individual, according to his position in life. However, if a minor contracts to purchase essential clothes he will be liable on the purchase contract but will not be liable on the cheque he writes out to pay for those goods: *Re Soltykoff* (1891).

Therefore any lending to a minor during his minority (ie, whilst he is under 18) is unenforceable, even if the borrowing was for necessaries. However, should a bank lend to a minor and be unable to recover its money, it will be subrogated to the rights of the supplier of the goods purchased by the loan monies. In *Nottingham Permanent Benefit Building Society* v *Thurstan* (1903), this amounted to a lien over the title deeds taken as security (despite the legal charge over them being absolutely void).

Furthermore, any borrowing undertaken during his minority is not automatically enforceable against him following his 18th birthday. For a debt undertaken during minority to be enforceable after reaching majority, the debt must be ratified and accepted in full, within a reasonable time of attaining the majority: s.1 Minors' Contracts Act 1987.

Also, under s.3 Minors' Contracts Act 1987 the courts have the discretion to enforce the minor to return the property to the other party in an unenforceable contract (eg, lending), providing the other party acted in good faith (honestly), and it is just and equitable to return the property.

(b) Minors and bank accounts

Where the depositor is under seven years of age the account must be treated as a trust account with the parents as trustees. Technically, with the above exception, banks are considered to be perfectly safe when dealing with minors where their account is maintained in credit, such as a deposit account or cheque account with auto-teller machine (ATM) access only. However, should the bank lend money to the minor this could cause complications for the lending banker, as seen above. The lending to the minor could take one of two forms. Firstly, the lending could be agreed to between the bank and the minor and perhaps supported by a guarantee from a parent. In the first instance, the bank will find recovery of the debt difficult, having to rely upon subrogation, ratification upon majority or approaching the courts for an order under s.3 Minors' Contracts Act 1987. In the second instance, s.2 Minors' Contracts Act 1987 provides that if a minor's debt is guaranteed and the minor is not liable, 'the guarantee shall not for this reason alone be unenforceable against the guarantor'. This is an important ruling for bankers and effectively overrules the decision in *Coutts & Co* v *Browne Lecky* (1947).

(c) Minors and other sundry matters

It is possible that the banker could deal with a minor not only as a sole account holder but also in some other capacity. For example, a minor can be a company director (if the company Articles allow), or an agent (an agent need not have contractual capacity). A minor can also be a partner but will not be liable on partnership debts incurred during his minority, unless he agrees to be so within a reasonable time of reaching his majority.

(d) Minors – summary

Banks need to take care when dealing with minors as customers, especially when issuing them with cheque books or cheque guarantee cards, as minors may not be liable on cheques drawn or debts created by them. However, the introduction of the Minors Contract Act 1987 has meant that greater protection is now available to persons dealing with minors and great comfort can be found within it for the banker.

Joint account holders

(a) Joint accounts – generally

A joint account is a bank account held by two or more persons. Joint accounts are most commonly seen between husband and wife or as a partnership banking account (discussed fully in Chapter seven). In these circumstances the banker must request identification, or references should be taken from each party. However, if one party is already a well-established customer then the introduction, by him, of the other party is usually considered sufficient. If the account is a partnership account and the partners are trading under a name other than that of the partners then a letter-head confirming the existence and the names of the partners should be sighted: Business Names Act 1985.

(b) The mandate

Unless specified to the contrary in the mandate, **all** parties must sign on all relevant documents, such as cheques, standing orders or direct debtis. It is normal practice for either party to the account to sign these documents, although if the parties require they can instruct the bank that only documents signed by both parties should be accepted. If the mandate states that both parties must sign on the account and the bank effectively ignores this instruction and pays on one signature, or one signature plus the forged signature of the other party, it is not necessary for both parties to sue the bank, this can be undertaken by just one party if necessary: *Baker* v *Barclays Bank Ltd* (1955).

Where the parties wish either party to sign cheques it is accepted that a cheque can also be stopped by either party, even if it is not the same party that signed the cheque: *Gaunt* v *Taylor* (1843). Parties to the joint account are automatically jointly liable on any debt on the account, although the mandate will normally state that the liability will be joint and several. Also, as previously mentioned, the bank will request that one party sign away his right to a separate statement.

(c) Death of a joint account holder

Joint and several liability gives the bank the advantage that if a party to a joint account should die, the bank will be able to claim any outstanding debt from the estate of the deceased; if the parties were only jointly liable this would not be so. Also, joint and several liability gives the bank the added protection of being able to rely upon security lodged by one party for his own liabilities, which will then be available for application to the joint account debt, as will any monies held in a credit account by one of the parties, in their own name.

One important aspect of the joint and several liability of a deceased party to a joint account is that his estate is liable only for the debts outstanding at the time of death, and to preserve the liability of the deceased party the bank must stop or 'freeze' the account as soon as notice of death is received and arrange to make alternative banking arrangements for the survivor. This will have the effect of preventing the rule in *Clayton's Case* operating to the detriment of the bank. For example, if on the death of a partner to a partnership account the balance is £1,000 overdrawn, then this is the limit of the liability of the deceased party. If the account should be allowed to continue, then any credits to the account will reduce the balance for which the deceased's estate is liable, and any debits will create a new debt for which the deceased's estate is not liable. This could be particularly important if the deceased is the wealthiest party to the account.

If the account is in credit and one of the parties should die, the surviving party will automatically be able to continue the account, without the need to apply for probate. In *McEvoy* v *Belfast Banking Co Ltd* (1935), the bank held a joint bank account between father and son. When the father died, the bank paid the money to the father's executors, and not to the son. The son sued for breach of mandate but was unable to prove that he was a party to the contract with the bank. If he had been able to do so the bank would undoubtedly have lost. This is the common law situation but it is also usually enforced by a specific clause in the mandate. Although the survivor can give a valid discharge to the bank, it is possible that he may have to report to the executors of the deceased for the proceeds from the account. Cheques drawn on the joint account by the deceased party should be returned 'drawer deceased', or alternatively confirmed, in writing, by the surviving party.

(d) Bankruptcy of a party to a joint account

Where a bankruptcy order is served on one party to a joint account, the effect is that that party automatically loses his contractual capacity, and as such the mandate is revoked, meaning that for any withdrawal on the account the document must be signed by **all** parties to the account, ie, the remaining parties plus the trustee in the bankruptcy of the bankrupt party.

If the account is in credit, the bank must await a written instruction from the trustee plus the remaining parties, before it can dispose of the monies in the account.

If the account is overdrawn the bank must stop the account to prevent the rule in *Clayton's Case* operating to the bank's detriment. It must also 'prove' in the bankruptcy for the full amount of the debt. This process is discussed fully in Chapter nine. The bank would usually also serve formal demand on the remaining parties to the account requesting repayment in full. The joint and several liability clause in the mandate also means that any funds held in private accounts in the names of any parties to the account will also be available for combination with the debt on the overdrawn joint account, and the bank will be able to realise any security held in the sole names of the other parties to the account.

Once notice of bankruptcy has been received the bank must return any cheques written on the account, marked 'refer to drawer' or 'refer to drawer − joint account holder involved in bankruptcy proceedings'; this careful wording is not thought to be defamatory. An alternative account can be opened for the remaining parties, and the remaining parties will be able to operate this account as the bank sees fit.

(e) Mental incapacity of a party to a joint account

Where the bank is made aware of the mental incapacity of a party to a joint account, the account should immediately be stopped until clear instructions are received from the receiver, appointed under the Court of Protection, and the remaining parties to the account. If the bank wishes to maintain the liability of the mentally incapacitated party it must once again stop the account.

Accounts of trustees

(a) Trustees – general

A trustee is a person to whom property is committed for the benefit of others. There are many different forms of trustees, for example:

(i) The trustees of a private trust. A trust for the benefit of an individual, or group, can be enforced by the beneficiaries. Other than the exceptions discussed later, the powers of a trustee of a private trust cannot be delegated to his co-trustees. This is the most common form of trust that as bankers you are most likely to encounter; an example of such a trust is a will quoting the executors as trustees.

(ii) The trustees of a charitable (or public) trust. A trust for the benefit of the public as a whole, or for sections of the public, such as education, religion, relief of poverty etc. These trustees can delegate either all or some of their powers to any of their number as they feel fit: s.34 Charities Act 1960. The activities of a charitable trust are closely supervised by a number of official bodies including the Charity Commissioners, a state department reporting directly to the Home Secretary.

(iii) Trustee in bankruptcy. A qualified insolvency practitioner appointed by either the courts, a general meeting of the creditors or the Secretary of State, to deal in the bankruptcy proceedings. Usually only one trustee is appointed, but, if there are more than one, the powers and rights of delegation are expressly provided for.

Just as there are many types of trustees, there are also a number of ways of identifying trust accounts; these include:

(i) Express notification. This is the approach by the trustees to open an account in the name of themselves acting as trustees. However, in *Re Gross ex parte Kingston* (1871), an account styled 'police account' was deemed to be express notice that the account was in fact a trust account.

(ii) Constructive trusteeship. This has been discussed fully in Chapter one, and I would suggest that you read again this section from Chapter one now. In general you need to know the difference between 'knowing assistance' (involving dishonesty, lack of integrity etc. which can mean the bank having to repay all losses to the trust fund) and 'knowing receipt', whereby the bank is liable only for money actually passing through the bank account.

(iii) 'Quistclose trusts'. (Discussed fully towards the end of Chapter one). These basically imply the placing of monies in the bank for one specific purpose and as such cannot be used for another, for example, combination.

In this chapter we will discuss the effects of express notification and how banks deal with trustees.

(b) Opening the account

As with the opening of all accounts, if the trustee (in effect the account holder) is not known to the bank then suitable identification or references should be taken.

If the bank is satisfied with the introduction procedures it will ask the trustees to sign the bank mandate. If the trust is a private trust this **must** be done by all the trustees, and cheques must also be signed by all the trustees, but if it is a charitable trust the power to sign the mandate and cheques can be delegated to one trustee or a number of co-trustees. If a trust deed is in existence there is no necessity for the bank to see it, but a cautious banker may wish to check the powers of the trustees.

The mandate will contain the following clauses:

- A request to open an account.
- Specimen signatures of all the trustees who are parties to the account (all, if it is a private trust).
- Joint and several liability of the trustees for any borrowing on the account.
- The number of signatures required on cheques (remember, if it is a private trust, this must be all the trustees).
- Confirmation that the items held in safe custody or safe deposit will be presented to the trustees upon express request by all the trustees.

Once the decision has been made to open the account, and the mandate signed, the account may be opened but must be styled clearly that it is a trust account, for example, 'trustees of Elizabeth Barton deceased'.

(c) Exceptional circumstances permitting delegation of powers of private trustees

(i) Where the trust deed permits.

(ii) By law, partial delegation is possible under s.23 Trustee Act 1925, whereby the trustees may appoint an agent (eg, a solicitor) to perform a specific duty. Under s.25 Trustee Act 1925, as amended by s.9 Powers of Attorney Act 1971, the trustee may delegate the whole of his powers by power of attorney. These cannot be delegated to the sole remaining co-trustee, unless that sole remaining co-trustee is a trust corporation. The delegation must be for a period not exceeding 12 months and the trustee is still responsible for the deeds of his attorney.

(d) Lending to trustees

When lending to trustees, the bank must satisfy itself that the express power exists to borrow and to charge the trust property as security. The bank cannot rely on an implied power and if no express power exists the bank must either:

(i) Request that the beneficiaries amend the trust deed. This is possible only if all the beneficiaries are over 18 and all agree.
(ii) Reliance on law. Section 16 Trustee Act 1925, states that if the trust document authorises the trustees to use capital money, borrowing for capital purposes is permitted as is the securing of such borrowing by mortgage. Section 17 Trustee Act 1925 states that where money is advanced by mortgage the mortgagee need not be concerned as to the use of funds borrowed in such a manner.
(iii) Application to court. As a last resort the consent of the courts may be sought, and they will give their permission on terms and conditions as they will see fit: s.57 Trustee Act 1925.

(e) Breach of trust by the trustees

As soon as the bank is aware that the account is a trust account, the bank must ensure that it does not knowingly become a party to a breach of the trust. It was held in *Gray v Johnson* (1868), that as the bank did not know of the breach of trust it could not be liable for the breach. This should be contrasted with the decision in *Rowlandson and Others v National Westminster Bank* (1978), where it was held that as the bank knowingly assisted the trustees in their dishonest and fraudulent designs, the bank was accountable to the trustees. Also, if the bank derives any benefit from the breach it will again be liable, as per *Foxton* v *Manchester and Liverpool District Banking Company* (1881), where funds were used to clear the overdraft of the trustees (executors).

Baden Delvaux and Lecuit v *Société Générale S.A.* (1983), listed five categories of knowledge and the courts decided that in the following circumstances the bank would be at fault:

(i) actual knowledge;
(ii) wilfully shutting one's eyes to the obvious;
(iii) wilfully and recklessly failing to make such enquiries as an honest and reasonable man would make;
(iv) knowledge of circumstances which would indicate the facts to an honest and reasonable man; and
(v) knowledge of circumstances which would put an honest and reasonable man on enquiry.

(f) Mixing of trustee's own personal funds and those held on trust

If the trustee should mix his own funds with those held in trust, there may be a problem in deciding whose funds are represented by the balance in the 'mixed' account. In normal circumstances the rule in *Clayton's Case* would be used to differentiate between the two. However, this is one instance where the rule does not apply. *Re Hallet's Estate* (1880) states that where monies held on trust are mixed with the trustee's own funds the balance on the account is presumed to belong to the trust until the amount owed to the trust has been exhausted. The remainder (if any) will pass to the trustee.

(g) Retirement, death or bankruptcy of trustees

A trustee may retire either by the consent of the beneficiaries, under the Trustee Act 1925 (with or without replacements) or, rarely, by order of the courts. In order to maintain the liability of the retiring trustee for any borrowing on the account, the bank will need to 'stop' the account and prevent *Clayton's Case* operating against the bank.

Upon the death of a trustee the bank needs to ascertain whether or not a new trustee is to be appointed. Section 18 Trustee Act 1925 states that the remaining trustees can continue the trust, exactly as before, unless there is a contrary provision in the trust deed. Either way if the bank wishes to maintain the liability of the deceased trustee for any borrowing on the account, the bank will need to 'stop' the account to prevent *Clayton's Case* operating to its detriment.

If a trustee is declared bankrupt he may continue as a trustee, although it is normal to ask him to retire, under which circumstances the bank will proceed as above.

(h) Personal accounts of trustees

Where a bank holds the personal account of a trustee (ie, not in his official capacity), then care needs to be taken that the trustee does not abuse his position. In *Midland Bank Ltd v Reckitt and Others* (1933), it was held that the bank was liable for conversion (and lost the protection of s.4 Cheques Act 1957 – for full discussion, see Chapter ten) due to its negligence in accepting for collection a cheque payable to a customer and drawn by him as agent. It is probable that the same conclusion would be arrived at if the trustee was misapplying the trust funds.

Accounts of unincorporated associations

(a) Unincorporated associations – generally

An unincorporated association is a group of people acting together for non-profitable purposes. The most common examples are charities (for example, RSPCA), enthusiasts' groups (such as MENSA) or drama, social or sports groups. The group is usually run by a number of its members acting as a board, or committee, the members of which are elected by the membership itself. The association will usually have a set of published rules by which it is governed.

The important point to note is that the unincorporated association is not a separate legal entity, as a limited company is, and as such the association comprises the membership and cannot sue, or be sued, in its own name. (Borrowing by these bodies is covered later in this chapter). One of the main dangers to banks is that of conversion of the funds belonging to the association. We have discussed fully the protections available to a collecting bank when faced with a charge of conversion; the main defence being s.4 Cheques Act 1957. However, to be able to rely upon this defence the bank must act without negligence. Where the bank has collected a cheque for a member of an unincorporated association and the cheque is either drawn by the association, or has supposedly been endorsed by the association, or the cheque is payable to him in his capacity within the association, then the collecting bank is undoubtedly at risk of losing its statutory defence under s.4. Although none of the following cases actually applied to an unincorporated association, the reason for the decision would apply equally if the account involved had been that of an unincorporated association:

- *Midland Bank Ltd* v *Reckitt and others* (1933). Here an agent drew cheques on his principal's account and paid them into his personal account. The collecting bank should have queried the collection and their failure to do so lost them the protection of s.4.
- *Ross* v *London County Westminster and Parr's Bank* (1919). Here cheques payable to 'The officer-in-charge, estates office, Canadian Overseas Military Forces' were endorsed and paid into the personal account of the officer-in-charge. Again the bank lost its statutory protection.
- *A.L. Underwood Ltd* v *Bank of Liverpool and Martins Ltd* (1924). Here the cheque was payable to A.L. Underwood Ltd, endorsed by the managing director and paid into his personal account. Theoretically, if the situation had involved an unincorporated association, and not a limited company, the position would be the same, the bank losing its protection under s.4.

As with any type of account if the bank does not know the committee members, or signatories on the account, then identification or references should be taken up.

Occasionally, a body such as a charity or club will in fact be a corporate body and registered as a limited company, usually limited by guarantee, and these bodies are covered fully in Chapter eight.

(b) The mandate

The normal method of opening the account would be by asking the committee members to complete the mandate, incorporating a resolution naming the bank as their banker. The resolution should be verified by the chairman and treasurer, and will state the signatories on the account, usually the treasurer plus one other from those authorised to sign. It is safer for the bank to use this format and not to name the signatories personally; if the latter course of action were adopted, a new mandate would be needed each time there was a change of treasurer.

The mandate will also state the name of the association, and it is normal practice for the account to be opened in this name. Alternatively, the account could be opened in a style such as 'Miss E. Davies for Chalfont Street Girl Guides'. This puts the bank on guard as per *Re Gross ex parte Kingston* (1871), and has the added benefit of making Miss Davies personally liable for any borrowings on the account.

(c) Borrowings by the unincorporated association

As previously mentioned, an unincorporated association is not a separate legal entity and as such cannot be sued for any borrowings on the account. However, the decision in *Bradley Egg Farm Ltd* v *Clifford and Others* (1943) held that under specific conditions it is possible that the appointed officers could be liable for the debt. Banks would not usually rely on this ruling and would lend subject to third party security, incorporating an indemnity clause (see Chapters 13 and 14); this would protect the lending bank against the ruling in *Coutts & Co* v *Browne Lecky* (1947) (see above mentioned chapters). Alternatively, the security offered could be held by trustees for the association, for example, a club house or sports ground. In these circumstances care needs to be taken and the rules and title documents must be carefully examined, with legal advice being sought if appropriate.

(d) Death or bankruptcy of a signatory

These happenings do not directly affect the association's account, and any cheque signed by the deceased or bankrupt party are still enforceable and as such can still be debited to the association's account. However, the executors, personal representatives, trustee or other party dealing with the bankruptcy cannot replace the deceased or bankrupt party and so replacement signatories, from the membership, should be organised as soon as practical.

Accounts of solicitors and financial intermediaries

When holding accounts for either of these bodies it is important that funds held on behalf of clients are not 'mixed' with the day-to-day banking requirements of the business or practice. Section 55 Financial Services Act 1986 states that firms regulated by the Act (see Chapter four) must maintain separate accounts with a recognised bank for client's funds and the account must be styled accordingly.

Solicitors are governed by similar Law Society rules, and by the Solicitors Act 1974, whereby each solicitor must have at least one client's account and if an amount of over

£500 is to be held for a period of over two months a separate client's account (known as a designated client's account) must be opened.

There is no right of set-off or combination between a client's account and any other account: s.283 Insolvency Act 1986. A client's account should never be overdrawn, as the existence of a client's account is solely due to the holding of credit balances on behalf of the client.

An important consideration when dealing with firms that should hold a client's account is that of constructive notice of a breach of trust. This has been discussed fully both in this chapter, and in Chapter one. In particular the decision in *Lipkin Gorman* v *Karnaple and Another* (1986), should be known, where it was held that the bank had constructive notice of the misappropriation of client's funds.

∎ Express termination of the banker/customer relationship

We have already discussed, above, the effects of death, bankruptcy or mental incapacity of parties on specific types of accounts. However, these are not the only events by which the relationship can be terminated. Perhaps the most common method of termination, either by the bank or the customer is the express method. If termination is by the customer it is usually by letter, or by a visit to the bank, the customer requesting to close the account and to be paid the balance as at that date, or by transfer request, asking the bank to transfer all banking facilities to another bank or another branch of the same bank. In these circumstances no notice is necessary (although the customer may lose interest on deposit monies if notice of withdrawal is normally needed). The bank will usually ask for the remaining unused cheques, the return of the cheque guarantee card and ATM card (if issued) and confirmation that any cheques already written can be debited to the new account. In the current competitive climate, it is not unusual for banks to charge a restrictive fee for the transfer, in an attempt to keep the account.

Alternatively, the account may be closed expressly by the bank. In these circumstances reasonable notice must be given: *Joachimson* v *Swiss Bank Corporation* (1921). The test as to what is reasonable will vary from account to account, with greater notice being necessary on more complicated accounts. In *Prosperity* v *Lloyds Bank Ltd* (1923) it was held that one month's notice was not adequate.

∎ Termination by operation of law

(a) Death of customer. However, s.75 Bills of Exchange Act 1882 protects the bank when paying cheques without notice of death.
(b) Mental incapacity. Defined by Mental Health Act 1983 as by reason of mental disorder being no longer able to manage his own affairs.
(c) Bankruptcy. See Chapter nine.

FACT SHEET

Basic types of customers

Account opening procedures
1. *Identification.* Movement away from references to actual identification (for example, passport, driving licence), important to retain protection of s.4 Cheques Act 1957. Business Names Act 1985.

2. *The mandate.* Protective clauses and effect of Unfair Contract Terms Act 1977, 'reasonableness' test.

Specific types of account holders

1. *Minors*

(a) Generally. Persons under 18. Contract for 'necessaries' is enforceable, but the cheque is a separate contract; Re Soltykoff (1891), but the bank could rely upon subrogation *Nottingham Permanent Building Society* v *Thurstan* (1903), or on s.3 Minors Contract Act 1987, providing it was taken in good faith and it is just and equitable to return the goods involved. Contracts undertaken during minority are not automatically enforceable upon reaching majority.

(b) Minors and bank accounts. Under age seven, the account is a trust account. Main problem is unenforceable lending. However, if supported by guarantee, the guarantee will not be unenforceable by reason of the principal debtor's minority alone, s.2 Minors Contract Act 1987. Minors can be directors or agents.

2. *Joint accounts*

(a) Generally. Identification necessary from each party, although an introduction by an existing, reputable customer is sufficient for second party to an account.

(b) The mandate. Additional clauses for joint accounts. Only one party needed to sue the bank, meaning that if the signature of one party is forged, either is free to sue for breach of mandate: *Baker* v *Barclays Bank Ltd* (1955). Cheque can be stopped by party other than the signatory on the actual cheque: *Gaunt* v *Taylor* (1843).

(c) Death, bankruptcy or mental incapacity of a joint account member. Joint and several liability means that each party is liable for full amount. If bank wishes to maintain liability it must stop the account to prevent *Clayton's Case* operating against the bank. Cheques signed by the deceased must be signed, countersigned or confirmed by remaining parties. Cheques signed by a bankrupt must be returned. On death, the remaining party automatically receives the balance. On mental incapacity or bankruptcy bank must await instructions.

3. *Trustees' accounts*

(a) Generally. Definitions, examples and methods of notification; particular emphasis on constructive notice.

(b) Opening the account. References, or identification, if trustees are not known. No need to sight trust deed. Protective clauses of mandate, general rule regarding trustee's inability to delegate powers, exceptions need to be known.

(c) Lending to trustees. Express power must exist to borrow and charge assets as security. Methods of obtaining express power.

(d) Breach of trust. Bank unaware: *Gray* v *Johnson* (1868), knowing assistance: *Rowlandson and others* v *National Westminster Bank Ltd* (1978); benefit to bank: *Foxton* v *Manchester and Liverpool District Banking Company* (1881). Knowledge defined in *Baden Delvaux and Lecuit* v *Société Générale S.A.* (1985).

(e) Mixing of funds. Rule in *Re Hallett's Estate* 1880, overriding *Clayton's Case*.

(f) Retirement, death or bankruptcy of trustees: retirement governed by Trustee Act 1925. Account to be stopped if necessary. Death: are replacements to be made? Again account to be stopped if necessary. Bankruptcy: can continue but it is normal to retire.

(g) Personal accounts of trustees – care with conversion.

4. *Unincorporated associations*

(a) Generally. Definition, not a separate legal entity. Care with conversion, possible examples of danger.

(b) The mandate. Clauses, resolution and style of account.

(c) Borrowings. *Bradley Egg Farm Ltd* v *Clifford and Others* (1943), signatories can be liable for debt, but banks usually do not rely on this and take either third party security incorporating indemnity clause (remember *Coutts & Co* v *Browne Lecky* (1947), or a direct charge on property held by the association; legal advice may be necessary.

(d) Death or bankruptcy of a signatory; no effect, but replacement signatories should be obtained as soon as possible.

5. *Solicitors and financial intermediaries*

Clients' accounts, when needed, no right of set-off: *Lipkin Gorman* v *Karnaple and Another* (1986).

Express termination

(a) By customer – closure of account, or transfer of account. No notice necessary but there could be a restrictive charge if account is being transferred.

(b) By bank – reasonable notice needed. *Prosperity* v *Lloyds Bank Ltd* (1923): one month not sufficient on complicated account.

Question

(a) When opening a personal account for an individual, what procedures should the bank follow and why?

(14 marks)

(b) What additional considerations should the bank bear in mind if the account is to be a personal joint account?

(6 marks)

Total 20 marks

Key words

(a) opening account, individual, procedures and why?

(b) additional considerations, joint

Answer

(a) 1. Identification. Obtain adequate identification of the prospective customer. If the bank fails to do this it may well lose its statutory protection against conversion should it collect a cheque for someone other than the true owner. One condition for protection is that the bank must not act negligently: past examples of negligence have included many cases of inadequate identification when opening the account. Historically, banks have relied upon references from mutual acquaintances, taking up a further reference on the referee not known to the bank. Unfortunately, this system proved both cumbersome and open to abuse (see *Hampstead Guardians* v *Barclays Bank Ltd* (1923), where the 'customer' gave his own real name as a referee and *Marfani* v *Midland Bank Ltd* (1968), where the 'customer' was known to the referee under the same incorrect name as the one used to open the account). Because of this most banks now confirm identity by asking the prospective customer to supply documentary evidence. The level of identification has been set by each bank individually and the basic documents required are usually a passport or full driving licence. Other details required include:

  (i) the name of the customer's employers, in order to prevent a recurrence of the facts in *Lloyds Bank* v *Savory* (1933), where a dishonest clerk passed cheques payable to his employer through his account; there is no obligation to keep up to date with changes in employers (*Orbit Mining and Trading Co Ltd* v *Westminster Bank Ltd* (1963)).

  (ii) the name of the employers of the customer's spouse.

  (iii) a credit reference search to satisfy the bank of the integrity of the customer.

2. Mandate. Once the bank is satisfied with the identity and integrity of the customer, he will then be asked to complete the standard bank mandate. The basis of the banker–customer relationship is enshrined in the implied terms as laid down in *Joachimson* v *Swiss Bank Corporation* (1921). If any of these implied terms are to be altered this must be done expressly (for example via the mandate) and the customer specifically advised: *Tai Hing Cotton Mills Ltd* v *Liu Chong Hing Bank Ltd* (1985). The terms of the mandate must satisfy the test of reasonableness, contained within the Unfair Contract Terms Act 1977, and will typically include: a request from the customer to open the account; details of agents powers, if applicable; and a statement that the mandate remains effective until cancelled in writing.

(b) When opening a joint personal account it is important that suitable forms of identification (or references) are obtained for both customers along with details of employers, so that the bank will be able to claim the protection of s. 4 Cheques Act 1957, should it face a charge of conversion in connection with the collection of a cheque. Other important points to note are:

  (i) The signing instructions must be expressly stated; it was held in *Husband* v *Davis* (1851) that unless specifically stated to the contrary it will be assumed that all parties to the account must sign. Thus, the mandate will expressly state the number of signatures required on cheques, direct debits, etc.

  (ii) The parties to the account will be made expressly joint and severally liable, the main advantage of this being that should one party die the deceased estate will still be liable for the debt. This is not so in the common-law state of joint liability.

  (iii) The survivorship clause ensures the continuation of the account should one party die, with the balance on the account being paid to the survivor.

  (iv) Under the Consumer Credit Act 1974 each party to the account should be forwarded a separate statement. However, banks usually state in their mandate that this right is expressly waived.

CHAPTER 6

Banks and agency

Syllabus requirements

● The main legal considerations to which a banker must have regard when dealing with agents (in relation to powers of attorney, trustees, directors and partners).

■ Introduction

As you can realise at first glance, the majority of items stated above are covered within other chapters of this book, and in an attempt to avoid repetition, I intend to outline the principles of agency and how they relate to each of the above items (partners are discussed in Chapter seven, directors are discussed in Chapter eight and trustees in Chapter five. I shall detail powers of attorney separately, and it is important that I should do so. I will discuss banks as agents and also banks dealing with agents. Before I do that we need to know what an agent is and how agency is created. This seems an appropriate point from which to start.

■ Definition and creation of agency

An agent is someone appointed to bring his principal into contractual relations with third parties and is rarely involved in the contract personally and incurs no liability. However, there are exceptions to this rule and these are discussed later. So, how is agency created? To help you to remember this there is a mnemonic, of I WONDER, and the memory prompt is 'I wonder how agency is created?', and the methods of creating agency are as follows:

Implication. This occurs when the principal implies by his previous actions that the person is in fact his agent; alternatively it can be stated that the nature of the relationship between the two parties implies that one is acting as agent for the other. The most relevant example to bankers is the collection of cheques by the collecting bank for its customers, and this implied duty of the bank has in fact been supported in case law: *Joachimson* v *Swiss Bank Corporation* (1921).

Writing. Naturally agents can be appointed in writing, for example, an instruction by a bank customer to accept the signature of a third party on the account. This is commonly brought into being by a 'third party mandate', an appointment in writing of an agent, stating quite clearly the powers of the agent.

Orally. Although agents can be appointed by word of mouth, this method is not acceptable to banks due to the difficulty of assessing the powers of the agent and the lack of supporting documentation should the principal later deny the appointment.

Necessity. Here a party, usually already dealing with the principal, will find it necessary to act as agent on his behalf. This form of agency is rare and subject to the following conditions:

- it was not possible to obtain instructions from the principal,
- there was a definite commercial necessity (ie, a loss to the principal would have resulted if the action had not been taken), and
- the agent acted honestly and took only the minimum action necessary.

One of the rare occasions on which this has occurred was in *Great Northern Railway* v *Swaffield* (1874), where the railway company was able to claim reimbursement for the overnight stabling of a horse, which was being transported by rail and which arrived late at the station, where no one had been sent to collect it.

Deed. This is an agent appointed under the Powers of Attorney Act 1971, or the Enduring Powers of Attorney Act 1985. Basically for an agent to be able to contract under seal (by deed, for example, to complete a legal charge) the agent must be appointed under seal. Powers of attorney are discussed fully later in this chapter.

Estoppel. This is an act or omission which prevents the principal from denying the existence of the agency. Estoppel can take two forms, which are both discussed in Chapter ten. They are basically:

(a) Estoppel arising from a misleading statement, as in *Brown* v *Westminster Bank Ltd* (1964), where an old lady confirmed numerous times that the signatures on cheques were either genuine or had been authorised by her. Eventually, the son became aware of the happenings and the bank was sued for breach of mandate. The claim failed as the previous statements by the customer meant that the customer was estopped from denying the genuineness of the signature.
(b) Estoppel arising from a breach of duty, as in *Greenwood* v *Martins Bank* (1933), where a husband was aware that his wife was forging his signature on cheques and yet failed to inform the bank. Upon his wife's death he tried to claim reimbursement for the cheques bearing his wife's forgery of his signature. His claim failed as the breach of duty to inform the bank of the forgery of his signature (a duty from *Joachimson* v *Swiss Bank Corporation* (1921)), meant he was estopped from denying the genuineness of the signature.

Ratification. This is the confirmation by the principal that he will be liable for the contract, despite the fact that the person entering into the contract at that time was not his agent or was acting beyond the powers given to him by the principal. There are a number of conditions, **all** of which must be satisfied before a contract can be ratified:

(a) The agent must have stated that he was acting as an agent and he must have named his principal, or else the principal can easily be identified. In *Keighley, Maxtead and Co* v *Durant* (1901), the non-disclosure of the agency meant that the contract was not enforceable against the principal.
(b) The principal must be aware of all material facts of the contract, at the time of ratification, or else he can waive this right.
(c) The principal must have been in existence and had contractual capacity both at the time of the contract and at the time of ratification. Examples of a lack of contractual capacity can include:
    (i) *Minors*: as you have read in Chapter five, minors have only limited contractual capacity, and so a contract for other than 'necessaries' cannot be ratified upon majority.

(ii) *Limited companies*: as you will see in Chapter eight, limited companies cannot commence trading until authorisation is received from the Company Registrar (by certificate of incorporation, if a private company, or by this certificate plus a certificate to commence trading, if a public company). Prior to this authorisation any contracts entered into are known as pre-formation contracts and are unenforceable, so they cannot be ratified: *Kelner* v *Baxter* (1866).

(iii) *Enemy aliens*: not as frightening as they might at first seem, as the phrase simply means nationals of a country at war with this country. If the principal is an enemy alien he cannot ratify a contract, even if entered into prior to the commencement of hostilities: *Boston Deep Sea Fishing and Ice Co Ltd* v *Farnham* (1957).

(iv) *Bankrupts*: a bankrupt cannot ratify a contract entered into prior to his bankruptcy.

(d) The whole contract must be ratified and not merely the favourable sections of it.

(e) Ratification must take place within the agreed time scale, and if none has been agreed, then within a 'reasonable' time.

▌ Types of authority of agents

Actual authority

This is the authority expressly delegated to the agent by the principal. The delegation may be in writing, by deed (power of attorney), or orally.

Implied authority

This is the authority that the principal intends the agent to have, but he has not expressed it in so many words, it merely being understood between the two of them. It is the authority needed by the agent to perform the tasks asked of him. In an interesting case, *Armagas Ltd* v *Mundogas S.A., The Ocean Frost* (1986), it was held that in the absence of a declaration by the principal that the agent had authority, the agent had none and the third party dealing with the agent could not rely upon a declaration by the agent.

Ostensible/apparent authority

This is the authority that it is 'reasonable' to expect the agent to have. What is 'reasonable' will depend upon the circumstances, the knowledge that the third party has of the agency and the facts at the time. For example, a partner of a joinery firm can have no ostensible authority to purchase a diamond ring on behalf of the firm, but he would have ostensible authority to purchase wood on behalf of the partnership. In *McLaughlin* v *Gentles* (1919), it was held that ostensible authority cannot exist if the third party does not know that the agent is acting on behalf of a principal.

An important point to note is that if an agent exceeds his actual authority but acts within his ostensible authority, the principal would be bound by the contract entered into by his agent. The exceptions to this rule are:

(i) Where the third party is aware of the limitation in the authority of the agent. He may acquire this awareness expressly or by constructive notice. In *Reckitt* v *Barnett, Pembroke and Slater Ltd* (1929), it was held that the third party could not rely upon the ostensible authority of an agent when they were aware that the agent was using his principal's monies to settle a personal debt.

(ii) Where a bill of exchange is signed 'per pro' (or on behalf of), this is held to be notice to a third party that the agent has only limited authority and as such the principal is bound only by a contract within the agent's actual authority.

An important example is a third party dealing with a director and relying upon the ostensible authority of the director to commit the company, or represent the board of directors.

∎ Rights of agent and principal

Rights of the agent (duties of the principal)

(a) The principal has a duty to give his agent a clear and precise mandate, where necessary.

(b) The principal has a duty to indemnify the agent against loss. In *Hichens, Harrison, Woolston and Co* v *Jackson and Sons* (1943), it was held that the principal had to reimburse the agents, a firm of stockbrokers. The stockbrokers had sold shares on behalf of the principal; unfortunately the principal later refused to sign the stock transfer form, resulting in the stockbrokers having to repurchase the shares at a loss. They were successful in claiming reimbursement from their principal.

(c) The agent has a right of remuneration from the principal. The level of remuneration can be expressly agreed between the two parties, for example, between an estate agent and client (the estate agent being the agent, the client, the principal) the level of remuneration is usually expressly agreed in the contract between the two parties at a percentage of the sale price. If the level of remuneration is not fixed, the agent will be able to claim remuneration at a reasonable level consistent with the trade or custom involved. Where the level of remuneration has been fixed by express agreement this cannot later be subject to any implied terms: *Luxor (Eastbourne) Ltd* v *Cooper* (1941).

(d) The agent has a right of lien (right to retain) over goods in his possession, belonging to his principal, should he not receive payment from his principal. For example, a solicitor can refuse to release the title deeds to a property, where he has acted on behalf of his client in the conveyance, until he has been paid in full. In banking terms this is useful where a cheque is returned unpaid to the collecting bank, resulting in a debit balance on the customer's account. In these circumstances the bank has a lien on the cheque and can enforce payment as a holder in due course (see Chapter ten for a full discussion of this point).

Duties of an agent (rights of the principal)

(a) The agent has a duty to exercise reasonable care. Again, 'reasonable' will depend upon the circumstances relating to the individual transaction, and especially whether the agent has been paid or not. If an agent has been paid he must exercise the due care expected of a professional; if he is unpaid, he must exercise the same standard as he would when acting for himself. As far as banks are concerned this differentiation is of little significance, as the standard of care expected from banks by both the public and the courts, is at the highest possible level.

(b) The agent has a duty not to delegate his authority. This is expressed in Latin as *'delegatus non potest delegare'*: he who is delegated to cannot delegate. This rule was further discussed in *De Bussche* v *Alt* (1878), where it was held that the exceptions to the rule were:

  (i) Where there is a trade custom to delegate.
 (ii) Where delegation is necessary to allow proper performance of the tasks, for example, a bank appointing a stockbroker to sell stocks and shares on behalf of the bank's customer.
(iii) Where the agent has the authority of the principal, express or implied, to delegate. An example of an implied authority is a builder delegating to a sub-contractor, such as a plumber or plasterer, the principal being aware that the builder is incapable of completing all the tasks himself.
 (iv) Where there is an emergency, such as illness, that necessitates the sub-delegation.

(c) The agent has a duty to avoid a conflict of interest. The interests that could conflict could be those of the principal (customer) and the agent (the bank), or between the agent (the bank) and two principals (two separate customers). It is unlikely that a bank will find itself in such a position, but if it does, the conflict must be disclosed and if necessary, the agency revoked.

(d) The agent has a duty not to take a **secret** profit or bribe. The key here is **secrecy**, since the agent is obviously entitled to remuneration, but he must not keep any other receipts secret from the principal, otherwise both the agent and the third party could be liable to prosecution under the Prevention of Corruption Act 1906. When the principal becomes aware of the agent taking a secret profit or bribe, he has a number of options:

  (i) The agent can be dismissed, without notice: *Boston Deep Sea Fishing Co* v *Ansell* (1888).
 (ii) The principal may claim the secret profit or bribe for himself.
(iii) The principal may refuse to pay the agent the commission due on the contract involving the secret profit or bribe, or if commission has already been paid, it may be reclaimed.
 (iv) The principal may refuse to be bound by the contract.
  (v) The principal may sue the agent or third party for damages incurred.

An obvious implication of this ruling to banks is the taking of a share of the stockbroker's commission when selling or buying stocks and shares on behalf of its customers. However, if you examine closely a contract note in respect of such a transaction you will note that the share of the commission is clearly stated in the contract note.

(e) The agent must keep his principal's affairs secret. The implications of this for banks have been fully discussed in Chapter one. This general rule of agency has been further supported in the banker/customer relationship by the case of *Joachimson* v *Swiss Bank Corporation* (1921).

(f) Other sundry duties of an agent include:

  (i) To obey his principal's mandate.
 (ii) To keep accurate accounts and produce these upon demand.
(iii) To keep his principal fully informed.
 (iv) To keep his property separate from that of his principal.

▌ Doctrine of the undisclosed principal

This doctrine applies where the principal is not disclosed, and it has two interpretations:

(a) Where the agency is disclosed but the identity of the principal is not. Here, the situation is no different from that where the agent names his principal, ie, if the agent acts within his ostensible authority, the principal will be bound.

(b) Where the agency is not disclosed and the agent acts as if he is the principal. The principal can take the benefit of the contract, but this will be subject to any equities or set-off between the agent and the third party.

On discovering the agency, and the identity of the principal, the third party can, within a reasonable time, take action against the principal or the agent but not both: *Scarf* v *Jardine* (1882). If the principal has already settled with the agent the third party can enforce the contract only against the agent.

Where the agent precludes the possibility of agency either expressly or implicitly (for example, by describing himself as the principal), then the contract cannot be enforced against the principal and neither can the principal seek to enforce the contract: *Said* v *Butt* (1920). The reason for this is naturally that if the third party had thought that he was dealing with the agent as the principal he might not have wished to contract with the actual principal. A banking implication of this could possibly be where the bank is lending money to an agent, say a company director, and it subsequently discovers that it is in fact dealing with the limited company. It would obviously be grossly unfair to the bank if it were bound to lend the money to the company.

▌ Personal liability of an agent

Under normal circumstances an agent will not be liable on any contract he enters into as an agent. However, the exceptions to this general rule are described below and in these circumstances the agent will be personally liable:

(i) Where the agent agrees to be liable.

(ii) Where he fails to disclose the agency; see the doctrine of the undisclosed principal, above.

(iii) Where he exceeds his actual authority. Although the principal will still be liable on a contract which exceeds the agent's actual authority, but is within the agent's ostensible authority, the principal will be able to sue the agent for breach of warranty of authority.

(iv) Where the principal does not exist or lacks contractual capacity, see *Kelner* v *Baxter* (1866).

(v) Where he signs a bill of exchange (or cheque) in his own name without indicating the agency: s.26 Bills of Exchange Act 1882. However, in *Bondina Limited* v *Rollaway Shower Blinds and Others* (1986), it was held that despite not signing per pro, the director (an agent for the company) was not liable on the cheque, as the cheque quoted both the name and account number of the company and so it should have been completely obvious that the cheque was drawn on behalf of the company and not by the director personally.

(vi) Where he contracts by deed without being appointed by deed (power of attorney).

(vii) Where trade custom makes him liable.

∎ Powers of attorney

As we have already discussed, for an agent to be able to contract by deed he must be appointed by deed. The method of appointment of an agent by deed is by a power of attorney. The principal is known as the donor and the agent is the donee, or attorney, and the agency will be drawn up under either the Powers of Attorney Act 1971 or the Enduring Powers of Attorney Act 1985. To be effective the power must be fully completed and not include any blanks: *Powell* v *London and Provincial Bank* (1893); must be signed, sealed and delivered by the principal to the attorney; and must be witnessed by at least one witness. An exception to this rule is where the donor is physically incapable of signing the document. In these circumstances the donor can direct someone else to execute the power of attorney on his behalf, providing this is done in the presence of two witnesses: s.1 Powers of Attorney Act 1971.

A power of attorney can be either:

(i) Specific, empowering the attorney to act for the donor for only one specific contract or number of contracts; the limits of the authority will be detailed in the power of attorney. The document may well include an 'omnibus clause' stating that the attorney can undertake any act that the donor can legally do. However, these further acts must be related to the items specifically mentioned in the power, for example, the attorney appointing an estate agent to sell a house, where the attorney himself had been appointed to sell the house. An important point for bankers to note is that an attorney appointed to operate the donor's bank account does not automatically have the power to borrow money on behalf of the donor.

(ii) General. An agent appointed under s.10 Powers of Attorney Act 1971, is said to be a universal agent and can act on behalf of his principal in any matter that can be legally delegated.

Under normal circumstances an agency is automatically cancelled upon the mental incapacity of the principal. However, if a power of attorney is drawn under the Enduring Powers of Attorney Act 1985 the attorney will be able to continue to act for the principal despite the mental incapacity of the principal. This can be of particular benefit either where the donor is elderly or where there is a family history of mental problems. In order to meet the conditions of this statute, the donor must be mentally capable at the time of completing the document and the attorney must be an adult or a trust company, and not an undischarged bankrupt. Joint attorneys are permissible. The power of attorney must state that the power is to continue despite the subsequent mental incapacity of the donor and contain a statement that the document has been read by, or to, the donor. As with a normal power of attorney, the authority delegated may be either specific or general.

Upon the mental incapacity of the donor:

(a) The attorney's authority is suspended.

(b) The attorney must apply to the Court of Protection for re-instatement of the power; notice must be served upon the donor and upon any specified close relatives of the donor.

(c) Upon application limited powers are automatically passed to the attorney. These are powers to maintain the donor and the attorney and to protect the donor's property.

(d) Upon full registration by the courts all the powers of the attorney are re-instated exactly as they were prior to the incapacity of the donor and cannot be cancelled, even by the donor, except with the court's consent.

When a power of attorney is produced before a banker, there are a number of items of which the banker must take special notice, and these are, mainly:

(i) Has the document been drawn up correctly? Items to check would be signing by the donor, witnessing and completion without blanks.

(ii) Is the document an original or certified copy? Under s.3 Powers of Attorney Act 1971, a copy certified as such by the donor, solicitor or stockbroker can be accepted as if it were the original.

(iii) Is the duration acceptable or has it lapsed? The power will either be for a specified time, or for the completion of a specific task or may be for an indefinite time. If the power has been revoked by the donor, the attorney and any third party are protected unless they are aware of the revocation: s.5 Powers of Attorney Act 1971. If the bank is aware of the revocation by the donor, it must ensure that any cheques signed by the attorney are countersigned by the donor. Also, the bank must make a note of the expiry date of the power, if there is one, as on expiry the attorney's powers automatically cease.

(iv) The extent of the authority of the attorney should be carefully checked and the bank must ensure that it limits the acts of the attorney to coincide with the authority quoted in the power of attorney.

(v) Is the power of attorney drawn up before 19 March 1985? If so, then the bank must ensure that it is correctly stamped. The stamp duty was abolished by the 1985 budget.

(vi) If it is drawn up under the Enduring Powers of Attorney Act 1985, has the power been registered at the Court of Protection? If so, it will bear the seal of the court.

In conclusion, a power of attorney is a very useful method of appointing an agent especially if the donor is leaving the country or will be unable to contract on his own behalf for a while (for example, hospitalisation etc.), and if drawn as an enduring power of attorney it will overcome the problems caused by the mental incapacity of the donor. An agent who is to transact under seal must be appointed under seal, and for this reason a power of attorney clause is included in the bank's memorandum of deposit when executed under seal. The benefit of this clause is that the chargor (the person signing the document) appoints the bank as his agent, under seal. Hence if the customer should default on the advance, the bank may execute a legal charge over the asset held as security and proceed as if it had a legal charge. This is fully discussed in the chapters on securities later in the book.

∎ Fraudulent acts by an agent

If an agent acts fraudulently it is possible that the principal may be liable for the fraudulent act by his agent. Thus if an agent commits fraud whilst acting on his principal's behalf and within his ostensible authority the principal will be liable: *Lloyd* v *Grace, Smith and Co.* (1912), even if the principal gains no benefit from the contract. One implication for bankers of this ruling is that they could be liable for the fraudulent acts of their employees.

∎ Termination of the agency

Revocation by the principal

The agency may be revoked by the principal at any time. However, for third parties with prior dealings with the agent the revocation is effective only once the third party has received notice of it and until that time the principal is still liable for contracts between the agent and the uninformed third party.

Some agencies, including powers of attorney, are said to be irrevocable. However, the agency can be revoked by the principal, but certain contracts undertaken by the agent may still be enforceable against the principal, for example, a contract for the sale of property.

Renunciation by the agent

The agent may renounce the agency at any time, but may be liable for breach of contract.

Death, mental incapacity or bankruptcy of the principal

These incidents automatically cancel the agency agreement and any contracts entered into by the agent are not enforceable against the principal or his estate. However, the third party may be able to sue the agent for breach of warranty of authority (for acting as if he has an authority he does not in fact have): *Yonge* v *Tonybee* (1910).

One exception to this general rule is a power of attorney drawn under the Enduring Powers of Attorney Act 1985, whereby the mental incapacity of the donor does not automatically cancel the agency.

Death, mental incapacity or bankruptcy of the agent

These events automatically terminate the agency. However, as it is not necessary for the agent to have contractual capacity, the bankruptcy of the agent does not automatically cancel the agency. Perhaps from the principal's point of view, express termination of the agency would be advisable.

Intervening illegality

Where the agency becomes illegal it is automatically terminated. The most common example of this is the declaration of war between the countries of the agent and the principal.

Fulfilment of purpose; expiry of time

Both of these are self-explanatory. A specific agency terminates upon the completion of the specific contract; an agency for a specified time is automatically cancelled upon the expiry of that time period.

■ Agency – Summary

Agency is a somewhat unusual concept as it can affect a bank acting as an agent and a bank dealing with agents. Examples of a bank acting as an agent will include the collection of cheques, safe custody, and the sale of shares. Examples of dealing with agents include third party mandates, powers of attorney, partners and directors. It is important that you should grasp the main principles of agency, especially how an agency can be created I WONDER, remember?), the duties and rights of an agent, and how an agency can be terminated. In particular, powers of attorney need to be known in detail, especially how they affect bankers, authorities, enduring or not, and clauses in equitable charge forms. All in all, a short but an important and a very practical chapter.

FACT SHEET

Banks and agency

Definition and creation 'to bring principal into contractual relations with third parties' 'I WONDER', and banking implications

Types of authority
(i) Actual
(ii) Implied: principal and agent intend to have the authority but it has never been expressed.
(iii) Ostensible authority: it is reasonable to expect the agent to have it? Exceptions – where the third party is aware of the limitations of authority, or where agent signs per pro.

Rights of agent
(a) Clear mandate
(b) Right of indemnity from principal: *Hitchens, Harrison, Woolston and Co v Jackson*
(c) Right of remuneration, either express or reasonable.
(d) Right of lien (NB returned cheque).

Duties of agent
(a) To exercise reasonable care.
(b) Not to delegate authority, exceptions; *De Bussche v Alt.*
(c) To avoid conflict of interests.
(d) Not to take secret profit or bribe; rights of principal, if taken.
(e) To keep his principal's affairs secret.
(f) Other sundry duties.

Undisclosed principal
(a) Agency disclosed but not the name of principal.
(b) Agency not disclosed. Enforceable against principal or agent, but not both *Scarf v Jardine*); once decision made, it is final.
(c) All possibilities of agency denied. Enforceable against agent only *Said v Butt*), but principal cannot take the benefit of the contract.

Personal liability of agent
Usually not liable but can be, where:
(i) He agrees to be liable.
(ii) Fails to disclose agency.
(iii) Exceeds his authority.
(iv) Principal does not exist or lacks capacity.
(v) Signs bills of exchange in his own name (s.26 Bills of Exchange Act; *Bondina*).

Powers of attorney
Under seal; conditions, authority either specific or general.
Enduring power of attorney; power remains valid despite mental incapacity of donor. Procedure necessary upon mental incapacity. Partial reinstatement of powers, full reinstatement, once power is registered. Items to look for when power is presented to bank – drawn up correctly, original, duration, authority, stamp duty.

Termination
Revocation, renunciation, death, mental incapacity and bankruptcy of principal and agent (NB., neither the bankruptcy of agent nor the mental incapacity of principal if under E P of A Act would cause termination), illegality, fulfilment of purpose, expiry of time.

Question

(a) Peter, a lecturer, has an account with the Loamshire Bank. As he is about to go on a one year visit to an American university, he grants to his colleague, Alfred, a power of attorney, which Alfred has just produced to the bank.
  (i) What is a power of attorney?
  (ii) What effect does a power of attorney have?
  (iii) To which provisions in a power of attorney should a bank pay particular attention? (14 marks)

(b) Two months ago Malade, an elderly man, gave a power of attorney in favour of his solicitor. Recently Malade became mentally incapacitated. What effect, if any, does this have on the power of attorney? (6 marks)

(total marks for question: 20)

Key words
(a) power of attorney	*(b) power of attorney*
What is?	*Recently*
What effect?	*Mentally incapacitated*
Which provisions?	*What effect?*

Answer

In (a), if an agent is to have authority to contract under seal on behalf of his principal, his own appointment must be under seal and this actual authority is known as a power of attorney. The former 50p stamp duty was abolished by the Finance Act 1985. By s.10 of the Powers of Attorney Act 1971, it is possible to confer power to do anything the principal can do (a form of general power of attorney for the purposes of s.10 is prescribed in the Schedule to the Act), and the bank should note whether this had been done. In the case of any power other than s.10, the bank would be particularly interested in the scope of the powers specifically given, e.g. authority to operate a bank account does not include powers to overdraw or give security; these powers must be specifically conferred, an 'omnibus' clause alone being insufficient. The bank would also look at the duration of the power and to what extent it is expressed to be irrevocable — often for one year, which would be appropriate here. Even so, as regards normal banking transactions, if the principal does in fact revoke it, and knowledge of revocation directly or indirectly reaches the bank, it must act on the revocation.

As regards (b), normally a power of attorney is automatically revoked by the mental incapacity of the principal (there is an exception for some special types of power in ss.4 and 5 of the 1971 Act). To avoid the power being automatically ended just when it is needed, the Enduring Powers of Attorney Act 1985 provides for a power to be made in a prescribed form which cannot be ended by the principal's subsequent loss of mental capacity unless the court otherwise directs. If this form has been used by the solicitor, then on Malade's loss of mental capacity the attorney must apply to the court for registration of the power; when this has been done, the power is once again fully effective.

Author's comment
Generally, I feel that this is a difficult question with many candidates struggling to justify 14 marks in (a). Many tend to repeat themselves in (i), (ii) and sometimes even in (iii). Also many candidates fail to realise that unless the power is drawn up under the Enduring Powers of Attorney Act 1985, the power will cease upon the mental incapacity of the donor. Additional marks should be available for a detailed discussion of the 1985 Act, for example if candidates realise that on the donor's mental incapacity the power is suspended and partial powers reinstated upon application to the courts with full powers reinstated when registration is complete.

CHAPTER 7

Partnerships

Syllabus requirements
- The main legal considerations to which a banker must have regard when dealing with partnerships. In particular, the following aspects are relevant: account opening, agency, death or mental incompetence of partners and the effect of insolvency.

■ Definition and methods of creation

Definition

A partnership is **'the relationship that subsists between persons carrying on a business in common with a view to profit'**: s.1 Partnership Act 1890. The important phrases from this definition are:

(i) **'between persons'** — hence the minimum number of partners is two. The standard maximum is 20: s.716(1) Companies Act 1985, but certain professional practices (solicitors, accountants, stockbrokers) have no maximum imposed upon them: s.716 (2) Companies Act 1985.

(ii) **'business in common'** — business is defined as including every trade, occupation or profession: s.45 Partnership Act 1890.

(iii) **'with a view to profit'** — the main aim of the partnership is to make a profit; it is not a charitable organisation (see Chapter eight).

A partnership is also known as a 'firm', but never as a company; this term is used exclusively for a limited company.

Creation

A partnership is usually created by agreement among the prospective partners; this agreement can be either oral, or by deed (known as a partnership deed) or in writing (known as partnership articles). A typical misconception by students is that every partnership will have a deed or articles of partnership; this is not correct. If a partnership does not have either of these formal documents it will be bound completely by the Partnership Act 1890. By the drawing up of a deed or articles of partnership the partnership is able to vary the rules laid down by the Partnership Act. For example, the Act states that upon the death of a partner the partnership will automatically be dissolved. This could make sense if it were a small building partnership with just two partners, but for a large solicitors' practice with 20 or more partners the effect could be very damaging. In these situations it is normal practice for the partnership agreement to include a clause stating that the death of a partner does not automatically dissolve the partnership.

An exception to the creation of partnership by agreement is its formation by 'holding out', which is discussed in 'Types of partners' below.

As well as the method of formation of the partnership, the partners must also decide on a name. They can use either the collective surnames of the partners or some other name. If they choose the latter they must ensure that the names of all partners and an address for legal correspondence is quoted on all stationery and displayed prominently at the business address: Business Names Act 1985. When opening an account for a partnership using such a name, the account-holding bank will ask for sight of the stationery, which must have been drawn up as described above. Without taking this action it is thought that the bank might well lose the protection of s.4 Cheques Act 1957, and be open to a claim of conversion should it collect a cheque for someone other than the true owner.

An important point to note is that a partnership is not a separate legal entity, as opposed to a limited company which is; a partnership is merely a collective body.

∎ Partners

Who can become a partner?

The basic answer to this question is that anyone can become a partner, with the exception of enemy aliens and convicts. As it is not necessary for a partner to have contractual capacity, a minor, bankrupt or mentally incapacitated person can become a partner. However, if a minor is a partner it is important to note that he will not be liable for debts incurred by the partnership during his minority, but he can commit the partnership to contracts and debts for which he may not be personally liable (see below). If a mentally incapacitated person is a partner the partnership will be voidable (avoided at the option of the injured party) if it can be shown that the partners either knew of the incapacity or took advantage of the mentally incapacitated person. A limited company can be a partner in a partnership.

Types of partners

General partner

This is the standard type of partner and every partnership must contain at least one general partner. Each general partner has a right to participate in the management of the partnership and a right to share in the profits. In return for these rights the general partner is liable for the liabilities of the firm up to the full extent of his personal assets.

Sleeping, or dormant, partner

This is in essence a general partner who wishes to have no active role in the management of the firm. He still however has a right to a share of the profits and is responsible for the liabilities of the firm. A typical example of a sleeping partner is a retired general partner or a wealthy person looking for a profitable investment opportunity.

Partner by 'holding out', a quasi partner

Such a partner is not a partner by agreement but is estopped (precluded) from denying that he is a partner, due to his previous conduct and/or statements: s.14 Partnership Act' 1890. Not only can a person be estopped from denying he is a partner of an existing partnership, but he can in fact also be estopped from denying the existence of a partnership, that is to say that a partnership can be created by the doctrine of holding out/estoppel. An example of a quasi-partner would be a person obtaining credit on behalf of the partnership leading the third party to believe that he was in fact a partner himself. A quasi-partner is liable for the debts of the partnership but has no right to a share in the profits.

Junior/salaried partner

Such a partner is usually new to the partnership and quite often unqualified. Instead of taking a share in the profit he draws a salary; if 'held out' as a general partner his liability will be to the full extent of his personal assets, but if the third party is aware of his status as a junior or salaried partner he should not be held liable.

Limited partner

A limited partner has a right to a share of the profits of the partnership but has no right to participate in the management of the firm. Also, his liability is limited to the amount of capital he **originally agreed** to contribute. The extent of his liability is important, and it is often misquoted as the amount of capital he actually contributes. This is obviously of importance to a limited partner as he could have agreed to contribute substantially more than his present contribution.

▌ Limited partnerships

The concept of a limited partnership was originally introduced to encourage investment in business ventures, whilst limiting the possible liability of the investor. This has largely been defeated by the popularity of limited companies, which are discussed in the next chapter. However, limited partnerships are still seen, albeit rarely, either for their original purpose or to protect an outgoing partner who may still wish to receive a share in the profits of the business.

A limited partnership is governed by the Limited Partnerships Act 1907, and the points to note in this Act are as follows:

(i) The fact that it is a limited partnership must be stated in the articles or the deed of partnership, and it must be registered as such at the Companies Registry: s.15 Limited Partnerships Act 1907.

(ii) There must be at least one general partner, the maximum membership being twenty: s.4 Limited Partnerships Act 1907.

(iii) As mentioned above, the limited partner cannot participate in the management of the firm; if he should do so he will be liable as if he were a general partner (ie, to the limit of his personal assets): s.6 Limited Partnerships Act 1907.

(iv) The limited partner's liability is fixed at the amount he agrees to contribute; if he should contribute less than this figure or if he should withdraw some of his capital he will still be liable up to the amount he **agreed** to contribute.

(v) The death or bankruptcy of the limited partner does not dissolve the partnership, neither does his mental incapacity but this can be grounds for the other partners to dissolve the firm.

(vi) To leave the partnership he must assign his interest, with the consent of the general partners.

▮ Rights and duties of partners

As mentioned in the introduction to this chapter, if there is a formal partnership agreement then the partners are bound by it. However, if there is no formal agreement, or if the agreement makes no mention of certain areas, then the Partnership Act 1890 will apply. Naturally, it is impossible to discuss each partnership agreement individually, and therefore the following duties and rights are discussed because they are contained in the Act and can be altered by the express agreement of all the partners, usually in the deed or articles of partnership.

1. Rights of a partner

General

(i) Each partner is entitled to the utmost fairness and good faith from his co-partners (*uberrimae fidei*).

(ii) Each general partner has a right to participate in the management of the firm.

(iii) All partners will share equally in any profits made by the partnership.

(iv) A partner is entitled to an indemnity from the firm when acting on partnership business.

(v) Each partner, or his nominated agent, has a right to inspect the books (accounts etc) of the partnership.

(vi) Where a partner advances a loan to the partnership, in excess of his agreed capital, he is entitled to a rate of interest of 5 per cent per annum.

(vii) Each partner is the joint owner of partnership property, if it is land, then as a tenant in common (see Chapter fifteen). This means that should one partner die, his share of partnership property will go to his estate and not to the surviving partners.

(viii) Under s.23 Bills of Exchange Act 1882, the partners can sign a bill of exchange (or cheque) in the name of the partnership and this will be the equivalent of it having been signed by all the partners. In *Central Motors (Birmingham) v P.A. & S.A. Wadsworth* (1983), it was held that the signature of one partner in the name of the partnership ('*pensagain*') was sufficient to make the partnership liable on the cheque despite the bank mandate stating that both partners had to sign.

Alteration of the partnership

(i) A new partner cannot be introduced without the consent of **all** partners.

(ii) An existing partner cannot be expelled by the remaining partners. The only option open to them is to dissolve the partnership and create a new one comprising the remaining partners.

(iii) A partner has the right to assign his share of partnership property or profits either absolutely or by way of charge.

(iv) The partnership's business can be altered only by agreement of **all** the partners.

Duties of partners

Many of the duties of partners are the mirror image of the rights of other partners. Examples of a partner's main duties are:

● To indemnify his co-partners against loss incurred whilst on partnership business.

- To act in the utmost good faith in his dealings with the other partners.
- To contribute equally to any losses incurred by the partnership.
- Not to carry on business in competition with the partnership, except with the consent of his co-partners. Any profits made by such a business must be paid over to the partnership.
- To be accountable to his co-partners for any profit made on partnership business. This prevents a partner profiting personally from partnership activities when the profit really belongs to the partnership.

▌ Partners' powers

Section 5 Partnership Act 1890 states that every general partner is the agent of the firm (for agency, see Chapter six). As with agents, partners have three distinct types of powers; these are actual, implied and apparent/ostensible. The easiest of these to understand is actual, this being the authority that the partners agree between themselves, that each of them shall possess. This can be agreed expressly, in which case it will appear in the partnership agreement, or orally. However, very few third parties dealing with partners will have notice of the actual powers of partners, or have sight of the partnership agreement, and therefore partners acquire implied or ostensible authority for certain transactions. These implied or ostensible powers may be more or less than the actual, agreed powers.

Implied powers

The implied powers of a partner in a trading partnership are greater than those in a non-trading partnership. A trading partnership was held in *Higgins* v *Beauchamp* (1914), to be one whose principal activity was that of buying and selling. This would involve most partnerships with which bankers come into contact, the exceptions being professional practices such as accountants, solicitors, doctors etc.

Implied powers of a non-trading partnership

The following are the implied powers of the partners in either a trading or non-trading partnership:

 (i) Power to buy or sell goods for the purpose of the business. This includes the purchase of goods on normal trade terms, where goods are supplied immediately and paid for later. The goods must be purchased only for the partnership business.
 (ii) Power to give legally binding receipts to debtors.
(iii) Power to employ and dismiss employees.
(iv) Power to draw cheques on the firm's behalf, providing this is in the normal course of business of the firm. This power is usually reinforced by the bank's mandate, quoting the number of partners needed to sign cheques.

Additional implied powers of a trading partnership

The partners in a trading partnership will have the following additional implied powers, as well as the ones stated above:

 (i) The power to contract and pay debts on behalf of the firm. This would include, for example, the partner contracting to settle a debt over a number of instalments, or the acceptance of a hire purchase agreement.

(ii) The power to draw, accept or discount a bill of exchange or other negotiable instruments (eg, cheques).

(iii) The power to borrow money on the firm's behalf. Many students fail to realise that this includes bank borrowing, be it on loan or overdraft.

(iv) Power to pledge goods and assets belonging to the partnership as security for the partnership's borrowing.

Items outside the implied powers of any partner

(i) The execution of deeds: remember that for an agent to be able to act under seal for his principal he must be appointed under seal.

(ii) The giving of a guarantee in the firm's name, unless the giving of guarantees is in the normal course of business of the partnership or there is a trade custom to do so.

(iii) The acceptance of property instead of money in settlement of an outstanding debt owed to the firm.

(iv) Authorising a third party to use the firm's name in legal or other proceedings.

(v) Submitting disputes to arbitration.

Summary

Three important points to note are, firstly, that the implied powers are exercisable by any individual general partner acting on behalf of the firm, and so one partner can exercise these rights (such as arranging a bank overdraft) on the firm's behalf. Secondly, a non-trading partnership can expressly authorise a partner to act on its behalf in any way (including those quoted as implied powers of a trading partnership), by quoting these powers in the articles or deed of partnership. Thirdly, any partnership can increase the actual powers of its partners by including specific powers in the partnership agreement.

Ostensible (apparent) authority

We have discussed ostensible authority fully in the previous chapter on agencies, but in essence the ostensible authority of a partner is the authority that a third party could reasonably expect the partner to have. The extent of this authority will vary depending on the circumstances and the knowledge that the third party has of the partnership. However, for a third party to be able to rely upon the ostensible authority of a partner and to be able to enforce the contract against the partnership the following conditions must be satisfied:

(i) The partner must have transacted as a partner.

(ii) The transaction must be in the course of the partnership business; the partner must not be acting on his own behalf.

(iii) The transaction must be in the ordinary course of the partnership's business; a classic example would be the purchase of a diamond ring or a holiday on behalf of a builders' partnership. These transactions would obviously be outside the ostensible authority of the partners whilst the purchase of bricks would be within the ostensible authority.

(iv) The third party must be unaware of any restrictions in the partner's actual authority. For example, if the third party is aware that the partner is not permitted to purchase bricks (due to a specific restriction in the partnership agreement) then the partnership would not be liable on the contract.

If a partner exceeds his ostensible authority he will be personally liable on the contract. If a partner exceeds his actual authority, but acts within his ostensible authority, the contract will be enforceable against the partnership. However, the firm will be able to sue the partner for breach of warranty of authority.

Actual authority

This is the authority expressly delegated to the partner by the partnership. This can either be by the partnership agreement or by another express mandate, for example, a bank mandate. The actual powers of a partner can either be greater or less than the implied or ostensible powers. It is normal for the bank to put the position beyond doubt by requiring **all** the partners to sign the bank mandate and expressly to inform the bank of the number of partners needed to sign cheques, or to borrow etc.

∎ Personal liability of partners to third parties

Generally

Section 9 Partnership Act 1890, states: 'Every partner in a firm is jointly liable with the other partners for the debts and obligations of the partnership incurred while he is a partner'. Hence, a general partner is liable jointly with all the other partners regardless of whether he himself, or any other partner, committed the partnership to the contract. A full discussion of joint liability is to be found in Chapter fourteen. Since the passing of the Civil Liability (Contribution) Act 1978, the difference between joint liability and joint and several liability has become minimal. The main difference is that should a partner die, his estate is released from liability on any joint debts existing at the time of his death. Obviously, bankers would not be willing to accept this and so bank mandates state that the liability between partners is joint and several. This means that should a partner die, the bank will be able to claim the balance from the deceased partner's estate, as well as from the surviving partners.

Since a general partner is liable to the full extent of his personal assets, then if there are insufficient partnership assets to meet partnership liabilities, the personal assets of the individual partners (for example, savings, property etc.) will have to be used to clear those liabilities.

Examples of partners incurring personal liability could include exceeding actual authority (thus becoming liable to the partnership for breach of warranty of authority); exceeding ostensible authority (therefore being solely and personally liable to the third party); and having insufficient partnership assets to meet partnership liabilities on the winding up of the partnership (fully discussed later). The most obvious example of a partner incurring liability for partnership transactions is via his joint (or joint and several) liability for all partnership liabilities.

Liability for torts

Section 90 Partnership Act 1890 states that the firm and the individual partners are jointly and severally liable for the torts (for example, negligence) committed by a partner in the ordinary course of business of the partnership and within the ostensible or actual authority of the partner. Also, the partner must actually be on partnership business and not acting on his own behalf.

∎ Dissolution of partnerships

The items discussed in this section are those contained in the Partnership Act 1890. As you should by now be aware, the effect of the provisions of this Act can be expressly altered by the partnership agreement. This is so with dissolution too, as it is with all matters involving partnerships. A partnership can be dissolved in the following ways:

Without reference to the court

(a) By statute

Subject to any express contrary statement in the partnership agreement, the following will bring about the automatic dissolution of the partnership without the need to approach the courts: ss.32–34 Partnership Act 1890:

(i) Where a partnership has been created for a fixed period, the partnership is automatically dissolved at the expiry of such a period.

(ii) Where a partnership has been created for a single purpose, for example the construction of a specific building, once the project has been completed the partnership is automatically dissolved.

(iii) The majority of partnerships are described as 'a partnership at will', this is to say that the partnership will continue until the partners decide otherwise. Such a partnership is dissolved by one partner giving notice to the others. The notice must be served in good faith and not merely to conceal his own fraudulent wrongdoings; *Walters and Others* v *Bingham* (1987). In fact in this case it was held that the serving of a notice in bad faith was sufficient grounds for expulsion of the partner serving the notice.

(iv) Death or bankruptcy of one partner. It is common for most large partnerships to include a specific clause in the partnership agreement excluding the provision of death bringing about the automatic dissolution of the partnership.

(v) Attachment of one partner's share of partnership property by court order in respect of a personal debt. Here dissolution is at the option of the partnership and is not compulsory.

(vi) When the partnership becomes illegal, for example a declaration of war between the U.K. and the country of which one of the partners is a national.

(vii) Where all partners agree.

By agreement of the partners

This is usually by express inclusion in the partnership agreement, and examples can include:

(i) Mental incapacity of one partner.

(ii) Where the formation of the partnership has involved fraud.

(iii) Criminal conduct of one partner.

(iv) Scandalous conduct of a partner, considered to be detrimental to the partnership.

In *Carmichael* v *Evans* (1904), it was held that travelling on a train without a ticket was sufficient to dissolve the partnership as the conduct was considered to be 'scandalous and detrimental to the partnership'.

Dissolution by order of the court

Dissolution of a partnership other than for the reasons mentioned above will be by order of the court and is covered by s.35 Partnership Act 1890. A partner may apply to the court for the dissolution of the partnership when:

(a) A partner, other than the one applying to the court, is temporarily or permanently incapable of performing his partnership duties. This could include mental or physical incapability or be due to some reason such as disqualification (eg, doctor, solicitor).

(b) A partner, other than the one applying, has been found guilty of committing a crime that is considered to be prejudicial to the firm's business: *Carmichael* v *Evans* (1904).

(c) A partner, other than the one applying, persistently breaches the partnership agreement, so that it is not reasonably practicable for the other partners to continue in partnership with him.

(d) The business can be carried on only at a loss.

(e) Where the courts consider it to be just and equitable.

Partnership insolvency

Insolvency is discussed in full in chapter nine and a detailed explanation of many of the insolvency terms will be found in that chapter, rather than here. However, should a partnership be insolvent (unable to meet its debts as they fall due), the partnership will have the option of seeking a voluntary arrangement (an alternative to insolvency). If this option is not exercised, the creditors (persons owed money by the partnership), under the Insolvency Act 1986 and the Insolvent Partnerships Order 1986, have three choices:

(a) wind up the partnership only (as an unregistered company), or

(b) present a petition for the bankruptcy of one or more partners, or

(c) wind up the partnership and concurrently petition for the bankruptcy of the partners.

However, recent case law has made the following modifications:

Marr v *Commissioners of Customs and Excise* (1989). It was held in this case that where the creditor has chosen the third course of action ((c) above) and the partnership debts have been fully satisfied from partnership assets, then bankruptcy of the individual partners would not be permitted. This cleared up a discrepancy in s.271 Insolvency Act 1986, as amended by paragraph 7 of Schedule 2 to the Insolvent Partnerships Order 1986. The Court of Appeal decided that s.271(1) was binding in that 'the court shall not make a bankruptcy order on a creditor's petition unless it is satisfied that the debt . . . has been neither paid nor secured or compounded for'.

Investment and Pensions Advisory Service Ltd and Another v *Gray and Another* (1989). In this case it appeared to the liquidator of the firm that there would be insufficient partnership assets to meet partnership liabilities and so he tried to serve an injunction preventing the partners disposing of their personal assets. However, the partners were not subject to insolvency proceedings and therefore the liquidator had no rights against the assets of the partners until it could be proven that the partnership was in fact insolvent; he could then rely upon the unlimited liability of the partners and claim re-imbursement from them. Ironically, if the partners had disposed of their assets merely in an attempt to defraud creditors, the liquidator could have claimed the assets back, if claimed within six months of the disposal: ss.423–425 Insolvency Act 1986.

Once the partnership has been declared insolvent (wound up) the assets of the partnership and the partners must be distributed as below:

(i) Partnership assets must first be placed to meet the costs of the winding up and secondly to meet partnership debts. If there is any surplus this will be distributed amongst the partners as per the partnership agreement, or equally if one does not exist.

(ii) Personal assets must be applied to the costs of the personal bankruptcies and then to personal liabilities. If there is any surplus then this is applied to partnership liabilities.

It is this ruling that will determine the choice of (a), (b) or (c) above, for example when the bank has lent money to a partnership (ie the bank is the partnership's creditor), and:

(a) The partnership has very few partnership assets but one of the partners is wealthy. In this situation it would be advisable to petition for the bankruptcy of the wealthy partner alone, since to petition for the winding up of the partnership concurrently could incur additional expense, for which the wealthy partner could be liable, if there were insufficient assets in the partnership to meet these costs.

(b) The partnership has many assets but the partners are known to have many personal liabilities, and a few assets. In this situation it may be advisable to wind up the partnership alone.

The effect of partnership insolvency on the bank account will depend upon the choice taken. For example, if a petition is served to wind up the partnership alone, then the partnership account should be stopped, but not the partners' personal accounts. If the partners are declared bankrupt, their personal accounts must be stopped, but not the partnership account, unless the partnership is also to be dissolved.

One important point to recall is that by ss.32–34 Partnership Act 1890 the bankruptcy of a partner is grounds for automatic dissolution of the partnership, unless expressly denied in the partnership agreement.

Permissible transactions after dissolution

Once dissolution has occurred due to either a court order or an occurrence which brings about automatic dissolution, the partners are allowed to continue to enter into contracts on the firm's behalf providing the contracts are either on-going transactions commenced prior to dissolution or new transactions entered into for the sole purpose of winding up the partnership.

∎ Sundry partnership details

Partnership property

This is property owned by the partnership, but as the partnership is not a legal entity in its own right it is effectively owned jointly by the partners (if the property is land, then it is held by the partners as tenants in common). If one partner dies, his share of partnership property will pass to his heirs and not to the surviving partners. Items included as partnership property will be assets brought into the partnership upon creation, property bought in the partnership's name or on the partnership's credit and property purchased by partnership money, unless a contrary intention can be proved.

The distinction between partnership and the partner's personal property is important because:

(a) An increase in the value of partnership property will accrue to the partnership and increases in the partner's personal property will accrue to the partner: *Robinson* v *Ashton* (1875).
(b) If the partnership is wound up, partnership assets will be applied to partnership liabilities, whereas the partner's own property will be applied to the partner's personal liabilities, as above.
(c) Where a bank is considering lending to the partnership and taking the property as security, ownership is obviously very important.

An obvious place to look to discover the owners of property is the partnership balance sheet; property quoted in the balance sheet of the partnership **should** belong to the partnership.

Upon dissolution, partnership property should be distributed to the partners in the same ratio as profits or losses are distributed, or as otherwise stated in the partnership agreement. This can result in the partners receiving back more, or less, than they originally contributed to the partnership, and if there are any creditors, the creditors obviously receive the money they are owed before the partners take their share of the partnership assets.

Change of partners

Incoming partner

As we have previously discussed, the appointment of a new partner must be agreed to by **all** the existing partners. An incoming partner is not usually liable for partnership debts incurred before he became a partner, but he can be by a process known as '**novation**'. This usually occurs when an incoming partner is replacing an outgoing partner (for example, on retirement) and the new partner agrees to be liable for debts incurred under the old partnership. For novation to be effective it must be agreed to by all the creditors and the partners. If the bank is a creditor (eg, by overdraft) its agreement is usually indicated by asking the new partners to sign a cheque on the new partnership account to clear the balance on the old partnership account.

Outgoing partner

The most common example of an outgoing partner is a partner who is retiring and this has been a favourite area for examination questions in the past. Normally an outgoing partner is liable only for debts up to the date of his retirement. However, a partner can be held responsible for future debts by 'holding out', a form of estoppel. The outgoing partner can have liability for both debts existing at the time of retirement and those incurred after retirement. In order to be released from liability the outgoing partner must act:

(i) **In the case of existing debts.** Normally an outgoing partner will still be liable for debts incurred during his time as a partner. However, s.17(3) Partnership Act 1890, states that this liability can be avoided by novation, subject to the agreement of the individual creditor involved and the remaining partners.

An important point for bankers to note is that if the partnership bank account is overdrawn on the retirement, or death, of a partner and the bank wishes to maintain the liability of the outgoing partner the bank must stop the account to prevent the rule in *Clayton's Case* operating against the bank (credits reducing the balance for which the outgoing partner is liable, and debits creating a new debt for which he is not liable).

(ii) **In the case of new debts**. Normally an outgoing partner will not have liability for debts created after his retirement. However, the following procedure will prevent him being 'held out' as a partner:

(a) s.36(1) Partnership Act 1890, states that third parties that have had previous dealings with the firm while the outgoing partner was a partner, have the right to assume he is still a partner until they hear otherwise. To overcome this the outgoing partner, or his executors or others acting on his behalf, should give written notice to the creditors of the firm.
(b) Notice of his leaving the partnership should be quoted in the *London Gazette*. This is thought to be sufficient notice to persons that have not dealt with the firm before.
(c) In removing his name from all business stationery. If he knowingly leaves his name on business stationery he can be held as 'knowingly holding himself out' to be still a partner: *Tower Cabinet Co* v *Ingham* (1949), and accordingly liable for future debts incurred.

As previously stated this is a common area for examination questions and so students should ensure they are familiar with novation, holding out and the implications of *Clayton's Case*.

∎ Summary: Partnerships as bank customers

Opening the account

(a) Firstly the bank must satisfy itself that the definition of partnership is met, ie, 'a business in common with a view to a profit'.

(b) If the partnership is trading under a name other than that of the partners, the bank must have sight of stationery quoting the trading name, business address and names of all partners. This information must be available under the Business Names Act 1985, and the production of it is taken as an attempt to meet the conditions of s.4 Cheques Act 1957 (acting without negligence), without which the bank could be open to a claim of conversion should it collect a cheque to the partnership account for someone other than the true owner.

(c) If the partners are not known to the bank, references should be taken up and/or identification asked for. Again failure to do so could mean the bank losing the protection of s.4 Cheques Act 1957.

(d) The standard bank mandate should be completed, establishing joint and several liability and expressly quoting the number of partners necessary to sign cheques etc.

(e) The account should be opened in the name of the partnership. If it is opened in the name of one of the partners the partnership will not be liable: *Alliance Bank Ltd* v *Kearsley* (1871).

Note: Banking practice is that the partnership agreement is not asked for, because, if sighted, the bank will be bound by it.

Operating the account

Cheques

(i) As previously mentioned, cheques signed in the partnership name are equivalent to having been signed by all the partners. This is particularly common with solicitors.

(ii) Care must be taken when collecting to the personal account of one of the partners cheques which are payable to the partnership. For an obvious example of the bank losing its protection of s.4 Cheques Act 1957 against conversion, see *Baker v Barclays Bank Ltd* (1955).

Borrowing

The distinction between a trading and non-trading partnership, and the implied powers of each must be known. The most important point is that a partner in a trading partnership has the implied power to borrow without the express consent of all of the partners (eg, one partner can arrange an overdraft/loan and it would be binding on the partnership and all the partners, but the execution of security by way of deed, such as a legal charge form, must be by **all** the partners with no one partner having the implied power to do so.

Ending the banker/customer relationship

Upon death, retirement, mental incapacity or bankruptcy of one partner

If the account is overdrawn and the bank wishes to retain the liability of the partner involved, then the bank must stop the account to prevent the bank's claim against the partner/estate being eroded. If the account is to continue, the cheques signed by that partner must be countersigned by the other partners and the bank must ensure that the partnership is not to be wound up. If the partnership is to continue, a new mandate should be taken, but if not, the account can be used to wind up the partnership.

Upon the dissolution/winding up of the partnership

The account should be stopped and only transactions necessary to wind up the business allowed. If the partnership is insolvent it is important that the bank acts only on the instruction of the insolvency practitioner dealing with that firm.

FACT SHEET

Partnership

Definition and creation
'business in common with a view to profit'
Creation can be express (deed or articles of partnership); if not Partnership Act 1890 will bind the firm. Max./min. number of partners and Business Names Act 1985.

Partners
Who? Anyone except convicts and enemy aliens.
Types? (a) General – most common unlimited personal liability, shares in profits and management.

(b) General/sleeping. Share in profits but no rights of management. Possibly retired partner or someone looking for an investment.

(c) Quasi-partner. By holding out s.14 PA. Assumes liabilities but no share in profits nor rights of management.

(d) Limited partner. Liability limited to amount of agreed contribution, even if more than amount actually contributed. No rights of management; if he does interfere he will be fully liable. Must be at least one general partner, and must be registered as a limited partnership at Companies House.

Partner's rights and duties

(a) *Rights*. Main ones are the right to manage, share equally in the profits; signature in name of partnership is equivalent to a signature by all partners; new partners and change of business only by agreement of **all** partners.

(b) *Duties*. Mainly the mirror image of the rights of other partners.

Note: These are the rights/duties quoted in the Partnership Act and can be varied by the partnership agreement.

Partner's powers

S.5 PA – every general partner is an agent for the firm.

1. *Implied powers*.
● Difference between trading and non-trading; *Higgins* v *Beauchamp* (1914).
● Implied powers of both: Buy and sell, give receipts, **sign cheques** (conditions).
● Additional powers of a trading partnership: power to **borrow** and to pledge assets as security (but not under seal).
● Items outside implied powers of both: execution of deeds, guarantees (exceptions) etc.
2. *Ostensible/apparent authority*.
Conditions: must have transacted as a partner, on partnership business, normal course of business, third party unaware of restrictions.
3. *Actual authority*.

Personal liability

● s.9 PA – every partner jointly liable for debts and obligations, banks insist on joint and several. General partners liable to full extent of personal assets.
● s.90 PA – every partner joint and severally liable for torts.

Dissolution of partnerships

1. *Without reference to courts*.
(a) By statute. Ss.32–34 PA:-fixed time period, single purpose, at will by agreement of partners, death or bankruptcy of partner, attachment of share of partnership property, partnership becomes illegal, partners agree.
(b) By agreement, for example mental incapacity, fraud, *Carmichael* v *Evans* (1914).
2. *By order of courts*: one partner incapable, crime, persistent breach, carried on only at loss, just and equitable.
3. *Insolvency*. Creditor has three options: wind up partnership only, bankrupt partner(s) only, concurrent winding up and bankruptcy. Recent cases *Marr* v *Commissioners of Customs and Excise* (1989), partner not bankrupt if all partnership debts satisfied; *Investment and Pensions Advisory Service and Another* v *Gray and Another* (1989), cannot serve injunction on partners' assets until partnership is declared insolvent. Partnership assets to partnership debts, surplus to personal estates. Personal assets to personal debts surplus to partnership.

Sundry partnership details

1. Partnership property. Important because of insolvency rules.
2. Change of partners. Retirement/death of partner typical exam question. Must know effect and procedure for novation, holding out and *Clayton's Case*.

Question – October 1989

(a) Three architects are in partnership as 'Grand Design'. One of them, John Brick, is asked if his partnership will guarantee the bank overdraft of a building contractor with which Grand Design often works. John Brick signs the guarantee below the words 'on behalf of Grand Design'. John Brick did not consult his co-partners before signing.
Is the guarantee binding on any of the partners? (5 marks)

(b) Sean Lamb, is a partner in 'Simply Offal', a firm which runs a butcher's shop. Simply Offal's bank agrees with Sean Lamb to grant the partnership a £3,000 trading overdraft on agreed terms as to the partnership account under the words 'Simply Offal'. One cheque is for £250 in favour of the partnership's meat wholesalers. The other cheque is for £1,000 in favour of a well known gardening shop, for the purchase of some garden furniture. Sean Lamb stops payment of this cheque.
Are any of the partners liable for the overdraft or the £1,000 cheque in favour of the gardening shop? (9 marks)

(c) Bill and Ben want to go into partnership, running a flower shop. Bill has inherited some money and agrees to purchase business premises for the partnership. However, the business will require a trading overdraft and, although Bill wants a share of the profits, he also wants to limit his liability to the bank and to any other creditors of the partnership. How can he do this and what rights will he have to manage the partnership's affairs? (6 marks)

Key words

(a) guarantee	(b) a butcher's shop	(c) Bill
John Brick signs	bank agrees with Sean Lamb	inherited some
'on behalf of Grand Design'	£3,000 trading overdraft	money
did not consult	Sean Lamb	trading overdraft
binding on any of the partners?	on the partnership account	Bill
	'Simply Offal'	share of the profits
	£250	limit his liability
	meat wholesalers	how can
	£1,000 cheque	rights will he
	well known gardening shop	manage
	partners liable	
	overdraft	
	£1,000 cheque	

Answer

(a) Under the Partnership Act 1890, s.9, general partners are jointly liable for the debts and obligerations of their firm. In the Partnership Act 1890, s.5, general partners are stated to be the agent of the firm and of the co-partners, with authority to enter into contracts in the name of the firm. However, the partners will not be liable for contracts entered into by an individual partner in the name of the firm, unless the transaction lies within the actual or ostensible authority of the partner.

Partners have various implied powers to act on behalf of the firm, the extent of these powers varying depending on whether it is a trading or non-trading firm. However, it is not within the implied power of a partner in any type of firm to execute guarantees which are binding on the firm. It would not, therefore, be possible to hold the firm liable under ostensible authority which exceeded the implied powers of a partner.

Thus, the co-partners will not be liable on the guarantee signed by John Brick unless they have expressly authorised him to act on their behalf. Since he has not consulted his co-partners, this seems unlikely. John Brick himself will incur a liability for signing on the guarantee when he lacked authority to do so.

(b) A trading partnership is one where the principal business objective involves buying and selling: *Higgins* v *Beauchamp* (1914). Individual partners in a trading firm have the implied authority:

(i) To borrow money in the firm's name and in the ordinary course of the firm's business.
(ii) To sign cheques on the firm's bank account in the ordinary course of the firm's business.

Thus, the bank will be able to hold the partners liable for a debt created by an individual partner in the firm's name, and for cheques signed by an individual partner, so long as the bank has no notice of a lack of authority on the part of the partner. This might arise, for example, where the bank holds a mandate from the firm specifying that more than one partner must sign cheques or arrange borrowings.

In the case of Simply Offal, the bank granted the overdraft facility to the firm on the authority of Sean Lamb. The overdraft was granted to support the trading activities of the firm, and would therefore lie within the ostensible authority of Sean Lamb, unless the bank was aware of any restriction on his actual authority.

In the case of the cheques:

(i) The cheque for £250 in favour of the meat wholesaler is clearly within the ordinary course of business of a firm of butchers. Therefore, unless the bank was aware of any restriction on Sean Lamb's actual authority, the firm and the co-partners will be liable for this cheque, and for the overdraft it creates.
(ii) The cheque for the garden furniture is clearly outside the ordinary course of business of a firm of butchers, and hence outside the scope of Sean Lamb's authority. The firm and the co-partners cannot be held liable on this cheque; but Sean Lamb could be held liable.

(c) Under the Limited Partnerships Acts 1907, it is possible for one or more partners to enjoy the status of 'limited partner'. This means that the partner has limited liability, and cannot lose more than the capital which he has agreed to contribute to the firm. Even if he later withdraws some of his capital from the business, he remains liable to the extent of the capital he originally agreed to contribute.

The principal conditions for the creation of a limited partnership are:

(i) There must be at least one general partner with unlimited liability for the firm's debts, as well as the limited partner(s).
(ii) The limited partnership must be registered under the Limited Partnerships Act 1907, s.8, otherwise the partner will have the same liability as a general partner.

Although a limited partner has the advantage of limited liability, he has no authority to manage the firm's business or to bind the firm contractually. He may advise the general partners; but, if he participates in the running of the firm, he will have the same liability for the firm's debts as a general partner.

Thus the solution for Bill will be to register himself as a limited partner, while Ben will be a general partner. However, Bill must then accept that he can advise Ben but cannot participate in the management of the firm's affairs.

Author's comment
This is a mainly factual type of question, which is typical of partnership problems. The students either know the answer or not with no area for common sense or a 'best guess'. Surprisingly many candidates did well in (c) with good knowledge being displayed on this relatively small part of the syllabus.

CHAPTER 8

Limited company customers

Syllabus requirements
The main legal considerations to which a banker must have regard when dealing with private and public limited companies. In particular the following aspects are relevant:
- account opening
- directors as agents
- termination of mandate and effect of insolvency.

∎ Introduction

Limited companies tend to be an area of the syllabus held in great awe by students. There is no reason for this other than that many of the 'high regard' customers they encounter throughout their careers will tend to be limited companies. However, it is the high respect given to this topic that in itself convinces candidates that it must be difficult. I liken this to sport and the high number of opponents who lose the match even before they leave the dressing room. Limited companies are not difficult to understand, once the basics are understood.

∎ Limited companies basics

Separate legal entity

A limited company is a legal entity in its own right; *Salomon v Salomon & Co Ltd* (1897). It is not made up of its shareholders (owners) nor its directors (as a partnership is comprised of the partners), the directors merely being the physical agents of the company. Hence a company, say Tony Grundy Electronics Ltd, is completely separate from its sole director, say Tony Grundy, and occasions could arise where the company was in dispute with the directors. In fact the *Salomon* case was based on whether the assets of the director could be claimed by the creditors of the company (the people owed money by the company). The court decided that this was not possible as the company was a separate legal entity.

Composition

As mentioned above, a company is a separate legal entity, but it does not have a physical presence. Hence it needs agents to transact on its behalf; these agents are known as directors. The minimum number of directors in a private limited company is one, and if there is only one then he cannot also be the secretary. As well as acting as agents the directors are also the trustees of the company assets.

Ownership/liability

The company and its assets are owned by the shareholders of the company. The minimum number of shareholders is two, there being no maximum, and the company must keep a register of shareholders. If the company is a company limited by shares (the most common type of company), the liability of the shareholders for the debts incurred by the company is limited to the contribution made when purchasing the shares, or the amount contributed plus the amount outstanding on partly paid shares. This is in contrast to a partnership where all partners are jointly liable for the debts of the partnership to the extent of **all** their personal assets and the partners are the joint owners of the assets of the partnership.

Formation

A limited company is formed by the completion of registration procedures. These procedures include the drawing up of a memorandum of association and articles of association; these are the rules of the company and are discussed in full later. These documents, plus others, need to be registered at the Companies Registry and confirmation received.

Public or private limited company?

A public limited company is capable of requesting the stock exchange for a quotation. Not every public limited company is quoted but the vast majority are. A private limited company cannot be quoted on the stock exchange and tends to be a smaller concern.

Name

A company cannot use the word bank in its name without meeting the requirements of the Banking Act 1987 (licensed deposit taker, paid up capital in excess of £5 million, subject to exceptions quoted in the Act). If the company is a public limited company it must contain those words in its title or the abbreviation PLC. If the company is a private limited company it must contain those words in its title or the abbreviation LTD. It has been normal for past exam questions to give the name of the company as LTD or PLC and from this the candidate must realise that the company is either a private or a public limited company; there will typically be no other reference to the type of company in the question.

Companies Act 1989

The above Act was introduced in 1990 after much anticipation and was introduced in part to meet the Seventh Harmonisation Directive issued by the European Community in 1983. It amends the Companies Act 1985, the Insolvency Act 1986 and the rules regulating the Monopolies and Mergers Commission. Due to its recent introduction, its implications have not yet been fully assessed and will not be until it is tested in the courts. However, the main impact of the Act will be in the areas of registration of charges given by the company, discussed in Chapter eighteen, and the acts of directors on the company's behalf, discussed later in this chapter. A large part of the Act also discusses accountancy procedures and will not be discussed at all in this text.

Types of limited companies

Company limited by shares

This is the most common type of company. The possible liability of the shareholders, should the company be unable to meet its debts or go into liquidation, is limited to the amount of capital contributed or the amount of capital contributed plus the balance outstanding on partly paid shares.

Company limited by guarantee

This type of company is typically formed by charitable institutions, the liability of the members being limited to the amount guaranteed. A company limited by guarantee cannot be created if the company is to have a share capital, ie, a contribution to the company by the shareholders.

Unlimited companies

These are very rare as the liability of the members is unlimited, and there is very little difference between such a company and a partnership.

Public limited companies

As mentioned above, a public limited company must quote public limited company or PLC in its name and is capable of seeking a stock exchange quotation. If such a quotation is sought, there must be no limitations on the transferability of its shares and the company must not have a lien on any shares that are not fully paid. For a PLC the minimum number of directors is two and the minimum authorised share capital is £50,000.

Private limited company

A private limited company must quote private limited company or LTD in its name. The minimum issued share capital must be £2 and the minimum number of directors is one, but if there is only one he cannot also be the secretary. Also, a private limited company cannot invite the public to subscribe for shares or debenture stock and such an action could lead to a fine. Many of the aspects of shares in a private limited company will be discussed in Chapter sixteen but in essence such shares could be difficult to value (not quoted on the stock exchange), difficult to sell (restricted market) and there could be restrictions on the transfer of shares (perhaps to an individual who is not a member of the owning family, or to another limited company, such as the bank's nominee company). A lien (a right to retain) on the company's shares could also exist for any debts owed to the company by the shareholders, such as any uncalled element of partly paid shares.

Limited company – formation procedures

As previously mentioned, limited companies are bound by rules known as the memorandum of association and articles of association. These are normally bound together in one document known as the memorandum and articles of association, or 'm & aas' or 'm &

as', and they also must be registered at the Companies Registry, based at Companies House, Cardiff. Once registered, the company will be issued with a Certificate of Incorporation. In effect this is the birth certificate of the company and prior to its issue the company does not legally exist, and upon its receipt a private limited company can commence trading. If the company is a public limited company it can commence trading only upon receipt of the Certificate of Incorporation plus the Certificate to Commence Business, issued by the Registrar of Companies (Companies Registry) once he is satisfied that the company has an issued share capital of £50,000.

Once formed, the company is referred to in all official documents and any communication with the Companies Registry by its company number quoted on the Certificate of Incorporation.

We shall now discuss in detail the memorandum and articles of association and the types of capital issued by limited companies.

Memorandum of association

This is the document that states the external rules of the company, and governs its dealings with outside parties. It contains the following five clauses:

The name of the company

It will state the name of the company, followed by public limited company or PLC or private limited company or LTD. Its name must not be similar to any existing company, and the conditions concerning the use of the word 'bank' have been discussed previously. The name of the company can be altered by special resolution of the shareholders (requiring 75 per cent of those members voting at the meeting): s.28 Companies Act 1985. However, s.113 Companies Act 1989 states that 'anything that may be done by a private limited company may be done, without a meeting and without any previous notice being required, by resolution in writing signed by or on behalf of all the members of the company who at the date of the resolution would be entitled to attend and vote at such meeting'. Hence, the need for a special resolution is removed for a private limited company.

The domicile of the registered office of the company

It will state whether this is England, Wales or Scotland. This is due to Scotland having different laws from England and Wales. The actual address is not usually quoted in the memorandum but is notified to the Registrar and available to third parties via a search at Companies House. The address can be changed by notification to the Registrar but the country of domicile cannot be changed.

Objects clause

This is discussed separately below.

Limitation of liability

This will state whether liability is limited by shares or guarantee or if, rarely, liability is unlimited. A PLC cannot have unlimited liability. The limitation can be transferred from limited to unlimited only by agreement of **all** members (shareholders), and obviously only for a private limited company.

Share capital

This will state the amount of authorised share capital and how it is divided, for example into ordinary and preference shares.

The objects clause

This tends to be the third clause in the memorandum of association and is historically by far the largest clause in the document. It is the clause that states precisely what the powers of the company are. Prior to the introduction of the Companies Act 1989, if companies undertook transactions outside the objects clause they were deemed to be '*ultra vires*' the company (outside the powers) and void. A transaction that is *ultra vires* the company cannot later be ratified and an *ultra vires* contract is totally unenforceable. This was supported by case law: *Re Introductions Ltd* (1969) where a company originally formed to introduce prospective clients at the Festival of Britain later entered into pig breeding. It was held that this transaction was *ultra vires* the company and void, as was the money lent to the company by the bank for this purpose and the security taken to support the lending.

The position was modified by s.35 Companies Act 1985, which stated that if anyone deals with the company in good faith, where the transaction is decided upon by the directors, it will be deemed that the directors have the power to bind the company, even if this is outside the memorandum, and the third party need not enquire as to the powers of the company. In *International Sales and Agencies Ltd* v *Marcus* (1982) it was held that good faith would be absent where the third party had actual knowledge that the contract was *ultra vires* or that the circumstances were such that the third party should have been aware that the transaction was *ultra vires*. This still left innocent third parties at risk and proposals were drawn up for the abolition of the *ultra vires* doctrine. The result is s.108 Companies Act 1989 which states that for s.35 Companies Act 1985 the following should be substituted:

'35(1) The validity of an act done by a company shall not be called into question on the ground of lack of capacity by reason of anything in the memorandum.

(2) A member of a company may bring proceedings to restrain the doing of an act which but for subsection (1) would be beyond the company's capacity; but no such proceedings shall lie in respect of a legal obligation arising from a previous act of the company.

(3) It remains the duty of the directors to observe any limitations on their powers flowing from the company's memorandum.

35A (1) In favour of a person dealing with a company in good faith, the power of the board of directors to bind the company, or authorise others to do so, shall be deemed to be free of any limitation under the company's constitution.

(2) For this purpose

(a) a person 'deals with' a company if he is a party to any transaction or other act to which the company is a party;

(b) a person shall not be regarded as acting in bad faith by reason only of knowing that an act is beyond the powers of the directors under the constitution; and

(c) a person shall be presumed to have acted in good faith unless the contrary is proved.

35B A party to a transaction with a company is not bound to enquire as to whether it is permitted by the company's memorandum or as to any limitation on the powers of the board of directors to bind the company or authorise others to do so.'

Thus the position would now appear to be that anyone dealing with a company has no duty to enquire whether or not the transaction is within the powers of the board of directors and even if he has notice that the transaction is outside the powers of the company, providing he acts in good faith apart from that, the transaction will be binding on the company. Also, where the third party is dealing with a director he will be able to rely upon the ostensible authority of that director to represent the board (see Chapter 6 for a full discussion).

However, a member (shareholder) of the company could restrain the company from acting outside the memorandum, but not if this was a legal obligation connected with a previous act of the company (eg, the sale of property contracted to previously).

Section 110 Companies Act 1989 declares that if the memorandum states that the object of the company is to carry on business as a general commercial company then:

(a) the object of the company is to carry on any trade or business **whatsoever**, and

(b) the company has power to do all such things as are incidental or conducive to the carrying on of any trade or business by it.

The position now is much more clear and the third party dealing with the company is in a protected position. The principle of transactions being *ultra vires* the company, as illustrated by *Re Introductions Ltd*, should not recur. There are, however, still thought to be problems with the interpretation of s.110 and the meaning of 'such things that are incidental or conducive to the carrying on of any trade or business by it'. For example, is the giving of a guarantee guaranteeing a supplier, or an inter-company guarantee guaranteeing the liabilities of a subsidiary 'incidental or conducive'? It is difficult to say but, subject to these minor grey areas, the new legislation is far-reaching and most welcome.

Articles of association

The articles of association are the internal rules of the company; in particular they state the authority delegated to the directors and the rules by which they are governed. A company may adopt a specimen set of articles known as Table A, and each major Companies Act will contain a Table A. Companies have three options when drawing up their articles. They can either draw up their own articles completely, adopt Table A completely or adopt some of Table A and omit or amend other clauses from Table A. If the articles are silent on one particular matter, then it is assumed that Table A of the most recent Companies Act will apply, which at present is the Companies Act 1985. The full effect of the articles of association and how they affect the role of the director is discussed in full later in this chapter.

Types of capital

There are many ways that a company can raise capital, be it to fund a capital venture (eg, new premises, expansion, takeover etc.) or to set up the company itself. These are discussed below.

Ordinary shares

These are the most common type of shares issued. The ordinary shareholders are paid a dividend depending on the profits of the company (typically, no profit means no dividend) and receive their capital back should the company be wound up only after all the other creditors and shareholders have been paid in full (see Chapter nine). In return for these disadvantages and greater risks (ordinary shares are sometimes known as risk capital) the ordinary shareholders acquire voting rights and are often the only type of shareholder to do so.

Preference shares

The name really tells you the nature of these shares. They are paid a dividend and receive their capital, should the company be wound up, in preference to the ordinary shareholders. Other characteristics include:

(i) A fixed dividend irrespective of the level of profits. Quite often the shares are referred to by the level of fixed dividend, for example 6 per cent preference shares. There is usually no extra dividend should the company produce large profits, unless the shares are participating preference shares.

(ii) They normally carry no voting rights.

(iii) Preference shares are usually cumulative; this means that should the company make insufficient profits in one year to meet the dividend on the preference shares, the unpaid portion remains as a liability and is 'rolled up' to the following year, or years. If the preference shares are non-cumulative, this must be stated on the share certificate.

Redeemable shares

These can be either ordinary or preference shares, and are redeemable at the option either of the company or of the shareholder. The conditions for the issue of redeemable shares are:

(i) There must be other non-redeemable shares in existence.

(ii) The issue of redeemable shares must be expressly provided for in the articles of association.

(iii) Redemption must come out of profits and not, for example, from another share issue.

(iv) The shares must be fully paid.

Deferred shares

These are also known as management or founder shares and are rarely seen now. In return for receiving their dividends after the ordinary and preference shareholders they carry loaded voting rights; for example a deferred shareholder may have three votes to one vote for an ordinary shareholder with the same share holding.

Debenture stock

This is a completely different concept from shares, in that debenture stock is a loan to the company, whereas shares are in effect an investment in the company, and a stake in the ownership of the company. Other differences include:

(i) debenture stock ranking before shareholders in respect of repayment of capital should the company be wound up;

(ii) interest payments to debenture holders being made irrespective of the amount of profit made (in fact being made even if the company makes a loss);

(iii) debenture holders do not have voting rights.

Director's loans

These are quite often referred to as 'quasi-capital' and represent monies input to the company by the directors, but are repayable to the directors, quite often on demand. It is not unusual for banks when lending to companies to ask the directors to postpone the director's loans. This in effect means that the directors agree that their loans will not be repaid until the bank has be repaid in full.

∎ The role of the director

Director's powers to bind the company

As previously mentioned, the director is in effect the physical agent of the company. His actions are limited by the articles of association and it is possible for a director to act *ultra vires* these powers, but within the company's powers quoted within the memorandum. Historically this has not really caused many problems for third parties as such a transaction can be adopted by the company, simply by amending the articles retrospectively. However, s.108 Companies Act 1989 states that the authority of the board of directors to bind the company shall be deemed to be free of any limitations under the company's constitution. Also, the third party is not bound to enquire as to any limitation of the powers of the board of directors to bind the company or authorise others to do so. Remember s.108 refers to the board of directors, third parties relying on the ostensible authority of the individual director to represent the board.

Interested directors

A recurring problem for bankers has been the area of interested directors. An interested director is accepted to be a director who will benefit either directly or indirectly from a transaction involving the company.

The articles of the company will state whether or not such an interested director can vote at the meeting deciding on the contract. The articles could state that the interested director can vote with or without disclosing his interest, or that he cannot vote at all. If the latter is the case then the bank must ensure that the quorum (minimum number of directors needed to be present to make the meeting effective) is made up of non-interested directors. The classic case in this area is *Victors Ltd* v *Lingard and Others* (1927), and if the above procedures are not followed, security taken by such a quorum will be void as against a liquidator. Examples of interested directors can be a contract with another company that contains common directors, or the taking of some form of direct security, for example a mortgage debenture (see Chapter eighteen, limited company security) where directors' guarantees already exist. The methods of overcoming such a problem have been to ensure that a non-interested quorum is present (as discussed above), or to amend the articles, allowing interested directors to vote.

However, the full implications of s.108 Companies Act 1989 have not yet been tested but would appear to mean that the problem of interested directors should no longer be present, as s.108 states that 'in favour of a person dealing with a company in good faith, the power of the board of directors to bind the company . . . shall be deemed to be free from any limitation under the company's constitution'. This presumably will also include the area of interested directors being precluded from voting on contracts from which they will personally benefit, either directly or indirectly. If this is so, the area of interested directors should no longer pose problems for bankers.

Due to the recent amendment of the law in this area it would be a sensible examination topic.

Power of one director to represent the board of directors

Many commentators on this area of the syllabus expected the Companies Act 1989 to state quite categorically that either any one director could represent the board of directors or alternatively that the managing director, if one exists, would assume all the rights of the board. However, the Act remains strangely silent on this area, apart from s.108 which states that: 'the power of the board to bind the company, or authorise others to do so, shall be deemed to be free of any limitation under the company's constitution.'

Therefore, it would appear that if a third party deals with a director in good faith, then he can assume that the director has authority to act of behalf of the company and on behalf of the boards of directors, without the necessity for a resolution etc. The authority that the third party relies on is the ostensible authority of the individual director representing the board.

Financial assistance to directors

Commercial transactions involving a director

Section 109 Companies Act 1989 'applies where a company enters into a transaction to which the parties include:

(a) a director of that company or of its holding company, or
(b) a person connected with such a director (spouse, child, step-child) or a company with whom such a director is associated,

and the board of directors exceed, in connection with the transaction, any limitation on their powers under the company's constitution.

The transaction is voidable at the option of the company.

Whether or not it is avoided, any such party to the transaction as mentioned in (a) or (b) above, and any director who authorised the transaction, is liable:

(i) to account to the company for any gain which he has made directly or indirectly by the transaction and
(ii) to indemnify the company for any loss or damage resulting from the transaction.'

The transaction ceases to be voidable if:

(i) restitution is not possible;
(ii) the company is indemnified for any loss or damage resulting from the transaction;
(iii) the avoidance would affect the rights of a person acting bona fide, for value and without notice of the exceeding of the director's powers;
(iv) the transaction is ratified by the company.
Note: 'transaction includes any act.'

The implication of all this to bankers is that where the bank is involved in a transaction and where the third party is either (a) or (b) above (for example, a loan to purchase equipment from a company with common directors) then caution must be exercised as the transaction could be voidable at the option of the company.

Loans to directors and guarantees or other securities given in support of a loan to a director by a third party

Transactions prohibited

By s.330 Companies Act 1985 both of these transactions are prohibited and for 'relevant' companies (PLCs or a private limited company that is a member of a group that includes a PLC), so are the following:

(a) 'quasi loan' to a director of the company or a director of the holding company, or a person connected with such a director (as defined above). A quasi loan is a payment or agreement to make payment by the company where the director is liable to make such a payment himself. Examples could include the agreed use of a company credit card for personal items, the company meeting the bill, or the payment of the interest on an advance for personal use, (eg bridging loan).

(b) the giving of a guarantee or other security to a third party in return for the provision of such a quasi loan.

(c) 'back to back' arrangements, for example the provision of a loan to a third party on the condition that that third party lend money to the director.

Exceptions

A number of exceptions exist and these include:

(i) loans to directors up to a total aggregate of £5,000 (increased from £2,500 by Companies Act 1989);

(ii) quasi loans for relevant companies up to a total aggregate of £5,000 (increased from £1,000 by Companies Act 1989);

(iii) director's business expenditure up to a maximum of £10,000, providing the assistance has the prior approval of a general meeting of shareholders, or if the assistance is not approved at such a meeting, the indebtedness is cleared in full within six months of the meeting;

(iv) inter-group transactions are permitted despite common directorship, as are transactions involving a holding company;

(v) where the company involved is a money-lending institution (for example, a bank) then providing the money is lent in the ordinary course of business and on terms no more favourable than those offered to an unconnected person the transaction is valid up to a limit of £100,000 (increased from £50,000 by Companies Act 1989).

Banking implications

Banks can be involved in financial transactions between companies and their directors (or connected persons) in a number of ways and when this is so the banker must be aware that the transaction may be prohibited, which could result in a guarantee being unenforceable or a debt irrecoverable, unless it meets the criteria of one of the exceptions. Such transactions could include:

● provision of a loan to enable the company to lend money to a director (a back to back agreement),
● lending money to a director of a company, the lending supported by a guarantee from that same company,

- allowing the company customer to make payments from its account to meet the indebtedness of a director.

Conversion and the director's bank account

When a bank holds an account of a company director, one of the main dangers is the possibility of the director converting funds belonging to the company. Thus the bank must be on guard in the following circumstances:

(a) When pressing for repayment of an out of order account.
(b) When collecting for the account of the director a cheque payable to the company and endorsed by the director (see *A.L. Underwood* v *Bank of Liverpool and Martins Ltd* (1924), Chapter ten).
(c) When collecting for the account of the director a cheque drawn by him in his capacity as an agent of the company (similar to *Midland Bank Ltd* v *Reckitt and Others* (1933).

If care is not exercised, the bank could be deemed negligent and, if so, would lose the statutory protection of s.4 Cheques Act 1957 and would be liable to the true owner (probably the company) for conversion.

∎ Personal liabilities of company directors

One of the main aims of the would-be directors when forming a limited company is undoubtedly the avoidance of personal liability. However, there are many circumstances when directors are unable to avoid this personal liability. Examples include the following cases.

Guarantees

The giving of a guarantee (limited or unlimited in amount) in favour of the company obviously means that the guarantor is personally liable for the company's debts. If an indemnity clause is included in the guarantee document, then the guarantor is primarily liable and this would override any lack of power of the company (eg, if the borrowing is *ultra vires* the memorandum or articles) and the guarantor/indemnifier would still be liable, although since the introduction of the Companies Act 1989 (s.108) the importance of such a clause is now substantially less than previously.

Exceeding of authority

If a company director commits the company to an *ultra vires* contract (eg, bank borrowing) but is acting within his ostensible authority, then it is possible for the third party (eg, the bank) to enforce the contract against the director: *Weeks* v *Propert* (1873). In this case the director negotiated a loan which, after taking into consideration existing debts, exceeded the maximum borrowing quoted in the memorandum. Again s.108 Companies Act 1989 should mitigate this peril.

The promoters

Any person who contracts for a company before it is formed is liable on the contract, even if that person signs per pro the company: *Phonogram Ltd* v *Lane* (1982). This is due to the fact that prior to the issuing of the certificate of incorporation (and Certificate to Commence Business if a PLC) the company does not exist.

Clause in memorandum

There may be a clause in the Memorandum of Association stating that the liability of one or all of the directors in unlimited.

Tort

Directors will be liable if they obtain a loan by negligent or fraudulent misrepresentation.

Cheques

Anyone who signs a bill of exchange or a cheque in his capacity as agent must state clearly that he is doing so by using the words 'for' or 'per pro' etc. But if he signs, only indicating his occupation, such as 'X' agent for 'Y' or 'X Managing Director of Y Ltd' this may not be sufficient. If a person signs a cheque bearing the name of the company printed on the cheque and an account number relating to the company the company alone is liable: *Bondina Ltd* v *Rollaway Shower Blinds Ltd* (1986). Here the court decided that it was obvious that the intention was for the company to be liable.

Fraudulent and wrongful trading

Fraudulent trading

The directors (or others) may be personally liable for fraudulent trading. Section 213 Insolvency Act 1986 provides that if in a winding up it appears that any business has been carried on with the intent of defrauding creditors (or for any other fraudulent reason), the court may declare that any 'knowing parties' are personally liable to make such contributions as the court thinks proper. In *Re William C Leitch Brothers Ltd* (1933) it was held to be fraudulent to continue to trade when the directors knew that there was no reasonable prospect of paying debts. *R* v *Grantham* (1984) showed that the onus is on the directors to prove the company's ability to repay the loan when due. Knowing that a creditor will not be paid may amount to intent to defraud. However, a stupid but optimistic director is not liable: *White* v *Osmond (Parkstone) Ltd* (1960)

Wrongful trading

Section 214 Insolvency Act 1986 relates to wrongful trading as opposed to fraudulent trading and applies when:

1. The company has gone into insolvent liquidation.
2. The directors 'knew or ought to have concluded that there was no reasonable prospect that the company would avoid insolvent liquidation.'
3. The person was a director of the company or a shadow director.

It is thought that the courts will show leniency (and in fact the Act is worded in such a way that leniency is provided for) where a director has realised that insolvent liquidation is likely and has taken every step to protect creditors.

Also, in *Re Marketing Consortium Ltd* (1989) it was held that the 'reasonable' standard of skill expected of a director will vary depending upon the size of the company. For example, it would not be equitable to compare the director of a small 'one-man' concern with the standard expected of a managing director of a large multinational company.

A worrying interpretation for bankers in s.214(7) is that personal liability may be attached to shadow directors – these are persons in accordance with whose directions or instructions the company is accustomed to act; professional advisers are excluded, but it is thought that where a bank is also a creditor then the exclusion available will not apply. It is not unusual for a company experiencing financial difficulties to approach its bank and to act on the instructions given. Thus banks must be careful to give advice only and not instructions or, if instructions are given, that the company is not 'accustomed to act' upon them.

Disqualified persons

If a person is disqualified under statutory provisions (eg, bankrupts – s.11 Company Directors Disqualification Act 1986) and is 'involved in the management of the company', he shall be personally liable jointly and severally with the company.

■ Company Directors Disqualification Act 1986

Persons may be disqualified from being directors or taking part in the management of companies for up to 15 years. The grounds for presentation of a disqualification order are:

1. Persistent defaults in complying with the Companies Act 1985.
2. Where in the course of a winding-up it appears that a person has been guilty of fraudulent trading (or of any other fraud) or of wrongful trading.
3. Where a director has been a director of an insolvent company and he is considered unfit to be involved in the management of a company.
4. A bankrupt cannot be a director.

■ Companies and the purchase of their own shares

A company giving financial assistance for the purchase of its own shares

A company cannot give financial assistance, either directly or indirectly, to a third party in the purchase of its own shares; s.151(1) Companies Act 1985. Examples of assistance could include the provision of funds to the third party, those funds to be used to purchase shares in the company; the use of company assets as security for the purchase of the shares in a transaction such as takeovers, acquisitions etc; or indeed any other transaction that reduces the net assets of the company: s.152(1) Companies Act 1985.

A company cannot give financial assistance to reduce or discharge a liability incurred by a third party for the purchase of the company's shares. For example, the commitment to reduce any borrowing undertaken by declaring a dividend that will be mandated direct to the lender.

However, there are many exceptions, applying to both private and public limited companies, including:

(A) Section 153(1) Companies Act 1985 states that financial assistance by the company for the purchase of its own shares is lawful where:

(i) the giving of the assistance is not the company's principal purpose, (for example, if the main purpose is the continuing existence of the company and this can be achieved only by the giving of financial assistance, say by guaranteeing the bank advance to a third party) and

(ii) it is given in good faith.

(B) Section 153(4) quotes the following exceptions:

(a) when the company's normal business is lending money, for example, banks and in particular the provision of loans by the TSB to its customers at the time of its flotation,

(b) for the purpose of an employee share-save scheme.

The following exceptions apply only to private limited companies:

● The private company's net assets must not be reduced or, where they are, the assistance must come from distributable profits, and

● the assistance must be authorised **beforehand** by special resolution, in a general meeting, and

● the directors must make a declaration of solvency stating that if assistance is given the company will be able to pay its debts within 12 months;

● the director's declaration of solvency must be accompanied by an auditor's report to the directors stating that the declaration of solvency is reasonable

This can be of significance to bankers, (and indeed was the topic of a recent, and poorly attempted, examination question) in the following circumstances:

(i) by making a loan to the company to allow it to offer financial assistance to a third party to purchase the company's shares; or

(ii) by accepting a guarantee from a company to allow the bank's customer to purchase the guarantor company's shares; or

(iii) by allowing the funds of a customer to be used for either the purchase of its own shares or the assistance of a third party for such a purpose: *Selangor United Rubber Estates Ltd* v *Craddock* (1968); or

(iv) advancing monies for the acquisition of a company, the security to be assets belonging to that company upon completion.

Purchase by the company of its own shares

A company may purchase its own shares, whether they are redeemable or not: s.162 Companies Act 1985, providing:

(a) There are not only redeemable shares left in circulation.

(b) Such an acquisition is expressly allowed for in the articles of association.

(c) Both private and public companies must inform the Companies Registry within 28 days of the acquisition and in addition a public limited company must state the total amount, minimum and maximum price per share paid: s.169 Companies Act 1985.

The shares can be bought either on-market (via a recognised stock exchange) or off-market. Obviously private limited companies will always be off-market, but PLCs could be either on-market or off-market (for example, by private agreement) and different procedures apply to each. The main differences are that if the purchase is on-market (s.162) the purchase can be approved by ordinary resolution of the shareholders and the resolution must be filed at the Companies Registry within 15 days, whereas an off-market (s.166) purchase needs to be approved in advance by special resolution of the shareholders and there is no need to notify the Companies Registry. In each case the authorisation is valid for only 18 months and when the purchase takes place it must be reported to the Companies Registry within 28 days.

▮ Limited companies as customers

Account opening procedures

Memorandum and articles of association

These documents must be present and their contents thoroughly checked. Items of special significance include:

- company name
- domiciled address
- objects clause (bear in mind the amendments to the *ultra vires* rule under the Companies Act 1989)
- directors'/shareholders' names if given
- interested directors and directors' powers (articles)

It is possible that since the changes implemented by the Companies Act 1989 banks will no longer wish to see the memorandum and articles, and if they are asked for, it cannot be doubted that the reliance upon them will decrease from the high level of importance placed on them presently.

Certificate of incorporation

The 'birth certificate', asked for every time whether the company is a private or public limited company.

Certificate to commence business

Only if a PLC.

Bank mandate

This normally incorporates a resolution appointing the bank as the company's bankers and will also state the number of signatures necessary on cheques etc, and other sundry account maintenance matters.

Companies registry search

This will confirm the details from the mandate and the memorandum and articles of association (directors' names etc), and will also provide the bank with a copy of the charges register. This is important to bankers for the main reason that if another bank has a debenture that incorporates a fixed charge over book debts (see *Siebbe Gorman* case and Chapter eighteen) and the bank accepts debtors' monies to the new account the bank will have to return **all** monies deposited to the account and not merely the balance of the account, to the debenture holder. Hence the potential risk is incredibly high.

Running the account

Paying cheques

The mandate will clearly state the number of signatures required to pay cheques. However, should a paying banker inadvertently pay a cheque bearing an insufficient number of, or incorrect signatories, the bank could have settled a legitimate debt of the company and if so the bank could rely on the right of subrogation and debit the account: *B. Liggett (Liverpool) Ltd* v *Barclays Bank Ltd* (1928).

Collecting cheques

Care must be taken when collecting cheques to an account of a limited company, where the payee on the cheque is another limited company. This is a very rare occurrence and the bank should make suitable enquiries immediately. If the bank fails to do so it could lose its statutory protection against conversion from s.4 Cheques Act 1957: *London and Montrose Shipbuilding and Repairing Co Ltd* v *Barclays Bank Ltd* (1926).

Lending to companies

Most of the technical hazards of lending to companies have been removed by the introduction of the Companies Act 1989, and the abolition of the *ultra vires* rule. However, the new legislation will take a while to be adopted fully by the banks and in the meanwhile students must have a knowledge of the law as it stands and understand the reasons for the procedures being implemented by the banks.

FACT SHEET

Limited company customers

Basics

1. Separate legal entity *Salomon* v *Salomon & Co Ltd* (1897)
2. Composition, no physical presence, hence the need for agents – directors.
3. Ownership/liability, company owned by shareholders, but their liability is usually limited.
4. Formation; memorandum and articles of association and registration.
5. Public or private limited company; PLC can request quotation on stock exchange.
6. Name; conditions on use of 'bank', must quote PLC or LTD.
7. Companies Act 1989, abolished *ultra vires* but the rulings not yet tested.

Types of limited companies

A. Limited by shares; most common, liability of shareholders is limited to amount contributed or amount contributed plus unpaid element of partly paid shares.
B. Limited by guarantee; typically charitable organisations, liability limited to amount guaranteed. Cannot be created with a share capital.
C. Unlimited companies; very rare.
D. PLCs; can apply for stock exchange quotation, but if does so there so there must be no restriction in the articles. Minimum number of directors two and minimum authorised share capital £50,000.
E. Private limited companies; minimum number of directors is one plus a secretary minimum share capital £2, cannot invite subscriptions from the public. Disadvantages of shares in a private company as security.

Formation procedures

1. Introduction; memorandum and articles to be drawn up and registered, certificate of incorporation (birth certificate) issued and certificate to commence business (if PLC), providing the PLC has £50,000 issued share capital.
2. Memorandum of association; external rules of company, includes name, country of domicile, objects clause, limitation of liability and share capital.

3. Objects clause; historical problems with *ultra vires* including *Re Introductions Ltd.* However, s.108 Companies Act 1989, reduced the problem providing the third party deals with company in good faith (knowledge of the lack of capacity will not be interpreted as bad faith) and there is no compulsion on the third party to enquire as to the limitations of the powers of the directors. S.110 Companies Act 1989 states that 'where the company describes itself as a general commercial company then it is free to carry on any trade or business and do such things that are incidental or conducive to that trade or business'. There could be a problem with the interpretation of 'incidental or conducive' especially with guarantees.
4. Articles of association, internal rules of little significance since introduction of s.108.
5. Types of capital:
   (a) Ordinary share capital most common, dividend paid in accordance with profits, receive their capital back last should the company be wound up. In return they receive voting rights.
   (b) Preference shares: dividend paid irrespective of level of profits, usually no voting rights, usually cumulative.
   (c) Redeemable shares: must be other non-redeemable shares in issue, must be expressly provided for in articles, redemption must come out of profits, must be fully paid.
   (d) Deferred shares: receive dividend and repaid after ordinary shares, in return have weighted voting rights.
   (e) Debenture stock: loan to company, interest paid even if no profit made, rank ahead of shareholders in winding up, no voting rights.
   (f) Director's loans: quasi capital, quite often postponed behind a lender's advance.

Role of the director

(a) Director's power to bind the company – *ultra vires* virtually banished since s.108 introduced.
(b) interested directors – as above see s.108.
(c) power of one director to bind the company – as above see s.108.
(d) financial assistance to directors.
   (i) Commercial transactions involving directors – s.109 Companies Act 1989, where a director is involved in a transaction with the company, and the company exceeds its powers, the transaction is voidable at the option of the company. Whether avoided or not, the director involved plus any director who sanctioned the transaction must indemnify the company against any loss **and** account to the company for any gain made. Transaction ceases to be voidable if the company ratifies the transaction, restitution is not possible or an innocent third party would suffer.
   (ii) Other transactions prohibited – includes loans to directors and guarantees by the company of an advance to a director and, for 'relevant companies', any quasi loans or guarantees for a quasi loan or back to back agreements. Exceptions are made by placing financial limits on the transactions plus inter group transactions and money lending institutions.
   (iii) Banking implications – care with transactions involving both the director and the company.
   (iv) The directors' bank account – care re conversion (*A.L. Underwood*)

Personal liabilities of directors

(a) guarantee – obivously.
(b) exceeding of authority – *weeks* v *Propert.*
(c) pre-formation contracts – *Phonogram* v *Lane.*
(d) unlimited company.
(e) tort.
(f) cheques – must be signed in representative capacity – *Bondina* case.
(g) fraudulent trading – s.213 Insolvency Act 1986 fraudulent purpose.
(h) wrongful trading – s.214 Insolvency Act 1986 plugged the gap left by s.213 where director 'knew or should have known' that the company could not avoid insolvent liquidation. *Re Marketing Consortium* (1989) knowledge of director will vary depending on size of concern. Care with shadow directors – s.214(7) could have serious implications for bankers.
(i) disqualified persons – jointly and severally liable with the company.

Company Directors Disqualification Act 1986

Companies and the purchase of their own shares

1. Financial assistance by the company not permitted s.151 Companies Act 1985, nor reduction of their assets to facilitate the purchase (s.152) nor reduction or repayment of liability incurred in the purchase.
   Exceptions: s.153(1) – purchase is not the main purpose and given in good faith, s.153(4) –

lending is normal business for the company and if private company by resolution etc. banking implications are obvious NB *Selangor United Rubber Estates* v *Craddock.*

2. Purchase by company of its own shares – conditions and can be on-market or off-market.

Limited companies as customers

1. Account opening – memorandum and articles, certificate of incorporation plus certificate to commence trading (if PLC), search at Companies Registry (fixed charge over book debts).
2. Running the account – dangers of paying and collecting cheques.

Question

Your long established customers Peter and Charles Ling, partners in a decorating firm, are considering changing from a partnership to a limited company. Mr P Ling states that they have been told that they will not be liable for the company debts. Is this correct and are there any other advantages or disadvantages that they should consider?

Key words

changing, not liable, other advantages and disadvantages

Answer

1. Re liability for company debts. Basically the statement is correct, as a company is a separate legal entity: *Salomon* v *Salomon & Co Ltd* (1897). However, there are instances when this is not so:

(a) Fraudulent trading (s.213 Insolvency Act 1986). The directors are personally liable for debts incurred when it can be shown that the company has been carried on with the intent to defraud creditors or for any other fraudulent purposes. However, the problem is the necessity to prove intent, although in *R* v *Grantham* (1984) it was shown that proof of the ability to repay a loan at the time of granting the facility lies with the directors. A stupid but optimistic director will not be found guilty of fraudulent trading: *White* v *Osmond (Parkstone) Ltd* (1960).

(b) Wrongful trading. Due to the difficulty of proving fraudulent trading, wrongful trading was introduced under s.214 Insolvency Act (1986) and applies when the directors knew or should have known that there was no reasonable prospect of avoiding insolvent liquidation. *Re Marketing Consortium Ltd* (1989) illustrated the fact that the reasonable level of skill will vary depending on the size of the company concerned.

(c) Pre-formation contracts. If the directors should sign a contract on behalf of the company before the company exists, the person contracting on the company's behalf will be personally liable: *Phonogram* v *Lane* (1982).

(d) Exceeding of authority. If a director should commit the company to a contract that is outside his powers (*ultra vires*) but within his ostensible authority he will be personally liable.

(e) Memorandum of Association. There may be a clause in the memorandum stating that any number of directors have unlimited liability.

(f) Cheques. Directors are merely the physical agents of the company. As such, if they sign a cheque and do not clearly state their representative capacity, they can be personally liable on that cheque. However, *Bondina Ltd* v *Rollaway Shower Blinds Ltd* (1986) stated that where the company name and account number are quoted on a cheque then it should be obvious that the company and not the signatory is liable.

(g) Disqualified persons. If a disqualified person is involved with the management of the company then they shall be jointly and severally liable along with the company.

2. Other advantages and disadvantages.

(a) Advantages
  (i)   opens other alternatives of raising capital (eg shares, debentures).
  (ii) succession. If a partner dies it is possible that the partnership would automatically dissolve. However, a company possesses 'perpetual succession', that is it will continue to exist until it is dissolved.
  (iii) tax position. The partnership profit is automatically classed as the partners' personal income and taxed as such. Shareholders only incur a tax liability on the company profit if it is distributed as dividends.

(b) Disadvantages
  (i)   loss of secrecy. All company affairs, including annual accounts, must be advised to Companies Registry, and are therefore available for anyone to inspect.
  (ii) setting up costs and procedures.
  (iii) powers. Partners are free from limitations. However, a company must comply with its Memorandum of Association.

CHAPTER 9

Insolvency and banks

Syllabus requirements
- The effect of insolvency on individual customers, sole traders, partnerships and limited companies.

■ Introduction

Since the introduction of the Insolvency Act 1986 insolvency procedures have been greatly simplified, and following the restructure of the syllabus in 1990 the emphasis on this topic has been greatly reduced. The candidate no longer needs to know the more complicated procedures involved but merely how insolvency affects the banker/customer relationship and securities taken to support bank lending. The latter is discussed in a later chapter, but this chapter will introduce you to the principles involved and the actions banks need to take when they become aware of insolvency proceedings involving their customers.

The natural starting point is the aims of existing insolvency law, and from there the chapter will be split between personal bankruptcy and corporate (limited company) winding up. Within each section we will discuss who can be made insolvent, the basic procedures involved, the assets of the bankrupt that can and cannot be claimed in the insolvency, the priorities of the creditors amongst themselves, the repercussions of insolvency and the possible alternatives.

■ Aims of the Insolvency Act 1986

The Act was introduced to simplify the existing legislation that was both complicated and fragmented, references to insolvency being found in many statutes. The Insolvency Act brought together all insolvency legislation into one Act and hence one point of reference. The Act is seen to protect the debtor (the person owing the money) by insisting that all his creditors are bound by the bankruptcy process, offering a number of alternatives to bankruptcy (for example, voluntary arrangements, administration orders) and rewarding the debtor if he realises the problems at an early stage. The Act also protects the creditor by, for example, ensuring that the assets are divided in an equitable manner and penalising company directors for failing to take early action that could have prevented loss being incurred by the creditors. Also the Act states that only qualified insolvency practitioners can deal with insolvency matters. If a practice wishes to involve itself in such dealings, then each individual must be qualified and not merely the practice. This prevents a practice being competent on the whole but perhaps having a minority of incompetent members.

■ Personal insolvency (bankruptcy)

Who can be made bankrupt?

The basic answer to this question is anyone who has power to contract; this includes:

- minors (but only for enforceable debts, for example, necessaries)
- married women
- imprisoned criminals – see criminal bankruptcy, later
- deceased persons, or, to be more accurate, the estate of a deceased person can be administered in bankruptcy if the liabilities exceed the assets
- mentally incapacitated persons, with the consent of the court of protection.

For each of the above examples the debtor must satisfy the residency rules contained in s.265 Insolvency Act 1986, in that he must:

 (i) be domiciled (based) in England or Wales, or
 (ii) be personally present in England or Wales when the petition is presented, or
(iii) at any time in the three years preceeding the petition has been:
  - ordinarily resident, or
  - had a place of residence, or
  - carried on business (in person, or via an agent, manager or partnership) in England or Wales.

Bankruptcy procedures

The petition

A bankruptcy petition can be served by either:

(a) the debtor,
(b) the creditor,
(c) the supervisor of a voluntary arrangement,
(d) the official petitioner in connection with a criminal bankruptcy.

Each of these will now be discussed more fully.

Debtor's petition

A debtor may petition for his own bankruptcy on the condition that he is unable to meet his debts as they fall due: s.272 Insolvency Act 1986. His petition must be supported by a statement of affairs quoting his assets and liabilities.

Once the petition and the statement of affairs have been analysed by the court, there will be three options available to the court:

(i) Court sponsored voluntary arrangement, subject to the following conditions:
- the value of the debtor's assets is over £2,000,
- the debts are below the 'small bankruptcy level', £20,000,
- debtor has not been an undischarged bankrupt or made arrangements with his creditors in the last five years.

Once this course of action has been decided upon, the court will usually serve an interim order, preventing the debtor disposing of his assets, and an insolvency practitioner will be appointed to report on the feasibility of the voluntary arrangement. If his report is favourable the courts will proceed, and if not, a bankruptcy order will be made.

Voluntary arrangements are discussed in full later in this chapter, under alternatives to insolvency.

(ii) Summary administration.

Subject to:

(a) liabilities below 'small bankruptcy level', £20,000.

(b) insufficient assets to justify realising the debtor's estate or making a voluntary arrangement.

If a summary administration is made, the debtor will be discharged after two years, compared with the normal three.

(iii) Bankruptcy order. This is fully discussed below.

Creditor's petition

A creditor (or more than one creditor jointly) may petition subject to the following conditions:

(i) the debt owed to the creditor(s) must be at least £750,

(ii) the debt must be unsecured, or
- secured by only third party security (security given by someone other than the debtor), or
- have an unsecured element of at least £750,

(iii) the debt must be a liquidated sum (ie, payable on demand and not a contingent liability),

(iv) the debtor must be unable to pay or have no reasonable prospect of paying. This is usually indicated by the failure to comply with a formal demand for repayment within 21 days of the demand being served, or an unsatisfied execution by the creditor on the debtor (for example, bailiffs calling at the debtor's property and being unable to realise sufficient assets to clear the debt).

The creditor's petition will be dismissed if the creditor has 'unreasonably' refused to accept the debtor's offer. 'Unreasonable' will vary from case to case and in some circumstances what would at first appear to be ludicrous offers may in fact be 'reasonable'.

Petition by the supervisor of a voluntary arrangement

This will be made when the debtor fails to keep to the terms of the voluntary arrangement.

Petition by the official petitioner in connection with a criminal bankruptcy

This occurs when the debtor is guilty of a criminal offence causing loss or damage of £15,000 or more.

Bankruptcy order

Once the bankruptcy order is made, the bankruptcy officially commences and the debtor becomes an undischarged bankrupt. Therefore:

(i) Any dispositions of property by the bankrupt are void, except those covered under s.284(5) Insolvency Act 1986, which states that where a bankrupt has incurred a debt after the commencement of the bankruptcy (the date of the order, for a personal bankruptcy) that would normal be void, the creditor (eg, a bank) is protected provided:

(a) the creditor was unaware that the debtor was bankrupt (difficult to prove if the bankrupt is an existing customer — as the bank would most probably have been informed by the trustee – and if the borrower is a new customer normal banking practice would be to obtain a credit reference search before lending), and

(b) it is not reasonably practicable to recover the monies from the recipient.

(ii) All the property of the bankrupt comes under the control of the official receiver, pending the appointment of a trustee in bankruptcy.

(iii) Any insolvency/debt recovery actions by creditors are stopped and the creditors must prove for their debt in the normal way – see below.

(iv) The official receiver will investigate the affairs of the bankrupt and **may** request a public examination, usually when the bankrupt is suspected of having acted fraudulently or of concealing assets or when the bankrupt is merely acting in an obstructive manner. Where a public examination is requested by 50 per cent of creditors, the official receiver **must** comply with such a request.

(v) Within 12 weeks of the order the official receiver must summon a meeting of creditors with the purpose of appointing a trustee in bankruptcy or of deciding to act himself.

Also the bankrupt is subject to the following restrictions:

(a) he is prohibited from obtaining credit (borrowing or hire purchase) of £250 or more, either solely or jointly, without disclosing that he is an undischarged bankrupt: s.360 Insolvency Act 1986;
(b) he cannot carry on business, directly or indirectly (eg, via a nominee), unless he does so in the name in which he was declared bankrupt or discloses this name to all parties he deals with: s.360 Insolvency Act 1986;
(c) he cannot act as a company director, or be involved in the management or formation of a company, except with the express consent of the court: s.11 Company Director's Disqualification Act 1986.

Once the order has been served and the trustee in bankruptcy appointed, it will be his function to realise the assets of the bankrupt and distribute them for the benefit of the creditors.

Distribution of the bankrupt's assets

Items that cannot be claimed by the trustee (known as non-divisible property), or will be disclaimed by the trustee (onerous property):

Non-divisible property

(i) Property held by the bankrupt as trustee: s.283(3) Insolvency Act 1986. In *Re Kayford (In Liquidation) Ltd* (1974), it was held that deposits received for advance orders and placed to a separate account could not be claimed, the monies being held on trust for the prospective purchasers.

(ii) Excepted items: s.283(2) Insolvency Act 1986. These include the tools of the bankrupt's trade (possibly including a vehicle if necessary) and the clothing, bedding and other household items of the bankrupt and his family. Where the trustee feels that any of these items could be replaced by one of a lesser value he can sell the existing item and replace it with a less expensive item, using the surplus funds to meet creditor claims.

(iii) Personal earnings necessary to support himself and his family. If the bankrupt earns in excess of this figure the trustee can apply to the courts for an 'incomes earning order' requesting a contribution be made towards the creditors.

(iv) Interests in property that are defeated by bankruptcy. A typical example would be leasehold land, where the lease contains a bankruptcy clause, whereby if the leaseholder is declared bankrupt the lease is automatically revoked and the situation reverts to one as if the lease had never existed (see Chapter fifteen).

(v) Rights of action to recover damages for injury to personal credit are not claimable by the trustee, but actions for damages for injury to personal property are.

(vi) Peerages and titles of honour.

Onerous property

This can be disclaimed by the trustee: s.315 Insolvency Act 1986 and includes:

(i) any unprofitable contract,
(ii) property that is either unsaleable or not readily saleable,
(iii) property that could give rise to a future liability.

Items that can be claimed (known as divisible property) or recovered by the trustee

Divisible property

(a) Bankrupt's existing property (assets). The whole of the property belonging to the bankrupt, except for those items listed above, is automatically vested in the trustee as soon as he is appointed; s.306 Insolvency Act 1986.

(b) After acquired property. This is property acquired by the bankrupt after the date of the bankruptcy order but before discharge. The trustee can claim such property for the benefit of the creditors by serving notice on the bankrupt, by which the property will be deemed to vest in the trustee from the date of acquisition by the bankrupt. Banking implications could include the claiming of deposit balances or items lodged as security. However, where the bank has taken after acquired property as security it will be protected provided it took the property in good faith, for value and without knowledge that the trustee had served notice on the bankrupt. There appears to be no case law in this area and it is difficult to assess where prior knowledge of the bankruptcy order would be sufficient to lose the bank this protection, but it would seem reasonable to believe so.

Recoverable property (previously disposed of by bankrupt)

(a) Preferences: s.340 Insolvency Act 1986 (s.239 if a company winding up).
A preference is deemed to have occurred when a person who subsequently is declared bankrupt has taken an action that has placed one or more creditors, or guarantors or other surety (depositor of third party security) in a more favourable position than any other. The trustee can reclaim the preference provided:

(i) the preference took place within six months of the presentation of the petition, or where the preferred party is an associate of the bankrupt (defined as a spouse, relative, partner, spouse of a partner, employer, employee or an associated company) and the preference took place within two years of the presentation of the petition, and
(ii) the bankrupt's decision was influenced by a desire to prefer (presumed where an associate is involved): *Re M C Bacon Ltd* (1989), and

(iii) at the time the preference was made the bankrupt was insolvent or became insolvent as a result of the preference.

An important point to note is that the trustee will be able to reclaim from a third party, even if the aim of the preference is not to prefer that party but another, for example, repayment of a loan so that the guarantor will no longer be liable.

Banks try to protect themselves against the possibility of being affected by the trustee reclaiming property, by proving a preference by:

● where an account is in default exerting pressure to repay (for example, by serving formal demand on the debtor), thereby ensuring that the repayment is not made voluntarily, as in (ii) above;

● where a debt secured by third party security is repaid, ensuring that the surety/guarantor is not released from liability until the 6/24 month period has elapsed. This is done by the insertion of a specific clause in the security document. This point is also discussed in Chapter fourteen.

This is an area of much case law, two main cases are quoted below:

Re F P & C H Matthews Ltd (1982). In this classic case the directors cleared the balances on accounts that were secured by their own guarantees. The court held that the transactions were indeed a preference.

Re F L E Holdings Ltd (1967). Here the execution of a legal charge was not held to be a preference because the intention was to remain on good terms with the bank so that future requests for facilities would be treated favourably. The claim failed due to the lack of intent to prefer.

(b) Transactions at an undervalue: s.339 Insolvency Act (1986).
A transaction at an undervalue is:

 (i) a gift (ie, no consideration passes),
 (ii) a transaction where the consideration that did pass was considerably less than the true value,
(iii) a gift in consideration of marriage.

The trustee can reclaim the asset passed on by the bankrupt providing:

● the transaction took place within five years of the order, and
● the bankrupt was insolvent at the time.

Note: if the transaction is within two years of the order, the bankrupt need not be insolvent at the time and if the recipient of the transaction is an associate (at any time), the insolvency of the bankrupt is presumed. However, if the disposal of the asset was done honestly and in an attempt to keep the company afloat, then this will be deemed an undervalue: *Re Welfab Engineers Ltd* (1990).

(c) Transactions which defraud creditors: ss.423–425 Insolvency Act 1986.
These include transactions at an undervalue but occur when the bankrupt has entered into the transaction with the intent of either putting the assets involved beyond the reach of his creditors or prejudicing the interests of creditors. One important difference between these and transactions at an undervalue is that there is no time limit applicable to transactions which defraud creditors.

If the court is satisfied it will make an order either to restore the position or to protect the disadvantaged party. Innocent parties that deal in good faith, for value and without notice of the relevant circumstances will be able to claim protection from such an order.

In *Moon and Others* v *Franklin* (1990), a transfer of the matrimonial home into the sole name of the spouse was held to be a fraudulent transaction at an undervalue as per s.423.

If the bank is concerned that a transaction may be one which defrauds creditors, the only methods of protection available to it are to ensure that at the time of the transaction either that the creditors are paid in full, or expressly agree to the transaction, or that there are sufficient liquid assets to meet the creditors in full, should they object.

(d) Extortionate credit transactions: s.343 Insolvency Act 1986.
This is a credit transaction where:

(i)   the terms require grossly exorbitant payments to be made, or
(ii) it grossly contravenes the principles of fair dealing.

Where such a transaction has taken place within three years of the bankruptcy order (note the difference between this and other reclaimable transactions), the trustee can approach the court for an order that will result in the whole or part of the transaction being set aside. Any sums recovered will be distributed as part of the bankrupt's estate.

The bankrupt's house

Strictly speaking the trustee has a right to sell the bankrupt's house, as he does any other asset of the bankrupt. However, complications can arise when the property is either jointly owned or when the spouse has a right of occupation under the Matrimonial Homes Act 1983, discussed in full in Chapter fifteen.

In these circumstances the trustee will acquire the bankrupt's legal interest in the property and if he wishes to sell the property he must approach the courts. When making their decision the courts will bear in mind the interests of the children (if any), the spouse, the creditors and the extent to which the spouse contributed to the bankruptcy. All in all everyone's interests but the bankrupt's are considered. If there are children under the age of 18 in the property the courts are unlikely to consent to the sale.

If the sale is either refused by the courts or is unlikely to be completed within a reasonable time, the trustee can apply for a charging order to be placed on the property which means that when the property is eventually sold the trustee will receive the bankrupt's share of the sale proceeds.

Proof

At this stage the creditors are staking their claim on the assets of the bankrupt, in that they are stating the net amount outstanding between themselves and the debtor. When claiming the creditor must state:

- the total amount outstanding
- the amount of the debt that is made up preferential creditors – see distribution order of assets later in this chapter,
- the details and value of security held.

When the bank is deciding on the amount to be claimed there are a number of items that must be taken into consideration. These include:

(a) Statutory set-off. Under s.323 Insolvency Act 1986 a creditor, before submitting proof, must take account of items that are mutually owed between the creditor and the bankrupt – in banking terms the accounts must be set-off. There are a number of rules that apply:

(i) debts incurred after the commencement of insolvency (for personal bankruptcy – the date of the order) cannot be set-off;

(ii) even where there is an express agreement not to set-off the bank must comply with s.323: *National Westminster Bank Ltd* v *Halesowen Presswork and Assemblies Ltd* (1972). This is contrary to the common law of combination discussed in Chapter two;

(iii) contingent liabilities can be set-off, as in *Re Chargecard Services Ltd* (1986). Again this is contrary to the common law situation, and in banking terms this allows a contingent liability (for example, a guarantee) to be set-off with a credit balance held before proving for the net amount in the bankruptcy of the guarantor;

(iv) as with the common law situation the accounts to be combined must be in the same right, owed to and by the same persons;

(v) if there is a preferential claim and a non-preferential claim (discussed later in this chapter) the credit balance must be combined with the two amounts on a proportionate basis: *Re Unit 2 Windows Ltd* (1985). For example, a preferential debt of £1,000 and a non-preferential debt of £500 must be combined with a credit balance of £300 in the same proportion as the debts, that is 2:1. Therefore £300 will be combined as £200 to the preferential debt and £100 to the non-preferential, leaving a total provable debt of £800 preferential and £400 non-preferential.

(b) Security. Security and insolvency is dealt with in Chapter nineteen but basically a creditor who holds direct security has four options:

(i) surrender the security and prove in the bankruptcy for the total debt – unlikely;

(ii) rely on the security and not prove at all – feasible only where the bank has an abundance of security and it is still unlikely. The trustee has the power to insist that the asset be disposed of and the surplus (after the secured creditor has been repaid) be used for the benefit of all the creditors;

(iii) realise the security and prove for any shortfall – useful where the security is of an easily realisable nature (eg, stocks and shares, life policies);

(iv) value the security and prove for any shortfall – useful where quick realisation of the security is not possible or is unlikely (eg, land).

If any third party security is held, then this can be totally ignored at the proof stage and any monies received from this source will be placed to a suspense account and not placed to the debtor's account. This course of action is possible due to the bank's whole debt clause included in its third party security documentation and was supported in *Re Sass* (1896). This will therefore not reduce the possibilities of the creditor receiving repayment in full, from a combination of monies from the surety/guarantor and the debtor, whereas without the clause included the amount proved for in the bankruptcy would need to be reduced by the amount received from the guarantor/surety. If the assets to be distributed amongst the creditors resulted in a dividend (say 50p for every £1 claimed) the bank could have a resultant loss.

Order of distribution

Once the assets of the bankrupt have been realised and all the claims of the creditors received, the trustee must then apply the funds to the debts of the bankrupt. This must be done in a strict order, as below:

Secured creditors

A secured creditor will receive reimbursement first, but only for the monies realised from the secured asset. There are three important points to note regarding secured creditors:

● If the monies realised by the secured asset are greater than the debt owed to the secured creditor, he will receive only the amount of the debt, the surplus being held by the trustee for distribution amongst the remaining creditors. As noted above, the secured creditor could wish to rely on his security and not prove in the bankruptcy at all, but if the trustee feels that the value of the security is much higher than the debt he can insist that the secured creditor realise the security and apportion the surplus to the remaining creditors.

● If the monies realised are lower than the amount of the debt owed, the secured creditor will appear in the order of distribution twice, once as a secured creditor for the amount of the secured portion of the debt and once as an unsecured creditor (see later) for the unsecured portion.

● When the bank realises its security it can then chose into which account it places the monies received. Where the bank has a preferential debt and a non-preferential debt it will be able to place the monies to the non-preferential debt leaving the preferential debt intact: *Re William Hall (Contractors) Ltd* (1967).

Trustee's expenses

These are the costs incurred by the trustee in realising the estate of the bankrupt and are met after the secured creditors have been paid.

Preferential creditors

These have been mentioned a number of times previously in this chapter (for example in relation to mandatory set-off or appropriation of monies raised from the realisation of security held) and they rank equally among themselves, but above all other types of creditor except for the two mentioned above. The main preferential creditors are:

 (i) Inland Revenue − for up to twelve months unpaid PAYE,
 (ii) Customs and Excise − for up to six months unpaid VAT,
(iii) certain social security and pension contributions,
(iv) non-payment of wages for up to four months previously, subject to a maximum of £800 per employee,
 (v) advances made to the bankrupt for the purpose of paying wages (up to the same limits as in (iv) above). An important alteration brought about by the Insolvency Act 1986 is that advances for unpaid wages by a sole trader, partnership or limited company are now preferential debts, whereas previously it was so only for limited companies.

This is an area of great importance to bankers and a favourite topic for examination questions. For this reason wages advances, usually via wages accounts, are discussed separately later in this chapter.

Floating charge holders

These are obviously unique to corporate (limited company) insolvency and the fact that a floating charge holder ranks higher than an unsecured creditor, up to the value of the assets charged, is a major advantage of a floating charge.

Unsecured creditors

This will normally represent the bulk of persons owed money by the debtor. They rank equally amongst themselves.

Claims for interest

When all previous creditors have been paid in full, the trustee will meet claims for interest accrued on debts from the date of commencement of the bankruptcy. The type of debt is irrelevant, as accrued interest on preferential, non-preferential and secured debts rank equally.

Shareholders

In a corporate insolvency the shareholders are the major risk-takers and their claims are met last. However, they may not rank equally amongst themselves and funds are paid in accordance with the articles of association, with for example, preference shareholders being paid prior to ordinary shareholders.

Deferred creditors

If the bankrupt's spouse should have advanced money to the bankrupt this debt will be repaid only if all other creditors have been repaid in full.

The above list of priorities must be complied with in all insolvency situations, with the trustee having no discretion at all.

Wages accounts

As discussed above, advances made in respect of wages are considered as a preferential creditor, for debts incurred up to four months prior to the commencement of the insolvency (date of order for personal bankruptcy or date of petition/resolution for corporate winding up) and with a financial limit of £800 per employee. The advance must be made in respect of employee's wages and not those of a director or sub-contractor: *Re C W & A L Hughes Ltd* (1966).

Many banks prefer to operate a separate wages account, especially when they feel that the customer is in financial difficulties. Although this is not strictly necessary in order to establish a preferential claim: *Rampgill Mill Ltd* (1967), it does give the bank the following advantages:

(a) It prevents the rule in *Clayton's Case* operating against the bank in that credits to a running current account could well extinguish debits made for wages. A full discussion of *Clayton's Case* was undertaken in Chapter two and if necessary you should re-read that section now. The opening of a separate account will prevent the bank's preferential claim being eroded by subsequent credits.

(b) It is administratively more convenient and prevents any possible disputes. The wages account will usually be allowed to operate on a normal basis until the statutory time limit of four months has been met. At this stage the banker will clear the amount of the debit of week one from the customer's current account and the wages for week seventeen will be debited to the account. This process will continue (at week eighteen the debit for week two will be cleared from the current account and week eighteen's wages will be debited etc.) and will result in the account balance always representing the last four months (16 weeks) wages.

One point to note is that there must be an actual advance. In *Re E J Morel (1934) Ltd* (1962), the bank had an arrangement with the debtor that the debit balance on the wages account must always be less than the credit balance on a separate account. The court held that in this situation the debit to the wages account was merely a bookkeeping entry and no actual advance had been made; hence the claim for treatment as a preferential creditor failed.

Duration of bankruptcy

Individual bankruptcy commences on the date of the bankruptcy order and continues until the bankrupt is discharged: s.278 Insolvency Act 1986. A bankrupt is discharged in the following circumstances:

(a) **Normal discharge** – three years after the date of the bankruptcy order. However, the official receiver can request suspension of the discharge where he believes that the bankrupt is not honouring his obligations under the bankruptcy order.
(b) **Summary administration** – two years after the date of the order. Again the official receiver can request suspension.
(c) **Criminal bankruptcy** – the bankrupt must apply to the court for discharge and may not do so until at least five years have passed since the date of the order. The court may grant the discharge unconditionally, grant the discharge subject to conditions or may decline the application completely.
(d) **Repeated bankruptcies** – this situation occurs when the bankrupt has previously been bankrupt in the preceding fifteen years. The bankrupt must apply to the courts for discharge and cannot do so until at least five years have elapsed since the date of the order.

Alternatives to bankruptcy

Voluntary arrangements

These are a new concept introduced by the Insolvency Act 1986 and are the main alternative to personal insolvency, giving the debtor the benefit of avoiding the stigma attached to bankruptcy and ensuring a better dividend for the creditors by avoiding the expensive bankruptcy procedures.

We have already mentioned a court-initiated voluntary arrangement when discussing a petition being presented by the debtor himself. There is a second type which is a debtor-initiated voluntary arrangement.

Court-initiated voluntary arrangement

As mentioned above, this course of action is undertaken when the debtor has presented his own petition and the courts do not deem it fit to declare the debtor bankrupt, with or without a certificate of summary administration. In these circumstances the court will appoint an insolvency practitioner to look into the feasibility of a voluntary arrangement, which, if accepted, will follow exactly the same procedures as those detailed in debtor-initiated voluntary arrangements below.

Debtor-initiated voluntary arrangements

Here the debtor proposes a scheme of arrangement or composition in satisfaction of his debt. The proposal must allow for an insolvency practitioner to supervise the arrangement: s.253 Insolvency Act 1986.

While the proposal is being considered the courts may issue an interim order which will have the effect of preventing bankruptcy proceedings being commenced or continued. The interim order will initially be for a period of 14 days (which may be extended by application to the court) and during the period of the order the nominee (the insolvency practitioner named in the proposal to deal with the procedures) must be supplied with the details of the debtor's proposals and must report to the court with a recommendation as to whether or not the proposals should be put to a creditor's meeting. If a creditor's meeting is agreed to, the nominee will ensure that **all** creditors are invited.

At the meeting the creditors will vote on the proposals and if accepted they will be binding on all creditors invited to the meeting (not only those that attended) and the nominee will become the supervisor of the voluntary arrangement.

As you should already be aware, if the debtor should default on the voluntary arrangement the supervisor can petition the courts for the bankruptcy of the debtor.

Deeds of arrangement

A deed of arrangement is governed by the Deeds of Arrangement Act 1914, and is an agreement between creditors and the debtor and assigns the debtor's property to the name of a trustee. However, a deed of arrangement is binding only on those creditors who agree to it (unlike a voluntary arrangement that is binding on all creditors regardless of whether they voted to agree to it or not), and prior to the introduction of the Insolvency Act 1986, those creditors not agreeing to it could petition for the bankruptcy of the debtor. Hence, deeds of arrangement have not been very popular and it is hoped that voluntary arrangements, introduced in the Insolvency Act 1986, will prove to be the main alternative to insolvency.

▌ Corporate winding up

Company winding up can be split into the two separate categories of voluntary winding up (commencing with a resolution by the shareholders of the company) or a compulsory winding up (commencing with a petition to the court). With each option the company may be solvent or insolvent.

Compulsory winding up

The petition

As stated above, a compulsory winding up commences with a petition to the courts, so the obvious questions are:

On what grounds can a petition be presented?

(i) Where the company itself passes a resolution to wind up the company. This is effected by a special resolution of the shareholders, the directors having no authority to act.

(ii) On technical grounds, for example, where the company fails to commence trading within twelve months, or the membership (shareholders) falls below two. Under s.440 Companies Act 1985, the Secretary of State may petition where he feels it to be in the public interest, based on a report from inspectors, or the Bank of England may petition under the Banking Act 1987 for banks to be wound up, subject to certain conditions.

(iii) Where the court is satisfied that it is 'just and equitable' to wind the company up. This method is rarely used but it is open to small private companies. Examples of its use are similar to those accepted in the dissolution of a partnership and would include the management being 'deadlocked' or one director being deliberately left out of the operation of the company: *Ebrahimi* v *Westbourne Galleries Ltd* (1973).

(iv) Where the company is unable to meet its debts. This is the most common reason for the presentation of a petition and is subject to the following conditions:

- an unsecured liquidated sum of £750 is owed. The definitions of unsecured and liquidated are exactly the same as in personal insolvency and if you cannot recall them the relevant section should be re-read, but basically they are that the debt is not a contingent liability and that it is either unsecured, has an unsecured element of more than £750 or the only security held is third party security; and
- the creditor has served a formal demand and the debtor has failed to pay, secure or compound the debt within 21 days; or
- the creditor holds an unsatisfied execution, again exactly the same as with personal insolvency; or
- the court is satisfied that the company cannot meet its debts as they fall due, because of its illiquidity rather than its liabilities exceeding its assets: *Re Patrick and Lyon Ltd* (1933); or
- where the court is satisfied that the company's assets exceed its liabilities.

Who can petition?

(i) the members (shareholders) of the company,

(ii) the directors. In *Re Instrumentation Electrical Services Ltd* (1988), it was held that a petition presented by the directors must be presented by **all** the directors,

(iii) creditor(s) of the company, owed at least £750, usually connected with the inability to meet its debts,

(iv) one or more contributories, ie, a person liable to contribute to the assets of the company should it be wound up: s.79 Insolvency Act 1986. Such a contribution would probably be either the unpaid call of any partly paid shares of the limit of any guarantee issued for a company limited by guarantee (see Chapter eight). The contributory must show that he had an 'interest' in the winding up, such as the expectation of making a contribution: *Re Othery Construction Ltd* (1966),

(v) the Secretary of State, possibly based on an inspector's report,

(vi) the official receiver, who can petition for a compulsory winding up only when he can satisfy the court that a voluntary winding up cannot continue with due regard to creditors' or contributories' interests.

(vii) official office holders. These can include the supervisor of a voluntary arrangement, (exactly the same conditions as with an individual insolvency) the administrator of an administration order or an administrative receiver (these two will be discussed in full later).

The winding up order

Once the court has decided to accept the petition, a winding up order will be made. The consequences of such an order are:

(a) the official receiver becomes the liquidator, except following an administration order or voluntary arrangement when the court will appoint the administrator or supervisor as liquidator,

(b) all actions and proceedings against the company must be stayed unless the court allows them to commence or continue on terms laid down by the court,

(c) a statement of affairs may be requested,

(d) a meeting of creditors and contributories must be arranged, within 12 weeks of the winding up order, unless dispensed with under s.136 Insolvency Act 1986,

(e) the directors' powers cease,

(f) the business of the company can continue but only by court sanction and for the purpose or benefit of winding the company up,

(g) dispositions of the company's property will be void unless sanctioned by the court: s.127 Insolvency Act, 1986, as confirmed in *Re Webb Electrical Ltd* (1988), where a disposition in the form of a transfer of funds to a director was declared to be void and ratification was declined due to the absence of a commercial benefit to the company, and

(h) the company's employees are automatically dismissed, although the liquidator may re-appoint some or all of them, at least temporarily.

The role of the liquidator

Initially the official receiver is appointed as the liquidator, with the exceptions mentioned in (a) above, but at the meeting of creditors an insolvency practitioner can be appointed as liquidator and a 'liquidation committee' can also be appointed to advise and assist the liquidator. the general duty of the liquidator of a voluntary or compulsory winding up is:

'to ensure that the assets are got in, realised and distributed to the company's creditors, and if there is a surplus, to those entitled to such surplus.'

In order to allow the liquidator to achieve this duty, and also to ensure a degree of accountability, the following are the duties and powers of a liquidator.

Duties

(i) He must exercise discretion in the management of the company's assets and their distribution. This is a personal duty and cannot be delegated: *Re Metropolitan Bank and Jones* (1876). He can appoint agents only in relation to duties that he cannot fulfil himself (eg, sale of property, shares etc), except for clerical or administrative duties that can be delegated to his staff.

(ii) Where the official receiver is not the liquidator, all books, documents, etc, must be made available for inspection by the official receiver.

(iii) On a compulsory winding up the liquidator must investigate the promotion, formation, business, dealings and affairs of the company and the causes for the company's failure, reporting to the court as he sees fit: s.132 Insolvency Act 1986. On the basis of that report he may apply to the court for a public examination of any person connected with the company: s.133 Insolvency Act 1986.

(iv) Also, on a compulsory winding up following the final creditor's meeting, he must seek the agreement of the creditors to his release and once obtained this must be notified to the Companies Registry.

(v) On a voluntary winding up the liquidator must prepare an account of the winding up showing how the assets have been disposed of and the general conduct of the winding up. This report must be made available at a meeting of the members and a separate meeting of the creditors, if it is a creditors' voluntary winding up (see later). Once these meetings have resolved that the liquidation is complete, the liquidator is released and must send a return and a copy of the report to the Companies Registry. The company is dissolved three months after submission of these documents.

Powers

(a) To seek a court order requiring the surrender of transfer of any property, books or other records to which the company appears to be entitled.

(b) To seek a court order to recover money or property disposed of by the company under a preference or transaction at an undervalue, discussed above.

(c) To bring or defend any action or other legal proceedings in the name of the company.

(d) To carry on the business of the company, to bring about the beneficial winding up of the company.

(e) To sell any assets of the company privately or by public auction. Should the liquidator seize or sell any assets of the company that he has reasonable grounds to believe he is entitled to sell or seize and later discover that they are not the property of the company, he is not liable for any loss incurred to any person and can claim a lien (right to retain) on the property for expenses incurred on the sale or seizure.

(f) To perform all acts and execute deeds or any other document, using the company seal if necessary.

(g) To prove in the insolvency of any contributory.

(h) To draw cheques on the company's behalf.

(i) To appoint agents to do any business he cannot perform himself.

(j) To do all other things necessary to complete the liquidation of the company's affairs and distribution of its assets.

Voluntary winding up

Whereas a compulsory winding up commences with a petition to the courts, a voluntary winding up commences with a resolution by the company. If the company is solvent when the resolution is passed the procedure is known as a members' voluntary winding up and if the company is insolvent, a creditors' voluntary winding up. The easy way to remember the difference is to concentrate on the people for whose benefit the company is being wound up. If it is a members' voluntary winding up, the members will probably gain as the assets are probably greater in value than the liabilities, and if a creditors' voluntary winding up the creditors will gain as the winding up should prevent the situation getting any worse.

Member's voluntary winding up

Examples include a condition in the articles (a single objective having been achieved or the expiry of the stated duration), or the wish of the members or directors. The winding up is initiated by a resolution by the members, and must be supported by a declaration of solvency from the directors: s.89 Insolvency Act 1986. The declaration must be made by a majority of directors (or both if only two), include a statement of the company's assets and liabilities and state that in the directors' opinion the company is able to meet all its debts within twelve months.

Due to the company being solvent it will be able to appoint an insolvency practitioner of his choice to act as liquidator. However, should the liquidator not be satisfied that the declaration of solvency is accurate he can request that proceedings be amended to a creditors' voluntary winding up.

Creditors' voluntary winding up

This again commences with a company resolution, but as well as the shareholders' meeting arranged to pass the resolution winding up the company, to appoint a liquidator and to appoint up to five representatives to be members of a liquidation committee of inspection, the company must also arrange a creditors' meeting, notice of which should be sent to every creditor and advertised in the *London Gazette* and two local papers.

The creditors' meeting will consider the statement of the company's affairs, appoint a liquidator and nominate up to five representatives to be members of the liquidation committee of inspection. Due to the company being insolvent, if the two meetings disagree as to the appointment of a liquidator the creditors' choice will act.

Other winding up matters

Claimable assets, proof and order of distribution

The assets claimable (special emphasis on preferences and transactions at an undervalue ss.238–240), the debts considered as provable, the method of proof and distribution of proceeds are almost exactly the same as for individual insolvency, and if necessary sections 3, 4 and 5 under personal insolvency (above) should be reread. Remember, the company (debtor) must be influenced by a desire to produce the effect of a preference s.239(5) Insolvency Act as supported by *Re M C Bacon Ltd* (1989) and a transaction at an undervalue can only be traced back for two years in a corporate winding up.

The order of distribution is particularly important as this is a typical area for examination questions, especially the impact of wages accounts.

Personal liability of company directors

Again this has been discussed in full previously and Chapter eight needs to be reread with special emphasis on fraudulent trading, wrongful trading and shadow directors. Basically a director can be liable to make a contribution to a company's debts where he is a director and the company has carried on trading with an intent to defraud creditors, or any other fraudulent purpose (fraudulent trading: s.213 Insolvency Act 1986) or where the director knew or should have realised that the company could not avoid insolvent liquidation (wrongful trading: s.214 Insolvency Act 1986).

Also, s.251 Insolvency Act 1986 introduced a new concept of shadow directors whereby 'persons in accordance with whose direction the company is accustomed to act' could also be held liable. This is a worrying concept for bankers who must now ensure that they offer only advice and not instructions to their customers. Indeed the first cases are being reported of banks being caught under this umbrella *Re M C Bacon* (1989); unless the company is 'accustomed' to acting under the banks' instruction then it is unlikely that the bank will be held to a shadow director.

Company Directors Disqualification Act 1986

The aim of this Act was to prevent unfit persons becoming directors. The Act gives the court powers to disqualify directors of insolvent companies from becoming directors of another company for a period of two to fifteen years. Any director who ignores this ban will be personally liable for the debts of the company of which he was a director while disqualified.

■ Alternatives to corporate insolvency

Voluntary arrangements

The rules and conduct of a voluntary arrangement for a company are very similar to those for an individual and so the section on voluntary arrangements as an alternative to bankruptcy under the heading of 'Personal insolvency' in this chapter should be reread. The only major difference is that for a corporate voluntary arrangement the proposal can be drawn up by the directors, the liquidator or the administrator (see below).

Appointment of an administrative receiver

This is discussed in full in Chapter eighteen and that section should be read, but in essence an administrative receiver is appointed by a floating charge holder and has powers to realise the assets of the company and distribute the proceeds accordingly. A major advantage to the bank of a floating charge is that it can block the appointment of an administrator (see below) by appointing its own administrative receiver.

Administration order

General

An administrator, acting under an administration order, can be appointed by the courts following a petition by either the directors, or the shareholders or the creditor(s). The company must be unable to meet its liabilities or likely to become so. The courts must feel that the order will achieve one of the aims of an administration order, which are:

(i) survival of the company as a going concern, or
(ii) approval of a voluntary arrangement, or
(iii) sanctioning of a scheme of arrangement, or
(iv) a more advantageous realisation of the assets than under a liquidation.

The effect of an administration order

   (i) the administrator must formulate proposals, and place these to a meeting of creditors for approval;

  (ii) once the proposals have been approved, the administrator becomes the manager of the company's affairs with the sole aim of achieving the objective(s) quoted in the proposals;

 (iii) no winding up resolution may be passed or winding up order made;

 (iv) no administrative receiver can be appointed (NB if one is already in existence then an administration order cannot be granted;

  (v) the administrator may insist on any existing receiver vacating office;

 (vi) except with the administrator's consent, or leave of court:

- no mortgagor or debenture holder (including a floating charge holder) can enforce any security held. This is a major disadvantage to a bank and can be one of the reasons why a bank will take a floating charge — to prevent the appointment of an administrator by the bank appointing its own administrative receiver under its floating charge,
- no hire purchase creditor can repossess goods caught under the agreement,
- no proceedings, executions, etc can be continued or commenced.

 (vii) the administrator is the agent of the company and does not acquire personal liability for contracts he enters into on the company's behalf.

In *Re Harris Simons Construction Ltd* (1988) it was held that an administration order can be granted even if the company was unable to meet its debts, providing the granting of the order met one of the objectives of an administration order as described above.

∎ Insolvency and its effect on the banker/customer relationship

Personal insolvency

Transactions after the petition, before the order

Although personal insolvency is held to commence at the date of the bankruptcy order, dispositions of the debtor's property after the date of the petition are void: s.284(1) Insolvency Act 1986. However, there are protections available to the bank:

(a) Validation/ratification by the courts. Where a debit has been passed to an account in credit after the date of the petition, the bank may approach the courts to have the disposition (obviously a debit to a credit account will have the result of transferring the debtor's property — the balance in the account — to another party) ratified. The courts will agree to the request only where it is satisfied that the bank acted in good faith and without notice of the petition. Once the bank is aware of the petition it should stop the account and allow no further transactions to pass through the account. However, if the bank is aware of future transactions due to pass through the account, for example standing order payments, or cheques written but not yet presented, the bank may approach the courts in advance for a validation order, allowing payment of these items. Such a step would be unusual.

    Where an account is in credit and a further credit is made to the account, then this will not affect the bank as the money will be classed as merely being held in trust for the trustee. However, normal practice would be to allow neither credits nor debits to the account.

(b) Where an account is in debit any credit to the account would be a disposition of the debtor's property (the money paid in) in favour of the bank and would therefore normally be void. However, s.284(4) Insolvency Act 1986 states that the disposition will not be void providing the court is satisfied that the bank acted in good faith, gave value (in this case the specific reduction of the debt) and had no notice of the petition.

(c) Where an account is in debit and the bank allows it to go further overdrawn, then this is a disposition of the bank's property and not the debtor's. Hence the problem is whether or not the bank can prove for the whole of the debt in the bankruptcy of the debtor. Section 382 Insolvency Act 1986 states that where the bank had no notice of the petition it can prove for the whole of the debt.

Transactions after the date of the order

After the bankruptcy order has been made, the bankrupt loses all contractual capacity and so all dispositions are void. However, the bank may be able to claim the protection of s.284(5) Insolvency Act 1986, providing it did not have notice of the bankruptcy order it is not reasonably practicable to recover the payment from the payee and the transaction occurred before the vesting date (the appointment of the trustee).

The bank should not accept credits to the account as technically these are the property of the trustee. The credit should be placed to a suspense account pending the trustee's instructions.

Action on receipt of notice

Upon receipt of notice of bankruptcy proceedings against a customer, whether in debit or credit, the account must be stopped. The reasons for this are obvious after reading the above, the onus on any protection available being the lack of notice.

Proof

The amount claimed by the banker will depend on many things, including:

(a) Preferential and non-preferential debts. As you should be aware, the bank will have a greater chance of recouping its money if it can claim as a preferential, as opposed to a non-preferential creditor. To this end it is not unusual for a bank to open a separate wages account for business customers, especially when there are concerns regarding the future viability of the business. This will allow the bank to claim for the balance of the wages account as a preferential creditor. Also, when realising any security it will look towards placing the proceeds to a non-preferential debt, maintaining its preferential claim.

(b) Statutory (mandatory) set-off. This has been discussed in full above. In brief, all debit and credit accounts must be combined (set-off) before proving for the resultant debt. Where the total debt includes a combination of preferential and non-preferential debts, the accounts must be combined in a proportionate basis (ie, the credit balance must be applied to the debit balances in the same ratio as the debts): *Re Unit 2 Windows Ltd* (1985).

The amount proven for can include both preferential and non-preferential debts.

(c) Security. Security and insolvency is discussed in Chapter nineteen. However, the basic position is that when proving for its debt the bank has four options:

- releasing its security and proving as an unsecured creditor – unlikely,
- relying on its security and not prove – unlikely,
- value its security and prove for any shortfall (useful for land), and
- realise its security and prove for any shortfall (eg, shares).

The bank will receive the proceeds from the security before any other creditor. Any third party security can be ignored for proof purposes, the money received being placed to a suspense account.

The undischarged bankrupt as a customer

Care must obviously be taken with any lending (no power to contract) and any credit balances held could be claimed by the trustee as an after acquired property. However, the bank would be protected where it could claim that it acted in good faith and without notice of the bankruptcy order: s.307(4) Insolvency Act 1986.

The effect of preferences

We have discussed in some detail the fact that banks retain third party security documents for a period of 6/24 months to prevent the bank being disadvantaged by the reclaiming, under a preference, of the credit used to clear the account secured by the third party security. You should be well aware of the potential risk in this area.

The other area in which preferences could affect the banker is the accepting as direct security (ie, security given by the debtor), which later is deemed to have been a preference. Such a claim is unlikely to succeed as the giving of the security will usually either be in response to a demand by the bank (therefore the debtor did not voluntarily prefer the bank) or in an attempt to obtain further monies (the intent was not to prefer the bank but to obtain the extra facilities).

Corporate insolvency

Generally

As mentioned above, the insolvency of an individual commences at (is effective from) the date of the bankruptcy order. An important difference for corporate insolvency is that the insolvency is effective from the date of the petition or resolution: s.127 Insolvency Act 1986.

Compulsory winding up

Due to the earlier commencement of the insolvency, plus the fact that winding up petitions are advertised in the *London Gazette* which is deemed to be notice to the world, a bank will not be able to claim any statutory protection for transactions after the date of the petition, unless the petition has not yet been gazetted. The only safe method by which the bank could continue to pay cheques is to approach the courts for a validation order authorising payment: *Re Gray's Inn Construction Ltd* (1980). Previous to this decision it had been normal bank practice to allow certain payments through the account to continue, as they were felt to be in the company's favour, relying on the courts sanctioning the transaction later (known as retrospective sanction).

Thus normal banking practice has become to stop the bank account upon receipt of notice of the petition, and to approach the courts should the bank wish to pay any particular item, as retrospective sanction is now thought to be unlikely following the *Gray's Inn Construction* case.

Once the winding up order has been made, the bank must exercise mandatory set-off as per s.323 Insolvency Act 1986, and prove for their debt, (if a debt exists after taking the necessary steps in respect of any security held), or pay over any credit balances held. The procedures for each of these steps are as described under personal insolvency above.

Voluntary winding up

The procedures are identical to those mentioned above, with the bank stopping the account upon receipt of notice of the resolution, and either claiming in the winding up for any outstanding debt (after security procedures have been followed) or paying over any resulting credit balances (after all the accounts have been set-off). One important difference is that the bank must await sight of the minutes of the creditors' meeting, to ensure that the liquidator approaching the bank is the liquidator appointed, or approved, by the creditors' meeting.

▊ Companies Act 1989 and insolvency

The above statute makes reference to insolvency and amends or introduces new rules. However, the act applies only to 'market contracts' which are defined by s.155 Companies Act 1989 as:

> '(a) contracts entered into by a member or designated non-member of the exchange which are made on or otherwise subject to the rules of the exchange; and
> (b) contracts subject to the rules of the exchange entered into by the exchange for the purposes of or in connection with the provision of clearing services'.

Hence the scope of the legislation in relation to insolvency is narrow and would not appear to encroach too greatly upon the syllabus.

▊ Summary: insolvency and banks

As you will now no doubt appreciate, despite the Insolvency Act 1986, and the restructuring of the syllabus in 1990, insolvency, be it personal or corporate, is an in-depth and complicated area of the syllabus. When revising this topic for the examination, candidates should concentrate on the following areas:

- aims of the present legislation,
- an outline of the procedures,
- claimable and non-claimable property with a special emphasis on recoverable property, for example preferences, etc.

- the order of distribution,
- the effect of fraudulent and wrongful trading, with a special emphasis on shadow directors,
- the alternatives to insolvency, but most importantly
- the risks to banks at certain stages and the protections available (if any),

FACT SHEET

Insolvency

Aims of the Insolvency Act 1986
a. simplify procedures
b. protect the debtor
c. protect the creditor
d. introduce the concept of insolvency practitioners

Personal insolvency
1. Who can be made bankrupt? NB residency rules.

2. Bankruptcy procedures
(a) the petition. Can be presented by:
    (i) any creditor(s) – minimum £750,
    (ii) the debtor himself – can result in summary administration, court sponsored voluntary arrangement or bankruptcy order,
    (iii) supervisor of voluntary arrangement – if debtor is in default or has not supplied all relevant information,
    (iv) official petitioner – for criminal bankruptcy.
(b) the bankruptcy order, the commencement of personal insolvency.
Transactions after the order are void, unless s.284(5) Insolvency Act 1986 applies. All property of bankrupt vests in the official receiver pending the appointment of the trustee (usually at the creditors' meeting).

3. Distribution of debtor's assets. Non-divisible assets, divisible property, recoverable property (special emphasis on preferences) and the debtor's house.

4. Proof. Important areas include mandatory set-off, preferential creditors and security.

5. Order of distribution. Must be learned, especially preferential creditors and wages accounts.

6. Duration.

7. Alternatives. Voluntary arrangements (court or debtor initiated) and deeds of arrangement.

Corporate insolvency
1. Compulsory winding up.
(a) Commences with a petition, students should know who can petition and on what grounds.
(b) The effect of the order must be known, as should the duties and powers of the liquidator.

2. Voluntary winding up.
Commences with a resolution. If the company is solvent (known as a members voluntary winding up) there must be a declaration of solvency. Most other procedures are similar to personal bankruptcy, (eg, proof, preferences etc) although the implications of fraudulent

and wrongful trading (especially shadow directors) and the Company Directors Disqualification Act 1986 should be realised.

Alternatives to winding up
Voluntary arrangements – similar to personal insolvency, administrative receiver – appointed by floating charge holder, administration order – the aims are fundamental.

Effect of insolvency on the banker/customer relationship

1. Personal insolvency
(a) Transactions after the petition, before the order. Automatically void.
   However, protections available:
      (i) Validation, ratification – by order of court.
      (ii) Section 284(4) Insolvency Act 1986, conditions – good faith, for value, no notice of petition.
      (iii) If account is already overdrawn, the debit will be a disposition of bank's, not debtor's, property and as such is a provable debt: s.382 Insolvency Act 1986.
(b) Transactions after date of order. Void. Protection s.284(5) Insolvency Act 1986, conditions – no notice of order and not reasonably practicable to recover.
(c) Action upon receipt of notice. Stop account immediately.
(d) Proof. The importance of beneficial position of preferential creditors, mandatory set-off (*Re Unit 2 Windows* (1985)) and the options of secured creditors.
(e) Undischarged bankrupts as customers. No power to contract, but bank is protected if did not know of order and acted in good faith: s.307(4) Insolvency Act 1986.
(f) Preferences. Position of repayment of debt secured by third party security, and taking of direct security affected by preferences.

2. Corporate insolvency.
(a) Generally. Insolvency commences at date of petition or resolution: s.127 Insolvency Act 1986.
(b) Compulsory winding up. Petition advertised in Gazette and as such removes the statutory protection. Only course of action available is to approach the courts for sanction. Since the decision in *Re Gray's Inn Construction* (1980), banks will now stop the account immediately on notice and seek court permission before payment of **any** items, and not afterwards.
(c) Voluntary winding up. Similar to compulsory winding up, but bank must take care that they deal with the liquidator appointed by creditors' meeting.
(d) Fraudulent and wrongful trading, shadow director implications.

Question (Autumn 1988)

(a) A small company customer of a bank directly employs 28 people. The bank (alone) has a fixed charge, but the company's supplier of stock has a floating charge. The company gets into difficulties, and the directors want to petition for the appointment of an administrator (under the Insolvency Act 1986).

Explain the grounds upon which an administrator might be appointed, and the purpose of the procedure, and say whether the bank or any other creditor could prevent the appointment, (You need not discuss the administrator's powers to dispose of charged assets). (10 marks)

(b) If an administrator of the same company is appointed, and the administrator needs continued funding, mainly in order to pay the wages of the employees, explain what sort of an account the bank (if it advances funds) should operate in respect of those payments, and the effect of maintaining such an account:
 (i) during the period of the administration, and
(ii) in the event of winding up, if it should later occur. (10 marks)
(Total marks for question – 20)

Key words

(a) small company, bank (alone), fixed charge, company's supplier, floating charge, directors, petition, appointment of an administrator, grounds, purpose, bank, any other creditor prevent appointment,

(b) wages what account, operate, and the effect (i) period of the administration (ii) in the event of winding up

Answer

This was an unpopular question and, where done, was not done well. Many who did it seemed unaware of the Insolvency Act 1986, and scored better on part (b).

(a) Under part II of the Insolvency Act 1986, the administrator can be appointed if any creditor or a majority of directors petitions the court. Application must be before a winding up resolution/petition. The court must be satisfied (1) that a company is, or is likely to become, unable to pay its debts; and (2) that an order is 'likely' to achieve one or more of the following purposes:

  (i) survival of the company or part of it as a going concern;
 (ii) approval of voluntary arrangement;
(iii) sanctioning of s.425 Companies Act compromise or arrangement;
 (iv) more advantageous realisation of assets than on a winding up. (i) & (iv) are the most common grounds).

The effect of the petition, and any subsequent order, is to 'freeze' the position of the company – no-one can realise securities, or sue it, or proceed against assets, etc. This, coupled with (i)–(iv) above, is the purpose of it: to freeze matters for those (i)–(iv) purposes.

The administrator must be an insolvency practitioner (hence, supposedly independent, competent, etc.). His job is to try to do (i)–(iv), and he prepares proposals for the creditors within three months. They consider these and may approve or reject them. He manages the company in the meantime, in accordance with the proposals.

A fixed charge holder cannot veto the appointment, though the court still retains its discretion to appoint the administrator or not. The holder of a floating charge can veto the appointment, if that charge (coupled, if necessary, with any fixed charges) gives him a charge over substantially all of the assets. He is then entitled to appoint an 'administrative receiver' (as opposed to a receiver under fixed charge). What happens is that the court must give a debenture holder five days' notice (time can be abridged), unless the floating charge holder consents. The veto, therefore, is exercised by (i) appointing a receiver; and (2) not consenting. Hence, the bank cannot veto but the supplier could if his charge covers substantially all of the assets.

(It does not seem necessary for this question to talk about his powers over charged assets).

(b) If the bank agrees to fund the administrator, it would wish to come to some sort of arrangement with him. One thing it can do is to ensure preference in relation to monies advanced for payment of wages of £800 over last four months. In winding up, the employees obviously have such preference, and so do those who advance money for the purpose. In the administration, s.19(5) Insolvency Act specifically says that any debts or liabilities incurred while he is an administrator for contracts which he enters, or for previous contracts of employment or for those adopted by him, have priority over floating charge assets. Thus, the bank's contract with him is not for wages (as well as in the winding up if for wages). As to the mechanics of the wages account for winding up purposes, it need not be, but usually is, a separate account (avoids *Clayton's Case*: *Re Rampgill Mill Ltd* problem). The money must actually be advanced for the purpose of wages and its application for the purpose is then presumed – *Re Rampgill Mill Ltd*. There must be an advance and not merely a juggling of accounts (*Re E.J. Morel Ltd*: contrast *National Provincial Bank* v *Freedman & Rubens*, *Re James R. Rutherford & Sons Ltd*).

Author's comment

As stated above this was not a very popular question, and indicates the 'false esteem' in which insolvency is held by many candidates. This was in fact a very straightforward question and if candidates had prepared themselves adequately they would, no doubt, have found it to be a rewarding question. As previously mentioned, although insolvency is one of the larger areas of the syllabus the questions asked do tend to be of an easy standard requiring mere knowledge and not very much interpretation of principles.

Question (Spring 1989)

In connection with the winding up of a company:
(a) briefly explain the priorities between different classes of creditors. (5)
(b) Briefly explain which debts are preferential. (5)
(c) Explain the use of a wages account in maximising the bank's preferential claim. (10)

(Total marks for this question − 20)

Key words
winding up of a company
(a) priorities, creditors
(b) which debts are preferential
(c) wages account, maximising preferential claim

Answer
This question was often well done, and was very popular, (c) being the weakest part.

(a) Priorities are generally in the following order:
  − holders of fixed charges
  − expenses of liquidation (this could be omitted, as may not be regarded as a 'creditor')
  − preferential creditors, *pari passu*
  − holders of floating charges (who cannot now jump to the class of fixed charge creditors by pre-crystallisation)
  − all other unsecured, non-preferential creditors, *pari passu* (Insolvency Act 1986 s.107)
  − interest on debts for unsecured creditors, including preferential ones, *pari passu*
  − the members of the company, according to the articles, or any subordination agreements (this could be omitted, as above).

Many candidates appear to treat floating charges as something different from a 'debenture' or a 'security'. Thus, in first place would come 'a debenture holder (secured creditor)' and in third 'a holder of a floating charge'. This was strange, but was not penalised. Many candidates, however, simply did not know where floating charges fitted in, at all.

(b) The preferential debts are:
  − certain Inland Revenue debts in the last twelve months (for PAYE and lump sum deductions)
  − certain Customs and Excise VAT debts in the last six months, and some other debts in the last twelve months (car tax, betting duty, etc.)
  − certain social security contributions
  − certain occupational pension scheme contributions
  − employee's unpaid remuneration, in the last four months, not exceeding £800 at present, plus holiday pay accrued, or money advanced for such purposes (eg, by banks).

The last of these is the most important for banks, and if sufficient detail here was given, a general treatment of others, such as 'certain tax or excise duties and contributions for social security and pensions' would be enough for full points.

(c) As discussed above, advances for wages are preferential for four months and £800 per employee, if advanced for the purpose of wages. This is 'statutory subrogation', the bank standing in the shoes of the employees. Wages accounts may be operated for administrative purposes (to keep an eye on the position) and to avoid *Clayton's Case* from eliminating the preferential element from a current account, and to avoid arguments about the purpose of advances from an account.

A separate account is not otherwise required: *Re Rampgill Mill Ltd*. The money must actually be used for wages, and if so, will be presumed to be advanced for that purpose.

There must be genuine advance, and if, as in *Re E.J. Morel (1934) Ltd*. an account is so conducted that any debit on the wages account is tied very closely to a credit on the current account, the bank will be held to be advancing nothing. In *Morel's case*, the credit in the current account was always to exceed the debit in the wages account, and the bank would not meet a cheque on either account without considering the combined position of the two accounts taken together. A bank may, however, refuse to meet wages cheques unless a sum is paid simultaneously into an account, for the money paid in will discharge the oldest sums on the account, and cannot necessarily be related to the payment out each month: *National Provincial Bank* v *Freedman & Rubens*; *Re James Rutherford & Sons*.

Administratively, what may happen with wages accounts is that each month (or maybe weekly, if employees are paid weekly) an amount equal to the debit on the wages account four months ago is paid from the current account, thus discharging the oldest, expired, debit.

Wages accounts are not opened only on liquidation, or when it seems likely, as many candidates thought.

Author's comment

A relatively straightforward question on insolvency, being merely a test of recall, requiring very little understanding of legal principles. The fact that the question was sub-divided also made the attainment of a pass mark much more likely.

Question (Autumn 1988)

In relation to companies, the Insolvency Act 1986 introduces a new concept of 'wrongful trading', in addition to the existing concept of 'fraudulent trading'.

Fully discuss these two principles, and also say how, if at all, they may operate to the advantage, or disadvantage, of banks. (20 marks)

Key words

wrongful trading   fraudulent trading   discuss how operate

Answer

Hardly anyone attempted this easy question. Candidates should have discussed: (i) what fraudulent trading is; (ii) what wrongful trading is and how it differs from fraudulent trading; and (iii) how, if at all, they affect banks.

Fraudulent trading

Section 213 Insolvency Act 1986. If a company is in winding up, and if it appears that its business is carried on with intent to defraud creditors, or for any fraudulent purpose, the court may, on a liquidator's application, declare that any persons who were knowingly parties are liable to contribute. cases: *Re William C Leitch Bros Ltd* (fraudulent to continue if they know there is no reasonable prospect of paying debts). *Re Patrick & Lyon Ltd* (must be actual dishonesty – real moral blame). *R Grantham* (need not be proved that there is no prospect of ever paying creditors – just that it knows no reasonable ground to think funds will be available). *White* v *Osmond (Parkstone) Ltd* ('sunshine') defence: stupid and optimistic directors not guilty – must be dishonest). *Re Sarflax* (can carry on business though assets transferred to parent company). Did this help banks or others? The threat of criminal or civil action may have restrained directors – they may have agreed to make themselves personally liable because of threat. But since dishonesty is needed, and negligence is not enough, scandals continue.

Wrongful trading

Section 214 Insolvency Act 1986.

(i) The company must be in winding up and insolvent on the 'asset test'. Actions start on a liquidator's application, as before.

(ii) The defendant must know or ought to have concluded that there was no reasonable prospect of avoiding insolvent liquidation (this introduces negligence).

(iii) The provision only applies to directors or shadow directors.

(iv) It is a defence if the director took 'every step' with a view to minimising loss to creditors which he 'ought to have taken'.

(v) In deciding what he knew/ought to know, the court is to look at the higher of:

(a) what a reasonably diligent person would think/do if he had the skill and knowledge which you would expect a person in that particular position to have (eg, is he the finance director, or an honorary/occasional director?); and

(b) the skill and experience and knowledge he actually has.

In *Re marketing Consortium Ltd* (1989) it was held that the level of skill expected will vary depending on the size of the concern, for example comparing a large multi-national company with a small 'one man' company.

How will this affect banks?

it is much stronger than fraudulent trading since it includes negligence. Actual dishonesty need not be proved. It puts directors in a difficult position: they must take 'every' step they ought. It should help to restrain fraud (together with other provisions in the Act on setting up in similar names, licensing of insolvency practitioners to avoid friendly liquidators, and new disqualification of director's provisions).

It may possibly affect banks' rescue operations, because banks may be shadow directors if they give instructions − see s.251; shadow director is a person in accordance with whose instructions the company is accustomed to act. Banks to be careful not to give instructions − only to state terms on which they will do business and continue loans; advise, do not instruct.

Parent companies may be particularly affected, as shadow directors.

Author's comment

The chief examiner has really summed up the position above and no further comment is necessary.

CHAPTER 10

Cheques, bank payment orders, banker's drafts and warrants

Syllabus requirements

- Forgery, fraudulent alteration, loss, theft and payment, and the respective rights and obligations of the payer/drawer, the paying and collecting banks and the payee are to be considered.
- The principles of transferability and negotiation (holder in due course, etc).

∎ Introduction

For ease of understanding I will cover each instrument in its entirety, separately. Firstly I will cover cheques, including the definition, rights and duties of each party (including the bank), the effects of certain happenings (forgery, fraudulent alteration, loss and theft) and the protection available to both the collecting and paying banks against wrongful action. I will then consider the other instruments in turn.

∎ Definition

A cheque is
'a bill of exchange drawn on a bank payable on demand'
see s.73 Bills of Exchange Act 1882. This is of little meaning unless you know the definition of a bill of exchange: s.3 Bills of Exchange Act 1882 states that a bill of exchange is

> 'an unconditional order in writing, addressed by one person to another signed by the person giving it, requiring the person to whom it is addressed to pay on demand or at a fixed or determinable future time a sum certain in money to, or to the order of, a specified person or to bearer.'

By combining these two definitions it is possible to arrive at the long definition of a cheque as:

> 'an unconditional order in writing, addressed by a person (the drawer) to another person, a banker, (the drawee, the paying bank), signed by the drawer, requiring the bank to pay on demand (ie, on presentation) a sum certain in money to, or to the order of, a specified person (the payee) or to bearer.'

It is now important to look further at this definition.

Unconditional

This in effect means that the payment of the cheque cannot be dependent upon any other possible event, for example, 'pay Joy Turner on her passing Law Relating to Banking Services exam'. This of course is a condition and as such prevents the instrument being a cheque. However, certain items that may appear, at first glance, to be conditions are acceptable. For example:

(i) The request for a receipt by the payee. Providing this request is addressed solely to the payee, and does not involve the bank, this is acceptable: *Nathan* v *Ogdens* (1905). These cheques are quite often indicated by a large block capital 'R' in the top right hand corner. If the request for a receipt is addressed to the bank not to pay unless receipted, then this is a condition and as such is not acceptable: *Bavins & Sims* v *London and South Western Bank* (1900).

(ii) An instruction to pay from a specific account is totally acceptable, for example 'pay from number 2 account' or 'VAT account'.

(iii) In *Thairlwall* v *Great Northern Railway Company* (1910) it was decided that a clause stating that the cheque must be presented within three months of issue was acceptable. The court held that this was merely an instruction to the payee and not a condition for the bank to fulfil.

Order in writing

The instruction must be an order and not a mere request. You will note that your own cheque book is pre-printed with the words

'Pay _____ or order'.

This is to eliminate the problem of customers not instructing their banks but merely requesting them to do something.

Although banks issue pre-printed cheque books, there is technically no necessity for customers to use them. For an instrument to be a valid cheque it merely needs to meet the definition, which does not include the use of banks' standard forms. The cheque must be in writing, but other than that it could be on any material at all (perhaps the most memorable ones I have heard of are on a pair of knickers, on a cow, and on a dustbin lid).

Addressed by a person to another person (a banker)

Although the definition refers to a person it is possible to have joint drawers, (the writers of the cheque) or corporate (limited company) drawers or other unincorporated drawers (such as local authorities, partnerships etc.). It is possible for a cheque to have joint drawees (although this is extremely unlikely in practice) but a cheque cannot have alternative drawees.

Signed by the drawer

Before a cheque is effective it must be signed by the drawer. However, a number of items must be taken into consideration:

(i) A forged signature is no signature, no matter how accurate the forgery: s.24 Bills of Exchange Act 1882 (see later in this chapter).

(ii) A signature by one of the partners in the name of the partnership is the equivalent of the signatures of all the partners of the partnership: s.23 Bills of Exchange Act 1882. This quote always reminds me of an occasion not long after I had joined my bank's mortgage department. I was dealing with the redemptions (early settlements) of the mortgages, and soon became acquainted with the signatures of local solicitors (almost always in the name of the firm). One day I thought I had detected a forgery on a cheque and, quite pleased with myself, brought this to the attention of my boss. After he had recovered from his bout of laughter he pointed out that all that had happened was that the cheque had been signed by a different partner. I won't forget section 23 in a hurry!

(iii) Many large concerns use a facsimile (reproduced) signature in an attempt to save time. The use of such a signature is supported by an indemnity insurance policy in case of misuse.

(iv) It is possible for an agent to become personally liable on a cheque, unless he stresses his agency: s.26 Bills of Exchange Act 1882. It is for this reason that persons acting as agent are advised to quote 'per pro', removing all doubt as to their agency.

Payable on demand

If a customer should complete a 'post dated cheque', this is obviously not within the definition of a cheque as it is not payable on demand. However, it will still be enforceable between the parties to it (the drawer, drawee and payee).

A sum certain in money

The normal banking interpretation of this is that words and figures must agree. However, if they disagree the bank may safely pay the words: s.9 Bills of Exchange Act 1882. Also if the amount is quoted in a foreign currency the sum is certain and as such is acceptable: *Barlow* v *Broadhurst* (1820).

To, or to the order of, a specified person or bearer

(i) *To a specified person*. This person is the payee and the person whom the drawer intends to receive the money; joint payees are acceptable (eg, Mr & Mrs Davies).

(ii) *Or to the order of a specified person*. It is possible that the payee may wish to pass the cheque on to someone else; to do this he merely endorses the cheque (see endorsements later in this chapter) and orders the cheque to be paid to the other person.

(iii) *Or to bearer (the person in possession of the cheque)*. It is rare for a cheque to be written payable to 'bearer', but it is possible for the cheque to become so by either the payee endorsing the cheque in blank (merely signing the reverse of the cheque) or if the cheque is payable to a fictitious or non-existent payee: s.7 Bills of Exchange Act 1882.

▌ Cheques as negotiable instruments

A negotiable instrument is an instrument which can pass 'the three tests of negotiability'. These are:

(i) that the title can pass by mere delivery or by delivery plus endorsement,

(ii) that the holder of the instrument can acquire absolute legal title by taking the instrument (a) in good faith, (b) for value and (c) without notice of defect in the title; and

(iii) that no notice of transfer needs to be given to the person liable on the instrument.

As far as cheques are concerned, condition (i) is obviously met as most of you should be aware by your day-to-day work on the counter of your branch. Condition (ii) is met, by the person holding an absolute legal title, which is known as a **holder in due course**. This is governed by s.29 Bills of Exchange Act 1882, and is covered in greater detail later. Condition (iii) is satisfied as notice need not be given to the drawer each time the cheque is endorsed or transferred.

▌Endorsements and cheques

When is endorsement necessary?

(i) When the cheque is payable to a named payee.

(ii) When the cheque has been specially endorsed. This is explained in greater detail later, but basically means where the endorser has negotiated the cheque to a specified person.

NB Where a cheque is payable to bearer or has been endorsed in blank (the holder merely signing his name on the reverse of the cheque), then no subsequent endorsement is required.

Types of endorsements

(i) **Blank endorsement** – where the endorser merely signs his name on the reverse of the cheque. This is known as an endorsement in blank and has the effect of making the cheque a bearer cheque, needing no further endorsement in order to transfer title.

(ii) **Special endorsement** – where the endorser specifies the person to whom the cheque is being transferred (the endorsee). In order for the endorsee to transfer title further he must endorse the cheque himself.

(iii) **Restrictive endorsement** – this type of endorsement is one which, as its name suggests, places a restriction on the subsequent transfer of the cheque. For example:
(a) It prohibits further transfer, such as 'pay A. Josephs only'.
(b) The endorsee must deal with the cheque as directed, for example, 'pay J Andrews for collection'.
A restrictive endorsee (someone receiving the cheque by a restrictive endorsement) has all the rights of a normal holder (can sue in his own name etc), but he is not free to transfer title and cannot be a holder in due course (see later).

(iv) **Conditional endorsement** – for example, 'pay L Barton on giving birth to her first daughter'. This type of endorsement can be ignored by the paying bank and although the bank is within its rights to ask for proof of the condition it is under no obligation to do so.

Forged or unauthorised endorsements

As previously mentioned, s.24 Bills of Exchange Act 1882 states that a forged signature is totally inoperative, and therefore 'a forged signature is no signature'. This has serious repercussions for cheques in that:

(i) Any person who receives the cheque subsequent to a forged 'essential endorsement' has no title to the cheque, an essential endorsement being one which is necessary for the transfer of title (see above: 'When is endorsement necessary?').

(ii) Where the person has taken the cheque subsequent to the forged endorsement, he can enforce the cheque against anyone subsequent to the forgery but not against anyone prior to the forgery (eg, the drawer).

(iii) Where the cheque is payable to a fictitious or non-existent payee, then the cheque can be treated as if payable to bearer: s.7 Bills of Exchange Act 1882. A fictitious payee is one whom the drawer never intended to receive the money, not necessarily one who does not exist (ie, contradictorily a fictitious payee can exist). In *Bank of England* v *Vagliano Brothers* (1891), the payee did exist but the fraudulent clerk did not intend that the payee should receive the money. The forged endorsement did not invalidate the bill as the endorsement was not essential, the bill being effectively a bearer bill.

∎ Types of holder

Holder

Section 2 of the Bills of Exchange Act 1882 defines a holder as:

> 'the payee or endorsee of a bill (cheque) in possession of it or the bearer thereof'.

The holder has the power to sue on the cheque in his own name and can enforce it against anyone who has signed it and against his immediate transferor (ie, the person who transferred it to him) whether that person signed it or not. A basic holder (not a holder in due course – see later) has only as good a title as his immediate transferor; hence if he receives the cheque from a thief (who obviously has no title to the cheque) then he will also have no title to the cheque.

Holder for value

Section 27 of the Bills of Exchange Act 1882 defines a holder for value as:

> 'the holder of a bill (cheque) for which value has at some time been given'.

It is important to note that it is not necessary for the holder for value to have actually given the value, merely that value must have been given on the cheque at some time. He is a holder for value as regards all parties prior to himself. The holder giving value and all subsequent holders are holders for value. A holder for value has the rights conferred upon him by the common law of transferability. He has precisely the same rights, with faults and failings if any, of the person who transferred the bill (cheque) to him.

Note: Giving value can include:
(a) any valuable consideration,
(b) the settlement of a debt, or
(c) where the holder has a lien on the cheque (see Chapter two).

A holder for value can enforce the cheque against anyone who was a party to the cheque prior to the giving of value (ie, anyone who actually received value). However, he only has as good a title as his immediate transferor.

Holder in due course

Section 29 of the Bills of Exchange Act 1882 defines a holder in due course, as being someone who:

(a) Takes the cheque, complete and regular on the face of it (which includes the reverse), which means that:
  (i) there must be no forgery of an essential endorsement,
  (ii) the cheque must be complete, without any missing sections (the cheque must contain the date, the amount in words and figures, payee's name and drawer's signature),
  (iii) the cheque must not be overdue, as mentioned previously, and must be taken without notice of previous dishonour.

(b) Takes the cheque in good faith and for value. Good faith is defined in s.90 Bills of Exchange Act 1882 as:

> 'something done honestly and without notice or intent of deceit or fraud whether negligently or not'.

This is an important, and easy, definition to remember and one which we will keep on coming back to in this chapter. If the holder is aware of circumstances which should cause concern, then failure to remove those doubts will effectively mean that he has not acted in good faith: *Raphael* v *Bank of England* (1855).

(c) Must **personally** give value on the cheque. The items that are considered to be valuable considerations are identical to those stated above under holder for value, but the important difference must be noted in that a holder for value need not have given value himself, whereas a holder in due course must give value personally.

(d) Must take the cheque without notice of defect in title of the person negotiating the cheque to him.
  It is important to realise that s.30 Bills of Exchange Act 1882 states that 'every holder of a bill (cheque) is prima facie deemed to be a holder in due course'. However, students must note that a payee cannot be a holder in due course: *R. E. Jones Ltd* v *Waring & Gillow Ltd* (1926), and also that it is possible for a holder in due course to have a better title than his immediate transferor, providing he can meet the criteria under (a) to (d) above.
  The rights of a holder in due course are that:

(a) He is the absolute legal owner of the cheque, his title cannot be disputed and it is not affected by any defect in a previous title or by any counter claims (eg, claims of set-off, see Chapter two) between prior parties: s.38 Bills of Exchange Act 1882.

(b) He can enforce payment of the cheque against any 'prior parties', sue all prior parties if necessary, in his own name, if the cheque is not paid by the drawee, ie, if it is dishonoured.

(c) He can pass a perfect title on to his immediate transferee.

Wrongful possessor

A wrongful possessor is a person who takes a cheque bearing a forged (or unauthorised) essential endorsement; for a full discussion see above. A wrongful possessor cannot be a holder, a holder for value or a holder in due course and has no title to the cheque.

■ Crossings and cheques

Types of crossings

General crossing

A general crossing is defined in s.76 Bills of Exchange Act 1882 and is basically two parallel lines across the face of the cheque, from top to bottom. This effectively means that it must be paid into a bank account and that the bank must not exchange the cheque for cash across the counter, the one exception being that the paying bank (the bank on which the cheque is drawn) will make payment to the drawer or his agent. Although strictly speaking this is not in accordance with the crossing there is no danger to the bank, as it is sure that it is paying its customer, or agent, by checking its own records (signature cards etc). Thus a general crossing on a cheque is instrumental in safeguarding against potential loss both to the drawer of the cheque and to the paying bank.

Special crossing

This is the addition of the name of a bank, with or without the addition of two transverse lines, on the cheque. The effect of this crossing is that the paying bank must make sure that it pays the proceeds of the cheque to the bank stated in the crossing. You will remember (it is hoped) from your day-to-day operations, that one of the functions undertaken when collecting a cheque, is that you stamp the cheque with a 'crossing stamp', which is essentially for the reason that, if the cheque is lost or stolen the paying bank can make payment only to the bank stated in the crossing. If the cheque is presented stating two banks, the cheque should be returned by the paying bank.

Not negotiable crossing

This is a general or special crossing plus the words 'not negotiable'. These words have a serious effect on the title of subsequent holders as they remove from the cheque the property of negotiability although the cheque is still a transferable document. The transferee (the person receiving the cheque) receives no better title than his immediate transferor, and since a payee cannot be a holder in due course it means that no one else can receive a better title either. This is of great importance to you both as bankers and as customers. As customers you should consider placing this type of crossing on most cheques, but especially those sent through the post. This will prevent you having to pay the amount twice should the cheque be stolen, once on a replacement of the original and again on the original cheque possibly to a holder in due course. As bankers, an important case for you to consider is that of *Ladup Ltd* v *Shaikh and Ritz Casino Ltd* (1982), where a 'not negotiable' cheque was issued in support of a gambling contract. However, as the cheque had been issued in return for an illegal consideration the payee had no title to it and as no subsequent party could have a better title, the cheque was unenforceable.

Account payee crossing

This crossing is not mentioned in any statute, but is recognised by banking custom and therefore case law has decreed that it is an instruction addressed to the collecting banker to collect the cheque for only the named payee's account. It in no way affects the negotiability or transferability of the cheque: *National Bank Ltd* v *Silke* (1891). However, as you will read later in this chapter, if a collecting bank acts negligently it will lose its statutory protection. A case of negligence was the collection of an 'account payee' cheque into an account other than the payee's without sufficient investigation: *House Property Company of London Ltd* v *London County and Westminster Bank* (1915).

Crossings and banks

One of the main reasons for crossing a cheque is to give protection to either the drawer or a holder. It is possible for a holder to cross an uncrossed cheque and to increase the restrictions imposed by a crossing, but he cannot decrease the restrictions. For example:

(i) A general crossing will increase the time taken for the cheque to be debited to the account, thus giving the drawer a longer period to stop the cheque.

(ii) A general crossing will make tracing of the beneficiary easier.

(iii) A 'not negotiable' crossing removes the possibility of a holder in due course enforcing payment against the drawer's wishes.

(iv) An 'account payee' crossing will put the collecting bank on enquiry when collecting the cheque, and it is hoped greatly reduce the possibility of loss due to fraud. Under the Cheques Act 1992, the "Account Payee" or "A/C payee" crossing now acquires the backing of statute for the first time. A cheque crossed in such a manner *must* be paid into an account of the payee and as such its negotiability is removed. At the time of writing many banks are considering issuing pre-printed cheque books with this crossing on.

▌ Rights and duties of each party to a cheque

The drawer

The drawer of the cheque is the person who writes it and orders the bank to pay it and by the very act of drawing it engages that, upon presentation to the bank, it will be paid: s.55(1) Bills of Exchange Act 1882. If it is dishonoured (returned unpaid) he will compensate the holder or any endorser who is compelled to pay on it (for a full discussion of the liabilities of holder or endorser, see later in this chapter). However, there are exceptions to this basic rule, some of which are as follows: if the drawer is a minor (under 18 years of age and as such lacking in contractual capacity); if there is an absence of valuable consideration; and if the drawer's signature was forged (the conditions for personal liability are discussed in full later). The drawer is also unable to deny the existence of the payee or the payee's capacity to endorse.

The holder

The holder of the cheque is the payee (the person to whom the cheque was originally made payable), or the person known as the endorsee (an endorsee is the person to whom the cheque has been endorsed by a special endorsement, ie, an endorsement specifying the person to whom it is endorsed), or the person in possession of a bearer cheque. The holder has the right to sue prior parties to the cheque in order to receive payment. There are basically three types of holder: a holder, a holder for value and a holder in due course – each of which has been discussed previously.

The endorser

The endorser is a holder to a bill (cheque) who signs on its back in order to pass title on to someone else. The endorser's liability is essentially the same as the drawer's in that he engages that the cheque will be paid upon presentation for payment and if not he will compensate the holder or any subsequent endorser who has to pay on it. He is precluded from denying the genuineness and regularity of the drawer's signature and all previous endorsements: s.55(2) Bills of Exchange Act 1882. The endorsee is also precluded from denying to a subsequent endorsee that at the time of his endorsement the cheque was a valid cheque and that he had a good title thereto.

Transferor by delivery

A transferor by delivery is the person who passes on the title of a bearer cheque by merely delivering the cheque to another. Normally he would incur no liability as he has not actually signed the cheque. However, he does warrant to his immediate transferee (the person to whom he passes the cheque) that the cheque is genuine, that he has a right to transfer it and that he is not aware of any fact that could make the cheque worthless.

An agent

Section 26 (1) of the Bills of Exchange Act 1882 states that where an agent signs a cheque and includes words that he is merely acting in a representative capacity (eg, 'per pro') then he will attach no liability to himself. However, if the words merely indicate his occupation (eg, 'director') then it is possible that personal liability will still attach. In *Bondina Limited v Rollaway Shower Blinds Limited* (1986) the court had to decide whether a cheque quoting the pre-printed name and account number of the limited company but signed by the directors in their name only, without any indication of agency, was enforceable against the company. The courts decided that it was clear that the intention was for the company to be liable and '. . . it shows plainly . . . that the drawer of the cheque was the company . . .'; hence the directors did not attach any personal liability and the cheque was enforceable only against the company.

Prior parties

The term 'prior parties' can be confusing, and therefore needs some explanation. The parties to a cheque, in chronological order, are:

- (L) drawer of the cheque;
- (M) drawee of the cheque;
- (N) payee of the cheque;
- (O) the endorsee who receives the cheque by endorsement from the payee; and
- (P) The endorsee who receives the cheque by endorsement from O, and so on.

Since a cheque is payable on demand, the holder, P, will present it for payment to M, the drawee. If M does not pay, P can sue all prior parties, except M; because M has not signed the cheque. Thus L, N and O are the prior parties to P. If P claims and receives payment from N, N can then sue all parties prior to him, ie, L, the drawer, who is the only party prior to N.

Note. If the cheque had been accepted (signed) by M, (for instance, a bank), then M would immediately go to the top of the list of prior parties and would be a prior party to all other parties.

▮ Rights and duties of the bank on a cheque

The paying bank

We have discussed in Chapter one the rights and duties of banks in general. We now need to analyse these in a little more detail. The paying bank has a duty to pay a customer's cheque when presented for payment. However this is not an absolute duty, in that there are the following exceptions.

The cheque must be unambiguous

(i) If the cheque is ambiguous, then the bank need not pay as its mandate is not clear and it may expose the bank to 'undue risk': *London Joint Stock Bank* v *Macmillan & Arthur* (1918).

(ii) An example of an undue risk could be that an undated cheque is overdue: *Griffiths* v *Dalton* (1940).

(iii) An endorsement in a foreign language could be incorrect and as such invalid: *Arab Bank* v *Ross* (1952).

(iv) If the words and figures on the cheque do not agree, then the bank need not pay as the amount is not for 'a sum certain in money', and so it is not a valid cheque. However, the bank can pay the sum in words; s.9 Bills of Exchange Act 1882.

There must be sufficient funds

(i) If there is a debit balance on another account, then the bank can exercise its right of combination (see Chapter two) and refuse to pay: *Garnett* v *McKewan* (1872). Additionally, if there is a credit balance on another account, then the bank need not combine the two, and pay the cheque; the bank can pay if it wishes to do so and debit the other account.

(ii) If the customer has paid funds in to meet a particular cheque (see 'earmarking', Chapter two) then the bank must comply with the request even if the account is overdrawn or is in excess of its limit: *Barclays Bank* v *Quistclose Investments Limited* (1970).

(iii) The bank does have a right to refuse to pay against uncleared effects, unless the customer can show that he has an implied or express agreement to pay against items not yet cleared: *A. L. Underwood Limited* v *Bank of Liverpool* (1924). An example of an express agreement could be where the bank has consistently paid against uncleared effects in the past.

(iv) Exceptions to the rule that there must be sufficient funds include, where there has been an agreed overdraft or where the cheque has been supported by a cheque guarantee card. Naturally, the card must be used in accordance with the cheque card regulations which include:

- the card must not have expired,
- the cheque must not exceed the card limit (presently £50, or £100).
- the cheque card number must be written on the reverse of the cheque by the payee, and
- the signature on the cheque must correspond with the signature on the card.

Payment must be demanded at the branch where the account is held

See *Joachimson* v *Swiss Bank Corporation* (1924). Also, the demand must be within the bank's normal opening hours or a reasonable time thereafter (to allow for the serving of customers in the branch prior to the closure of the doors). In *Baines* v *National Provincial Bank Limited* (1927), five minutes after closing was deemed to be reasonable.

The cheque must not have been in circulation for an unreasonable time

By banking custom, and not decreed by statute, a cheque which is over six months old is considered to be 'stale' and banks would refuse to pay it. However, they have no legal justification for so doing and are technically in breach of their mandate. Under s.36 of the Bills of Exchange Act 1882, a cheque that has been in circulation for 'an unreasonable' time is overdue and may be the explanation of the banks' actions.

There must be no legal bar to payment

A legal bar could include:

   (i) Notice of death or mental incapacity of customer.
  (ii) Insolvency of customer.
 (iii) Closure of account.
 (iv) Court proceedings against the customer such as a garnishee order or injunction.
  (v) Outbreak of war between the country of the bank and the country of the customer: *Arab Bank Ltd* v *Barclays Bank (Dominion, Colonial and Overseas)* (1954).

Payment must not be countermanded by the drawer

See later in this chapter.

Where the bank is aware, or should be aware, that the money is held on trust

See constructive trusts in Chapter one.

The cheque must be in proper form

This means that it must meet the definition of a cheque as discussed earlier in this chapter. One of the most important features under this heading is the genuineness of the customer's signature. Also, the bank could check that the endorsements are all genuine. This is naturally an impossible task for the paying bank and as we will see later, the Cheques Act 1957 was introduced to remove the necessity for endorsements and thus remove this onerous duty from banks. Failure to comply with this duty, prior to the introduction of the Act, led to the bank being open to a claim of conversion (unlawful interference with the property of another).

The collecting bank

The rights and duties of the collecting bank (the bank at which the cheque is paid in) are as follows.

Clearance of cheques

The collecting bank, acting as its customer's agent, must exercise reasonable care in presenting cheques for payment and must use the quickest method available according to normal banking practice, as was confirmed in *Forman* v *Bank of England* (1902). It is important to note that 'special presentations', where the cheque is sent by post to the paying bank and the collecting bank telephones for confirmation of payment the following day, are not included in the options of 'normal banking practice'. This case involved the practice of clearing cheques via the town clearing system if the paying bank and the collecting bank were both in London. The town clearing system is merely a truncated clearance system where cheques are presented for payment on the same day as received; if the collecting bank receives no message to the contrary they assume the cheque to be paid. However, the bank did not take advantage of the quicker system and was held liable as the delay had meant the returning of other cheques presented for payment to the payee's account.

The duty of the collecting bank is discharged only when the cheque is received by the paying bank: *Barclays Bank plc and Others* v *Bank of England* (1985). Although this case was principally concerned with the responsibility for costs of presentation of cheques, the decision is important as it confirms the extent of duty for the collecting bank, which is not discharged until the cheque is received by the paying bank. It is not discharged when the cheque is received by the clearing centre as was previously thought in some quarters.

Where the collecting bank/branch and the paying bank/branch are one and the same (ie, the holder and the drawer of the cheque have accounts at the same branch of the same bank), then the holder of the cheque has the right to expect a reply on the same day, but only if he asks for confirmation. It was held in *Boyd* v *Emmerson* (1834), that unless the customer asks for confirmation the branch need only decide on the fate of the cheque the day after it is paid in.

Notice of dishonour

The collecting bank has a duty to inform its customer of the dishonour of a cheque deposited for collection. This duty includes the information of the fate of cheques which would normally be immediately represented, for example 'refer to drawer please represent' or 'post-dated' where the date for presentation has now arrived. Most banks write to their customers on the same day they receive notice of the dishonour, enclosing the dishonoured cheque (s.49 Bills of Exchange Act 1882) and debiting their customer's account accordingly. It is important to realise that if the bank wishes to maintain its right of lien (right to retain – see Chapter two), then it must retain the cheque and **not** return it. If the bank releases the cheque it will not only lose its right of lien but it may also lose its power to act as a holder in due course, as the holding of a lien is classed as giving value.

If the customer should wish to retain the liability of any previous party to the cheque (endorser, payee etc.), then he must also give notice of dishonour to each of these parties, but notice to the drawer is not necessary: s.50 Bills of Exchange Act 1882. Like the bank, if the customer wishes to maintain his lien on the cheque he must retain the cheque.

No duty to advise on particular collection

A recent case, *Redmond* v *Allied Irish Banks* (1987), came as great relief to all banks. It was decided in this case that the collecting bank does not owe a duty to its customers to advise as to the risks associated with a particular collection. This case referred to a 'not negotiable' cheque, which was returned unpaid. As mentioned above the customer was unable to set himself up as a holder in due course (as the cheque was crossed 'not negotiable') and likewise unable to enforce the cheque against the drawer. He failed to recover his loss from the bank despite feeling that they should have advised him of the risk. However, the court did state that the bank did owe a duty not to mislead the customer by giving incorrect information and must answer any direct questions accurately.

■ Summary

We have now discussed cheques in general, their definition as a negotiable instrument, the effects and importance of endorsements and crossings, the different types of holders and the rights and duties of each party to a cheque, including the banks. We now need to look more closely at the roles of the paying bank and the collecting bank. There are risks involved for each bank but each has its own protections available for each risk and the remainder of this chapter will be associated with the respective risks and protections of the paying and collecting banks. To follow the natural progression of a cheque, I shall start with the risks facing the collecting bank.

■ Risks facing the collecting bank

Conversion

By far the greatest risk for the collecting bank is that of conversion. Conversion was defined in *Hiort* v *Bott* (1874) as 'an unauthorised act which deprives another person of his property permanently or for an indefinite time'. (Note that it is the lack of 'foundation' knowledge, the basics of Law Relating to Banking Services, such as the understanding of conversion, which tends to be one of the main reasons for failure in the examination.) The most common example of conversion is in the collection of a cheque for a person who has no title to it, such as a thief or the possessor of a cheque bearing a forged or unauthorised essential endorsement. The collecting bank, by facilitating the conversion, even though innocently, will be interpreted as a party to the conversion and liable to the true owner who will have a choice whether to bring an action against the bank or the individual who actually originated the conversion. Naturally, the true owner would normally choose the bank as he will have a greater chance of recovering his loss than he might have from most individuals.

Obviously, when a bank collects a cheque for its customer there is a possibility that the customer may not be the true owner and so is depriving the true owner of possession of his property. Realistically, it is impossible for a collecting bank to ensure that its customers are the true owners of all cheques they present to it; to be sure of this, banks would need to check every endorsement for validity. The bank is therefore potentially at risk each time it collects a cheque on behalf of its customer.

No notice of dishonour

If the collecting bank fails to notify its customer of the dishonour of a cheque within a reasonable time and as a result of the delay the customer suffers a financial loss, the bank could be held liable for damages. An example of the customer suffering a loss would be if the customer were unable to enforce the cheque against previous endorsers.

Incorrect clearance procedure

As mentioned previously, one of the duties of the collecting bank is to collect cheques for its customers, by the quickest method available. If the bank fails to do so it will be liable for any losses incurred by its customer.

Protections available for the collecting banker against conversion

Section 4 Cheques Act 1957

The collecting bank will be able to claim statutory (that is by virtue of a statute) protection against a claim of conversion from the true owner under s.4 Cheques Act 1957. However to be able to claim this form of protection the collecting bank must be able to satisfy the following conditions:

(i) the bank must have acted in good faith
(ii) for a customer, and
(iii) without negligence.

The interpretation of each of these terms is as follows.

In good faith

As mentioned previously, s.90 Bills of Exchange Act 1882 defines in good faith as 'something done honestly, . . . whether negligently or not'. Good faith is usually presumed in dealings between a bank and its customers. However, should the bank be guilty of fraud or dishonesty, then the protection of s.4 would not be available.

For a customer

We have previously discussed 'What is a customer?' in Chapter one and I would suggest that you re-read that section. In summary, we saw that since there was no statutory definition of a customer, the banks had to look to case law, for guidance, which is as follows:

(a) The mere cashing of cheques for a person does not make that person a customer of the bank: *Great Western Railway* v *London and County Banking Corporation* (1901).
(b) The opening of an account, with or without a deposit, is sufficient for the depositor to become the bank's customer: *Barclays Bank* v *Okenhare* (1966).
(c) The duration of the bank/customer relationship is irrelevant: *Commissioners of Taxation* v *English, Scottish and Australian Bank* (1920).

Without negligence

As stated above it is generally presumed that the bank acts in good faith, and the vast majority of transactions undertaken at the counters of most clearing bank branches are for customers. Hence, it is not surprising that the most disputed area for the bank to satisfy is 'acting without negligence'. Unfortunately, as with 'a customer' there is no statutory definition for 'acting without negligence' and we have to turn to case law and, in particular, to judicial comments in coming to a conclusion. There are two main cases and quotations to be taken into account:

(a) *Lloyds Bank Ltd* v *E. B. Savory and Co* (1933)

'The standard by which the absence, or otherwise, of negligence is to be determined must in my opinion be ascertained by reference to the practice of reasonable men carrying on the business of bankers, and endeavouring to do so in such a manner as may be calculated to protect themselves and others against fraud.'

As with most legal quotations this needs to be translated into everyday English! The judge was in fact saying that the level below which the bank will be deemed to have been negligent is that level which can be expected from 'reasonable . . . bankers'. Another important point is that the banks are 'protecting themselves and others from fraud', the 'others' is interpreted to be the true owner of the cheque.

(b) *Marfani* v *Midland Bank Ltd* (1964)

'What the court has to do is to look at all the circumstances at the time of the acts complained of, and to ask itself: were those circumstances such as would cause a reasonable banker, possessed of such information about his customer as a reasonable banker would possess, to suspect that his customer was not the true owner of the cheque?'

Once again, the judge is stressing the acts of 'a reasonable banker', but he is also introducing a new concept, that of the knowledge that a 'reasonable banker' should have about his customers. Many of the cases concerning negligence come back to this point concerning the knowledge the bank should have had of its customers.

(c) A further quotation from the judgment of *Marfani* v *Midland Bank Ltd* (1964), is:

'. . . cases and decisions of thirty years ago may not be a reliable guide to today's banking business.' Thankfully, this is self-explanatory!

Examples of banks losing their statutory protection include poor account opening procedures and poor collection procedures for a particular cheque. We will also consider later on cases where the banks have been able to retain their statutory protection, despite a claim of negligence being made against them.

Account opening

Not taking, or not following up, references

In *Ladbroke* v *Todd* (1914), it was held that a bank had acted negligently in collecting a cheque for a customer, where it had not ascertained the correct identity of the customer by the then popular method of taking references. In this case an account was opened, fraudulently, by a thief in the name of the payee of a stolen cheque. The taking up of references would have uncovered the fraud but since this was not done, no protection was available to the bank.

Furthermore, in *Hampstead Guardians* v *Barclays Bank Ltd* (1923), an account was fraudulently opened under a false name, the 'customer' giving his own name as referee. It was decided that where a referee was not known to the bank, then it should have followed up the reference and established whether it was genuine (usually by enquiring of the referee's bankers). Failure to do so was interpreted as negligence and the bank lost its statutory protection available under s.4 Cheques Act 1957.

However, to gain an accurate and up-to-date picture of the taking of references we must refer to the second quotation from the *Marfani* case quoted above: '. . . cases and decisions of thirty years ago may not be a reliable guide to today's banking business'. As many of you will be aware, today's banking practice is moving away from the time-absorbing method of taking references and moving towards the taking of suitable identification when opening accounts, possibly supported by a reference from a credit reference agency. The banks hope to achieve two objectives from this action:

(i) Swifter account opening procedures which should give the competition (other banks, building societies etc.) less chance of attracting business away from 'their' customers.

(ii) Enjoying protection under s.4 Cheques Act 1957 against conversion. The banks feel that as long as suitable identification is taken, then they are satisfying their responsibility to identify their customer and are confident that circumstances such as *Ladbroke* v *Todd* or *Hampstead Guardians* v *Barclays Bank* would be prevented by the procedures adopted. This 'confidence' has not yet been tested in the courts, only time will tell!

Not taking note of customer's employers or the employers of customer's spouse

Many cases in this area include the involvement of 'fraudulent clerks', stealing or misappropriating cheques belonging to their employers. One such case is *Lloyds Bank Ltd* v *E. B. Savory & Co* (1933), where the proceeds were placed into accounts, in the name not only of the employee but also of the employee's wife. The bank was found guilty of negligence as it should have known the name of its customer's employer and also the employer of the female customer's husband because if it had, it should have been aware of the possibility of fraud and would have prevented it. Although this case referred to the wife's employer, it is a natural assumption that it would also refer to the wife of a male customer.

However, it was held in *Orbit Mining and Trading Co Ltd* v *Westminster Bank Ltd* (1963), that the bank has no responsibility to make regular enquiries to ensure that it is aware of any possible change in employer of the customer.

Trading names

Where a person (or company) is trading under a name other than his own, then the bank must satisfy itself that it is not leaving itself open to the possibility of conversion. Banking practice now is that the account holding branch will, before opening the account, ask to see the stationery stating the trading name and the name of the proprietor. As no official registration of business names is now necessary (Business Names Act 1985) it is thought that this is the only method of realistically ensuring that the account holder is also the proprietor of the business. This is one area of banking practice which causes almost daily headaches for branch bankers. In a recent incident, I declined to open an account for a person since he was trading under a name very similar to the trading name of his brother (say, Jones Commercial compared with his brother's Jones Commercial Transport). He stated that his brother was away on holiday and that he did not have any stationery connecting himself to Jones Commercial. I declined to open the account as I felt the danger of conversion was too great, I made an appointment to meet him on the return of his brother from holiday. The appointment was not kept which assured me that I had made the right decision.

A further complication on this theme is the use of 'nom de plume' or pseudonyms. These are used extensively by authors to keep their true identity secret. Before accepting a cheque payable in such a name the collecting bank must satisfy itself that the cheque is actually meant for the benefit of its customer. This is usually undertaken at the account opening interview by obtaining a letter from the publisher or exceptionally by a cover photograph easily identifying the customer as the 'nom de plume' user.

Collection of a particular cheque

As well as being negligent when opening the account, it is also possible for the bank to be negligent when collecting a particular cheque. An important case to remember in this connection is *Commissioners of Taxation* v *English, Scottish and Australian Bank* (1920), where it was stated that 'the test of negligence is whether the transaction of paying in any given cheque, coupled with the circumstances antecedent and present, was so out of the ordinary course that it ought to have aroused doubts in the banker's mind, and caused him to make enquiries'. To make this quote more understandable we need to realise that the banker must receive such replies as would satisfy a reasonable banker and merely to enquire is not sufficient. Examples of bankers acting negligently in the collection of a particular cheque include:

(a) Collecting, without enquiry, cheques drawn on the private account of an individual payable to a company and endorsed by that individual in his capacity as an official of the company: *A. L. Underwood Ltd* v *Bank of Liverpool* (1924). In this case the cheque was made payable to A. L. Underwood Ltd endorsed by the sole director and paid into his account. Naturally, this is not a normal transaction and so the bank should have enquired and received a reasonable explanation. This the bank did not do.

(b) Collecting cheques, without sufficient enquiry, that are out of character for the account. In *Nu-Stilo Footwear* v *Lloyds Bank Ltd* (1956), the bank was held to have been negligent when collecting a cheque for a large amount which was not consistent with the standing of the account holder or the account. An easy way to recall this case is to remember that the transaction was 'out of step', and the case was *Nu-stilo FOOTwear*!

The second case in this area is *Motor Traders Guarantee Corporation Ltd* v *Midland Bank Ltd* (1937), where an account had been in default and the debtor (customer) cleared the indebtedness with the deposit of one large cheque. The bank procedures laid down that the cheque should have been referred to the manager but it was not and the cashier merely made enquiries himself. It was held that the non-compliance with bank procedures was not in itself negligence, but the cashier had been too easily satisfied with the replies received and the manager would not have been so easily misled. This case is important for three reasons:

(i) Banks must be on their guard when collecting cheques after pressurising their customers for repayment of a debt. The circumstances behind the cheque received for collection need to be investigated.

(ii) It is not sufficient merely to ask the right questions; the bank must also receive answers which are acceptable to 'a reasonable banker'.

(iii) Non-compliance with bank procedures is not necessarily tantamount to negligence. However, you must remember that the procedures are usually there for very good reasons (usually to protect the bank), and not merely to ensure that you don't leave work too early!

(c) Collecting, without sufficient enquiry, cheques payable to a partnership, into the private account of a partner. In *Baker* v *Barclays Bank Ltd* (1955), the bank made enquiries but received inadequate replies and hence lost its statutory protection.

(d) Collecting, without sufficient enquiry, for the private account of an individual cheques payable to him in his official capacity. In *Ross* v *London County Westminster and Parr's Bank* (1919), the bank was held negligent when collecting cheques payable to the account holder in his capacity as officer-in-charge of the administration of the estates of deceased

Canadian soldiers. In a not too dissimilar case the bank was held negligent when collecting cheques, payable to 'D. McGaw for Marquess of Bute', to the agent's (i.e. D. McGaw's) personal account: *Bute* v *Barclays Bank Ltd* (1954).

(e) Collecting, without sufficient enquiry, for the private account of an individual a cheque payable to him but also drawn by him in his capacity as agent on his principal's account. In *Midland Bank Ltd* v *Reckitt* (1933), Sir Harold Reckitt's fraudulent attorney (a form of agent, see 'agency' section) drew a number of cheques on Sir Harold's personal account. It was held that the collecting bank should have enquired into the transaction as it was one which obviously held possibilities of fraud. As it did not enquire, it was found to be negligent and lost its statutory protection.

(f) Collecting, without sufficient enquiry, a cheque payable to a limited company for an account other than the company's. It is unusual for a cheque payable to a company to be negotiated to any other person, or company, except for companies within the same group. Hence, where this happens the collecting bank should make reasonable enquiries. Failure to do so will be interpreted as negligence and loss of protection will result: *London and Montrose Shipbuilding and Repairing Co Ltd* v *Barclays Bank Ltd* (1926).

(g) Collecting cheques, without sufficient enquiry, payable to the collecting bank for the private account of an employee, where the cheque is signed by that employee. In *Lloyds Bank Ltd* v *Chartered Bank of India, Australia and China* (1929), a chief accountant drew cheques on his employer's account and paid them into his own personal account. The bank did not enquire and was therefore held to be negligent. However, one of the judges concerned stated: 'in my view, a bank cannot be held liable for negligence merely because they have not subjected an account to a microscopic examination. **It is not expected that officials of banks should also be amateur detectives.**'

(h) Collecting, without sufficient enquiry, cheques crossed 'account payee' for an account other than the payee's. As mentioned previously an account payee crossing is not recognised by statute, but is merely accepted by banking custom as an instruction to the collecting bank. However, in *Bevan* v *National Bank Ltd* (1906) it was held that a collecting bank would be held negligent when collecting for other than the payee, unless it had ensured either that the payee had already received the proceeds or would receive them as a result of the collection.

As you can see, the main connection throughout each of the cases above is the fact that '. . . the transaction . . . was so out of the ordinary course . . . [of the collection that it should have] . . . caused them to make enquiries'. This you should recognise from the *Commissioners of Taxation* v *English, Scottish and Australian Bank* (1920) case. However, there have been cases where the banks have made sufficient enquiries and received replies that would satisfy a 'reasonable banker', and then, although the conversion took place, they were successful in claiming the statutory protection available and were not liable. These cases include:

● *Slingsby* v *Westminster Bank Ltd* (1931). Here a bank manager had asked the customer about the circumstances surrounding the particulars of a certain transaction and he had received a reasonable reply which seemed all the more adequate as the customer was a solicitor of the (then) highest repute.

● *Penmount Estates Ltd* v *National Provincial Bank Ltd* (1945). In this case the bank manager asked for an explanation from a solicitor customer and received suitable replies.

With hindsight the explanation did not seem very feasible but the court realised that there was no way the bank manager could have been aware of these facts at the time of his decision.

The collecting bank as a holder in due course or a holder for value

The second protection available for the collecting bank, when faced with a claim of conversion, is that it could set itself up as a holder in due course or a holder for value. As you will recall from your earlier reading in this chapter, if someone can satisfy all the conditions of a holder in due course he will have an absolute legal title to the cheque and can enforce it against all previous parties: s.29 Bills of Exchange Act 1882. In brief, to qualify as a holder in due course the collecting bank will have to take the cheque (complete and regular) (i) without notice of defect in title, (ii) in good faith, and (iii) for value.

A holder for value is a holder of a cheque on which value has at sometime been given: s.27 Bills of Exchange Act 1882. You should now realise that the condition which is the most difficult for the bank to fulfil is the giving of value, something we discussed in detail earlier in this chapter. However, there has been much case law involving banks and the giving of value and the current position is as follows:

Payment against uncleared effects

There must be an express or implied agreement to allow the customer to draw monies against cheques not yet cleared. Absence of such an agreement will mean that the transaction will not be accepted as 'giving value': *A. L. Underwood Ltd* v *Barclays Bank Ltd* (1924). An example of an implied agreement to pay against uncleared effects can be if the bank has done so on a regular basis in the past. However, where the bank's stationery expressly forbids the drawing against uncleared effects or where the bank has charged interest on uncleared effects, then the possibilities of claiming an implied agreement will be slim: *Westminster Bank Ltd* v *Zang* (1966).

Reduction of a debt

If a cheque is collected in reduction of a debt, then the effect must be a specific or permanent reduction of the debt and not merely a temporary decrease in the balance: *M'Lean* v *Clydesdale Banking Co.* (1883). An example of a specific reduction would be the reduction of the limit on an overdraft or a reduction in the outstanding balance of a loan.

Where the bank holds a lien

As previously mentioned (Chapter two) a lien is a right to retain, and if a bank holds a lien on a cheque, then it is deemed to have given value: s.27 Bills of Exchange Act 1882. However, the bank must retain the cheque and if it is returned to the customer the bank will lose its lien and with it its right to act as a holder for value, or in due course: *Westminster Bank Ltd* v *Zang* (1966).

In exchange for services

Where the bank is paid for services by cheque, then it is deemed to have given value. Examples of this include foreign currency transactions, safe custody of valuables or perhaps in recent times estate agency fees.

Where cheque is 'cashed'

Naturally, where the bank exchanges the cheque for cash over the counter, then the bank has effectively given cash for the cheque and will be able to set itself up as a holder in due course or for value.

As a defence, the bank setting itself up as a holder in due course has two main defects, other than the necessity to give value; these are that the cheque can bear a forged endorsement or a 'not negotiable' crossing. Both of these matters have been fully discussed previously and I suggest that if you are not familiar with them you re-read those sections now.

Contributory negligence

If all else fails and the bank is guilty of facilitating the conversion it is possible that the bank can reduce the damages it must pay due to the contributory negligence of another party. In *Lumsden and Co* v *London Trustee Savings Bank* (1971), it was held that the TSB could reduce the damages by 10 per cent after bearing in mind the fact that the negligence of the drawer (he had left spaces in the cheque which enabled easy alteration) had contributed to the conversion. In this case it was also suggested that when opening an account for a newly arrived immigrant, the account holding bank should ask for sight of the prospective customer's passport as a means of identification.

A claim of contributory negligence is not literally a form of defence against conversion, but is more a means of reducing the damages when a bank is found guilty of inadvertently facilitating the conversion.

Summary – Collecting banks and their protection against conversion

Where a collecting bank is faced with a claim of conversion, it will first of all try to stand out of the litigation and allow the other parties to continue without its involvement; it will do this by claiming its statutory protection under s.4 Cheques Act 1957. In order to claim this protection it will need to satisfy the conditions of acting for a customer, in good faith and without negligence. Where this protection is not available (due to non-compliance with one of the conditions), then the collecting bank will attempt to set itself up as a holder in due course and enforce the cheque against a prior party. Again, the bank will need to satisfy the relevant conditions of taking the cheque complete and regular on its face, without notice of any defect, in good faith and for value. If the bank is unable to claim either of these defences it will attempt to reduce any damages payable by claiming contributory negligence of a previous party.

▌ Protections against wrongful dishonour or incorrect clearance procedure

There are few protections available to the collecting banks when they fail to conform to their duties when giving notice of dishonour or collecting cheques. Hence, a bank needs to comply carefully with the laid down procedures. Theoretical protections could include setting itself up as a holder in due course or for value (providing notice of default has been given to other parties, other than the customer) and the fact that the delay in clearance was justified (postal strike etc).

■ Risks for the paying bank

Breach of mandate

One risk for the paying bank when paying its customer's cheques is that it may not be paying in accordance with the customer's instructions as per the mandate between the customer and the bank. The mandate breached could be either the original mandate completed when the account was opened (for example, forged signature), or non-compliance with the cheque itself as a mandate in its own right (for example, material alteration), or other mandates (payment of countermanded (stopped) cheque instructions). Now let us look at each of these breaches of mandate affecting the paying bank in more detail.

Non-compliance with drawer's signature instructions

As mentioned previously, a forged signature is totally invalid, no matter how good the forgery: s.24 Bills of Exchange Act 1882. Remember: a forged signature is no signature. An unauthorised signature is likewise invalid. Examples of an authorised signature can include an agent's signature, the use of a facsimile signature stamp, and a partner's signature in the name of the partnership. Also, where the original mandate referring to a joint account states that both members of the account must sign each cheque, then failure to comply with this mandate will result in the non-signing party to the account having a right of action against the bank. This was supported in *Catlin* v *Cyprus Finance Corporation (London) Ltd* (1983).

Inchoate instruments and alterations to cheques

An example of an inchoate instrument is an incompleted cheque. Under s.20 Bills of Exchange Act 1882, the holder of such a cheque has authority to complete it. However, to be able to enforce the cheque against the drawer the holder must complete the cheque within a reasonable time and strictly in accordance with the authority he holds. A holder in due course can enforce the cheque against the drawer, providing that when he received the cheque it was 'complete and regular'. Hence the person who completes an inchoate cheque cannot be a holder in due course. Naturally, inchoate instruments are open to abuse and many problems have been seen.

Any alteration to a cheque should be initialled, or preferably signed, by the drawer(s). A bank paying a cheque bearing an unauthorised alteration is not complying with its customer's mandate (the cheque as originally drawn) and as such could be liable to its customer for breach of mandate. Alterations could include the payee, crossing etc. and the most typical fraudulent alteration is of the amount by an employee, agent and others. If the alteration is apparent the bank should return the cheque unpaid. If the alteration is non-apparent the bank is entitled to debit its customer's account with the original amount only and will need to obtain the difference from the beneficiary, this could obviously be difficult especially if the beneficiary has 'disappeared' or a large amount is involved.

Payment of countermanded cheques

An obvious example of the bank not complying with the instructions of its customer is in paying an item that it had previously been instructed not to pay. For a countermand to be effective it must be:

(a) In writing. Where a telephone request is received it is normal banking practice to accept this, but only as a temporary measure, with the account holder being requested to confirm his request in writing. If the cheque is presented in the meanwhile it should be returned 'payment countermanded awaiting drawer's confirmation'. This type of reply can also be used for other reasons (including a past examination question) where the countermand was requested by the payee and the paying bank was unable to verify the instruction immediately with the drawer.

(b) Communicated to the bank. A countermand is not effective until it is actually in the hands of the bank. In a fairly controversial decision, *Curtice* v *London City and Midland Bank Ltd* (1908), the stop instruction was placed in the bank's post box, but due to an oversight by the bank the post box was not completely emptied and the stop instruction was overlooked. It was held that the bank was entitled to debit the account as the cheque had not been effectively countermanded at the time of presentation of the cheque. The countermand must be communicated to the account holding branch; if it is sent to another branch and the cheque is presented in the time taken to pass the instruction onto the account holding branch then the stop is not effective: *London Provincial and South Western Bank Ltd* v *Buzzard* (1918).

(c) Unequivocal. This means that the instruction must not be able to be misinterpreted. In *Westminster Bank* v *Hilton* (1926) it was held that the only accurate way of identifying a stopped cheque is by the cheque number. In this case the customer quoted the wrong number on his stop instruction, that numbered cheque having in fact already been paid. When the cheque which the customer intended to stop was presented the bank thought it to be a replacement and paid it. It was held that the number of a cheque is the one exact method of identification and also that the bank has no duty to check whether or not the cheque number quoted has been paid.

When a bank has paid a previously 'stopped cheque' the bank is left with a potentially unenforceable debt as the cheque cannot be debited to the customer's account.

Wrongful dishonour

Unfortunately banks have been known to return cheques when they should have paid, and perhaps the most typical example is where the bank has previously paid an item that it should not have done (eg, payment of a countermanded cheque) which has resulted in an insufficient available balance to pay the item.

Where a bank returns an item wrongfully it is open to two claims:

(a) Breach of contract. The scale of damages awarded will depend upon the loss experienced by the customer and whether this should have been foreseen by the bank. It has been established in *Gibbons* v *Westminster Bank Ltd* (1939), and more recently in *Rae* v *Yorkshire Bank* (1988), that a personal customer will be awarded only nominal damages (£20 in the *Rae* case) for breach of contract; damages for a commercial customer are likely to be substantially higher.

(b) Libel. This is a very grey area, and the bank is possibly committing a written defamation of character should it wrongfully return a cheque containing words which could be harmful to the name or reputation of the drawer. Examples of wordings which have been decided to be libellous include:

'*not sufficient*': *Davidson* v *Barclays Bank Ltd* (1940), on a wrongful return following payment of a countermanded item.

'*present again*': *Baker* v *Australia and New Zealand Bank Ltd* (1958), a New Zealand case, not binding on British courts.

'*account closed*': *Russell* v *Bank of America National Trust and Savings Association* (1977). Here the customer alleged that he had made arrangements for the cheques to be debited from an account in Jersey.

'*refer to drawer*': no case has been decided in British courts concerning this wording since *Plunkett* v *Barclays Bank Ltd* (1936), when it was held not to be libellous. However, the increased usage of the phrase by banks has meant that in the eyes of the public it has come to mean 'insufficient funds'. In *Jayson* v *Midland Bank Ltd* (1968), it was surprising that this matter was not brought before the Court of Appeal, despite the fact that the lower court had held the words to be libellous. Also, in 1972 the Post Office settled out of court for an undisclosed sum when faced with a claim for libel when it returned items marked 'refer to drawer'.

It is possible that libel damages could be reduced if the bank apologises and take steps to reduce the loss to the customer by writing to the payee stating that no responsibility for the return of the item was the customer's and that the bank accepts full blame for its error.

Conversion

The second main area of risk for the paying bank is the possibility of conversion, where the bank pays the proceeds to someone other than the true owner of the cheque. If this should be the case, then the paying bank is obviously open to a claim from the true owner for re-imbursement.

∎ Protections available for the paying bank

Re: breach of mandate

Estoppel

As mentioned before 'a forged signature is no signature': s.24 Bills of Exchange Act 1882, and so the bank has no mandate to debit its customer's account with a cheque bearing a forged signature, no matter how good the forgery. Another important point is that a forged cheque cannot later be ratified (accepted as genuine) by the drawer. However, it is possible that the drawer may be **estopped** from preventing the debiting of the cheque to his account.

Hence the first defence against the debiting of a cheque bearing a signature which is not in compliance with the original mandate is estoppel. The literal definition of estoppel is 'anything which prevents a person by his own acts or words from denying or confirming a fact or the validity of a document.' A short definition, for ease of recall, would be: 'prevented from denying'. There are two main, well established, illustrations of estoppel:

(i) Estoppel arising from a misleading statement from the customer: *Brown* v *Westminster Bank Ltd* (1964). In this case an old lady's signature had been forged on over 300 cheques and the bank had questioned her on several occasions and on each occasion they were informed that the signatures were either her own or had been authorised by her. Eventually, her son became aware of the situation and the bank was taken to court in respect of the forged cheques. The court held in favour of the bank deciding that the customer was estopped from denying that the signatures were genuine. It is thought that this form of estoppel would apply not only to forgery of the drawer's signature but also to other forgeries or fraudulent material alterations (ie, if the customer is questioned and confirms that the alteration was his own, then estoppel could arise).

(ii) Estoppel arising form a breach of duty by the customer: *Greenwood* v *Martins Bank* (1933). In this case a husband was aware that his wife was forging his signature but was 'persuaded' not to inform the bank (I am not quite sure how). When the wife died the husband claimed against the bank. However, it was held that the husband was in breach of his duty to inform the bank of forgeries (see Chapter one) and was estopped from denying the genuineness of the cheques.

In *London Joint Stock Bank* v *Macmillan and Arthur* (1918), the customer did not take due care when drawing cheques, leaving a space for fraudulent alteration of the amount in figures from £2 to £120 and there was no amount written in words. It was held that the customer was in breach of his duty to take due care when writing cheques and as such estopped from denying the genuineness of the cheque. The duty to report forgeries or to take due care when drawing cheques is an example of the customer's duty and the customer could well be estopped in respect of the breach of these and some other duties. It is important at this stage that you recall *Tai Hing Cotton Mill Ltd* v *Liu Chong Hing Bank Ltd* (1985), which stated that the customer does not have a duty to check his statements and report any forgeries to the bank. This was decided in spite of the bank inserting an express condition to the contrary in its contract with its customers. Also from the *Tai Hing* case it was stated that the customer does not owe a duty to the bank to ensure that his employees take due care.

Subrogation

Where a bank has paid a cheque in breach of mandate, then it has a right of subrogation (a right to step into the shoes of the creditor). The most common example of subrogation is the ability of the bank to claim back from the customer the goods purchased by a wrongly paid 'stopped cheque', in order to prevent the unjust enrichment of the customer. A memorable example for me is one where a seaside branch received a countermand instruction in respect of a cheque used to buy donkeys which turned out to be lame. The customer stopped the cheque but unfortunately the bank paid the cheque. As soon as the bank realised their mistake they re-credited the account and apologised to the customer. The branch manager, knowing his banking law, demanded receipt of the items bought with the stopped cheque. The bank became the owners of six lame donkeys!

A further example of subrogation is where the bank can prove that the payment extinguished the debts of the customer. In *B. Liggett (Liverpool) Ltd* v *Barclays Bank Ltd* (1928), the court held that the bank could be subrogated to the position of the trade creditors and enforce the cheque. The rationale behind the decision was to prevent, once again, the unjust enrichment of the customer.

Payment under mistake of fact

It is possible that a paying bank may use this defence to reclaim any money paid in breach of mandate from the person benefiting from the payment. There are three conditions:

(i) Payment must not be made under mandate. Hence payment must be as a result of a forged signature, payment of a stopped cheque or some other breach of mandate, payment in excess of the agreed overdraft limit will not be sufficient.

(ii) Payment must be as a mistake of fact, not as a mistake of law (a difficult and impractical distinction).

(iii) Payment must be as a result of the mistake.

All three of these conditions were present in *Barclays Bank Ltd* v *W. J. Simms, Son and Cooke (Southern) Ltd and Sowman* (1979), which related to a stopped cheque, and so the bank was able to claim the monies paid from the beneficiary. In a forgery case: *National Westminster Bank Ltd* v *Barclays Bank International Ltd and Ismail* (1975), the bank was again able to reclaim the monies paid out.

However, it is possible that the bank could be estopped from claiming that the monies be refunded. For a claim of estoppel to defeat the bank's claim for repayment under mistake of fact the beneficiary must prove:

(a) That the bank made a representation to the beneficiary stating that the payment had been made, or there was some breach of a duty owed by the bank, other than the payment itself: *Cocks* v *Masterman* (1829).

(b) That the recipient must have relied on the representation, making repayment inequitable (unfair). In *United Overseas Bank* v *Jiwani* (1976), the claim of estoppel failed because the claimant had not changed his position following the error; had he done so the claim would have succeeded.

(c) That the beneficiary must not be at fault.

Cocks v *Masterman* (1829) also laid down an easier form of estoppel, which states that the instrument must be held by a holder (see above, in this chapter), negotiated to him with an intrinsic defect on which he has received payment. This easier form of estoppel by the beneficiary means that it cannot be claimed by a payee: *R. E. Jones Ltd* v *Waring and Gillow Ltd* (1926), nor can the defence apply to forged instruments: *National Westminster Bank Ltd* v *Barclays Bank International and Ismail* (1975). However, it can be easier to claim than the alternative form of estoppel as there is no need for the bank to have made a representation or to have committed a breach of duty.

Re conversion

As you should now be aware, conversion is defined, in *Hiort* v *Bott* (1874), as 'an unauthorised act which deprives another person of his property permanently or for an indefinite time'. Hence a paying bank that pays the incorrect person is obviously committing the tort of conversion. Every day examples occur of paying a cheque bearing a forged or unauthorised endorsement, or even paying a cheque bearing no endorsement when such an endorsement is necessary to transfer title. It is almost impossible for the paying bank to ensure that every endorsement on a cheque is valid or even more so to ensure that every necessary endorsement is present. It is for these reasons that a bank comes to rely on the statutory protections available to it when faced with a claim of conversion. The following are the statutory protections available to the paying bank:

(i) Section 59 Bills of Exchange Act 1882. This statutory protection is available to the paying bank when paying 'in due course'. To be eligible for this protection the paying bank must:

(a) Pay to the holder, ie the payee, or endorsee in possession, of an order cheque or to the bearer of a bearer cheque. If you cannot remember the conditions for a holder and the differences between a holder and a wrongful possessor, you must now go back and re-read the earlier section of this chapter. However, briefly, a wrongful possessor is someone in possession of the cheque bearing a forged, unauthorised or missing essential endorsement. A bearer cheque is one made payable to bearer, endorsed in blank or payable to a fictitious or non-existent payee: s.7 Bills of Exchange Act 1882.

(b) In good faith: 'something done honestly whether negligently or not' s.90 Bills of Exchange Act 1882.

(c) Without notice of any defect in the holder's title.

(d) Payment must be made by the bank; for the payment to be made by any other source is not sufficient.

Obviously, (b), (c) and (d) in the previous paragraph are usually easily satisfied, but the problem arises with the satisfaction of condition (a), ie, payment to a payee, or endorsee in possession, of an order cheque or bearer of a bearer cheque. The first impression may be that a bank would rarely be guilty of conversion when paying to a holder. However, examples to the contrary could include the theft of a cheque payable to bearer, or the theft of an order cheque endorsed in blank prior to the thief stealing it.

Although *Auchteroni & Co.* v *Midland Bank Ltd* (1928) refers to the payment of a bill of exchange by the paying bank, the principles are thought to remain for payment of cheques. The cheque (an order cheque, endorsed in blank, and as such, a bearer cheque) was presented by a clerk for payment, but then unfortunately the clerk absconded with the money. The bank claimed under the protection afforded by s.59. It was held that the payment to a clerk was not sufficiently 'out of the ordinary course' for the bank to lose its protection. However the judge stated that payment over the counter to a tramp, postman or office boy would be very special circumstances calling for enquiry.

However, there will still be many examples of possible conversion where the paying bank will not be making payment to a holder, and hence the extent of the protection of s.59 is limited. This is identified by the law and therefore a number of other protections are available. For example:

(ii) Section 60 Bills of Exchange Act 1882 protects the paying bank liable to a claim of conversion where it pays a crossed or open cheque bearing a forged or unauthorised endorsement. You should be aware that a forged endorsement is no endorsement: s.24 Bills of Exchange Act 1882, and that an unauthorised endorsement is one added to the cheque without the authority of the principal or where an agent exceeds his authority (see Chapter six). In order to claim this protection the paying bank must pay:

(a) in good faith (see s.90 above); and
(b) in the ordinary course of business.

Yet again there is no statutory definition of 'in the ordinary course of business' and we need to turn to case law and interpretation:

● *Baines* v *National Provincial Bank Ltd* (1927), stated that the bank had a reasonable time after closing to serve the customers already on the premises.
● We have already discussed *Auchteroni & Co* v *Midland Bank Ltd* (1928).
● Payment must be in accordance with the crossing (for example, a crossed cheque must be paid to a banker and not cashed over the counter: s.76 Bills of Exchange Act 1882, except to the account holder or his named agent under a pre-arranged agreement (known as third party mandates/authorities).
● Banks must take care when requested to make a payment that is so unusual that it may be deemed to be outside the ordinary course of business. Such requests could be the

postal request to exchange an open cheque for cash, and the proceeds to be forwarded to the customer by post, or, as per the *Auchteroni* case, a request for payment by a tramp, postman or office boy.

(iii) Section 80 Bills of Exchange Act 1882 offers protection to a paying bank where it pays a **crossed cheque only** bearing a forged endorsement. The conditions for this protection are that payment must be made:

(a) in good faith (see s.90),
(b) in accordance with the crossing; for example if crossed generally to a bank and if crossed specially to the bank named in the crossing; and
(c) without negligence (see earlier in this chapter for the extent of the implications of negligence and the collecting banker).

As you may well imagine, there are not many recorded instances of banks using this form of protection, due mainly to the onerous condition of having to act without negligence. From comparing the two defences against a forged endorsement (ie, s.60 and s.80), you can see that the only time that a bank would possibly use s.80 is where it has acted outside the normal course of business. However, there is a school of thought along the lines that if the bank should act so far outside the normal course of business as to lose the protection of s.60 that it is in fact acting negligently and should lose the protection of s.80. This has not been substantiated by case law and is an area of debate which I suspect will continue until satisfied by the courts.

(iv) Section 1 Cheques Act 1957. This offers protection to the paying bank when open to a claim of conversion after paying a cheque missing an essential endorsement. The conditions that the paying bank must satisfy to claim this protection are that is paid:

(a) in good faith (s.90); and
(b) In the ordinary course of business (s.60).

However, a memorandum from the Committee of London Clearing Banks (CLCB) in 1957 stated that an endorsement was still necessary in the following circumstances:

(a) cheques requiring a receipt by the payee, usually identified with a large 'R' in the top right hand corner,
(b) cheques presented for payment at the counter,
(c) travellers cheques, and
(d) ordinary bills of exchange.

■ Situations where the collecting bank is also the paying bank

Where a bank collects a cheque for a customer which is coincidentally drawn on another of its customers, then the bank will be acting as both collecting bank and paying bank. If the bank should be faced with a claim of conversion, then to claim the statutory protection available (say, s.1 and s.4 Cheques Act 1957), it must satisfy the conditions necessary for both the paying and collecting bank: *Carpenters Company* v *The British Mutual Banking Company* (1937). This could mean the bank losing its protection as a paying bank, despite fulfilling all the conditions necessary for s.1, because it acted with negligence and lost the protection of s.4.

■ Summary – Bills of Exchange Act 1882 or Cheques Act 1957?

Quite often I see exam scripts and homework assignments where candidates have obviously got themselves confused between the above two Acts. The easiest method of distinction between the two is to remember that the main aim of the Cheques Act 1957 was to remove the need for endorsements and it therefore offers protection for banks where the cheque has no endorsement or an essential endorsement is missing. The Cheques Act 1957 has only four sections to remember and so if you refer to s.60 Cheques Act 1957 you should immediately realise that you have made a mistake and correct your authority by switching to s.60 Bills of Exchange Act 1882.

■ Other paper-based payment systems (banker's drafts, banker's payment orders and warrants)

Banker's drafts

A banker's draft is referred to in s.4 Cheques Act 1957, as 'any draft payable on demand drawn by a banker on himself, whether payable at head office or some other office of his bank'. The bank is both the drawee and drawer of such an instrument and therefore it does not meet the definition of a bill of exchange or a cheque as defined earlier. In practice banker's drafts are used where a customer requests a guaranteed form of payment and are regularly used to satisfy the purpose of advances (eg, a draft payable to the seller of a car, enabling the customer to pick up the car immediately without the need to carry a lot of cash) and are popular where transfer of title is to take place (eg, purchase of property). Their popularity in these areas is due mainly to the fact that they are viewed by the public as being as good as cash, their payment rarely being refused.

A banker's draft must not be payable to bearer as this would be the equivalent of a banknote and under the Bank Charter Act 1844 only the Bank of England can issue banknotes (in England and Wales).

Drafts and conversion

Unfortunately, the bank is still open to a possible charge of conversion from the true owner of a banker's draft should it be paid to anyone else. This is a real risk for both the collecting and paying bank. Fortunately, there is statutory protection available for both banks against conversion:

The paying bank

(i) Section 1 Cheques Act 1957 protects the paying bank when paying a crossed or uncrossed draft, bearing an irregular endorsement or missing an essential endorsement, providing that the bank acts in good faith and in the ordinary course of business. Both of these conditions have been discussed in full detail earlier.

(ii) Section 80 Bills of Exchange Act 1882 protects the paying bank when paying a crossed draft bearing a forged endorsement, providing the bank acts in good faith, without negligence and in accordance with the crossing. These conditions have also been discussed in full previously.

(iii) Section 19 Stamp Act 1853, protects the paying bank when paying an uncrossed draft over the counter when the draft bears a forged endorsement. The draft must purport to be endorsed by the payee.

The collecting bank

The collecting bank is protected by s.4 Cheques Act 1957 when collecting drafts for someone other than the true owner. The conditions are exactly the same as for cheques, that is, in good faith, without negligence and for a customer.

Lost drafts

It is possible that the bank's customer could inform the bank that the draft issued to him has been lost and as such request that the bank 'stop' the draft and issue a replacement. The possible risk to the bank of this course of action is that the bank could be asked to pay both the original and the replacement drafts, particularly if both have fallen into the hands of holders in due course. There are two possible defences for the bank:

(a) Take an indemnity from the customer. In effect this means the customer promising to re-imburse the bank should it have to pay out twice. However, the strength of an indemnity is the standing of the customer and if the customer is either untrustworthy or has little financial standing then the indemnity would be of little value.

(b) Ensure that the draft has been crossed 'not negotiable'. As previously mentioned it is not possible for a party to a cheque (or draft) crossed 'not negotiable' to become a holder in due course.

Due to the seriousness of the consequences, however, the bank will firstly try to delay having to issue a replacement draft, giving time for the original to appear and be presented.

Banker's payments

A banker's payment is similar to a banker's draft except that the banker's payment is payable to another banker. It is quite often used for settlement of inter-bank transactions, for example, cash transfers or collections, clearance of cheques and special presentations.

Other payment orders

These items include conditional payment orders, money orders or postal orders, and each is discussed below:

Conditional orders

An example of such an instrument would be a travellers cheque (the payee having to countersign the cheque before the paying agent can effect payment), or an insistence by the drawer on the bank ensuring that the cheque be receipted by the payee before it is paid, hence this instrument is not a cheque, (not an unconditional order). However, the paying bank is still protected by s.1 Cheques Act 1957 for a missing or irregular endorsement and s.80 Bills of Exchange Act 1882 for a forged endorsement. The collecting bank will be protected by s.4 Cheques Act 1957.

Money orders

These are issued by a post office and are not negotiable instruments, and therefore the statutory protections are not available to the paying bank or collecting bank as when dealing with cheques. Hence if the post office should decide to claim payment back from the bank, the bank would have to comply and if it has allowed its customer to draw the funds, it could make a loss in this situation. The bank would ensure that it has the right to claim re-imbursement from the customer, as was stated in *London & Provincial Bank Ltd* v *Golding* (1918), but this may well prove fruitless if the customer is unavailable or unable to pay.

Postal orders

These are also issued by a post office and are usually for a smaller amount than money orders. Section 21 Post Office Act 1953 protects a bank when obtaining payment of a postal order as an agent. However, banking practise is that the bank will usually exchange a postal order for cash or treat it as cash when crediting to a customer's account. In these circumstances the bank is not acting as agent but collecting the monies for itself, and so s.21 will not be applicable and the bank should again credit the post office with recourse to the customer. As the amounts are usually small the risk is thought to be negligible.

Dividend warrants

A dividend warrant is a method of distributing the dividends payable on a shareholding with a limited company. It is drawn in the form of a cheque, usually with the signature being in the form of a facsimile; (these are acceptable if supported by a suitable indemnity from the company). Hence the statutory protections available for the collection (s.4 Cheques Act 1957) and payment (s.1 Cheques Act 1957 and s.80 Bills of Exchange Act 1882) of cheques are also available for dividend warrants. If a warrant states that it must be presented within a certain period then this does not make it a conditional order: *Thairlwall* v *Great Northern Railway Company* (1910).

Paymaster general warrants

These are orders for payment from a government department or a public official authorising payment by the paymaster general. These are not cheques as they are not drawn on a bank and so there is no need for any protection for a paying bank. The protection of s.4 Cheques Act 1957 is available for the collecting bank.

Note: (i) s.60 Bills of Exchange Act 1882 does not apply to 'analogous instruments' (payment instruments which appear to be cheques, but are not, including drafts, conditional orders and warrants). (ii) s.5 Cheques Act 1957 states that the crossed cheque sections of the Bills of Exchange Act (sections 76–81) shall apply to analogous instruments. Section 4 Cheques Act 1957 protects collecting banks in respect of the same.

Cheques – general

1. Definition
(a) unconditional – what is a condition? what is not a condition? *Bavins & Sims* v *London & S. W. Bank* and *Thairlwall* v *G. N. Railway*
(b) order in writing – must not be a mere request, can be on any material but usually on pre-printed standard bank forms
(c) addressed by one person to another – joint drawers acceptable but not alternative ones
(d) signed by the drawer – forged signature is no signature: s.24 Bills of Exchange Act 1882, signature in name of partnership (s.23), facsimile signatures (supported by indemnity) are acceptable, liability of agent (s.26).
(e) payable on demand – post dated cheques?
(f) a sum certain in money – amount in words and figures must agree, but banks can safely pay amount in words (s.9), amount expressed in foreign currency acceptable
(g) to or to the order of a specified person or to bearer – joint payees acceptable, fictitious or non-existent payees can make cheque payable to bearer (s.7).

2. Cheques as negotiable instruments
(i) conditions – title passes by mere delivery or delivery plus endorsement, absolute legal title possible, no notice of transfer necessary
(ii) endorsements – when is endorsement necessary? types of endorsement and effects of each, forged endorsements (s.24)

3. Types of holder
(i) holder – (s.2), can enforce against any signatory plus immediate transferor, but will only get as good a title as the person that transferred the cheque to him.
(ii) holder for value – (s.27), value must **at some time** have been given, (it is important that you learn what can be classed as value (eg, valuable consideration, settlement of debt, having a lien), can enforce the cheque against any party prior to giving of value
(iii) holder in due course – (s.29), conditions (complete and regular, in good faith as per s.90, for value and without notice of any defect); rights (absolute legal owner, can enforce against all parties, passes on absolute legal title)
(iv) wrongful possessor – cheque bearing forged essential endorsement, has no title to cheque.

4. Crossings
(a) types
(i) general crossing – two transverse parallel lines, means payment must be made to another bank; sole exception is payment over the counter to the account holder or his known agent
(ii) special crossing – contains the name of a bank. The paying bank must make payment to the bank named in the crossing
(iii) 'not negotiable' crossing – removes the negotiability of the cheque and prevents any one becoming a holder in due course: *Ladup* v *Shaikh & Ritz Casino*
(iv) account payee – instruction addressed to collecting bank, does not affect negotiability or transferability: *National Bank* v *Silke*, if ignored by collecting bank, bank could lose its statutory protection: *House Property Co of London* v *London County & Westminster Bank*

(b) general – inserted to protect drawer or holder.

5. Rights and duties of each party
  (i) drawer – promises that it will be paid when presented, unable to deny the existence of the payee or his ability to endorse
 (ii) holder – see previous discussion
(iii) endorser – promises that cheque will be paid, and that drawer's and all previous endorsers' signatures are genuine
 (iv) transferor by delivery – only liable to immediate transferee
  (v) agent – s.26, must make his agency clear: *Bondina* v *Rollaway Shower Blinds*
 (vi) paying bank – duty to pay is not absolute; exceptions: ambiguous cheque (*London JSB* v *Macmillan & Arthur*; *Griffiths* v *Dalton*; *Arab Bank* v *Ross*), sufficient funds (*Garneth* v *McKewan*; *Barclays* v *Quistclose Investments*), uncleared effects (*A. L. Underwood* v *Bank of Liverpool*), payment demanded at account holding branch (*Joachimson*), overdue or stale cheques, legal bar to payment, payment countermanded, money on trust
(vii) collecting bank – clearance of cheques, (*Forman* v *Bank of England*; *Barclays* v *Bank of England*; *Boyd* v *Emerson*), notice of dishonour (care with right of lien s.49), no duty to advise on particular collection (*Redmond* v *Allied Irish Bank*)

FACT SHEET

Cheques – collecting bank, paying bank and analogous instruments

1. Collecting bank

A. RISKS
(i) conversion – definition: *Hiort* v *Bott* – 'an unauthorised act depriving another person of his property . . .' – a collecting bank can be guilty of conversion merely by allowing it to occur. Main problem is with forged or missing endorsements.
(ii) no notice of dishonour
(iii) incorrect clearance procedure

B. PROTECTIONS
i. conversion
(a) s.4 CHEQUES ACT 1957 – conditions
● in good faith, s.90 Bills of Exchange Act 1882: 'something done honestly, whether negligently or not'
● for a customer: *G.W. Railway* v *London & County Bank*; *Barclays Bank* v *Okenhare*, *Commissioners of Taxation* v *English, Scottish and Australian Bank*
● without negligence,
  Definition – quotations from *Lloyds* v *E. B. Savory*: 'reasonable bankers', *Marfani* v *Midland Bank*: 'were the circumstances such as to cause a reasonable banker . . . to suspect that his customer was not the true owner?', and 'cases of thirty years ago might not be a reliable guide'
  Negligence in account opening: poor identification of customer, formerly by references (*Ladbroke* v *Todd* etc.), not taking note of customer's employer or the employer of customer's spouse (*Lloyds* v *E. B. Savory*), but no need to know of changes in employers: (*Orbit Mining & Trading* v *Westminster Bank*), trading names
  Collection of a particular cheque – *Commissioners of Taxation* v *English, Scottish and Australian Bank*: '. . . transaction . . . so out of ordinary course . . . that . . . bank should enquire' and receive replies that satisfy a 'reasonable banker'. Examples: collecting cheques to a private account, a cheque payable to a limited company and endorsed by

the customer: *A. L. Underwood v Bank of Liverpool*, collecting cheques out of step with the account: *Nu-Stilo Footwear v Lloyds; Motor Traders Guarantee Corporation v Midland*, collecting cheques payable to a partnership for the account of a partner: *Baker v Barclays*, collecting cheques payable to an individual in his official capacity: *Ross v London County Westminster and Parr's Bank; Midland v Reckitt*, collecting a cheque payable to a company for an account other than the company's: *London and Montrose Shipbuilding and Repairing Co Ltd v Barclays*, collecting a cheque payable to the collecting bank for the private account of an employee: *Lloyds v Chartered Bank of India, Australia and China*: 'it is not expected that officials should also be amateur detectives', collecting cheques crossed 'account payee' to an account other than the payee's: *Bevan v National Bank*.

Sufficient enquiry can protect the bank: *Slingsby v Westminster Bank, Penmount Estates v National Provincial Bank*

(b) holder in due course or for value – main problem is the giving of value, quite rare for a collecting bank, examples: paying against uncleared effects (must be agreement): *A. L. Underwood v Barclays; Westminster Bank v Zang*, reduction of debt (must be specific): *M'Lean v Clydesdale Bank*, holding of a lien: *Westminster Bank v Zang*, in exchange for services, cashing of cheque.

(c) contributory negligence – last resort, only reduces damages: *Lumsden v London TSB*

(ii) no notice of dishonour and wrongful collection method, no protections are available for these two occurrences, other than good banking practice.

2. **Paying bank**

A. RISKS
(a) breach of mandate: non-compliance with drawer's signing instructions: *Catlin v Cyprus Banking Corporation*, inchoate instruments and material alterations (s.20), payment of countermanded cheque (to be effective countermand must be in writing, communicated to the bank: *Curtice v London City and Midland Bank; London Provincial and S.W. Bank v Buzzard* and unequivocal *Westminster Bank v Hilton*); wrongful dishonour – bank guilty of breach of mandate: *Rae v Yorkshire Bank* and libel *Davidson v Barclays* etc.
(b) conversion.

B. PROTECTIONS
(a) re breach of mandate
(i) estoppel, misleading statements: *Brown v Westminster Bank*, breach of duty by customer: *Greenwood v Martins Bank; London JSB v Macmillan & Arthur*
(ii) subrogation, 'stepping into the shoes of': *B. Liggett v Barclays*
(iii) payment under mistake of fact: *Barclays v W. J. Sims; Nat. West. v Barclays Bank International*, conditions: must not be under mandate, must be a mistake of fact (not law), payment must be as a result of the mistake. It is possible for repayment under mistake of fact to fail due to a claim of estoppel by beneficiary, conditions: representation by bank: *Cocks v Westerman*, representation relied upon: *United Overseas Bank v Jiwani*, beneficiary not at fault. Or easier form of estoppel by holder providing cheque negotiated to him with an intrinsic defect: *Cocks v Westerman*

(b) re conversion
(i) s.59 – payment in due course, conditions: payment to a holder (this is usually the most difficult condition to satisfy), in good faith, without notice of defect, by bank: *Auchteroni & Co v Midland*
(ii) s.60 – crossed or open cheque bearing forged or unauthorised endorsement. Conditions: in good faith, ordinary course of business *Baines v National Provincial; Auchteroni v Midland*
(iii) s.80 – crossed cheque only, bearing forged endorsement. Conditions: in good faith,

in accordance with crossing, without negligence (no case law on this section due to this condition)

(iv) s.1 Cheques Act 1957 – a cheque missing an essential endorsement, conditions: in good faith and in ordinary course of business. Some items must still be endorsed (learn them).

When collecting and paying bank are the same – in order to claim the statutory protection available to either the collecting or paying bank the bank will have to satisfy **all** the conditions applicable to both: *Carpenters Co v British Mutual Banking Co.*

3. Analogous instruments

(a) Banker's drafts – definition (s.4), conversion:

(i) paying bank protected by s.1, s.80; or s.19 Stamp Act 1853.

(ii) collecting protected bank by s.4.

Lost drafts, care needs to be exercised due to possibility of having to pay out twice.

(b) banker's payments – drafts payable to banker

(c) other payment orders

(i) conditional orders: paying bank protected against conversion by s.1 and s.80, the collecting bank by s.4.

(ii) money orders – no protections available hence only collect with recourse to customer: *London & Provincial Bank v Golding*

(iii) postal orders – s.21 Post Office Act 1953 protects a collecting bank when acting as agent, but collecting banks usually collect postal orders for themselves, again, collection should be with recourse.

(d) dividend warrants – definition: can be treated as cheques for protection purposes (paying bank s.1 & s.80, collecting bank s.4)

(e) paymaster – general warrants – drawn on a government department, protection of s.4 available for collecting bank.

(f) general – s.60 not available for analogous instruments: s.5 Cheques Act states ss.76–81 are available.

Question

A corporate customer had a trusted employee, Smoothe, who being unsupervised over a period of years, forged cheques drawn on his employer's current account. Unknown to the bank, the cheques were all made payable to the owner of a local gambling casino, and were to pay Smoothe's gambling debts. Smoothe's immediate superior knew of his substantial gambling losses, but made no attempt to supervise Smoothe. No investigation was carried out until Smoothe's retirement, when the forgeries were discovered and the corporate customer demanded that the bank should repay.

Fully discussing the relevant legal principles, state:

(A) whether the bank must recredit the customer's account; and   (10 marks)

(B) whether the bank may demand repayment from the casino.   (10 marks)

Key words
unsupervised over a number of years
unknown to the bank
superiors knew of . . . gambling losses but made no attempt to supervise legal principles

Answer

(A) Under the Bills of Exchange Act 1882, s.24, a forged drawer's signature on cheque is wholly inoperative, and the instrument is void. If a cheque is simply looked at as the customer's mandate to the bank to make payment, clearly a cheque bearing a forged signature is not the customer's mandate. Thus, the bank cannot debit the customer's account with cheques bearing a forged drawer's signature. If it has already done so, it must re-credit the account.

The bank cannot:

(a) Look to the customer to ratify, even if willing, since forgery is an illegal act and incapable of ratification.

(b) Claim a defence based on contributory negligence since this is no defence against an action for debt.

The bank's only possible line of defence is estoppel: that the customer, through words or actions, led the bank to believe the signature was genuine, and is therefore estopped (prevented) from denying the genuineness of the signature. In order to establish a defence of estoppel, **three things must all be true**:

(a) The customer made a statement suggesting the signature was genuine (as in *Brown* v *Westminster Bank*); or the customer owed a duty to the bank which he failed to fulfil (as in *Greenwood* v *Martins Bank*).

(b) The bank relied on the statement or the fulfilment of the duty.

(c) The reliance was detrimental to the bank, so that it would be inequitable to expect the bank to repay.

The bank did rely on a belief that the signature was genuine, and this reliance was detrimental. So the crucial point is whether condition (a) is fulfilled. Clearly the customer had made no statement suggesting the signature was genuine, and the bank would have to establish a breach of duty to succeed. However, case law suggests that customers only owe two basic duties to their bankers:

(i) A duty promptly to notify the bank where they become aware that their signature has been forged: *Greenwood* v *Martins Bank Ltd*. But the customer only became aware of the forgeries after Smoothe left its employment.

(ii) A duty to exercise care when drawing cheques, so not to facilitate a fraudulent alteration: *London Joint Stock Bank* v *Macmillan & Arthur*. This clearly is not relevant here.

The only possible breaches of duty are that:

● The customer failed to exercise proper supervision over its employee, so as to prevent fraud; or

● The customer failed to check its statement which would have revealed the forged items.

However, in *Tai Hing Cotton Mills Ltd* v *Liu Chong Hing Bank*, the Privy Council specifically rejected the view that a customer has a duty to supervise an employee; and it reconfirmed the established principle that there is no duty on a customer to check statements, and this does not estop the customer from later setting up a forgery claim against the bank. Thus, the bank would not be able to set up an estoppel defence, and avoid re-crediting the customer. To do so, it would have had to incorporate a specific contractual requirement that the customer must do something (say, check its statement); and the *Tai Hing* case suggests the clause will only be effective where its full impact has been explained in advance to the customer. There is also a possibility that such a clause might be regarded as breaching the Unfair Contract Terms Act 1977.

(B) Money paid under a mistake of fact is recoverable from the recipient, in this case the payee of the cheques. In order that recovery can lawfully be made, **three conditions must all hold true**:

(a) Payment must not be made under mandate.

(b) There must have been a mistake of fact, rather than a mistake of law.

(c) The mistake must have been the cause of the payment being made.

Looking at the facts of the question, the bank clearly has no mandate from the customer to debit its account since the cheques bore forged signatures. Inadvertently paying cheques bearing a forged drawer's signature is a mistake of fact; and clearly the bank would not have paid the cheques had it realised they were forged. Thus, the bank would appear to have a good case to make recovery from the payee; and the ability of a bank to do this was confirmed in *Barclays Bank Ltd* v *W J*

Simms, Son & Cooke (Southern) Ltd and Sowman.

The recipient, the casino, may be able to resist the bank's claim for reimbursement by itself setting up a defence of estoppel. In order to establish an estoppel defence, the casino would have to show **all** of the following were true about the payments:

(a) That some representation was made to the payee that the money was due, and this would have to be additional to the mere payment of the money.

(b) The payee relied on the misrepresentation so that it is inequitable that he should repay. This would require spending the money or entering into commitments to spend it, which would not have been made but for the misrepresentation.

(c) The payee was not at fault.

It seems very unlikely that the payee will be able to resist the bank's claim in law, since it is very unlikely the bank made any representation to the casino that the money was due, other than simply paying the cheque which is not sufficient. There is an 'easier estoppel' route established in *Cocks v Masterman* requiring only that the money was paid. However, this defence only applies to the holder of a negotiable instrument who has had it negotiated to him. Since technically the payee has the cheque issued to him rather than negotiated, he cannot claim this easier defence.

Question

Albert Brown promises £500 to his niece, Bertha, when she passes her AIB examinations. When Bertha does so, Albert hands her a cheque for £500 payable to 'Bertha Brown'. Bertha endorses the cheque to her poor fiancé, Carl, as a present. Carl uses it to pay for a rare first edition of a book on Bills of Exchange, sold to him by Dave, to whom the cheque is indorsed.

Consider who is liable to whom in both of the following alternative cases:

(a) Dave presents the cheque for payment, but finds that Albert has stopped payment, because he disapproved of Carl having the cheque. (10 marks)

(b) The cheque is stolen by Tim who pretends to be Dave and forges an indorsement to Erica to pay for goods received, and Erica transfers the cheque to Fred for value (10 marks)

(Total marks for question – 20)

Key words

promises £500 . . . hands	*Who liable?*
Bertha endorses . . . as present	*(a) stopped*
Carl . . . pay	*(b) forgery*

Answer

There tended to be a lot written about stopped cheques, without answering the question. The terms 'holder for value/ in due course' often mentioned, but not necessarily understood. Often assumed that Bertha gave value. Many failed to recognise that holder in due course could sue anyone, not just Carl. Part (b) often better than (a). The effect of the forged signature was frequently not appreciated, so many thought Dave was no longer true owner, and lost interest in him. Even where the forgery was noticed, many referred to Erica and Fred as holders for value or in due course (not possible because of the forged essential endorsement)

Part (a)

Bertha and Carl are endorsers so the question of their liability to Dave, the holder, arises, as do the liabilities of Albert, to Dave as drawer. Albert's position: he may be liable under s.55(1)(a) as drawer to any holder or any indorser compelled to pay the bill. But he is liable only to a holder for value (or in due course), or to a stranger-indorser (not having been a holder) after consideration was given (within s.27). An answer to this really answers the position of Bertha or Carl.

Bertha's position: it was a gift, without past or present consideration, so Bertha is not holder for value (and anyway, as payee, can't be holder in due course). Because of s.27, therefore, Bertha has no right of recourse against Albert, (despite s.55(1)(a)).

Carl's position: he also got it as a gift and as Bertha did not give consideration, Carl cannot be a holder for value and cannot sue Albert or Bertha.

Dave's position. Dave is holder for value, under s.27 and if he meets s.29 is holder in due course. To meet the conditions of s.29 the bill must be complete and regular on its face, Dave must become holder before overdue and without notice, etc., and he must take for value without notice of defects, etc. Unlike s.27 and the holder for value, this means that he must have a lien (within s.27(3)) or must himself give value; he cannot rely on value given by others. But here he gives value. If he is a holder in due course he will have perfect title, (despite defects in the title of Bertha and Carl) and he can sue any previous party to the cheque. Albert is therefore liable to him.

Part (b)

The cheque was an order cheque and is not payable to anyone but Dave unless Dave endorses it.

A forged indorsement is of no effect: s.24, so the bill is payable still to Dave, who is the true owner.

Erica's position. Though she gives value, she is not owner or 'holder' (so cannot be holder in due course) and is liable in conversion to Dave. She cannot sue any parties before the forgery, though she can sue Tim if she can find him (and if worth it when she does). She is liable to Fred because, by transferring it to him, she warrants that she is entitled to transfer the bill: s.55(2)(c).

Fred's position. Though he gives value, he is not owner or holder and is liable in conversion to Dave. He cannot sue any parties before the forgery, though he can sue Erica or Tim.

CHAPTER 11

Direct debits and credits

Syllabus requirements

- Direct debits and credits: whether paper based or electronically effected through CHAPS or BACS.
- Forgery and fraudulent alteration: the respective rights and obligations of the drawer/payer, the paying and collecting banks and the payee.

■ Introduction

Direct debits and credit transfers are merely uses of the same system but in opposite directions; for example, a direct credit is known as a 'push' transaction (the money being pushed through the system by the payer), and a direct debit is known as a 'pull' transaction (the money being pulled through the system by the payee).

The pull or push transactions can be electronic-based, using either BACS (Banker's Automated Clearing System) or CHAPS (Clearing House Automated Payment System), both of which are discussed in more detail later, or, alternatively, they can be paper-based, by direct debit mandates and/or credit transfers. For ease of understanding I intend to cover each individually, but as you can imagine there may be times when one particular aspect will refer to more than one payment system.

■ Direct debits

A direct debit is a claim for payment initiated by the beneficiary/payee, whereas a standing order is initiated by the payer. In order to effect the payment the payer (bank customer) must sign an authority (the direct debit mandate) and the beneficiary/payee must obtain the written permission of the Committee of the London Banks Clearing House to use the system. This permission is usually automatic, once the application has been approved by the benficiary's own bankers. The beneficiary/payee must also issue an undertaking to indemnify all banks using the system against claims of payments being either in error or unauthorised. The mandate may state the amount and frequency of the payments to be made (although the recent trend is for a mandate to state an unspecified amount and frequency), and will state the account to be debited (usually account name and account number) and the beneficiary. Payment will be made by either:

(i) Forwarding a supply of credit transfer forms to the head office of the paying bank; a credit transfer will be despatched to the collecting bank by the paying bank's head office upon receipt of a debit advice from the paying branch, or

(ii) Using BACS, by supplying a magnetic tape bearing the details of the accounts to be debited and credited. BACS then sorts the details into bank order and provides each paying bank with its own relevant details. A printout of all the accounts to be debited is also provided and this is received by each branch on the day of the debit. No doubt each bank has its own name for this printout but I know it as the BACS report and it will do no harm at all to request sight of the one received by your branch.

If a paying bank is unable to pay a direct debit, for whatever reason, eg, insufficient funds, cancelled mandate etc, the paying bank must advise the beneficiary's bank by 12.00 noon on the day following the debit claim.

Cancellation of the mandate

The payer (bank customer) can revoke or cancel the mandate at any time by informing both the bank and the beneficiary (initiator) in writing. Naturally, any payments claimed after the cancellation should not be paid. However, should the paying bank inadvertently pay under the direct debit it will be able to reclaim the money from the beneficiary as the payment was made under a mistake of fact: *Barclays Bank Ltd* v *W. J. Simms and Cooke (Southern) Ltd* (1980).

Parties to a direct debit

- Payer – person making the payment.
- Paying bank – bank that debits the account and forwards the funds to the collecting/originating bank.
- Collecting/originating bank – bank that demands the money from paying bank.
- Beneficiary/originator/recipient – self-explanatory.

Wrongful payment

As mentioned above, where wrongful payment is due to a cancellation of the mandate then the paying bank is entitled to reclaim the funds from the recipient. A claim could also be made on the recipient's bank for the amount still held in the recipient's account; the bank cannot be liable to a claim exceeding the balance on the account: *National Westminster Bank Ltd* v *Barclays Bank International Ltd* (1975).

Instances of fraud concerning direct debits are rare, due mainly to the difficulty of gaining a benefit from the fraud. For example, a forgery of the payer's signature would be of little benefit to anyone other than the person named as beneficiary on the mandate, from whom the funds could be reclaimed under mistake of fact, as mentioned above. One possible fraud could be the beneficiary making claims outside the scope of the mandate, for example, claiming a figure greater than that intended, when the mandate is for an unspecified amount. In these circumstances the paying bank would be protected by the unspecified amount in the mandate and the payer would have a right of recourse against the beneficiary for fraud, or a claim under mistake of fact, and against the collecting bank under mistake of fact.

■ Credit transfers

A credit transfer is a method of payment whereby the payer presents a form to the paying bank detailing the bank, branch, account number and name of the beneficiary. The payer will also furnish the paying bank with either cash or cheque on his account at that bank. At the end of the day the paying bank forwards them to the clearing centre to be processed and passed on to the recipients' banks. The time period between the payer presenting the credit transfer to the paying bank and the recipient receiving the funds is generally three full working days. Due to this delay in payment one of the key questions is, 'when and how is the payment made, and when is it irrevocable?'

Parties to a credit transfer

- Payer/debtor – the party making the payment.
- Paying bank – bank forwarding credit transfer form on payer's behalf.

- Collecting bank – bank receiving payment for credit of its customer's account.
- Beneficiary/recipient/payee – party that eventually receives payment.

When and how is the payment made?

As mentioned above, there is generally a three day delay between the payer presenting the instrument to the paying bank and the payee receiving the money. This is quite a complex area of discussion and the argument can be summarised as follows: (i) The payment is not effected immediately on deposit of the funds with the paying bank as there is no instruction from the payer to the paying bank, and so the payer would not have a right of recourse to the paying bank for breach of mandate should an immediate transfer not take place. (ii) The money is not held on trust by the paying bank because a separate account is not opened with the intent of holding the money on trust for the payee: *Barclays Bank Ltd* v *Quistclose Investments* (1970). (iii) The credit transfer does not constitute a legal assignment of funds, even if the money comes from the customer's account: *Scott* v *Porcher* (1817). (iv) If the payer's bank and the recipient's bank are different, then payment could be said to have been made when the credit transfer form comes into the possession of the recipient's bank, or when the computer procedures necessary to credit the payee's account have been commenced, as countermanding instructions would not be accepted after this time: *Momm & Others* v *Barclays Bank International Ltd* (1976). (v) A contrary argument could be put forward for payment being effected at the time of payment being passed between the two banks as at this time the paying bank commits funds for the benefit of the payee and prior to this time the collecting bank could recall the transfer form. (vi) If the payer's bank and the recipient's bank is one and the same, then payment is effected only when the payee's account has been credited: *Gibson* v *Minet* (1971).

Examples of payee's (beneficiary's) title being defective

(i) Forged or unauthorised credit transfers. As with direct debits, forgery of a credit transfer is rare and of little practical benefit unless the details of the credit are also altered, (for example, to settle the debt of the forger), and/or the transaction is linked to the debiting of the account. If the bank receives a limited mandate from its customer to effect credit transfers on, say, the signature of a director, and acts outside that mandate, then the signature is in effect a forgery; the bank should not have debited the account. However, the paying bank will have a claim against the agent for the tort of deceit or for breach of warranty of authority: *Collen* v *Wright* (1857). (ii) Transfer made for an illegal consideration or in support of an illegal transaction. Examples of this could be the credit transfer being in settlement of a gambling debt or to settle a debt connected with drug trafficking or terrorism. (iii) Payment made under mistake of fact. This has already been discussed fully above. Examples could include where the payer believed that he was liable to pay the amount, or that he completed the transaction believing it to be something else (this is known as '*non est factum*' and is described in more detail in Chapter fourteen). However such a plea cannot succeed if the claimant did not exercise due care as per *Saunders* v *Anglia Building Society* (1970), where the claimant did not put her spectacles on to read the document in question. (iv) The payer was influenced by a misrepresentation, or for some other reason the transaction was voidable (eg, undue influence). If this is so, then the payer or the paying bank can claim the money back from the payee.

Protections available

(i) Against forgery. The only protection available for the paying bank when paying against a forgery, other than that available under payment made by mistake of fact discussed below, is to claim against the agent for the tort of deceit or for breach of warranty of authority: *Collen* v *Wright* (1857).

(ii) Against illegal consideration. The payer or the paying bank will be able to claim the money back from the payee or from the collecting bank, but only to the extent of the funds still held by them: *National Westminster Bank Ltd* v *Barclays Bank International Ltd and Ismail* (1975). However, it is thought that s.4 Cheques Act 1957 will also protect the collecting bank from personal liability, providing it satisfies the conditions (as discussed in Chapter ten) ie, in good faith for, without negligence and for a customer.

(iii) Against payment under mistake of fact. We have already discussed reclaiming of payments made under mistake of fact as it applies to cheques; the same line of thought can be applied to credit transfers. However, the collecting bank may be protected by s.4 Cheques Act 1957 subject to the standard conditions. If the payer is mistaken as to the identity of the payee he may recover the amount paid from the payee: *Cundy* v *Lindsay* (1878). Naturally, as the paying bank has merely obeyed the mandate of the payer, it will not be liable to the payer unless it was actually aware of the mistake.

(iv) Against misrepresentation. If the payment is induced by a misrepresentation, then the payer or paying bank will be able to reclaim the funds from the payee. Recovery from the collecting bank is not possible if it has acted in good faith: *Babcock* v *Lawson* (1879). The collecting bank is also protected by s.4 Cheques Act 1957.

Direct debits and credit transfers generally

As you can see there is a greater possibility of problems being experienced with credit transfers than with direct debits, due to the fact that direct debits are strictly controlled by the direct debit mandate and the indemnity given by the originator. Hence, in most disputes involving direct debits the solution is easily arrived at by referring to the mandate and assessing whether or not the payee has acted in breach of the mandate. Also, with credit transfers the collecting bank could well be protected in most circumstances by s.4 Cheques Act 1957.

BACS

The Bankers Automated Clearing System was registered as a private limited company (BACS Ltd) in 1971. Its function is to enable easy transfer of funds between participating members. The transfers can relate to standing orders, direct debits or the corporate customers of members using the system for payment of wages, salaries, rentals, trade debts etc. All the major clearing banks are members of BACS but membership has grown to include foreign banks and the larger building societies and is expected to continue growing.

The system of operation has already been discussed under the direct debit section above. Briefly, the originator provides BACS with the magnetic tape detailing payments to be claimed, or credits to be made, two days prior to the due date. BACS will then sort transactions and categorise them into bank and branch order, producing a computerised list for each branch. Once the transactions are sorted, each bank is advised of the net debit or credit figure allocated to it and the settlement is made on the same day.

One grey area when considering BACS is when is payment made and uncancellable? Is payment made when the inter-bank settlement is made, when the beneficiary's account is credited or when the time limit for recall has expired (up to two days after the instruction)? The answer is that payment is made when the paying bank is committed to making it and payment cannot be revoked by the payer. With BACS this is generally held to be the time at which the settlement between the banks has been made, generally on the second day of processing at BACS.

■ CHAPS

The Clearing House Automated Payment System (CHAPS) was introduced in 1984 by the member banks (of which there are now 13). The system provides a **guaranteed** method of same-day-payment chiefly to settle large financial transactions for which records of payments, made and received, are all wasily accessible. The restrictions to the system are that the minimum transaction has to be of at least £5,000, with no maximum limit; the acceptable hours of business are 9.30 am to 3.00 pm, the reason for this relatively early closure being to allow the net settlement figure to be calculated and settled by 4.30 pm; and that the physical settlement is transacted through accounts held by each of the settlement banks with the Bank of England.

The method of operation is that each member bank (known as settlement banks) will be instructed by its customers, either in writing or by telephone, to effect a CHAPS transfer. The instruction will contain all the relevant details, including the amount, the name of the payee and his banking particulars (account name, number and sort code) plus the payer's banking particulars, and will be acted upon via the bank's head office or certain designated branches. These will then transmit the message electronically by a computer terminal to a concentrator known as the gateway, which will then transmit the message onwards to the settlement bank of the payee. It is the precise moment of **guaranteed** payment which removes the area of doubt present with BACS. In CHAPS transactions the time of payment is clear and precise – the time of the passing of the transaction through the 'gateway' – at this stage the receiving bank issues a Logical Acknowledgement (LAK) and the transaction is deemed complete.

Again, as with BACS, it is hoped to increase the usage of the system, and it is possible that CHAPS could be incorporated within the EFTPOS system (Electronic Funds Transfer at the Point of Sale, which is discussed in more detail in Chapter twelve). At the very least it is hoped that more large corporate bodies will have their own access to the system, thus bypassing the banks, other than for settlements.

Possible risks

Forged or unauthorised payment instructions

It is possible, although rare, for the payment instruction to be forged or unauthorised, and the same rules apply to a forged signature on a CHAPs instruction as for a cheque. Hence, the rules previously discussed in *Catlin* v *Cyprus Finance Corporation* (1983), and s.24 Bills of Exchange Act 1882 (this applies only to bills or cheques, of course) will also apply to CHAPS instructions and so an instruction bearing a forged signature cannot be debited to the payer's account.

Ambiguous instructions

The items expected to be included in the payment instruction have been listed above. However, it is possible that the instructions could be ambiguous as to the amount or payee and if the paying bank makes an incorrect assumption it could theoretically be at risk.

Customer mistakes

It is possible that a mistake by the customer could lead to an incorrect payment being made.

Payment made for an amount different from that authorised

It is possible for this to occur either by mistake or by fraudulent alteration.

Payment delayed

As previously mentioned, CHAPS is meant to be a same-day- payment service and it is for this reason that banks will accept instructions up to only one hour prior to the 3.00 pm deadline imposed by CHAPS.

Fraud

There are two main types of fraud that could affect banks and CHAPS. The first is fraud by a bank employee and the second by an outside source (for example, a computer 'hacker').

Breach of duty of care

The banks have a duty to the customer to exercise due care when acting on his behalf. When applied to CHAPS this is thought to mean that the bank must ensure that all security precautions are adhered to. The system has a number of 'built-in' security measures and these include the use of codes and passwords for the payment or receipt of funds. The main concern in this area must once again be fraud and the liability of a bank not taking sufficient steps to prevent the fraudulent alteration of a message or the fraudulent instruction of a bank.

Possible protections

Against forged or unauthorised instructions

As previously mentioned, a forged signature is no signature and the only protection available to a paying bank that acts on a forged instruction is estoppel: *Greenwood* v *Martins Bank* (1933) or *London Joint Stock Bank* v *Macmillan & Arthur* (1918) (both in respect of a breach of duty by the customer) or *Brown* v *Westminster Bank Ltd* (1964) in respect of a misleading statement by the customer. Estoppel has been discussed fully in Chapter ten.

Against ambiguous instructions

Since the bank is acting merely as an agent for the customer, then the bank may rely upon *Westminster Bank* v *Hilton* (1926) (see 'countermanded cheques' in Chapter ten) or *Broom* v *Hall* (1859), both of which state that where the instruction is ambiguous and the agent makes a reasonable interpretation of it, then no liability will rest on the agent, as he should have been supplied with a precise, unambiguous mandate.

Against customer mistake

If the customer discovers a mistake in the underlying transaction (for example, the purchase of equipment, for which the CHAPs instruction is the financial payment), this does not invalidate the secondary transaction (ie, the CHAPS instruction): *Pollard* v *Bank of England* (1871). Hence, the CHAPs transaction will still be valid between all parties to it.

Against amount transferred differing from that in the original instruction

The protections available against mistake have been discussed above.

Against delay of payment

Since CHAPS is meant to be a same-day-payment system, the banks have attempted to protect themselves by placing a 2.00 pm deadline on all outgoing CHAPS transactions. However, even if the bank were for some reason (eg, system malfunction, heavy workload) unable to take action on the instruction on the day of receipt, it would still be protected by *Hare* v *Henty* (1861), which stated that the obligation of the paying bank is merely to act expeditiously (promptly) in carrying out its customer's mandate.

Against fraud

If the fraud is committed by the bank's employee, then it is unlikely that the bank will be able to avoid liability: *Lloyd* v *Grace & Co* (1912). The same is thought to be true of a contractor (eg, computer engineer) engaged to fulfil a contract. However, should the fraud originate from outside the bank, then it is thought that the bank would be protected as long as it had acted with reasonable care and provided an adequate security system. Obviously one interpretation of 'adequate' would be whether or not the system contained the up-to-date technology necessary to defeat computer crime.

■ Summary of BACS and CHAPS

Although both systems have their similarities it is important that you remember their differences. Both systems naturally have a payer and a payee and the equivalent of a paying bank and a collecting bank and the rights and duties of these are basically the same as the rights and duties in dealing with cheques (see Chapter ten). However, CHAPS is wholly computer-based and as such much quicker (same day), whilst BACS is still quite time-consuming but is designed to handle a greater volume of lower-value transactions than could ever be handled by CHAPS. The legal problems and protections are again similar both to each other and to cheques.

The main difference between BACS and CHAPS is the **guarantee** of same day payment under CHAPS. Hence, once payment has passed through the 'gateway' it is deemed to be both received by the beneficiary and rendered uncancellable by the payer. However, BACS is seen by most as an electronic credit transfer system and as such the time of settlement is not quite as black and white, with a sensible, rather than statute- or case law-supported, view being taken.

FACT SHEET

Direct debits and credits (including BACS and CHAPS)

Direct debits
General – meaning of a direct debit, whether paper – or BACS – based, cancellation of mandate and wrongful payment.
Credit transfers
General – meaning, when is payment effective? (with cases), defective title of beneficiary (forged signature, illegal consideration, mistake, misrepresentation) and protections (estoppel, mistake of fact, s.4 Cheques Act 1957. *Cundy* v *Lindsay* and *Babcock* v *Lawson*).

BACS
Method of operation and procedures (typical transactions, amounts and time taken). Time delays and consequences.

CHAPS
Method of operation and procedures (minimum amount and types of transactions, guaranteed same-day-payment). Possible risks (forgery, ambiguity, mistake, amount difference, delay in payment, fraud, breach of duty of care) and protections (estoppel, *Westminster Bank* v *Hilton*, *Broom* v *Hall*; *Pollard* v *Bank of England*; *Hare* v *Plenty*; *Lloyd* v *Grace & Co*), keeping abreast of technological developments.

Question

Briefly describe the operation of CHAPS and BACS transactions. When is a CHAPS transaction considered complete and irrevocable? How, if at all, does this differ from a BACS transaction?

(20 marks)

Key words

briefly describe operation, when CHAPS complete and irrevocable, how differ from BACS

Answer

(a) CHAPS operates as follows:

- the payer will instruct his bank to make the payment (unless he is a member of the system himself – unlikely, but possible). The payment must be at least £5,000 and must be advised to the bank before 3.00 pm
- his bank will debit his account with the stated sum
- his bank, known as the settlement bank, will pass the payment through a concentrator, known as a 'gateway'
- the beneficiary's bank (payee bank) will credit the beneficiary's account and issue a Logical Acknowledgement to the settlement bank
- the financial settlement will be made between the banks centrally at 4.30 pm on the same day.

The main aim of CHAPS is to provide a wholly electronic same-day guaranteed payment system for large one-off transactions. Once the message has been passed through the gateway it is deemed to be effective and is irrevocable. The basic rule from *Warlow* v *Harrison* (1859), that a bank's customer is committed to a transaction at the same moment as his banker, holds firm with electronic transactions, in that as the paying bank cannot reclaim the transaction once passed through the gateway then neither can the payer. If the payee bank holds the funds, but as yet has not credited the payee's account, the payment is still deemed complete. The crediting of the account is looked upon as a purely administrative step; *Royal Products Ltd* v *Midland Bank Ltd* (1981). Also, it is not necessary, in order to make payment complete, to inform the payee of receipt of funds; *Momm* v *Barclays Bank International Ltd* (1977).

However, there are possible problems connected with ambiguous instructions, fraud and mistakes. The basic rules are:

(i)   ambiguous instructions – the principal (payer) has a duty to supply his agent (the bank) with a precise mandate, and if he supplies the bank with an ambiguous instruction, and the bank interprets it reasonably, but incorrectly, the primary responsibility will be with the payer;

(ii) if the transaction is a forgery the bank has no authority to debit its customer's account; *Catlin* v *Cyprus Finance Corporation* (1983). If the transaction has already passed through the gateway then the CHAPS transaction is irrevocable and as such the paying bank will have to attempt to recover the money from either the beneficiary or his bankers. Another possible defence could include estoppel (see *Greenwood* v *Martins Bank* (1933) or *Brown* v *Westminster Bank* (1964);

(iii) where payment is made by mistake of fact then it is possible to reclaim the monies as per *Barclays Bank* v *W. J. Simms, Son and Cooke (Southern) Ltd* (1980). This does not revoke the original CHAPS payment: the reclaiming of the funds (or those still held by the beneficiary) is a separate transaction in its own right.

(b) BACS is a partially electronic payment system designed to cope with a high volume of individually small transfers (either debits such as direct debits, or credits such as salary payments).

The system operates as follows:

- the originator (the beneficiary if debits, the payer if credits) supplies his banker or BACS direct with an electronic tape of payments
- this tape is then run by BACS and each branch of each bank involved will receive a computer listing of the transactions involving accounts held at that branch
- the debit (or credit) is usually passed through the account named by the originator on the third day (including the day of receipt) following receipt, with the originator's account receiving a corresponding entry on the same day
- the financial settlement is made between the banks centrally.

As the whole process takes three days, it is this processing time that is the main difference between CHAPS and BACS and which leads to the most common cause of dispute in BACS transactions: 'when is payment actually made?' As mentioned above, the payer is committed to the payment at the same time as his bank; *Warlow* v *Harrison* (1859). Payment is deemed to be made when it is irrevocable, that is it cannot be cancelled by the payer. As a BACS transaction can either be a 'pull' transaction (eg a direct debit payment) or a 'push' transaction (eg a salary credit) the method of revocation is important. In the context of the question there would be little benefit in the originator (beneficiary) of a direct debit cancelling payment; this would normally be done by the payer, and banking practice is that such a cancellation is accepted up to (and including) the day of payment. With a credit payment, the revocation is likely to come from the originator (payer), not the beneficiary. The payment can be recalled by the originator any time during the three day cycle. However, once the credit has been placed to the beneficiary's account the transaction is deemed complete and any action for recovery will need to be between the originator and the beneficiary via other channels (eg through the courts).

CHAPTER 12

Automated tellers and EFTPOS systems

Syllabus requirements
- Description of the available systems.
- The effects of fraud, systems failure and error.
- The duties and rights of customers (third party beneficiaries, if applicable) and banks.

■ Introduction

As you should be aware, the area of automated tellers, also known as auto-teller machines or, for ease, ATMs, is one of great competition amongst banks, with each bank varying the wording on its claims to appear the most impressive. For example, 'the bank with the greatest proportion of branches with ATMs' or 'the bank with the highest number of ATMs per branch' and 'the bank with the highest number of ATMs'. All of this of course is totally irrelevant except to serve to show the public the emphasis that banks now place on what is termed ATM penetration, that is, the number of transactions via the ATMs as a percentage of the transactions conducted over the counter. Once you realise that transactions conveyed by ATMs cost substantially less than those done over the counter (after allowing for staff training, time and other costs) you will see why the banks place such importance on this ratio.

Further recent developments include:

(a) **Reciprocity**. (a word which, to me, is totally unpronounceable. I have to write it on the board during lessons and let one of the bright sparks at the front pronounce it!) It means one bank allowing another bank's customers to use its ATMs in return for its customers using the other bank's ATMs. As far as I am aware, the largest such agreement is one between the Midland, National Westminster and TSB, referred to as MINT (a bit of poetic licence I think!).

(b) **Telephone banking**. This again is one of the main competitive areas amongst the banks, with each striving to be the first on the market with a fully-electronic home banking service. Most banks now have a telephone banking service in one form or another. One of the main areas of difference is whether the system is voice-activated (ie, the 'customer' talking to the computer and the computer reacting to his voice and complying with his instructions, say, to transfer funds from one account to another), or electronically activated, the customer having to place a tone-pad over the mouth piece of the phone and certain numbers representing a certain transaction. For example, 05 meaning to pay a bill and when this is followed by 13 then the 'customer' is telling the computer to pay his credit card bill, and he will then proceed to tell the computer how much to pay and when. Another main area of difference is the level of service offered by the telephone banker; for example, most offer transfer of funds from one account to another, payment of regular bills by the customer providing the recipient's bank details beforehand, and the ability to request a statement to be posted. However as the systems become more advanced, further facilities are being placed on them, such as applying for a loan/overdraft, requesting an immediate statement by fax; (this is quite impressive for the customer as the statement can appear in front of the customer whilst he is actually on the phone to the computer), or checking whether a particular cheque has been presented. No doubt many other facilities will evolve in time. Many of the facilities described above are also, of course, available on ATMs, for example, bill payment systems and transfers.

(c) **EFTPOS** stands for Electronic Funds Transfer at Point Of Sale. EFTPOS has always been viewed as a very futuristic payment system but recent advancements are now bringing it further into the realms of possibility. In essence the 'customer' would arrive at the payment counter with his goods and, instead of writing out a cheque or using a credit card (or even that out-moded method of payment known as cash), will produce an EFTPOS card. After being satisfied with the identity of the bearer the cashier will 'swipe' the card through an amazing electronic device, the retailer will enter the amount and the 'customer' will then enter his personal identification number (PIN). The 'customer's' bank account will be debited and the retailer's account, regardless of where he banks, will be credited, at present, within 24 to 48 hours. It is hoped to reduce this time period in the future. One of the main advantages to banks is again one of costs, because a purely electronic system is substantially less expensive than the incredible number of items being processed by the clearing system at present. As previously stated, the system is not yet fully operational in this country, although a number of experimental systems have been set up with isolated retailers (usually petrol stations) and have been moderately successful. The system is fully operational in a number of European countries (mainly in Scandinavia) and the Scandinavian system has been adopted by many as their role model.

As you can imagine, each of the above systems has its own legal complexities, but they all tend to fall into the same categories:

(i) When is a payment made, accepted and irrevocable?
(ii) What are the rights and duties of the customer, recipient (the retailer), the creditor (in a bill payment system) and the banks under an EFTPOS system?
(iii) What are the effects of fraud (possibly by the customer, bank employees, installers of the system or other third parties), system failure and error?

As you can imagine, as each system is relatively new on the banking scene there is one statute that deals solely with electronic banking and much of the discussion will take the form of interpreting existing statute and case law and trying to apply their terms or decisions to this new topic.

▌ Details of the available systems

When is a payment made, when is it accepted and when does it become irrevocable?

In general the principal is committed to the transaction as soon as his agent is committed to it: *Warlow* v *Harrison* (1859). In the transaction of an electronic funds transfer, this means that the customer (the principal) is committed as soon as the bank (the agent) is committed to make the payment to the retailer or creditor. As we have already seen in the previous chapter, payment under CHAPS becomes irrevocable when the message is passed through the 'gateway' and the appropriate acknowledgement is sent. However, in *Re Chargecard Services Ltd* (1986), a full discussion of the parties to a credit card transaction was undertaken. The facts of the case are that the card holder used the card to pay for petrol. Unfortunately, the card company became insolvent and the petrol station tried to claim the funds from the card holder. The court held that **absolute payment** by the card holder was made upon the completion of the contract by the card holder, and as such the petrol station could not claim repayment off the card holder, but had to prove in the insolvency of the card issuing company. It was held that there were basically two contracts here: (a) the acceptance of the card conditions in return for the goods; (b) the guarantee by the card company to pay the supplier.

This case is thought to apply equally to EFTPOS transactions with the secondary contract being between the bank and the supplier.

Rights and duties of the parties concerned

Duties of the paying bank

(a) The basic duty of the bank making the payment, be it to the customer direct via an ATM, or to a third party beneficiary through either EFTPOS or some form of bill payment facility, is that the payment must be made in accordance with the customer's mandate: *Joachimson* v *Swiss Bank Corporation* (1924). The case is described in full detail in Chapter one and if you are not familiar with the case I suggest that you refer to the chapter. If the bank pays an amount other than the amount quoted, or pays to someone other than the intended beneficiary, then the customer will be able to seek recompense from the bank.

Also, if the customer's instruction be forged, or unauthorised (eg, forged cheque or similarly forged EFTPOS transaction), then the bank has no mandate with which to debit its customer's account: *Orr* v *Union Bank* (1854).

(b) The bank must warn the customer of the dangers of handing over his ATM card to an untrustworthy person, who by watching the customer key in his PIN, could himself gain access to the customer's account: *Ognibene* v *Citibank* (1981). In this case the customer was requested to hand the card to a third party and was informed that he was acting on the instruction of the bank to test the system. Unfortunately, the third party was a criminal and, having previously memorised the customer's PIN, withdrew £400 from the customer's account. The decision was reached after the court had taken into account a number of recent similar cases and felt that the bank had a 'notional' duty to inform its customers of the risks involved. It is a topic for discussion as to whether or not a similar decision would be reached in today's climate, without the unusual precedent of a number of similar, recent cases. No doubt time will tell.

(c) The bank has a duty to act with an expected level of skill, the level being that of a reasonably competent banker acting in accordance with the accepted current practice: *Selangor United Rubber Estates Ltd* v *Craddock (No. 3)* (1968). You will notice that there is nothing exceptional in the standard of skill expected. This is basically a constructive trustee case but the principle applies to any banking transaction. The bank was found to be negligent for not enquiring into the circumstances behind a large cheque drawn payable to a company, endorsed and deposited into Craddock's account, followed by a large withdrawal on Craddock's account. It was held that the bank had not acted in a manner expected of a reasonably competent banker and should have enquired from the company's directors about the origins of the cheque and not merely accepted Craddock's explanation.

(d) The bank may incur liability on the s.75 CCA 1974 which attaches to a debtor/creditor/supplier transaction and results in the creditor having joint and several liability for the breach of contract or misrepresentation of the supplier. However, there are exceptions: • charge cards – as the card holder does not obtain credit (he must settle the balance in one payment); • debit cards – the Banking Act 1987 gives protection to electronically-based transactions. Debit cards are sufficiently electronic to qualify for this exception.

(e) The bank has a duty to ensure that it engages a fully effective security system. This means that it is essential that the banks remain 'one step ahead' of the criminal fraternity, and that they are constantly researching areas of improvement of electronic security to ensure that their systems are not easily accessible to anyone without their customers' consent.

(f) The paying bank has a duty to accept a notice countermanding payment up to the time that the payment is actually made. As discussed previously, a CHAPS payment is complete when the relevant acknowledgement is received, and other electronic payments are complete apparently when the bank is committed to the payments. Therefore, up to such time as described above, the bank must 'stop' the payment if requested to do so by the customer: *Morrell* v *Wooton* (1852). Naturally, once the stop instruction has been received it must be complied with.

Duties of the customer

(a) A relevant case is *London Joint Stock Bank* v *Macmillan and Arthur* (1918), which underlined the fact that the customer has a duty to draw his cheques in such a way as not to facilitate fraud. It is thought that the customer will have a similar duty with either ATM or EFTPOS transactions, ie, he will be expected to act in such a way as not easily to facilitate fraudulent use of the ATM or EFTPOS system. One example of a breach of this duty is thought to be the storage of the card and the Personal Identification Number (PIN) together. The rationale behind this line of thought is that if the two were kept separate, then individually they could be of no possible benefit to the thief or anyone else into whose possession they might fall. However, if they are kept together and stolen, the 'thief' will have access to the computer system and the customer's account.

(b) As previously discussed in Chapter three, s.84(1) Consumer Credit Act 1974 (as amended by the Consumer Credit [Increase in Monetary Amounts] Order 1983) states that if the customer should lose his credit card he is liable for the first £50 of any loss suffered by the credit card company. Under the same legislation the customer is also liable for the first £50 of any loss suffered by the bank on an ATM/EFTPOS transaction due to the revealing of the PIN by the customer. Also underlined in Code of Banking Practice.

(c) There is usually an express term in the ATM/EFTPOS contract between the customer and the bank that the customer will keep his PIN secret. Any breach of this duty will render the customer liable for any loss incurred by the bank due to misuse of the card.

Additional rights of the paying bank

(a) As previously discussed in Chapter ten, the paying bank has the right of recovery from the receiving bank or beneficiary if the loss was due to a mistake of fact: *Barclays Bank* v *W. J. Simms, and Son and Cooke (Southern) Ltd* (1980). Although this is essentially a countermanded cheque case, it is thought that exactly the same principles will apply to an ATM/EFTPOS transaction, in that if the payment is made to a wrong person (due solely to a mistake of fact, not a mistake of law) the paying bank will be able to reclaim the amount of the payment from either the receiving bank or the recipient. However, the paying bank will be able to claim only the balance of the payment remaining undrawn in the recipient's account: *National Westminster Bank Ltd* v *Barclays Bank International Ltd* (1975).

(b) We have also previously discussed the effect of estoppel on the relationship between the paying bank and the customer in Chapter ten. You should recall (and if not, you should read again the relevant section) that there are two examples of estoppel enabling the paying bank to enforce a transaction against the customer despite the absence of his consnet or authorisation. The two instances are (i) where there is a misleading statement from the customer: *Greenwood* v *Martins Bank* (1933); (ii) where there is a breach of duty owed by the customer: *Brown* v *Westminster Bank* (1964). It is possible for the bank to use estoppel in ATM/EFTPOS disputes in a similar way to cheque disputes. For example the permitted use of an ATM card by a relative could not later be contested if the relative should exceed the amount of the agreed withdrawal.

Effect of the Unfair Contract Terms Act 1977 on ATM/EFTPOS transactions

The main aim of the introduction of the Unfair Contract Terms Act 1977 is to introduce the concept of 'reasonableness' into contracts between parties especially where one party is in a stronger bargaining position than the other (for example, lender/borrower where the borrower is in need of money, and landlord/tenant where the tenant is in need of accommodation). For a contract to be enforceable it will now be necessary for each individual clause to pass the test of 'reasonableness', which is defined in s.11 of the Act, as

> 'the term shall have been a fair and reasonable one to be included having regard to the circumstances which were, or ought reasonably to have been, known to, or in the contemplation of, the parties when the contract was made'.

Where there is a dispute as to the reasonableness of the clause, the onus of proof will fall on the bank. In a recent case (*Tai Hing Cotton Ltd* v *Liu Chong Hing Bank Ltd* (1985)) the bank wrote into its contract with its customer that the customer had to check the bank's statements, and report to the bank any disputed transactions, and, furthermore, to sign a slip confirming that the statement was correct. The clause was not contested under the Unfair Contract Terms Act 1977 but no doubt if it had been it would have been deemed 'unreasonable', taking away the customer's previously held rights under *Wealden Woodlands (Kent) Ltd* v *National Westminster Bank Ltd* (1983). The bank cannot place any unreasonable terms in the contract for EFTPOS/ATM facilities which would not pass the test of s.11 as discussed above. Possible items which would almost certainly be dismissed as unreasonable would be the customer accepting sole liability even if the bank had been negligent (or indeed fraudulent), the customer being unable to contest any ATM/EFTPOS transaction on his account and the customer being liable for an unlimited financial amount in the event of the misuse of the card by another due to fraud.

What are the effects of fraud, system failure and error?

Fraud

In relation to electronic funds transfer, a fraud has been defined as

> 'an unauthorised instruction, alteration of the account to which an entry is to be made or alteration of the amount of the entry'

(from United Nations Commission on International Trade Law 1984–85, known as UNCITRAL). There are a number of possible types of fraud including fraud by either the bank's or the customer's employees, or by any other third party.

Instances of fraud could include a fraudulent bank clerk accessing the customer's account using information gained from an interview with the customer or from information held at branch level (the latter being most unlikely), an untrustworthy employee of the customer using information gained during normal working practice (PIN's, cypher codes etc.) in order to process unauthorised transactions for his own benefit, or a criminal third party gaining access to the customer's account by fooling the customer into divulging his PIN to the criminal (as per *Ognibene* v *Citibank* (1981), discussed in full above), unauthorised use of the card and PIN following a breach in the customer's duty to keep his PIN confidential, or fraudulent access to the communication system (by a probably unconnected third party) by, say, intercepting and changing the message.

As there are many different types of fraud, so the reactions and liabilities also vary. One of the main points to bear in mind is that the burden of proof will lie with the person making the claim. So, if the customer is accusing an employee of the bank of fraud then there must be a level of proof which leaves no doubt as to the identity of the fraudster. Mere suspicion is not sufficient and neither is the lack of other possibilities (for example: 'It wasn't me, so it must have been him'). The burden of proof will be coupled with an examination of the duties of each party before the courts will make their decision. If one party is in breach of one or more duties, then this will usually be the main guiding factor in the courts coming to their decision. For example, has the employer made the fraud easy by allowing the employee access to certain information, (possible similarities with the *London JSB* v *Macmillan & Arthur* (1918) decision) or has the bank not installed a sufficiently sophisticated security system making the entry into the system by the 'hacker' far too easy?

It is feasible for the party found responsible for the fraud to be able to make a claim of contributory negligence, as per *Lumsden & Co* v *London Trustee Savings Bank* (1971), in an attempt to reduce the damages awarded, where it is felt that the incident was partly facilitated by the negligence of the other party. In the above case, the damages awarded were reduced by 10 per cent when the way that the altered cheque was later completed by the customer was taken into account.

Finally, under s.84 Consumer Credit Act 1974 (as amended by the Consumer Credit [Increase in Amounts] Order 1983) the customer is liable for the first £50 of any misuse of the ATM card where the misuse is due to the loss of the PIN by the customer.

System failure

In the possible instance of the customer suffering financially due to an ATM or EFTPOS system failure, the customer may well seek recompense from the bank. The question raised will be 'can the bank avoid the claim, or can it pass the settlement of the claim onto another party?'

The first point of reference will be the formal contract between the banker and his customer and the express and implied terms in the contract (see Chapter one, especially *Joachimson* v *Swiss Bank Corporation* (1921), and the effect of express terms). Obviously any express terms will need to pass the 'reasonableness' test as per the Unfair Contract Terms Act 1977 discussed above.

If it can be established that the loss should have been reasonably foreseeable (*Hadley* v *Baxendale* (1854)) and that negligence by a third party (for example, software manufacturers, installation company) was present, then a claim can be made against the third party providing there is also sufficient proximity between the parties: *Junior Books Ltd* v *The Veitchi Co Ltd*, (1982).

Error

In essence a payment made under a mistake of fact (for example, payment to the wrong person, payment of a countermanded transaction) can be recovered from the collecting bank or the beneficiary *Barclays Bank* v *W. J. Simms, Son & Cooke (Southern) Ltd* (1979), up to the extent of the funds remaining in the beneficiary's account. The mistake itself must be a fundamental mistake; a mistake between the payer (paying bank) and payee (beneficiary) and cause the payment to be made: *Aiken* v *Short* (1856). However, there are exceptions to this rule that would prevent recovery under mistake of fact. These would include, for example, where the payment has been passed on by an agent to this principal, the payment can be recovered only from the principal: *National Westminster Bank Ltd* v *Barclays Bank International & Ismail* (1975). The bank could be estopped from retrieving the payment, the estoppel requiring a representation other than the actual payment. If the benficiary has relied upon the representation and changed his position, the bank will be unable to reclaim the monies: *Lloyds Bank Ltd* v *Brooks* (1950). In *United Overseas Bank* v *Jiwani* (1976), the beneficiary failed to prove that he had changed his position as a result of the mistake. There is an easier form of estoppel available which requires no representation other than the actual payment *Cocks* v *Masterman* (1829); however this form of estoppel is available only to negotiable instruments and as ATM or Electronic Funds Transfer (EFT) transactions are not negotiable instruments, this defence will not apply.

In conclusion, for an erroneous payment to be reclaimed under a mistake of fact the payment must be made: (i) not in accordance with the mandate; (ii) the mistake must be one of fact, not law; (iii) the mistake must have caused the payment to be made; (iv) if payment has been made to an agent and passed on to his principal the payment can be reclaimed only from the principal; and (v) the beneficiary must not be able to claim estoppel.

■ Other sundry EFT/ATM transactions

Cheque truncation

Cheque truncation is a method of reducing the amount of paper and time consumed in the current cheque clearance procedures. Basically, the information is gathered centrally (either at the collectin bank's branch or the clearing centre) and passed electronically to the paying bank. At present this system is used by some banks between their own branches and it is possible that it will eventually be extended to branches of other banks as well. It would require the customers' consent before the system could be extended to include all other banks.

The possible cost savings could be substantial and it is mainly this reason that is leading the banks to investigate this process further. However, there is much discussion as to whether or not the paying bank and/or collecting bank would lose their statutory protection under the Bills of Exchange Act 1882 or Cheques Act 1957 due to the inclusion of conditions such as 'ordinary course of business', 'duly presented for payment' etc. It is thought that the most preferred method of introduction would be by legislation.

USA Electronic Funds Transfer Act 1978

Much of the ambiguity of the current legal position involving EFTPOS ATMS and, to a certain degree CHAPS and other items discussed in the previous chapter, is due to the lack of specific legislation and also to a lack of relevant case law. The situation is not the same in the USA, since the above statute was introduced; the procedures are strictly governed and all persons involved have a set of rules and guidelines to fall back on. For example, s.909 of this Act states that a consumer is liable for an unauthorised EFT transaction only if the card is used with the PIN (or equivalent). The loss is limited to fifty dollars if the report is made to the relevant body within two days of the loss of the card, or of the unauthorised transaction, or to five hundred dollars if the loss is reported within two to sixty days. Such legislation would be most welcome and is much needed in this country.

The Jack report

This report, discussed in Chapter 1, was commissioned to investigate the banker/customer relationship. One of the main recommendations of the report was the introduction of regulatory codes applying to electronic banking transactions. The Jack report prefers codes to statute due to the rapid changes seen in this area, and this approach is surely correct. The areas for regulation are quoted as countermand of payment, completion of payment and access to funds. However, the report does threaten that if the codes of practice are not effective, then legislation in the form of statute will be introduced.

FACT SHEET

Automated teller machines and EFTPOS systems

Introduction
Types of systems, reasons for development.

When is payment made, accepted and irrevocable?
Principal bound when the agent is: *Warlow* v *Harrison* (1859). *Re Chargecard Services Ltd.*

Rights and duties of parties involved
(a) Duties of paying bank. Compliance with mandate: *Joachimson* v *Swiss Bank Corporation*, to warn customer against handing card and PIN to stranger *Ognibene* v *Citibank* (1981) (is it relevant under normal circumstances?), to act with reasonable level of skill: *Selangor United Rubber Estates Ltd* v *Craddock* (what level is expected?), s.75 CCA liability to implement fully effective security system, act on countermand up to time of payment.

(b) Duties of customer: *London JSB* v *Macmillan & Arthur*, to act in such a way as not to facilitate fraud, s.84(1) CCA, customer liable for first £50 if due to loss of PIN, to keep PIN secret (usually an express term).

(c) Rights of paying bank. Recovering under mistake of fact: *Barclays* v *W J. Simms* etc., *Nat West* v *Barclays International*, estoppel: *Greenwood* v *Martins Banks* – breach of duty by customer, *Brown* v *Westminster Bank* – contrary declaration).

(d) Unfair Contract Terms Act 1977 and ATM/EFTPOS – test of 'reasonableness' – *Tai Hing's* case.

Effect of fraud, system failure and error
(a) Fraud – definition (source UNCITRAL) and examples. Onus of proof and breach of duty. Possible claim of contributory negligence: *Lumsden & Co* v *London TSB*.

(b) System failure – firstly refer to contract. Can recompense be claimed from a third party? (examples), conditions – reasonably foreseeable: *Hadley* v *Baxendale*, negligence and sufficient proximity: *Junior Books Ltd* v *The Veitchi Co Ltd* (1982).

(c) Error – conditions for recovery, mistake of fact: *Barclays* v *W. J. Simms* etc, not in accordance with mandate, mistake caused payment to be made, only claimable from principal, beneficiary unable to claim estoppel. Also, if beneficiary relied upon a representation from bank and changed his position then the funds cannot be reclaimed: *United Overseas Bank* v *Jiwani*.

Other matters
(a) Cheque truncation – description, reason and possible drawbacks (loss of protection).

(b) USA Electronic Funds Transfer Act 1978 – removes the ambiguity and 'limbo' situation that is present in this country. Such legislation is needed here.

(c) Jack report – Recommends 'codes of conduct' for regulating electronic banking, with threat of statute if necessary.

Question

(a) When would a bank be liable, to the customer, following the obtaining of cash from the bank's ATM by the unauthorised use of the customer's ATM card? (14 marks)
(b) What duties does the customer owe to the bank to prevent such an occurrence? (6 marks)

Total 20 marks

Key words

(a) when liable to customer, unauthorised use ATM card
(b) duties customer owe prevent occurrence

Answer

(a) This question deals with the bank's duty to comply with its customer's mandate and the rights of the bank against the customer in certain situations. The basic principle is that if the customer has not used the card then the bank does not have a mandate to debit the account. However, the bank has a number of defences which may enable it to enforce the transaction against the customer. These are:

 (i) the customer was aware of previous unauthorised transactions and did not inform the bank. In these circumstances the customer may well be estopped from denying the genuineness of the transaction: *Greenwood* v *Martins Bank* (1933);
 (ii) the customer has not kept his PIN secret or has been careless in keeping his PIN and card together;
 (iii) the customer has, by way of his conduct, given his implied consent to the transaction;
 (iv) the customer may be liable for the first £50 of any third-party transaction either by a specific clause in the card mandate, or by s.84 Consumer Credit Act 1974. If the transaction was authorised by the customer (and the authority abused) the customer's upper liability limit of £50 will not apply.

However, the bank will *not* be able to enforce the transaction where:
- the bank has failed to implement a suitable security system
- the bank fails to act with a 'reasonable' level of skill: *Selangor United Rubber Estates Ltd* v *Craddock* (1968)
- the bank fails to act upon a valid countermand instruction (whether by telephone or in writing). All banks must provide an address and telephone number at which card holders can advise the bank of theft or loss of cards; s.84(4) Consumer Credit Act 1974
- the customer can prove that the fraud was committed by an employee of the bank, or a sub-contractor employed by the bank (eg an outside contractor repairing computer equipment), as a direct result of information gained from his employment. The onus of proof is on the customer and mere suspicion or lack of alternatives will not be sufficient. Following a number of frauds in which the customer had disclosed his PIN to a third party it was held in an American case (*Ognibene* v *Citbank* (1981)) that the bank had a duty to inform the customer not to disclose his PIN to any other party. However, whether such a duty would be enforceable against a British banker without a history of previous frauds is thought to be unlikely.

(b) The duties owed to the bank by the customer to prevent such a fraud are:

 (i) by an express clause in the account mandate or request for a card the customer undertakes that he will not disclose his personal identification number to any other party. It is this clause that is the first line of defence for most banks faced with a 'phantom', or disputed ATM withdrawal;
 (ii) the customer has a duty to act in such a way so as to not facilitate fraud: *London Joint Stock Bank* v *Macmillan & Arthur* (1918);
 (iii) the customer must inform the bank as soon as he becomes aware of fraud on his account: *Greenwood* v *Martins Bank* (1933);
 (iv) under s.84(i) Consumer Credit Act 1974 (as increased by Consumer Credit (Increase in Monetary Amounts) Order 1983), the customer is liable for the first £50 of any loss incurred by the bank due to the customer revealing his PIN to another party.

CHAPTER 13

General securities

Syllabus requirements
- Bank's duty on taking security from individuals (<u>undue influence</u>), standard terms in bank security documents and the special considerations where a mortgage or guarantee secures current account borrowing.

■ Introduction

The aim of this chapter is to give a basic introduction to securities and provide you with a foundation and point of reference for the more difficult areas to follow. In this chapter we will discuss why banks take their security on standard forms, what duties a bank incurs when taking security, the difference between legal and equitable charges and between direct and third party security and the special problems associated with lending on a running current account.

■ Parties to a security transaction

Principal Debtor

This is the person to whom the money is lent, the customer.

Creditor

This is the institution lending the money, as far as we are concerned, the bank.

Mortgagor

This is the person who signs the bank's legal charge form, and will always be the owner of the security. If the mortgagor is not a debtor then the security taken will be known as 'third party' (see below). An example would be <u>where the bank's security is a property owned by husband and wife</u> and the bank is lending only to the husband, or where the security is a life policy on the husband with the wife as the beneficiary and the bank is lending to the husband.

Mortgagee

Where a facility is secured the creditor is also known as the mortgagee.

Guarantor/surety

A guarantor is the person who gives the guarantee, ie, the person who promises to repay the creditor should the principal debtor fail to do so. He is also sometimes known as the 'surety' and this term is used to describe a third party mortgagor, who is not a principal debtor.

Generally, if you find yourself struggling to remember which party is the mortgagor and which is the mortgagee, one easy method of remembering this is:

The mortgagOR is the 'ownOR' (sic) of the security;
the mortgagEE is the 'trustEE' savings bank'.

Standard bank security forms

The standard security form has evolved over many years (in most cases, over centuries) into the form we all use today. Each time a bank loses money on a point that could have been avoided with the insertion of a clause in the form, the form is altered and that additional protective clause inserted. At this stage it would be helpful if you could obtain a specimen security form from either your branch security clerk or from your centralised securities department; you will then be able to read the form and confirm for yourself the existence of the clauses I shall discuss below.

Continuing security

This clause is inserted with the sole intention of enabling the security to cover all future advances and thus overcome the rule in *Clayton's Case (Devaynes* v *Noble* (1816)), see Chapter two). Without this clause any future credits to the account would reduce the amount secured/guaranteed and any further advances (or debits) would be new debts and not covered.

All moneys clause

The charge covers all moneys owing to the mortgagee (the bank) by the mortgagor (the 'owner' of the security and the person who signs the charge form) including all accounts, interest and any expenses incurred in the perfection of the security. The clause also prevents the mortgagor proving in the insolvency of the principal debtor, or claiming subrogation or repayment from the principal debtor unless the debt has been repaid in full.

Repayable on demand clause

Under s.2(1) Limitation Act 1980 no action can be taken on a simple contract unless such an action is taken within six years of the date of the cause for the action. The insertion of the repayable on demand clause means that the 'cause for the action' is the serving of a formal demand for repayment: *Bradford Old Bank* v *Sutcliffe* (1918). Without the insertion of the clause the six-year period will start to run from the granting of the loan as in *Parr's Banking Company* v *Yates* (1898).

Preclusion of Clayton's Case *clause*

This clause is a direct preclusion of the rule in *Clayton's Case*. The effect of this clause is that if the bank does not stop the debit account when it should have done (for example, on determination of guarantee by guarantor) the bank will still be able to claim the full amount of the debt outstanding as in *Westminster Bank* v *Cond* (1940).

Guarantor/mortgagor to remain liable despite change in the constitution or principal debtor or bank

The reason for this clause is self-evident in that the intention is to protect the bank should the principal debtor change in constitution (for example, from joint to sole account, or if trustees should alter) or the bank may do likewise (for example, Trustee Savings Bank forming a PLC, or the change of Williams and Glyn's to Royal Bank of Scotland). Thus, despite a change in constitution of either party, the mortgagor/ guarantor will still be liable.

Laws applicable

In almost every situation the bank will state in its charge form that the security will be subject to the law as it applies in England and Wales. Hence a foreign national will be unable to claim that he thought he signed the guarantee under the law of his own country.

Consideration

As you should be aware, most contracts need to be supported by consideration. However, one of the main exceptions is a contract executed under seal, and it is normal for banks to execute their security under seal. It is not necessary for a contract to be supported by consideration in every case, for example, guarantees and memoranda of deposit. In these forms there will be a clause stating that the consideration will be 'affording bank accommodation . . . time/credit . . . continuing the account.' So the main problem of taking new or additional security to secure an existing account without lending any further monies will be overcome by this clause.

There are also specific clauses which apply to individual forms, for example, guarantees and charges over land, these will be discussed fully in Chapters fifteen and sixteen respectively.

▌ Legal or equitable charge?

Before discussing the relative merits of each type of charge it is important that you understand the difference between the two types of charge. The basic difference (and the one which leads to all the others) is that with an equitable charge the title to the asset being used as security remains with the mortgagor and sometimes the actual physical possession of the asset is left with the mortgagor. However, if the bank takes a legal mortgage the asset will be held by the bank and in many circumstances the actual ownership of the asset will transfer to the mortgagee.

Lending bankers are quite often faced with the question 'should I take a legal charge or an equitable charge?' Unfortunately, there is no hard and fast rule about this, with each decision being totally different from any other and dependent solely on the circumstances relevant to that particular case. There are advantages and disadvantages with each type of charge and on top of this there are also circumstances which apply to only one type of security such as shares. In essence, from the bank's point of view a legal charge would usually take a little longer but would result in the bank having more rights than if it had taken an equitable charge. The main disadvantage is that the legal mortgagee will have the power of sale without the necessity of approaching a third party (except the courts, if it is a residential property), whereas an equitable mortgagee will usually have to approach a third party to execute a power of sale (either the mortgagor for his improbable consent or the courts for an enforcement).

When taking an equitable charge the mortgagee will decide how 'strong' he wishes his equitable charge to be. The most simple form of equitable charge will be a mere retention of the document of ownership of the asset to be taken as security; for example, the share certificate or a life policy. However, this course of action is open to a claim from the mortgagor that the asset was understood to be left under safe custody. The most common form of equitable charge is the retention of the title document, plus the execution of a Memorandum of Deposit (MoD) by the mortgagor. The execution of the MoD has the following advantages:

(i) It puts the intent beyond doubt.
(ii) It gives the mortgagee the benefit of the protective clauses contained therein (continuing security, whole debt etc.).
(iii) If the MoD is executed under seal (as opposed to under hand) the mortgagee will have the additional benefit of being appointed the agent of the mortgagor, under an irrevocable power of attorney. This will have the effect of the mortgagee being able to act on the customer's behalf either to sell the asset or to execute a legal charge form.
(iv) Where the security is said to be third party (as discussed above – where the mortgagor is not a debtor), the MoD will give the mortgagee the protection of the clauses included in a guarantee, such as whole debt, the mortgagor being unable to accept security from the debtor and so on.
(v) Other specific advantages depend upon the type of security, for example, the equitable mortgagor of shares would undertake to forward to the bank any further shares acquired under a bonus or a rights issue (see Chapter sixteen), adequately to insure the property charged, or to comply with any covenant in a relevant lease.

The advantages and disadvantages of equitable and legal charges as they relate to individual types of security will be discussed further under their own individual chapters. The intention in this chapter is merely to introduce the concepts and act as a point of reference.

■ Duties of the mortgagee/creditor

It is perhaps initially difficult to accept that when the bank is taking security in respect of lending by it, that it actually owes a duty to the prospective mortgagor or guarantor. However, the case is that the mortgagor or guarantor does have certain rights and the bank must ensure that these are not violated. The duties of the mortgagee fall under the following areas.

Misapprehension

Where it is obvious that the mortgagor/guarantor is under a misapprehension (for example, the guarantor thinks that the debtor has no other liabilities, yet the bank is aware of many other debts including loans with the bank), then this must be corrected at the first opportunity. However, the bank must be aware of its duty of secrecy to its customer:

Tournier v *National Provincial* (1924). As such, if the security is third party it will normally arrange a meeting between the bank, the debtor and the mortgagor/guarantor.

Misrepresentation

The bank must not deliberately or innocently misrepresent the situation to the mortgagor/guarantor. In *Mackenzie* v *Royal Bank of Canada* (1934), it was held that where the bank mistakenly advised a potential guarantor that other securities would be realised unless she entered into the guarantee, then the guarantee was deemed unenforceable.

The general rule is that **the bank must correct any misapprehensions and not create any misrepresentations**.

Explaining the document

The bank does not owe a duty to explain the document to a non-customer: *O'Hara* v *Allied Irish Banks* (1984). However, judicial comment following recent cases would suggest a movement towards imposing such a duty to customers: *Cornish* v *Midland Bank* (1985). Either way, if a bank does explain the form to a mortgagor/guarantor he is under a duty of care not to misrepresent the contents of the document (*Lloyds Bank* v *Waterhouse* (1989)).

Undue influence

This occurs only in third party security and exists where the surety is in a position where he cannot exercise his own free will. The main reason for this is that he is totally dominated by the principal debtor. There have been many cases where this has been so and these are discussed fully in Chapter fourteen. However, in exceptional circumstances the undue influence can actually be exerted by the bank: *Lloyds Bank Ltd* v *Bundy* (1974). Before you get too excited by this concept, it is important for you to realise the very small likelihood of the circumstances of the *Bundy case* being repeated. Firstly, Mr Bundy was an old farmer who had become totally reliant on the bank for advice on all financial aspects of his life. Secondly, the bank had lent substantial sums to Mr Bundy's son, and the bank was considering calling in the lending, by serving a formal demand and insisting on full repayment. The offer to increase his guarantee (and charge over the farm) to support the son's borrowing did not come from Mr Bundy senior but from the assistant manager of the bank, and bearing in mind the fact that the form was brought to the farm by the bank, the courts held that the burden was placed on the bank to prove a lack of undue influence, which it was unable to do.

The fact that the circumstances leading to the somewhat unusual decision in *Bundy* are unlikely to be repeated was underlined in *Tai Hing Cotton Ltd* v *Liu Chong Bank and Others* (1985).

It is possible that the undue influence could be effected by an agent of the bank, for example, where the guarantee form is handed to the principal debtor to obtain the guarantor's signature. Whether the guarantee is handed to the principal debtor by the bank *Avon Finance Co. Ltd.* v *Bridger* (1985)), or to the solicitor instructed to act (*Kings North Trust* v *Bell* (1985)) does not make a difference. If the principal debtor goes on to exert undue influence on the guarantor, it is interpreted as having been exerted by an agent of the bank and hence by the bank itself.

Thus, although undue influence by the bank is unlikely *Tai Hing*), banks need to take care when appointing others to act on their behalf. In general, the principal debtor should never be instructed to obtain the guarantor's signature and where a solicitor is instructed (the usual practice with a third party security and quite common with other forms of security) he should be informed not to delegate his duties to anyone else.

∎ Why are charge forms/guarantees completed in the presence of a solicitor or senior bank official?

There are basically four reasons why the banks insist on legal charge forms/guarantees being completed in the presence of (and witnessed by) either a senior bank official or a solicitor. Although it is unlikely that an exam question will be set on this topic alone, it is important that you do understand the following reasons which are behind the practice.

Prevention of forgery

In general a forged signature is no signature and so a forged signature on a legal charge form/guarantee will automatically release that person from liability. However, the effects of the forgery can be quite different as in the following two cases.

(a) *James Graham Timber Co Ltd* v *Southgate Sands* (1985).
Here the signature of a joint and several guarantor was forged and as he was obviously no longer liable on the contract, the other three guarantors, each of whom signed under the impression that he would be one of four co-guarantors, were also released from their liabilities under the guarantee. The guarantee was totally unenforceable, due to the forgery.

(b) *First National Securities* v *Hegarty* (1985).
In this case the form in question was a legal charge form over land, and Mr Hegarty called at the bank to complete the form. He came with a woman and introduced her as his wife, though she was in fact his girlfriend. Mr Hegarty signed the form and the girlfriend forged the signature of the wife. Naturally, Mrs Hegarty incurred no liability, but the question arose as to the liability of Mr Hegarty. The courts decided that his signature created an equitable charge over his interest in the property (a legal charge would have given the bank a power of sale – obviously unfair to Mrs Hegarty), and so did not invalidate the document.

In each of the above cases the forgery had a detrimental effect on the bank's security and its detection could have prevented a possible loss for the lending bank. The witnessing of the document in the presence of a senior bank official or solicitor should, it is hoped, overcome this problem and not expose the bank to the risk.

Prevention of a claim of '*non est factum*'

The literal translation of *non est factum* is 'not my deed', and it is a defence claimed by the signatory to the document, whereby he is stating that the document he signed was not the document that he intended to sign. However, the possibility of a claim of '*non est factum*' succeeding was drastically reduced following the decision in *Saunders* v *Anglia Building Society* (1970). In this case the court decided that a claim could not succeed where the claimant had been careless as in this case, where an old lady failed to put on her glasses to read the document in question. In *Lloyds Bank Plc* v *Waterhouse* (1989), the illiterate farmer claimed '*non est factum*' when the bank sought to enforce an unlimited guarantee. The Court of Appeal stated that to establish a defence of '*non est factum*' a defendant had to show:

(a) that he was under a disability,

(b) that the document was fundamentally or radically different from the one he thought he was signing,

(c) that he was not careless, but took the precautions he ought to have taken to ascertain its contents and significance.

In this case Waterhouse thought he was signing a guarantee covering a new advance to his son to enable his son to purchase a farm. It was in fact an unlimited guarantee covering all his son's liabilities to the bank. Waterhouse attempted to ascertain the nature and extent of his liability by asking questions. The words and conduct of the bank employees led Waterhouse to believe that he was signing something other than that which he did in fact sign.

The claim of *non est factum* failed, but the Court of Appeal held in favour of Waterhouse, due to the bank's failure to comply with its duty to avoid a misrepresentation.

Prevention of undue influence

As briefly mentioned above, undue influence happens when the signatory has signed the form without being able to exercise his own free will, and it is presumed in a number of situations:

● Parent and dependent child
● Doctor and patient
● Solicitor and client
● Guardian and ward
● Trustee and beneficiary
● Religious advisor and disciple

It is important to remember that although in the above six instances undue influence is presumed, there are many other times where it is not presumed but must be proved, the most obvious (and most common) being between husband and wife. You should automatically realise that this condition can arise only in third party security, where the person signing the document is not a party to the lending.

It is possible for undue influence actually to be exercised by the bank (*Lloyds* v *Bundy* (1974)), but is highly unusual (*Tai Hing Cotton Mill Ltd* v *Liu Chong Hing Bank* (1985)). It is more likely to be exercised by the debtor (as in *Kings North Trust* v *Bell* (1985)). However, it has been a subject of many recent cases, which are discussed fully in chapter fourteen, and the current position appears to be that for a claim of undue influence to succeed the following conditions must be present:

either (i) The undue influence must be exercised by either the bank (*Bundy*) or by its agent. In *Kings North Trust* v *Bell* (1985), the guarantee was actually handed to the principal debtor to obtain his wife's signature. It was held that the debtor was acting as an agent of the bank. (*Rej.* 1974.)

or (ii) The bank must have actual or constructive notice (eg, where presumed) of the undue influence. In *Midland Bank* v *Perry* (1987), the claim of undue influence failed as the bank was not aware of the total dependency of the guarantor (wife) on the principal debtor (her husband), despite the fact that she was unduly influenced by her husband.

and in all situations (iii) The transaction must be 'manifestly disadvantageous' to the claiming party. In *National Westminster Bank* v *Morgan* (1985), Mrs Morgan's claim failed because she actually benefited from the transaction which was a re-finance of an existing mortgage under which the mortgagee was starting re-possession proceedings.

One of the easiest methods of defeating a claim of undue influence is to ensure that the surety is actually making the decision to sign of his own free will. The form, therefore, is sent to a solicitor who will ensure that this is so.

Correction of any misapprehension and prevention of any misrepresentation

As previously mentioned, the position must not be misrepresented to the signatory and if he/she is under any misapprehension, then the situation must be corrected; failure to do so could result in the security being unenforceable. In *Lloyds Bank* v *Egremont* (1990) a wife was bound by a charge over the matrimonial home. Her claim of misrepresentation failed, as the form was completed in the presence of her solicitor, who had explained the contents to her.

No SOLICITOR PRESENT 1990!

■ Priorities

One of the more difficult areas for students to grasp (and as such one of the favourite areas for the examiner!) appears to be that of priorities. The problem is 'if there are two mortgagees, how is it decided who gets their money first, ie, who take priorty?'. The order of priority will vary from security to security, but it is important that you should be able to answer the above question for each type of security on the syllabus: land, stocks and shares, and life policies.

■ Limited company security

As you will now be aware a limited company is a separate legal entity *Salomon* v *Salomon & Co Ltd* (1897), and is therefore able to offer a unique form of security (mortgage debenture). However, there are also certain additional formalities to undertake when taking security from a limited company, and these include checking the memorandum and articles of association (to ensure that the company has the power to give the security and that the directors have the power to act on behalf of the company) and its registration at Companies House within the 21 day period. All of the relevant procedures are discussed fully in Chapter eighteen.

■ Special security considerations when lending on current account

As we have already discussed (see 'appropriation', Chapter two) it is important that we do not look at a debit balance on a current account (an overdraft) as merely a single amount, because the balance is made up of a series of debits and as such a series of debts. It is possible that some event could happen that would make this fact have great implications for bankers. In Chapter seven it was pointed out that if the lending bank wished to retain the liability of a deceased partner it must 'stop' the account on receipt of notice of death, as the deceased partner is liable only for the liabilities up to the time of his death. If the bank failed to stop the account then the rule in *Clayton's Case Devaynes* v *Noble* (1816) would operate against the bank, with the first credits clearing the debits in chronological order. Hence the first credits would clear the debits which the deceased partner would be liable for, and the new debits, after his death, would create new debts for which he would not be liable. As you can imagine on an active current account it would not take long for the whole of the balance at death to be cleared by subsequent credits and the deceased would no longer be liable for the resulting debit balance.

A similar situation arises when the bank is lending on a secured overdraft, say by a first legal charge over the residential property belonging to the debtor, and the bank receives notice of a subsequent charge. The effect of the subsequent mortgagee (for example, a finance company) giving notice is that it 'fixes' the lending caught under the prior mortgagee's charge, and any further lending by the bank will rank behind any advances by the subsequent mortgagee.

If the bank were lending on loan, then the bank would need merely to note in its records that any further lending would not be covered by its first charge. However, if the bank were lending on overdraft then the situation would be much more serious. Due to the overdrawn balance being made up of a series of debts, any credits made after receipt of notice of the subsequent charge would reduce the amount secured by the bank's charge and any debits made to the account would create a new debt which would not be secured by the bank's first charge. These were exactly the circumstances of *Deeley* v *Lloyds Bank* (1912), where the bank's first legal charge secured nothing, the court deciding that, to prevent the rule in *Clayton's Case* applying, the bank should have made a specific appropriation of the later credits by stopping the overdrawn account and opening a new account for future transactions.

Also, if a bank is lending on overdraft secured by a joint and several guarantee and the bank receives notice of the death, mental incapacity or insolvency of one of the guarantors, then, in order to preserve the liability of the deceased, mentally incapacitated or insolvent guarantor the bank must stop the account to prevent the rule in *Clayton's Case* operating against the bank. If the account is not stopped then credits to the account would reduce the balance for which the deceased, mentally incapacitated or insolvent guarantor was liable and debits would create new debts for which he/she would not be liable.

It could well be that the bank does not wish to protect the liability of the deceased, mentally incapacitated or insolvent guarantor (due to his being relatively poor, or the bank being satisfied with the remaining guarantors), and if this is so, no further action is required and it would not be necessary to take a new guarantee, due to the protection offered to the bank by the guarantee's change in constitution clause. However, should the bank wish to maintain the liability of the deceased, mentally incapacitated or insolvent party then it would be necessary to stop the account as discussed above.

A bank lending on overdraft, therefore, needs to be alert to the circumstances which could possibly result in the security or guarantee being rendered valueless.

Protections available

(i) The main form of defence against *Clayton's Case* operating to the bank's detriment is to stop the overdrawn account, thus 'freezing' the liability of the guarantor to the debt secured by the bank's security. The bank would then open a separate account to be maintained to the bank's order, either in credit, secured by some other form of security, or otherwise at the bank's discretion. This would be seen by the courts as a specific appropriation by the bank (see rules of appropriation in Chapter two) and as such would prevent the default rule of appropriation *Clayton's Case*) from operating.

(ii) A secondary defence is the insertion in a bank's standard forms of a clause stating that *Clayton's Case* does not apply, despite the fact that the bank may not stop the account. The effectiveness of such a clause has been supported in case law: *Westminster Bank* v *Cond* (1940).

■ Conclusion

The aim of this chapter has been to introduce you to the principles involved in secured lending, to be used as points of reference should you come across a difficult section of a subsequent chapter, and to assist you with your revision by giving you a summary of the main points of secured lending.

FACT SHEET

General securities

Standard clauses in a bank security form
(i) Continuing security: security covers all future debts, defeating the rule in *Clayton's Case*.
(ii) All monies clause: security covers **all** debts owed to the creditor by the debtor. If the security is third party, the surety cannot sue or enforce any obligation against the principal debtor unless the whole of the debt has been repaid, not merely the limit of the guarantee (if applicable).
(iii) Repayable on demand: precludes Limitation Act.
(iv) Change in constitution: security still enforceable despite change in constitution in creditor or debtor.
(v) Consideration: defeats common law rule that past consideration is no consideration.

Legal or equitable charge?
Basic difference, and advantages of taking a memorandum of deposit.

Duties of the mortgagee/creditor
(a) bank must correct any misapprehension and not create any misrepresentation *Lloyds* v *Waterhouse*);
(b) explaining the document to a customer: *Cornish* v *Midland*;
(c) undue influence: undue influence by bank is rare: *Lloyds* v *Bundy*, undue influence by an agent of the bank is a possible problem: *Avon Finance* v *Bridger*.

Why are charge forms/guarantees executed in the presence of a solicitor or senior bank official?
1. Forgery; compare the decisions in *James Graham Timber Products Ltd* v *Southgate Sands* with *First National Securities* v *Hegarty*.
2. *Non est factum*; *Saunders* v *Anglia Building Society* and *Lloyds* v *Waterhouse*.
3. Undue influence; where presumed and conditions for affecting the bank.
4. Correction of misapprehension and prevention of misrepresentation.

Priorities and limited company securities
These are discussed in full in their own chapters.

Special considerations when lending on current account

Clayton's case and *Deeley* v *Lloyds*. Effect of receipt of notice of subsequent charge, death/bankruptcy/mental incapacity of joint account holder/partner/guarantor. Method of protection.

Question (April 1986)

Advise the Grand Bank on the legal position in the following situations, where the bank's claims are being resisted (assume that both transactions exceed £15,000):

(a) Martyn guaranteed an advance by the bank to his neighbour, Norman, to enable him to buy a motor coach in order to operate tours at weekends. Norman failed to make repayments to the bank because of heavy gambling losses, so the bank called on Martyn to pay up under his guarantee. Having found out about the gambling, Martyn refused to pay on the ground that for a long time the bank must have known from the payees of his cheques that Norman was a persistent gambler, and had the bank told him this at the time, he would not have signed the guarantee.

(b) As part of a financial re-arrangement, Anna mortgaged to the bank her interest in the house jointly owned by her and her husband. She did this in order to secure a loan made to her husband so that he could discharge an earlier loan secured on the house and made to him by a finance company, which was pressing for payment. Recently the bank called in the mortgage. Anna, who did not have independent legal advice at the time the mortgage was executed, now alleges that she signed it because of undue influence by the bank.

[Total marks for question – 20]

Key words
re introduction
  legal position
  resisted
  less than £15,000

re (a)
  failed . . . because of heavy gambling losses
  refused . . . because bank must have known
  had bank told him . . . would not have signed

re (b)
  mortgaged . . . house jointly owned
  in order to secure a loan to husband
  discharge earlier loan . . . finance company . . . pressing for payment
  did not have independent legal advice
  because of undue influence by the bank.

Answer

Overall, this was reasonably well answered. In (a) it was usually seen that a guarantee is not a contract of the utmost good faith, and the correct conclusions were drawn. It was gratifying that numerous answers cited the House of Lords case, *National Westminster Bank Plc* v *Morgan* (1985), on which part (b) was based, though a sizable proportion of the answers stopped at *Lloyds* v *Bundy* (1974).

In (a), since a guarantee is not a contract *'uberrimae fidei'* (of the utmost good faith), the bank is not legally obliged to disclose known facts: *Hamilton* v *Watson* (1845). Moreover, as answers usually stressed, a bank owes a duty of secrecy to its customer: *Joachimson* v *Swiss Bank Corporation* (1921). The guarantor should make his own enquiries about the debtor, and is unable to avoid liability.

Cooper v *National Provincial Bank* (1945), or *National Provincial Bank* v *Glanusk* (1913), could have been mentioned. However, if the guarantor asks the bank questions, the bank must make unequivocal replies. If he shows he is under any misapprehension as regards the debtor, the bank must correct it: *Royal Bank of Scotland* v *Greenshields* (1914).

The allegation against the bank in (b) should fail, as the facts are based on *National Westminster Bank Plc* v *Morgan* (1985), where the bank's appeal succeeded in the House of Lords, which upheld the bank's legal charge on the grounds that it was a normal business arrangement between the banker and a customer, not one where the bank manager had a dominating influence, and furthermore as the transaction was not unfair to the wife, the bank had not been under a duty to ensure that she had independent advice. The existence of undue influence depends on a 'meticulous examination of the facts', and so it seems that *Lloyds Bank Ltd* v *Bundy* (1974), where the Court of Appeal held that the charge was procured by undue influence exerted by the bank manager, is a case decided on its own special facts in which the bank had 'crossed the line'.

Author's comment
This is basically a straight forward question, but the length of the question itself means that without underlining the key words the chance of misunderstanding the problem or missing a key point is very likely. In (b) a key point which tends to be missed is the fact the charge of undue influence is actually being levelled against the bank. As quoted in both *Lloyds* v *Bundy* and more recently *Tai Hing Cotton Mills Ltd* v *Liu Chong Hing Bank Ltd* (1985), undue influence by the bank is rare and unlikely to be repeated.

Candidates with a reasonable level of knowledge and a good exam technique (see UPRAY in the introduction to this book) tend to gain excellent marks on this question.

CHAPTER 14

Guarantees

Syllabus requirements

● The legal principles of taking, protecting, enforcement, and the effects of insolvency on guarantees as security.

▮ Introduction

In this chapter we shall discuss not only guarantees but also indemnities and the complexities of all forms of third party security, such as the mortgaging of a property in the name of the husband and wife to secure borrowing in the sole name of the husband. But the main emphasis will be on guarantees.

You will soon see that guarantees are vastly different from all other types of security we have discussed, in that they do not require the deposit of any document of title and are really a commitment from a party, other than the principal debtor, to be responsible for the debt. It is not uncommon for banks to ask for some form of 'supporting security' to support the guarantee. This means that the guarantor as well as being responsible for the debt will also provide some form of security (eg, shares or a life policy) which the bank could realise should the monies not be forthcoming. If a guarantee is supported, the bank needs merely to follow the procedures described below for the taking of a guarantee and at the same time to follow the procedures for the taking of the additional security.

As a form of third party security the guarantee will acquire its own characteristics and will provide several new areas of danger of which the bank must be aware and attempt to overcome.

▮ Types of guarantee

Parties involved

A guarantee will be either a sole party (a guarantee given by one individual) or a multi-party guarantee. If there is more than one guarantor, then the bank will require that each guarantor is fully liable for the whole amount of the debt guaranteed. This is known as joint and several liability and gives the bank the following advantages:

(i) The bank can enforce the whole debt against each guarantor, either separately, consecutively (one after another) or jointly (all at once). This gives the bank a greater chance of obtaining repayment of the debt in full, although obviously the bank cannot obtain more than the amount due.

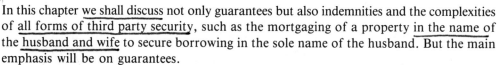

(ii) If any of the guarantors should die, become bankrupt or mentally incapacitated, the bank will be able to claim from their representatives or estates. If the guarantee was merely a joint guarantee the estate would automatically be released from liability.

(iii) If any security or a credit balance is held in the name of the guarantor, then this can also be used to recoup monies owed under the guarantee liability.

Liabilities covered

A specific guarantee

This will cover one specific transaction only, for example, loan number . . . As you have read in chapter three, the Consumer Credit Act 1974 actually insists on guarantees covering regulated agreements (ie, loans to non-corporate bodies of £15,000 or less) being specific, as the Act states that the document must refer to the agreement and the guarantor be supplied with a copy of the completed loan agreement. Also the Act does contain specific wording for guarantees and these should now include words such as, '**you may have to pay instead**' and be headed '**a guarantee under the Consumer Credit Act 1974**'.

Continuing guarantee

This covers debts owed by the principal debtor now or in the future, so it covers present borrowing and any future advances the bank may make to the principal debtor. If the bank is lending on overdraft this clause is important as it prevents the rule in *Clayton's Case* operating to the bank's disadvantage, in that without this clause any new debits to the overdrawn account would be considered to be new debt and not covered by the guarantee (for a full explanation of *Clayton's Case*, see Chapter two). A continuing guarantee will be either:

(i) unlimited – the guarantor will be liable for the full indebtedness of the principal debtor, whatever the amount; or
(ii) limited – here the guarantee will state his maximum liability, for example, £20,000. However, on top of the maximum liability the guarantor will also be liable for charges and interest, therefore his true final liability could well exceed the limitation quoted in the guarantee.

Guarantee or indemnity?

[handwritten: Bank has 6 year limitations on its actions / Not so customers!! Bank knowing of 1974 Charge (guarantee?) also knowing of £1,500.00 debt in 1990 (16 years later) did NOT consider / mentioning this FACT at time of signing of 3rd Charge in 1990, FURTHER — Bank never NSY/ual MM that £5,500.00 debt was owing at time they took action.]

A guarantee is 'a written promise by one person to be responsible for the debt, default or miscarriage of another incurred to a third party': s.4 Statute of Frauds 1677. In other words, it is a written promise that if the principal debtor does not pay, then the guarantor will. For a guarantee contract to be enforceable the contract between the creditor (bank) and the principal (debtor) must also be enforceable: *Coutts & Co v Browne Lecky* (1947) (the one exception to this is s.2 Minors' Contracts Act 1987 which states that if the principal debtor is a minor, then the guarantor will not escape liability for this reason alone). Despite the *Browne Lecky* case concerning a minor as the principal debtor and minors now being specifically excluded under the Minors' Contracts Act, it is thought that the case will still be relevant for other cases regarding principal debtors lacking in contractual capacity, such as undischarged bankrupts or limited companies acting *ultra vires* (see Chapter eight).

To overcome this problem banks insert an indemnity clause in all third party security, which instead of stating 'if he does not pay I will', in effect states that the indemnifier is saying, 'I will pay'. One other major difference between a guarantee and an indemnity is that a guarantee must be in writing, whereas this is not so with an indemnity which can occur by implication. Two examples we have previously discussed are firstly an agent's right of indemnity from his principal should he suffer loss and, secondly, on a forged transfer form passing through a bank when taking legal charge over shares; in such a case the bank indemnifies the issuing company as to the genuineness of the signature: *Sheffield Corporation v Barclay* (1905).

[handwritten at bottom: Bank did NOT consider M.M's situation. No attempt to warn/notify of situation knowing of highly probable 'undue influence' of husband.]

203

∎ Initial security considerations

Signatures

If the document is a joint and several guarantee, then it is vital that all the guarantors sign the unaltered form. This is because each guarantor thinks that he is signing the form along with all the other guarantors indicated on the document. The case law on this area includes the following cases:

- *National Provincial Bank* v *Brackenbury* (1906). Three guarantors signed the guarantee but the fourth guarantor died before signing. He (and his estate) were therefore not liable and accordingly neither were the other co-guarantors.
- *James Graham & Co (Timber) Limited* v *Southgate Sands and Others* (1985). Three guarantors had signed the guarantee. However, the signature of the fourth guarantor was forged. As the guarantee was not enforceable against the forged party it was likewise not enforceable against any of the other guarantors.
- *Ellesmere Brewery Company* v *Cooper* (1896). Three guarantors signed the guarantee, the fourth guarantor altered the amount that he was liable for before signing it. The guarantee was unenforceable against any of the guarantors.

If the guarantee is to be given by a partnership, then in almost all situations the guarantee **must** be signed by all partners, as the giving of guarantees is outside the ostensible authority of partners (see chapter seven for more detailed discussion of ostensible authority). The exceptions to this rule are if the giving of guarantees is in the normal course of business of the partnership (unlikely), or if all partners authorise one partner to sign the guarantee (impractical).

Guarantees given by limited companies

For a full discussion of this see chapter eighteen, but in essence it means that the bank must check the memorandum of association (to ensure that the company can give guarantees), and the articles of association (to check the internal procedures necessary and to ensure that the directors can give a guarantee on behalf of the company). The bank must also be aware of the possibility of interested directors (*Victors Ltd* v *Lingard* (1927)), of the modification brought about by the Companies Act 1989; and ensure that commercial justification is present (*Charterbridge Corporation* v *Lloyds Bank Ltd (1969)*) and take extra care with inter-company guarantees (*Ford & Carter Ltd* v *Midland Bank Ltd* (1979)).

Duty of disclosure

The first point to note is that a guarantee is not a contract *'uberrimae fidei'* (of the utmost good faith): *Hamilton* v *Watson* (1845). As such the bank does not have a duty to volunteer information to the guarantor regarding the principal debtor, which may have influenced the guarantor's decision to sign the guarantee. Legally this means that non-disclosure of a material fact does not render the contract voidable at the option of the injured party and this situation should be compared with life policies, where non-disclosure of a material fact usually means that the insurance company will be able to avoid the contract. Also, the bank needs to bear in mind its duty of secrecy to its customer (as confirmed in *Joachimson* v *Swiss Bank Corporation* (1921) and *Tournier* v *National Provincial Bank*

(1924), which means that it cannot disclose information regarding the principal debtor (or the principal debtor's account) to the guarantor without the principal debtor's consent.

There has been much case law in this area, an important case being *Cooper v National Provincial Bank* (1945), where it was held that the bank had no duty to advise the guarantor that the principal debtor's husband was an undischarged bankrupt, that he had access to the principal debtor's account and that the account had been operated irregularly.

Not only is the bank not under a duty to disclose material facts to the guarantor at the time of signing the guarantee, but it is also not under any compulsion to disclose a change in the circumstances of the principal debtor: *National Provincial Bank v Glanusk* (1913).

However, the guarantor does have a right to know the limit of his liability, and therefore the bank has a duty to inform him accurately, without breaching its duty of secrecy to the principal debtor (its customer). The method of achieving this compromise depends upon the balance on the guaranteed account at the time of the enquiry:

(a) If the balance is less than the limit on the guarantee (in all cases on an unlimited guarantee) – the balance will be given as the current liability, but the guarantor will be reminded that the potential liability is the limit on the guarantee, and that notice will be required to determine (be released from) the guarantee and that the balance could alter during this period of notice (for further explanation, see later in this chapter).

(b) If the balance is greater than the limit on the guarantee – the guarantor should be told that the guarantee is being fully relied upon.

Misapprehension/misrepresentation

Despite the above points, if the guarantor is under a misapprehension as to the status of the principal debtor or any other relevant fact (eg, purpose of guarantee) the bank has a duty to correct the misapprehension. However, the bank must also bear in mind its duty of secrecy. The usual solution is to call the guarantor and principal debtor together for a tri-partite meeting with the bank when the guarantor can put questions direct to the principal debtor with the bank's representative present.

Also, the bank must not misrepresent the position to the guarantor; to do so would render the guarantee unenforceable: *Royal Bank of Scotland v Greenshields* (1914). Even if the misrepresentation is an innocent misrepresentation this is still the case. There are many examples of possible misrepresentation by the bank and these include the giving of incorrect information (*MacKenzie v Royal Bank of Canada* (1934)) and not answering direct questions of the guarantor (*Royal Bank of Scotland v Greenshields* (1914)). In *Lloyds Bank Plc v Waterhouse* (1989), it was held that the bank had misled an illiterate farmer and due to this they could not rely on the guarantee signed whilst under the misrepresentation. Interestingly, a concurrent claim of '*non est factum*' would not have succeeded due to the fact that the guarantor did not disclose his illiteracy, but this did not detract from the claiming of misrepresentation due to the words and deeds of the bank. In *Lloyds Bank v Egremont* (1990) a claim of misrepresentation failed as the document had been witnessed and explained to the claimant by her solicitor.

The golden rule in this area is that the bank must correct any misapprehension and **not** create any misrepresentations.

Undue influence

General

Undue influence occurs where one party to a contract is unable to exercise his own free will on deciding whether or not to enter the contract. This affects guarantees in that the guarantor could be unduly influenced to sign as the guarantor by the principal debtor, or, very rarely, by the bank (the creditor). There are certain accepted situations where undue influence is presumed and must be disproved by the party attempting to enforce the contract (the bank); in **all** others it must be proved by the party attempting to avoid the contract (the guarantor). If present, undue influence can result in the contract (the guarantee) being set aside and unenforceable.

The circumstances in which undue influence is presumed are:

- parent and dependent child,
- guardian and ward,
- doctor and patient,
- solicitor and client,
- trustee and beneficiary,
- religious adviser and disciple.

Note

 (i) In each of the above circumstances the guarantor is the second named party.

(ii) From a banker's viewpoint there are two important exceptions to this list, the first obviously being banker and customer and the second husband and wife. In each of these two situations undue influence must be proved by the guarantor.

Undue influence by the bank

It was in *Lloyds Bank* v *Bundy* (1975), that undue influence by the bank was found. However, the circumstances in this case were exceptional in that the guarantor was an old farmer who had become totally reliant on the bank for financial advice. When the bank asked the old man to sign a new guarantee, increasing his total liability, the courts decided that the facts of the case amounted to undue influence by the bank.

However, this case (and the exceptional circumstances surrounding it) have been referred to in at least two other cases: *National Westminster Bank Plc* v *Morgan* (1985) and *Tai Hing Cotton Mills Ltd* v *Liu Chong Hing Bank Ltd* (1985), both of which confirmed that undue influence by the bank is rare.

Undue influence by the principal debtor

There has been much recent case law on this topic and it has been a favourite topic for examination questions. In fact one chief examiner has been quoted as saying 'I am not an undue influence freak and the fact that it has appeared on each examination I have set is purely coincidence'. Make of that what you will!

The current position appears to be that the following conditions need to be met before a claim of undue influence can succeed:

(i) The guarantee must be 'manifestly disadvantageous': *National Westminster Bank Plc* v *Morgan* (1985). In this case Mr and Mrs Morgan re-mortgaged their house with the bank, funds being used to settle a building society mortgage under which the building society was threatening to repossess the house. When Mrs Morgan claimed undue influence the courts decided that Mrs Morgan's sole concern was to prevent the house being taken away from her and her young family. As she had succeeded in this aim (albeit only for a short time), her claim failed. One easy way to remember the facts of this case is that Mr Morgan was an earth moving contractor, ie, he made the earth move for a living and by coincidence had a young family and no means to support his mortgage.

This 'manifestly disadvantageous' condition has since been confirmed in a more recent case of *Bank of Credit and Commerce International Société Anonyme* v *Aboody* (1988).

(ii) The bank must have actual or constructive notice of the undue influence (eg, where presumed): *Midland Bank* v *Perry* (1987). In this case the attempts to have the guarantee set aside failed due to the fact that, despite the presence of undue influence on the wife by the husband, the bank had no notice of it.

(iii) The undue influence must be executed by an agent of the bank: *Kings North Trust* v *Bell* (1985). Here the guarantee document was actually handed to the principal debtor (the husband of the guarantor) to obtain the signature of the guarantor. Ironically it was not handed to him by the bank but by solicitors acting on the bank's behalf. It was held that as the husband was effectively acting as an agent of the bank and he exercised the undue influence, then the guarantee must be set aside. An identical decision was arrived at in *Avon Finance Co Ltd* v *Bridger* (1985), where the guarantee was handed to the principal debtor to obtain the signatures of his elderly parents. (This case may easily be recalled by linking the names of the parties: '*bridge*' over the river '*Avon*'.) In *Coldunell Ltd* v *Gallon* (1986), it was decided that although Mr & Mrs Gallon's son had undoubtedly exerted undue influence over his parents he was not acting as an agent of the bank. Hence the claim failed and the bank's security was still enforceable.

How undue influence can be overcome

As stated previously, undue influence in guarantees occurs when the guarantor has not been able to exercise his own free will when deciding to sign the guarantee, due to the dominance of another party (usually the principal debtor). The easiest way to detect the presence of undue influence is to insist on the guarantor receiving independent legal advice from a solicitor acting for neither the bank nor the principal debtor. If the guarantor has his own solicitor then it is sensible for him to be used. The solicitor will explain the contents of the form to the guarantor and will attempt to ascertain whether ot not undue influence is present. Remember, that if it is present then the guarantee can be set aside. If the solicitor is satisfied that undue influence is not present then after the guarantor has signed, the solicitor will witness the signature and add an attestation clause along the lines 'signed by the above-named after the contents had been explained to him by me'. As yet this method of protection has not been tested in the courts but it is thought to be effective and it is difficult to see what else the bank could do to protect itself.

It is now normal practice for most banks to insist on all guarantors or third party mortgagors to have the benefit of independent legal advice. However, if the guarantor should NEVER not wish to take this route then he will be asked to sign a 'free will clause' along the lines of OFFERED. 'I confirm that independent legal advice has been offered to me, but declined, and that I have signed this document of my own free will'. Again this has not been tested in the courts but it is difficult to imagine any extra protection given by it, because if a prospective guarantor is unduly influenced to sign the guarantee, then surely he could also be unduly influenced to sign the free will clause.

Additional duties owed by the bank to a guarantor

We have already discussed a number of duties owed by the bank (the creditor) to a prospective guarantor. These have included a duty to correct any misapprehensions and not to create any misrepresentations: *Royal Bank of Scotland* v *Greenshields* (1914), to avoid undue influence: *Lloyds* v *Bundy* (1975), and to inform the guarantor of his liability when requested to do so.

However, in *Cornish* v *Midland Bank Plc* (1985), it was put forward that the bank had a duty to explain the nature of a guarantee document to a customer guarantor. It is felt that referring the customer to a solicitor for independent legal advice would be sufficient to meet this duty. The problem arises should the customer/guarantor refuse the independent legal advice, and the bank then relies upon the 'free-will' clause.

In *O'Hara* v *Allied Irish Banks* (1984), it was held that the bank had no duty to explain the nature of the document to a stranger (non-customer) guarantor.

Finally, on this topic, in *Midland Bank Plc* v *Perry* (1987), the failure of the bank to explain the effect of signing a third party legal charge document amounted to negligence by the bank (not undue influence, as claimed) and damages had to be paid by the bank.

One other duty owed to the guarantor arises when a security, as well as a guarantee, is taken. In *Standard Chartered Bank Ltd* v *Walker and Walker* (1985), it was held that a receiver (appointed by the bank) owed a duty to the guarantor to obtain the true market value of any direct security (ie, security from the principal debtor himself). In this unusual case the bank was also liable as it had interfered in the receivership by advising the receiver to achieve a quick sale. This resulted in a lower than expected price being obtained and therefore the liability of the guarantor was higher than expected. The bank attempted to claim the protection of the variance of arrangements clause, but the courts held that this breached the 'reasonableness' test under the Unfair Contract Terms Act 1977 and so could not be relied upon. The bank's liability to the guarantor remained intact.

This should be contrasted with the Privy Council decision in *China and Southsea Bank Ltd* v *Tan* (1989), where the increased reliance on the guarantee was due to a fall in the price of shares, also held as security. It was held that 'no creditor (bank) could carry on the business of lending if he could become liable to a **mortgagee or surety** for a decline in the value of a mortgaged property, unless the creditor was personally liable for the decline'.

■ Specific clauses seen in bank guarantee/third party security forms

Due to the fact that these documents are different from other security documents, in that the security (be it guarantee or third party security) is given by someone other than the principal debtor, the banks feel it necessary further to protect themselves by the addition of extra protective clauses. These clauses may include:

Whole debt clause

If the guarantor/third party mortgagor pays off the debt, then he has a right of subrogation (stepping into the shoes of) to the principal debtor, in that he has a claim to any other security deposited (either direct or third party), a right to sue on the debt in his own name, and seek compensation from any co-guarantors for a contribution. The whole debt clause means that he cannot exercise this right of subrogation until the bank has been repaid in full. Thus, if the debt is, say, £10,000 and the guarantor pays £5,000 (the limit on the guarantee) he cannot sue the principal debtor or prove his bankruptcy, until the whole debt of £10,000 is paid in full. This protects the bank as it reduces the number of persons able to claim from the principal debtor and increases the bank's chances of obtaining full recovery of its debt.

Also, the whole debt clause enables the bank to place any monies received to a suspense account and not to the principal debtor's account. This again increases the amount that the bank can claim from the estate of the principal debtor and ensures a greater possibility of full recovery. For example:

Debt	Recovered from guarantor	Value of estate	Recovered with clause	Without clause
10,000	5,000	5,000	10,000	7,500
20,000	5,000	10,000	15,000	12,500

Note: In the above example, the following assumptions have been made: that the only creditors are the bank, and the guarantor, and that all of the guarantor's estate is available for settlement.

You can see from the above example that the inclusion of the clause greatly enhances the amount recovered.

Determination of guarantee by notice

By common law the guarantor has the right to determine (terminate) the guarantee at any time. However, a clause will be inserted into the guarantee insisting on a period of notice prior to determination. This will enable the bank to interview the principal debtor with a view to making alternative arrangements in order either to continue the lending facilities or reducing them or asking repayment of the facility. The account will be allowed to continue until the expiration of the period of notice; the liability of the guarantor will be the balance at the date of expiration. Without the clause the guarantor will be able to determine the guarantee and clear the indebtedness when the debit balance is low or even when the account is in credit.

Death does not determine the guarantee

It was held in *Beckett* v *Addyman* (1882), that the death of one joint and several co-guarantor does not release other co-guarantors from liability. However, if the bank decides to determine the guarantee upon the death of a co-guarantor (say, the wealthiest of the guarantors), then the bank may determine the guarantee and call in the debt, proving in the estate of the deceased party.

Continuation of the account despite the determination of the guarantee

Upon the expiration of the period of notice of determination, the account should be stopped to prevent the rule in *Clayton's Case* operating to the detriment of the bank by credits to the account repaying debts for which the outgoing guarantor was liable, and new debits to the account creating new debts for which the outgoing guarantor is not liable. However, banks include a clause stating that the guarantor will be liable for the debt at the date of determination regardless of the continuation of the account. This clause effectively defeats the rule in *Clayton's Case* and was confirmed in *Westminster Bank* v *Cond* (1940).

Consideration

A contract under hand must be supported by consideration: s.3 Mercantile Law Amendment Act 1856. However, where the account is an existing account with existing facilities, then no additional consideration will usually be offered. The bank has two options:

(a) to have the guarantee executed under seal, as no consideration is necessary on contracts executed under seal, and

(b) to serve formal demand on the principal debtor, execute the guarantee and in consideration of the guarantee extend the term of the facility and rescind the formal demand.

Power to open new accounts on determination

It was held in *Re Sherry* (1884), that the bank can open a new account for the principal debtor after the guarantee has been determined, without affecting the liability of the guarantor.

Guarantee remains the property of the bank

As we have seen in Chapter nine it is possible that any disposition within six months (or 24 months, if an associate is involved) of the insolvency of an individual or company could be classed as a preference and recalled. Thus, banks refuse to release the guarantor from his liability as soon as the debt is settled. The most obvious example of such a situation affecting a bank occurs when the principal debtor repays the debt, improving the position of the guarantor and reducing the possibility of him having to pay under the guarantee. The bank will insist on retaining the guarantee and with it the guarantor's liability for a further six or 24 months.

Conclusive evidence clause

The guarantor accepts as absolute any statement by the bank or the guarantor as to his liability: *Bache & Co (London) Ltd* v *Banque Vernes et Commerciale de Paris S.A.* (1973), and he cannot insist on sight of any other documentation to support the statement.

Other clauses

These include the guarantor undertaking that he will not accept security from the guarantor, that the guarantee is additional to, and not in replacement of any additional document, and an indemnity clause, which has been fully explained above in this chapter.

■ Realisation (determination) of the guarantee

The guarantee can be determined by either the guarantor or the bank. Determination will have the effect of freezing the liability of the guarantor and making repayment due. As we have already seen if determination is made by the guarantor, then the bank will require a period of notice (usually three months) in order to make arrangements with the principal debtor as to the continuation of the account. The account will be allowed to continue during the period of notice and the liability of the guarantor will be the outstanding balance as at the expiry of the period of notice. If the account continues after the expiry of the period of notice *Clayton's Case* will not apply and the guarantor's liability will remain at the balance on the above date. If the account balance is substantially increased during this period up to determination, even if drawn to the limit on the account, the guarantor is still liable for the full balance, or to the limit of his guarantee if lower than the balance: *Lloyds* v *Harper* (1880).

If the guarantor submits notice of determination to the bank, then he has a right to expect the bank to serve formal demand on the principal debtor and obtain payment from him: *Thomas* v *Nottingham Incorporated Football Club* (1972). This protects the guarantor from the bank merely expecting repayment in full to come from the guarantor.

As well as the guarantor serving written notice of determination, we need to discuss the effect of death, mental incapacity or insolvency of the guarantor:

Death of guarantor

As mentioned above, death of the guarantor does not automatically determine the guarantee; the bank will ask for three months notice of determination from the personal representatives. If the guarantor is one of a number of joint and several guarantors then the bank may decide not to determine the guarantee but to allow the account to continue and rely upon the remaining guarantors.

Insolvency of guarantor

Immediately upon the commencement of the guarantor's insolvency, or as soon as the bank receives notice of it, the principal debtor's account should be stopped as any further debits will not be provable in the insolvency of the guarantor. It is important to note that although the guarantee is a contingent liability, the bank will be able to prove for the debt. If the guarantor is one of a number of joint and several guarantors the bank will need to decide whether or not to determine the guarantee. If the bank decides to determine the guarantee it should stop the account and prove in the insolvency (see Chapter nine).

Mental incapacity of guarantor

As with insolvency and death, the mental incapacity of the guarantor means that he loses all contractual capacity. Upon receipt of notice of mental incapacity the bank should inform the representatives that three months' notice of determination is required. The remaining guarantors will still be liable for any future advances and the account could continue and the guarantee still be enforceable against the other co-guarantors.

Determination by the bank

It is possible that the bank may wish to call in the guarantee, due to either the mental incapacity, death or insolvency of the principal debtor. In each case the bank would claim the debt from the principal debtor's estate, as well as from the guarantor. Any funds received from the guarantor will be placed to a suspense account as well as the full amount of the debt claimed from the estate of the principal debtor. This will have the effect of increasing the amount claimed from the principal debtor and therefore increasing the possibility of receiving full repayment. In *Re Sass* (1896), the placing of funds received from the guarantor to a suspense account and the proving for the full debt in the insolvency of the principal debtor was confirmed as acceptable. The bank will not be able to obtain more than 100 per cent of the amount owed and will need to make a refund to the guarantor of any surplus receipts. Another reason for the bank determining the guarantee could be default by the principal debtor. The account should be stopped and formal demand served on the principal debtor with a copy to the guarantor.

Where determination is made by the bank, no notice is required to be served.

▌ Repayment of the debt

Repayment by the guarantor

Once the guarantor has repaid the full debt owed to the creditor (the bank) by the principal debtor, the guarantor will then acquire certain rights. It is important to remember that by the inclusion of the bank's whole debt clause the **whole** of the debt must be repaid, even if this amount should exceed the limit of the guarantee. The rights acquired by the guarantor upon the repayment of the whole debt would be:

Subrogation

(i) He would step into the position of the principal debtor. This is the ability of the guarantor to 'step into the shoes of' the principal debtor and acquire any rights or claims that the principal debtor would have. This includes the right to any security deposited by the principal debtor (up to the extent of any monies paid by the guarantor), and any other third party security that exists, but only on a rateable basis. This means that the additional third party security will be divided amongst the other persons involved in relation to the total liability of each party.

(ii) Step into the position of the bank. The guarantor, once the debt has been repaid in full, will be able to sue in the name of the bank. If the guarantor has repaid the liability of the principal debtor in full he will then be able to sue the principal debtor for recovery of the monies paid. This will be possible only if the original debt was due for repayment, for example, if the principal debtor was in default and formal demand had been served on him. Without this preclusion the principal debtor would always be under the theoretical threat of the guarantor repaying the debt and claiming full repayment from the principal debtor.

To the right of contribution from co-guarantors

Even though each guarantor is jointly and severally liable for the whole debt guaranteed, if one guarantor should repay more than his proportionate share of the debt he will have a right to claim the amount that should have been their contribution from the other co-guarantors.

If the principal debtor is solvent then he must be included in any action against the co-guarantors for a contribution: *Hay* v *Carter* (1935). If the principal debtor makes a payment to the guarantor then this needs to be taken into account when a contribution is sought from the co-guarantors.

If the principal debtor is insolvent (or indeed if there is any other legal bar preventing him making a contribution) an action could be made against the co-guarantors alone.

Repayment by the principal debtor

The main danger of an unrequested repayment by the principal debtor is that the payment may later be recalled as a preference. Preferences have already been discussed in Chapter nine. All we need to say at this stage is that if a voluntary payment is made which (whether innocently or not) has the effect of improving the position of one creditor as compared with other creditors. Obviously if the bank has released the guarantor from his liability under the guarantee, and subsequently the credit is recalled, the bank will be left with an unsecured debt. If it retains the guarantee however until the expiry of the relevant period, then should the credit be recalled the resulting debt will still be secured by the guarantee. The guarantee should be retained for six months (24 months if an associate is involved), after which the credit cannot be recalled.

Also, if repayment is made in response to a demand by the bank, then the transaction is not said to be made voluntarily, but in response to the bank's formal demand, and it is not a preference.

▌ Other sundry items

Supported guarantees

Quite often guarantees are taken alone. However, it is not unusual for some other form of security, for example, a second charge over a house, to be taken behind the guarantee. This principle is perhaps best explained by way of an illustration: the bank is unwilling to lend to Mr Ian Glyn, a young man with no assets, but his rich uncle Mr Brian Smith is willing to act as guarantor and Mr Smith has a property worth, say, £75,000 with a mortgage to the building society of £15,000 outstanding. One problem could be that the bank would be lending to Mr Glyn but the asset is in the name of his uncle. There are two possible solutions to this problem:

(i) take a guarantee from Mr Smith, supported by a direct charge over his property, or
(ii) take a third party charge from Mr Smith in favour of Mr Glyn.

There is technically little difference between these two options, except that if an unlimited guarantee is taken, Mr Smith (the guarantor) would be liable to the full extent of Mr Glyn's (the principal debtor) liabilities as opposed merely to being liable to the extent of the value of the property as in the second option.

No matter which option is taken, the bank will still need to be wary of each of the initial security considerations, as discussed earlier in this chapter and in Chapter thirteen, such as, undue influence, misapprehension/misrepresentation, *non est factum*, disclosure of information and additional duties owed to the guarantor, especially if he is a customer (*Cornish* v *Midland Bank* (1985)).

Guarantee given by a partnership

As you have read in Chapter seven, there are various actions which are assumed to be within the powers of partners and many which are not. These powers depend upon whether the partnership is a trading (eg, retailers) or non-trading (eg, solicitors) partnership: *Higgins* v *Beauchamp* (1914). However, it is important to realise that no matter whether the partnership is a trading or non-trading partnership, unless a partnership deed or articles of partnership have been drawn up and include a clause to the contrary, a guarantee executed by the partnership (as guarantors) will not be effective unless signed by all the partners. A guarantee signed by less than all the partners will not be binding on the partnership, but the persons that do sign will incur personal liability, in their own names.

Letters of comfort

Where a bank is lending to a subsidiary of a larger parent company, and where security from the subsidiary is lacking, it is not unusual for the bank to ask for a letter of comfort from the parent company. The letter of comfort will usually state that the parent company will support the subsidiary in the future, but this letter is merely a gentleman's agreement. The letter of comfort is not usually legally binding due to a lack of consideration, or a lack of an intention to create a legally binding agreement, possibly by express quotation in the actual letter of consent.

There have been two recent cases involving the wording of letters of comfort and their enforceability:

● *Kleinwort Benson Ltd* v *Malaysia Mining Corporation Berhad* (1987). In this case the courts discussed the difference between a guarantee and letter of comfort. The Court of Appeal, reversing the decision of the lower court, decided that the main difference was that a guarantee was entered into with the intent of entering into a legally binding contract, whereas a letter of comfort was usually lacking in the intent that it be legally binding.
● In *Chemco Leasing S.P.A.* v *Rediffusion* (1987), a legal commitment was entered into, and was legally binding.
  The deciding factor as to whether the letter of comfort is binding or not depends upon the wording of the document and the presence (or otherwise) of intent and consideration.

■ Advantages/disadvantages of guarantees as security

Advantages

1. Easy to take.
2. Lac of formality, registration procedures, expense, etc.
3. Gives a moral dimension, in that the borrower is less likely to default due to the embarrassment caused by the bank approaching the guarantor for repayment.
4. If the guarantee is given by a director in favour of a limited company it gives the bank recourse to the director's assets. Again possibly increasing the commitment of the director/guarantor to ensure the project succeeds.
5. As third party security the guarantee can be ignored when proving in the insolvency of the principal debtor, any funds received are placed in a suspense account.

Disadvantages

1. Unless supporting security is taken, the strength of the security is the financial stability of the guarantor, which is liable to variation over a period of time.
2. Bad feeling could result if the bank calls in the guarantee, where the guarantor is not expecting the guarantee to be relied upon. This could be especially relevant if the guarantor is also a customer.
3. Litigation could be necessary should the guarantor attempt to disclaim liability on the grounds of undue influence, *non est factum* etc.
4. Possible danger in early settlement by the principal debtor, by credit being reclaimed as a preference.

FACT SHEET

Guarantees

Types of guarantee
   (i) sole or joint and several
  (ii) specific, NB, CC Act regulated agreements
 (iii) continuing and limited or unlimited
 (iv) guarantee or indemnity – if guarantee, the guarantor is secondarily liable (take care: *Coutts & Co* v *Browne Lecky* (1947)). If indemnity the indemnifier is primarily liable (remember: s.2 Minors' Contracts Act 1987).

Initial security considerations
   (i) signatures – all must sign, several cases, but mainly *NP Bank* v *Brackenbury* and *James Graham* cases
  (ii) limited company guarantees – check memorandum and articles and take care with interested directors: *Victors* v *Lingard* (1927), and commercial justification: *Charterbridge Corporation* v *Lloyds* (1969).
 (iii) duty of disclosure – take care: *Tournier* case, guarantor has the right to know his liability.
 (iv) Misapprehension/Misrepresentation – bank must not create any misrepresentation and must correct any misapprehension
  (v) undue influence – when presumed creditor must prove a lack of undue influence, in other cases the presence of undue influence must be proved by the claimant (several cases). NB conditions. Undue influence is usually claimed against the principal debtor and rarely against the bank. Protection is usually taken by insisting on independent legal advice, free will clauses are not thought to be effective.
 (iv) additional duties incurred by the bank – explanation of the document by the bank to customer/guarantor (*Cornish* v *Midland Bank*), not necessary to non-customer guarantor (*O'Hara* v *Allied Irish Banks*), possible claim of negligence: *Midland* v *Perry*. *Standard Chartered* v *Walker & Walker*, duty to obtain a fair price when realising other security held.

Specific Clauses
   (i) whole debt – must be settled before guarantor acquires any rights, even if balance exceeds guarantee limit.
  (ii) determination by notice – allows for renegotiation with principal debtor.
 (iii) death does not determine guarantee – self explanatory.
 (iv) continuation of account after determination and power to open new account on determination.
  (v) consideration – time is classed as consideration, providing formal demand has been served.

   (vi) guarantee remains property of bank – protection against preference.

  (vii) conclusive evidence clause – guarantor must accept the word of the principal debtor or bank as to extent of liability.

Realisation of guarantee

(a) written notice by guarantor.

(b) death, insolvency and mental incapacity of guarantor.

(c) by bank due to default or death, insolvency and mental incapacity of principal debtor.

Repayment of debt

  (i) by guarantor – right of subrogation, to bank or principal debtor and right of contribution from co-guarantors.

 (ii) by principal debtor – take care with preferences.

Other sundry items

  (i) supported guarantees – access to security in name other than the principal debtor.

 (ii) guarantees by partnership – all partners must sign unless contradicted by deed or articles of partnership.

(iii) letters of comfort – normally gentleman's agreement, but if mis-worded can be legally binding.

Question (Autumn 1988)

Five terms which you might find in a bank's guarantee are stated below. Referring to relevant legal principles and authority, discuss the reason for, and effect of, THREE of these terms:

(a) the 'whole debt' clause and a proviso limiting liability to a stated figure;

(b) the 'determination by notice' clause;

(c) the 'change in constitution' clause;

(d) the 'continuing security' clause;

(e) the 'variation and release' clause.

[20 marks]

Key words

relevant legal principles and authority   *effect of*

reason for   *THREE*

Answer

(a) A 'whole debt' clause gives the bank a number of distinct advantages (which would not be relevant if the clause was omitted) including:

  (i) the guarantor must repay the whole debt outstanding before he can exercise his common law right of subrogation, the ability to step into the shoes of the creditor (bank) and claim any security taken in respect of the debt or sue the debtor in his own name.

 (ii) the creditor can place any money received under the guarantee to a suspense account and prove in the bankruptcy for the full debt and the guarantor will not be able to prove in the debtor's bankruptcy at all.

Without this clause the dividend payable to the creditor in the bankruptcy of the debtor would be reduced due to the figure claimed by the guarantor in respect of the amount paid by him under his guarantee liability.

    The limitation of liability is inserted because without this proviso the guarantee would be unlimited and possibly unacceptable to the guarantor. It is important to note that the limit quoted in the guarantee does not include interest and hence the total amount claimed from the guarantor can exceed the financial limitation quoted in the guarantee document.

(b) Even though the guarantee may be for a fixed or unspecified time period it will be revocable by the guarantor giving reasonable notice, in writing, of his intention to withdraw from his guarantee: *Offord v Davies* (1862). Most guarantees state that the minimum notice of revocation is three months (but this can vary). The account will be allowed to continue until the notice has expired and the liability of the guarantor will be the balance outstanding at the date of expiration. The clause gives the creditor the opportunity to seek other security and the debtor time to make alternative arrangements should the creditor decide that it cannot allow the debt continue without the benefit of the guarantee.

Where there is more than one guarantor then it is possible that the withdrawal of one co-guarantor will release all the others. It has been decided in *Beckett v Addyman* (1882) that the death of a joint and several co-guarantor does not release the others from their liabilities, but it is not certain what effect the withdrawal of a co-guarantor would have.

Without the clause the guarantor would be able to clear the indebtedness when the debit balance is low (or the account in credit) and then demand immediate release from his guarantee liability.

(c) In normal circumstances a change in constitution of the principal debtor or the bank would automatically result in the guarantee being determined. However, in many circumstances this could be to the disadvantage of the bank (for example on the conversion of TSB to a PLC) hence a clause is usually inserted in the guarantee stating that a change in constitution of the bank or debtor will not determine the guarantee.

However, a change in constitution of the guarantor(s) would not normally determine the guarantee. For example the death of a co-guarantor does not determine the guarantee but notice of death does mean that the bank can serve demand and enforce the guarantee if it deems it necessary.

(d) The insertion of a continuing security clause is specifically to prevent the rule in *Clayton's Case (Devaynes v Noble* (1816)) operating against the bank. Without this clause the guarantee would be described as a 'single' guarantee and would apply only to the first advance made after the guarantee had been executed. This would obviously be satisfactory if the bank was lending on loan account but would create problems should further advances be made or if the bank were lending by way of overdraft, where *Clayton's Case* states that credits are applied to the earliest debits in chronological order and new debits create a brand new debt, in the event of a 'single' guarantee a new debt not covered by the guarantee.

(e) It is possible that an agreement between the bank and the debtor could innocently (or not) affect the guarantor, subsequently causing the guarantor to be in a worse position than he was previously and hence release him from his liabilities under the guarantee: *Ward v National Bank of New Zealand* (1883). Examples of such an agreement could be the replacement of the principal debtor with another (*Bradford Old Bank v Sutcliffe* (1918)), the creditor deciding not to take security which he had suggested would be taken (*Royal Bank of Canada v Girgulis* (1980)), or the release of additional security taken at the time of the execution of the guarantee.

Hence, in order to protect themselves banks include in their guarantee documents that they are free to vary their arrangements between themselves and the debtor in any way as they consider appropriate without seeking the consent of the guarantor.

Author's comment

Although this proved to be a popular choice with candidates (with some attempting all five sections and not the three instructed in the question — in those circumstances examiners take the first three attempted regardless of which gain the highest marks), very few achieved a good mark, with many failing to obtain the standard required to pass. The problem appeared to be a lack of sufficient knowledge to obtain the marks alloted. Simple arithmetic should tell people that if you are to answer three sections for a total of 20 marks each sub-section must be worth approximately 7 marks each. Too many scripts did not include enough information to be awarded the marks required (say 4 marks on each clause). This was a great pity because the question was a straightforward test of knowledge with no interpretation or application necessary, surely an advantage to the less well prepared candidate.

CHAPTER 15

Land

- The legal principles of taking, protecting, priority over, enforcement and realisation of, and the effect of insolvency on legal and equitable mortgages on freehold and leasehold land.

∎ Introduction

There can be little doubt that the law relating to land is one of the most difficult areas for students to grasp. At this stage let me emphasise that by land we automatically include any property that happens to be built on the land. The main reason for the difficulties which students experience, I feel, is the number of options involved and how these options are covered by teachers. Each option on its own is relatively simple, it is only when they are put together into one tongue twisting phrase that students, if they have not got the foundations (no pun intended) solid, will become confused. For example, as you will see later, the differences between leasehold and freehold, registered and unregistered, legal and equitable and first and second charges are not in any way complicated. However, if a student should try to grasp the complexities of a second legal charge over freehold registered land without the basic understanding of each option then he will undoubtedly struggle. I am a firm believer in 'foundations', as in *Joachimson v Swiss Bank Corporation* as a foundation for the banker/customer relationship, and *Salomon v Salomon & Co Ltd* in the consideration of limited companies. The basic foundation in land is the understanding of the options and the first part of this chapter is structured to make them clearly understood.

∎ Legal estates in land – freehold or leasehold?

People tend to talk of 'owning' land, but alas, this is a fallacy as all land in this country is effectively 'owned' by the Crown. The individuals involved actually hold the tenure (or term) of the estate, be it either freehold or leasehold. The fundamental difference between a freehold and a leasehold title is the term of the 'ownership' of the land. If the estate is freehold, then the current holder (or his heirs) is deemed to be the holder of the estate for ever, or until it is disposed of by him (eg, sale, gift etc). The holders of the leasehold title hold the title only for the length of the lease (eg, 7, 25 or 999 years). To every parcel of land there will be a freehold title; if the freeholder has decided to allow a third party to use the property for a determined length of time, then he may do this by creating a lease. Within the lease there will be many clauses, known as covenants, some of which will be restrictive in their nature and others will have little effect. The most obvious clause is naturally the term, or length, of the lease. This is of great importance to lending bankers, as it would not be prudent to lend money over, say, 25 years taking as security a leasehold property with only 10 years left to run on the lease. In fact many banks will tend to attach a security value only to leasehold land with at least 25 years left to run at the end of the lease. By s.1 Law of Property Act 1925, both freehold and leasehold titles have their own legal definition, freehold being fee simple absolute in possession and leasehold term of years absolute. A breakdown of this definition follows:

Freehold (fee simple absolute in possession)

Fee

Means that the title is inheritable by the present freeholder's heirs. This does not mean that the freeholder **must** pass his title on to his general heirs, he is still free to pass it on to whom ever he pleases, but he may pass it to them if he wishes.

Simple

Means that it may be inherited by his general heirs, as opposed to an entailed freehold title which passes only to a particular type of heir (eg, male only). An entailed freehold title is an equitable, as opposed to a legal, interest.

Absolute

Means that the title is not subject to any conditions, apart from various sundry statutory restrictions, for example, under the Town and Country Planning Acts.

In possession

Means not only physical possession but also the right to receive rents (of particular relevance where the property is leased).

Leasehold (term of years absolute)

Term of years

Refers to the fact that the lease is for a fixed period. Although the definition refers to 'term of years', it does include parts of years.

Absolute

Again means that the title is not subject to any conditions, unless it ends earlier due to forfeiture of the lease as a result of non-compliance with the covenants.

There are many other interests in land which do not satisfy the conditions above and so are said to be equitable interests. Examples include entailed freeholds as above and conditional freeholds. Many leases do not satisfy the definition either, as the term is not definite, eg, weekly rental agreements which are merely repeated until either party gives notice to terminate the agreement (usually the person entitled to receive the rent on the occurrence of non-payment). Other interests in land are discussed later in this chapter.

Additional security considerations for leasehold land could obviously include the close examination of the lease, ensuring that no matters that could cause problems in the future are overlooked. These could consist of:

Restrictive convenants

These come in many guises, many irrelevant to the lending banker. For example, in a 'posh' area in my home town the residents are not allowed to hang out their washing on a Sunday and are not permitted to keep a caravan on their own drives (but only in the front, as they can park them in the rear), and no red bulbs are permitted if they can be seen from the road (presumably the freeholders are not concerned with residents running brothels, so long as no-one knows). However, some restrictive covenants can be of serious consequence to the banker and these include:

(i) The leaseholder may have to insure with a particular insurance company.

(ii) A bankruptcy clause whereby if the leaseholder is declared bankrupt the lease is automatically forfeited; that is to say that it will be as if the lease had never existed and the bank will lose its security. This is an obvious danger area to banks as the time when the bank wishes to realise (enforce) its security is the one time when the bankruptcy of the leaseholder is a possibility.

(iii) The permission of the freeholder to the bank's charge may be necessary. This can be either definite (ie, under no circumstances will permission be given) or restrictive (permission usually given, sometimes on the payment of a fee).

Term

As mentioned above, the term remaining of the lease is important, and is always compared with the term of the advance being considered.

Ground rent

Usually a leaseholder will have to pay a ground rent at regular intervals, normally annually. A lending banker will ensure that the ground rent is up to date (by sight of the latest ground rent receipt), as non-payment could result in forfeiture of the lease.

The value of the leasehold property

There could also be problems when valuing leasehold property for, as the term approaches maturity, the demand for the property and therefore its value, falls. As previously mentioned, this is the reason that short term leases are not viewed as good security except in exceptional areas, such as central London.

The Leasehold Reform Act 1967

This could possibly operate in the bank's favour. The Act gives the leaseholder of residential property only (commercial property is covered only if living accommodation is included) the legal option to purchase the freehold title from the freeholder. The price depends upon the rateable value of the property and at present the effect of the community charge is not clear. The purchase of the freehold title usually enhances the value of the property, and removes many of the problems discussed above, and so the mortgagee is unlikely to object.

Forfeiture of lease

If the leaseholder fails to meet any of the covenants of the lease, the freeholder can forfeit the lease without notification to the mortgagee. In *Bilson* v *Residential Apartments Ltd* (1990) the lease was forfeited because the leaseholder commenced works without the freeholder's consent.

Other interests in land

An interest in land is a right to claim against the property of another, but does not amount to possession.

Legal interests

These must be created by deed. There are five legal interests which are:

Easement

For example, a right of way, or a right to remove something such as when fishing or hunting. An easement can be for ever or for a term of years absolute.

Rent charge

This can be either for ever, or for a term of years absolute. This typically refers to a ground rent on freehold property.

A charge by way of legal mortgage

This is naturally the one of greatest concern to banks and will be discussed in full later in this chapter.

Land Tax, or other charge imposed by law

Rights of entry

These are usually attached to a lease (or rent charge) and exercisable upon a breach of a covenant in the lease, for example, non-payment of rent.

Equitable interests

These include any other interests in land and include:-

(i) Any of the above legal interests not executed by deed (example, equitable charge)
(ii) Entailed freehold.
(iii) Conditional freehold.
(iv) Beneficial interest (see *Parker-Tweedale* v *Dunbar Bank Plc* (1989)).

Legal or equitable interests are not enforceable against a bona fide purchaser for value unless it can be shown that he had notice of the charge. Hence a method of registration of interests was evolved which superseded the method of giving notice and replaced it with the doctrine that a registered charge was notice to any purchaser of the interest. This is discussed in full later when registered and unregistered land are considered.

Co-ownership

Joint tenancy

Both parties own the property and their 'share' is not identifiable. Upon the death of a joint tenant the title will automatically pass to the survivor(s). There can be a maximum of only four legal joint tenants. If there are more than four named, the first four are held to be the legal joint tenants holding the property in trust for themselves and the other remaining equitable joint tenants. In *London Building Society* v *Flegg* (1987), it was held that the legal joint tenants can execute a legal charge without the consent of the equitable joint tenants and that the legal charge would rank in priority to the claims of the equitable joint tenants. The equitable joint tenants (if the bank exercised its power of sale under its legal charge — see 'remedies of a legal mortgagee' later) would have to dispute the sale proceeds with the legal joint tenants and would have no rights against the bank.

Tenants in common

Each person owns a share of the property (usually unidentified) and not necessarily proportionate. If one party should die, that share of the property will pass to his heirs. Tenancy in common is an equitable title to the land and is sometimes common with partnership property, to protect the interest of the partner's family as opposed to the surviving partner. Where the estate is legal, then the co-ownership must be by legal joint tenants, although they can hold the title in trust for tenants in common.

Where a legal mortgage is to be taken over jointly owned property, then each owner must be a party to the legal charge.

▋ Title: registered or unregistered?

Prior to the introduction of the Land Registration Act 1925, all title to land was evidenced by a bundle of title deeds. Each time there was a change in title or a legal charge (taken or vacated) another document was added to the bundle. This meant that investigation of title (deciding whether the present owner had a good title or not) and transfer of title were both complicated and expensive.

The Act was introduced to simplify matters by creating a system of transfer and evidence of ownership similar to stocks and shares, and also to create a method of state guaranteed title to land. Unfortunately, in order to register the title initially there was a charge and this made the system slow to be accepted. However, there is now a system of compulsory registration in most built-up conurbation areas in England and Wales, which means that on each transfer of title the new title must be registered. In time it is to be expected that unregistered land will become less and less common, with registered title becoming the dominating title system. The details of both registered and unregistered land are now discussed in full below.

Unregistered land

Title

As previously mentioned, title to unregistered land is evidenced by a bundle of title deeds and documents and transfer of title is by a document known as a conveyance (if freehold land) or assignment (if leasehold). Once this document has been completed (signed, sealed and delivered) by both the vendor (seller) and the purchaser it is then placed with the title deeds. Another document regularly seen within the bundle is an extract of title which summarises the position and the constituents of the bundle at that particular date. Other typical documents contained could be wills, death certificates, assents (a document completed by the personal representatives of a deceased owner), legal charge forms (it is to be hoped that these will be vacated/released) and marriage certificates. One of the first tasks undertaken by a securities clerk is to check the items quoted on the schedule (if enclosed) back to the actual documents. Then he must try to ascertain whether or not the proposed mortgagor has a good title to the property or not. The method of achieving this is by following the title from the current owner back through the documents to a document which is at least 15 years old and fully identifies the property, the owners at that date and if there were any equitable interests. If the parties follow on from that document, then the owner/mortgagor is said to have a **'good root of title'** and the bank will accept the property for security purposes. However, should it not be possible for the security clerk to confirm the presence of a good root of title, usually due to a missing document or complicated transactions, the title deeds are forwarded to a solicitor who will be asked to prepare a report on title on the bank's behalf with his fee, naturally, being met by the customer.

The Land Charges Register

General

The bank will also undertake a search at the Land Charges Department in Plymouth to check if any other interests are registered. Within the Land Charges Register at the Land Charges Department there are many separate registers and various entries could be revealed. The entries are recorded with an alphabetical entry, sometimes followed by a Roman numeral. The main entries, as affect bankers, are:

C(i) Puisne mortgage – a legal mortgage without the deposit of the title deeds (as you will see later in this chapter, this is the typical entry made by a second or subsequent mortgagee).

C(iii) General Equitable Charge – an equitable charge taken without the deposit of the title deeds.

C(iv) Estate contract – contracts to sell, convey or create a legal estate in the land. For example, a contract of sale or an agreement to offer the first right of refusal to the local authority when selling the property: *First National Securities Ltd* v *Chiltern District Council* (1975).

D(i) A charge registered by the Inland Revenue in respect of inheritance tax due.

D(ii) Restrictive covenants – self-explanatory and discussed previously.

D(iii) Equitable easements – for example, rights of way not executed by deed.

F Spouse's right of occupation under the Matrimonial Homes Act 1983 – discussed in full later.

One obvious item missing from the above list is a legal or equitable charge taken with the deposit of the title deeds. This is because the deposit of the title deeds is sufficient notice of a previous charge and does not require registration.

As we have already mentioned, failure to register a registerable interest (including legal and equitable charges) could render the charge unenforceable against a purchaser for value (including any subsequent mortgagee).

Priority of charges

First priority is determined by the holder of the title deeds, providing a clear Land Charges

Department search is also held. Absence of the title deeds is constructive notice to a prospective mortgagee of the existence of a prior charge. Priority between subsequent mortgagees is decided by the **date of registration** of the charge, not the date of the charge itself: s.97 Law of Property Act 1925. This is an important concept and one that has important repercussions for bankers, in that if a bank takes a charge but fails to register the charge until later, it is possible for another mortgagee to have taken a charge, searched the Land Charges Register, and registered its charge in priority to the bank's. Also, where an equitable charge is registered (as a C(iii), mentioned above), then it will be impossible for a subsequent legal mortgagee to take priority by the mere fact that his is a legal charge.

Searches

A search of the Land Charges Register may be conducted by personal appearance at the Registry, over the telephone or by mail using a pre-printed form. The latter is the most likely and a written reply is considered to be conclusive proof of the search having taken place, and if clear is proof of a lack of detrimental entries. The search also gives the searcher a 15 working day protection period within which the Land Charges Department promises that the entries will not change. It is felt that in certain circumstances this protection may not be valid and banks tend to ignore this promise and search after execution of the charge form and any necessary registration. If the charge is registered the mortgagee will receive a confirmation of registration from the Land Charges Department, quoting a reference number. When the subsequent search is made the only alteration to the entries on the initial search should be the registration of the bank's charge, identified by the reference number quoted.

The mnemonic SCENT may be of assistance when dealing with unregistered land:

Search,
Check the search for detrimental entries,
Execute the legal charge form, remember where the legal charge form should be executed (in presence of senior bank official or solicitor) and why (protect the bank from *non est factum*, forgery, undue influence etc),
Now register (if necessary). The bank cannot register before execution and to wait too long afterwards could be detrimental.
Then search again, to ensure only alteration from the initial search is the entry of the bank's charge. If the charge does not need to be registered (if the deeds are held), then there should be no difference between the searches.

Loss of priority

It is possible that the bank could lose the priority offered to it by the above. Examples of this could be:

(a) Notice of subsequent charge. This has been discussed previously in Chapter two and will be mentioned again later. In essence when the bank receives notice of a subsequent charge (usually either a C(i), C(iii), or Class F) its priority is fixed at the balance of the secured debt on the date of receipt of the notice: *Deeley* v *Lloyds Bank Ltd* (1912). If the bank is lending on current account and does not stop (other expressions such as freeze or break are also used) the account but allows it to continue to run, then *Clayton's Case* will operate to the bank's disadvantage, in that credits to the account will extinguish the element of the debt that ranked in priority to the subsequent mortgagee's debt and new debits to the account will create a new debt that ranks behind the subsequent mortgagee's debt. The bank does have two defences; firstly it could come to an agreement with the subsequent mortgagee that the bank's charge will have priority upto a certain figure (this document is known as a deed of priorities), or the bank could rely on a clause in its security document precluding the operation of *Clayton's Case*, as held in *Westminster Bank Ltd v Cond* (1940).

(b) Non-retention of the title deeds. The bank's priority hinges on the fact that a charge taken with the deposit of the title deeds does not need to be registered and has ultimate priority. There are a number of possible dangers for the bank if reliance on this priority is taken too far and the title deeds released from their possession. Two examples could include,

● Firstly, the release of the deeds to the customer for inspection. If the deeds were to be released to the customer they could be offered as security to an unsuspecting lender as in *Agra Bank Ltd v Barry* (1874). Even if the new/prospective mortgagee were to search at the Land Charges Department nothing would be revealed as the bank's charge does not need to be registered. Hence, if an inspection of the deeds is requested, this is usually undertaken on bank premises and in the presence of a bank official. If this is not possible, then inspection in front of a solicitor is arranged, which brings us nicely to:

● Secondly, release of the deeds to a solicitor, for example, acting in the sale of the property. There is a feeling that whilst the deeds are held by the solicitor the mortgagee is at risk and indeed some mortgagees have even gone as far as adopting the practice of registering a C(i) or C(iii) entry, depending on their charge, when deeds are released to solicitors. This is not a very common practice as it is felt that the solicitor is acting on the bank's behalf as its agent, and so the deeds have in fact never left its possession.

(c) If mortgagees agree between themselves to alter the order of priority, the mortgagor's agreement is not necessary; *Chea Theam Swee v Equiticorp Finance Group Ltd* (1991).

Registered land

Title

Title to registered land is evidenced by a land certificate, a large booklet quoting on the cover the title number and bearing the seal of the District Land Registry dealing with the title. Inside the cover to the certificate is a section quoting the last date that the certificate was compared with the records held by the District Land Registry. The rest of the certificate comprises copies of the registers, up-to-date as at the date quoted on the inside cover. Finally, there may, or may not, be a basic street map showing the location of the land/property and on the inside of the back cover general information relating to the certificate.

Transfer of title is achieved by the vendor (seller) completing a simple deed of transfer, which is then passed to the District Land Registry along with the land certificate. A new land certificate will be issued bearing the name of the purchaser, replacing that of the vendor.

If a legal charge is taken, the mortgagee will be issued with a charge certificate, which is identical to a land certificate except that the colour of the seal on the front of the document is green (as opposed to red on a land certificate) and the details of the charge will be recorded inside the document in the charges register, discussed in full below. If a charge certificate has been issued it is necessary for the land certificate to have been surrendered to the District Land Registry.

The District Land Registry
General

H.M. Land Registry is divided into District Land Registries for ease of administration, each areas being served by a District Land Registry. The first two letters of the title number indicate the District Land Registry dealing with the title (eg, LA titles are dealt with at Lytham District Land Registry). There are three Registers held at the District Land Registry, and reproduced in the land certificate or charge certificate:

(i) Property Register. This will quote the title number, and a brief description of the property, for example, '41, Percy Street, Bolton' (and not 'a rather run-down two bedroom terraced house'). If it is not possible to refer to the property accurately, then the location will be quoted, for example, 'the land at the intersection of Whitecroft Road and Sherbourne Road bounded on the north side by Whitecroft Road and on the west by . . . etc.'; a street map will also be enclosed in these circumstances. The property register will also inform you whether the title is freehold or leasehold and if leasehold, brief details of the terms of the lease will be quoted.

(ii) The Proprietorship Register. This register will quote the name and address of the present owners of the property and any restrictions or cautions registered against the title. Both of these items are discussed in full later in this chapter. Also this register will quote the class of title held by the owner. These comprise:

● *Absolute title* – This is a state guaranteed title and is subject only to overriding interests (discussed in the initial security considerations later) and any minor interests or other items quoted in the registers. Due to the presence of the state guarantee the title is unchallengeable and can relate to freehold or leasehold titles, although it will only apply to leasehold titles where the originating freehold title is also registered with absolute title.

● *Good leasehold title* – obviously, this can apply only to a leasehold title and occurs when the leasehold title is guaranteed but no mention can be made of the freehold title from which it has originated.

● *Possessory title* – here the District Land Registry can speak only for items after the date of registration of the title, items prior to that date are not covered. The reason for the registration of such a title is usually the inability of the District Land Registry to satisfy itself as to the title of the possessor on first registration, due to a missing document or lost title deeds to unregistered land. Possessory title can be converted to absolute title 15 years after the first registration, or to good leasehold 10 years after first registration.

● *Qualified title* – rarely seen and granted due to a defect in the title of the possessor.

Where registered property is offered as security banks will accept only the first two classes of title (ie, absolute or good leasehold).

Priority of charges

Priority of charges is decided purely upon date of registration. The one exception to this rule is agreement between the mortgagees. The mortgagor need not be party to the agreement; *Chea Theam Swee* v *Equiticorp Finance Group Ltd* (1991). One important difference between registered and unregistered land is that a first charge of unregistered land does not need to be registered; this is not so with registered land, where **all** charges must be registered to protect their priority.

Searches

When a bank is considering taking a registered property as security there are two types of search available to it. The first is merely a request for office copies, which the bank will request should the land certificate not be available to it, or if it wishes to confirm that the land certificate held is up to date. The District Land Registry will provide the bank with up to date copies of each register, from their records, which could differ from the land certificate if it has not been updated since the latest entry on the register.

The second search available is known as an official search and will quote a date from which the search is required. For example, if the last time the land certificate was compared with the register is 20 June 1990, then this will be the date which the bank will quote on the official search form. The response from the District Land Registry will quote any alterations on the title from this date and will also guarantee that the details will not alter for a further 30 working days. This period is known as the protection period and is a great advantage to mortgagees when taking a charge over registered land. Since December 1990 the consent of the title owner is no longer necessary when undertaking a search at the District Land Registry.

Loss of priority

As mentioned when discussing unregistered land above, it is possible to lose priority due to not stopping or breaking the running current account upon receipt of notice of a subsequent charge. This is fully discussed in the above section on unregistered land and if you are not familiar with the mechanics of its operation you must re-read the implications of *Deeley* v *Lloyds Bank Ltd* (1912), and *Clayton's Case* operating against the bank.

Other items which could appear in the land or charge certificate

(i) Caution. This is registered to protect the interests of a lender or other interested party and does not require the production of the land certificate to be registered. Once a caution has been registered, then any alteration to the register will be notified to the person registering the caution, who will then have 14 days to act, by either seeking a court injunction or registering a legal charge. Due to this 14 day period and the fact that no fee is payable to register a caution, many banks use a specific form of caution, a notice of deposit, to take a legal charge by registering a caution and holding a legal charge form unregistered. This is discussed in full later in this chapter.

(ii) Notice. This can be registered only by an interested party if the land certificate is held by that party.

(iii) Legal Charge. Self explanatory and discussed in full later.

(iv) Restriction. This is an entry in the register to protect an interest in the property, and examples can include a restriction on the distribution of any sale proceeds, or a mortgagee (say a bank) restricting the creation of any subsequent mortgage except with the consent of the party registering the restriction. Unfortunately the restriction alone is not effective unless registered as a caution, supported by the 14 day protection period, within which the bank could apply for a court injunction against the perceptive subsequent mortgagee.

▌ Charges

First/second or subsequent?

One of the characteristics that makes land so complicated (or interesting) is the relatively high popularity of second or subsequent charges. Land is not the only security where it is possible to take a second charge (it is also possible with life policies) but the trend of constantly increasing values of property has meant that owners of property quite often hold a reasonable 'equity' (the difference between the value of the property and the outstanding balance of the mortgage on the property) and it is not unusual for this to be the only asset many people hold, and thus the only item they can offer as security. Hence, if the bank wishes to lend and protect its advance with security, it needs to take a charge over the property that will rank after the first mortgagee. The subsequent charge must be registered at the District Land Registry (if registered land) or the Land Charges Register (if unregistered) and notice will need to be given to the first mortgagee. The giving of this notice will fix the value of the first mortgagee's charge at the balance outstanding at the date of receipt of the notice.

If the first mortgagee is lending on overdraft then the ruling in *Deeley* v *Lloyds* will apply (as described above), with *Clayton's Case* operating against them. If the first mortgagee is lending on loan or mortgage, then no action is necessary other than to note in their records that if they lend any more money their advance will rank after the debt of the subsequent mortgagee, unless either the two mortgagees agree to a deed of postponement or the first mortgagee is obliged to make further advances, known as tacking, and the subsequent mortgagee should have been aware of this fact.

Equitable or legal?

Remedies

Essentially, the major difference between an equitable and a legal charge is the means by which the mortgagee can obtain repayment of his debt. Either mortgagee can sue the debtor for the recovery, this would mean taking legal proceedings against the debtor following the serving of formal demand. To sue in your own name is a right of any creditor and is not limited to mortgagees. However, mortgagees (either legal or equitable) have further remedies as follows:

Equitable mortgagee

Normally, an equitable mortgagee cannot enforce its security without approaching a third party. This third party will either be the equitable mortgagor, approached to comply with his promise in the memorandum of deposit to execute a legal mortgage if asked to do so by the mortgagee, or if this is not successful the mortgagee will approach the courts asking them to allow the bank rights as a legal mortgagee, despite holding only an equitable charge. Bearing in mind the fact that the customer has defaulted on his promise to repay, it is unlikely that the equitable mortgagor (the customer if a direct charge, or the owner if a third party security has been taken) will keep his promise to execute a legal charge.

However, one solution to this problem is to have the memorandum of deposit executed under seal, as opposed to under hand as described above. A memorandum of deposit executed under seal will appoint the bank as an agent for the equitable mortgagee by power of attorney (for a full discussion of powers of attorney see Chapter six). Once appointed, the bank will be able to execute a legal mortgage on the mortgagor's behalf. This will give the mortgagee the same remedies as a legal mortgagee, as discussed below.

Legal mortgagee

Once again I rely on a mnemonic to help remember the remedies of a legal mortgagee. The question to ask yourself is what does the mortgagor need to fear should he default on the advance and the mnemonic is FEAR, made up as below:

Foreclosure. This is an order of the courts, which removes the mortgagor's equity of redemption and effectively means that the whole of the asset (in this case the land or property) will vest in the name of the mortgagee and that whatever proceeds are received should the asset be sold will belong to the mortgagee, irrespective of the level of the debt between the two parties. Due to this removal of the mortgagor's equity of redemption it is very unusual for the courts to agree to the application.

Exercising of power of sale. This is a remedy provided for under s.101 Law of Property Act 1925, whereby the mortgagee can sell the property without the consent of the mortgagor, and tends to be the most popular option of mortgagees. By law the power of sale is exercisable only after the following has occurred:

(a) the borrower is in default for at least three months' capital or two months' interest, and formal demand has been served: s.103 Law of Property Act 1925.
    Note: this time limit is excluded by a specific clause in the legal charge form/mortgage deed and is easily defeated by banks; or
(b) the mortgagor is in default of some other clause in the legal charge form; and
(c) where the transaction is a regulated agreement under the Consumer Credit Act 1974, and the property is residential the mortgagee must apply to the courts for their consent, unless the mortgagor agrees to the sale.

When exercising its power of sale, the bank will usually sell the property at auction, or via an independent estate agent, selling only on a written recommendation from the estate agent that the offer can be accepted.

When the mortgagee is selling the property he owes duties to the mortgagor and to the depositor of other third party security as follows:

● The mortgagee must obtain the true market price for the property:
Cuckmere Brick Company v *Mutual Finance Limited* (1971), where it was decided that the non-disclosure by the bank that planning permission was held for a number of flats on the land had adversely affected the resulting sale price.

● The mortgagee has no duty to wait for a favourable time at which to sell; *Bank of Cyprus* v *Gill* (1979), where the mortgagor tried to claim that the bank sold at a time when property prices were deflated, and if the bank had waited, a better price would have been obtained.

● If the bank should interfere in the sale, then the bank may owe a duty to the surety (depositor of any third party security) as well as to the debtor; *Standard Chartered Bank* v *Walker & Walker* (1982), where the bank insisted on a quick sale, which resulted in a lower than expected attendance at the auction and the price obtained was less than anticipated, resulting in the third party being asked to contribute a greater than expected amount.

● If the land is unregistered the mortgagee must undertake a search at the Land Charges Department (known as a surplus proceeds search), to check the existence, or otherwise, of any subsequent mortgagee(s). Such a search is dispensed with if the land is registered as the District Land Registry would have informed the bank should a subsequent charge have been registered.

● Once the property has been sold the proceeds must be distributed in the following order:

To discharge the debt of any prior mortgagee(s).
To meet the cost of the sale (eg, estate agents, solicitors etc.).

To discharge the debt of the mortgagee exercising the power of sale.
To discharge the debt of any subsequent mortgagee(s).
The remaining sale proceeds (if any) will be forwarded to the mortgagor.

Returning to the mnemonic, FEAR:

Appoint a receiver. Under s.101 Law of Property Act 1925, the bank can appoint a receiver to manage the property. It is important to note that although appointed by the mortgagee, the receiver is in fact an agent of the mortgagor. The mortgagee is not responsible for any breach of duty, or negligence of the receiver. However, should the mortgagee interfere with the receiver he will be liable; *Standard Chartered Bank* v *Walker & Walker* (1982). The appointment is subject to s.103, as described above and once again the bank will specifically prevent s.103 applying, with a clause in the charge form. Receivers are rarely appointed, except where the property is complicated or let, for example, a block of flats or a mill containing many small units. The receiver will collect any income derived from the property and will distribute it in the following order:

To discharge any rents, rates or other direct outgoings connected with the property.
To meet the receiver's expenses and costs.
To payment of the interest on the mortgagee's debt.
To reduction of the capital outstanding on the mortgagee's debt.

Repossess. Once again this is an option rarely exercised by the mortgagee. This is so because if the mortgagee enters into possession, he acquires the rights and duties of the mortgagor. Thus he is liable for any negligence associated with the up-keep of the property (for example, a slate falling off the roof and maiming a passer-by), and he is liable to the mortgagor for the difference between what the mortgagor actually received and what he might have received with greater care on behalf of the mortgagee; *White* v *City of London Brewery* (1889).

Taking the charge

In general the formalities associated with taking a legal charge are greater than with taking an equitable charge. Hence, if the security, for whatever reason, must be completed quickly it is usual to take an equitable charge. The actual procedures for taking the charge are discussed in full later in this chapter, but for example, an equitable charge can be taken by the mere deposit of the title deeds, with or without the completion of a memorandum of deposit.

Initial security considerations

Charges registered under the Matrimonial Homes Act 1983

Under s.1 Matrimonial Homes Act 1983, it is possible for a spouse (usually, but not definitely, the wife) to have a right of occupation in a property of which she is not a legal owner, by which she cannot be evicted from the property except by court order. As the charge is classed as an equitable charge over the property it must be registered as either a Class F charge (unregistered land) or a notice (registered land). Failure to register the charge would render it unenforceable against a subsequent purchaser for value (including a mortgagee). A bank as mortgagee can be affected by such a charge in one of two ways:

(i) when taking the charge the bank's search reveals a charge registered under the Act.

Here the bank must agree with the spouse that her charge will rank behind that of the bank (deed of postponement) or the spouse must agree to remove the charge. If neither of these matters occur, then it is usual for the property to be classed as unacceptable for security purposes.

(ii) having taken the charge the bank is notified of the subsequent registration of a charge under the Act. Here the bank must bear in mind the rule in *Deeley* v *Lloyds*, described above and stop the account to prevent *Clayton's Case* operating against the bank.

Overriding interests and registered land

Overriding interests are listed in s.70 Land Registration Act 1925 and are not subject to registration in order to be effective. The main items included as overriding interests are:

(i) leases for any term not exceeding 21 years (ie, short term leases of less than 21 years cannot be registered and will not receive their own separate land certificate)

(ii) the rights of every person in actual occupation, save where enquiry is made of such a person and the rights are not disclosed.

As previously mentioned in certain areas of the syllabus there are 'foundation cases', upon which other cases have been built. In the area of overriding interests the foundation case is *Williams & Glyn's Bank Ltd* v *Boland* (1981). In this famous case (surely in the top five of any list of the most important cases affecting bankers) it was decided that a spouse can have a right of occupation to a property of which she was not a title holder. This interest took the effect of an overriding interest (as per (ii) above) and so registration was not necessary, or indeed possible. However, since the *Boland* case there have been many more cases and the actual conditions for a spouse to achieve an overriding interest are now accepted to be:

(a) The spouse must have contributed directly to the property. In *Winkworth* v *Edward Baron Development Company Limited* (1986), the spouse attempted to claim that a contribution to the company that two years later purchased the property in question, should be accepted as a contribution to the property. The court held that the two transactions were totally separate and in no way connected. Also, in *Midland Bank Ltd* v *Dobson* (1985), the spouse tried to claim that the fact that her earnings contributed to the household budget and that she paid for the redecoration of the property, should have been sufficient. Again the claim failed.

Thus the condition is quite specific, the spouse **must** have contributed directly towards the property.

(b) The spouse must be in actual occupation, as per s.70 Land Registration Act 1925, and mentioned above. However, in a rather surprising case, *Lloyds Bank Plc* v *Rossett* (1990), the court accepted a claim from a spouse that a daily cleaning and decorating visit to the property, which was in the process of extensive repair, was sufficient to satisfy the meaning of 'occupation' as per s.70.

In *Abbey National Building Society* v *Cann* (1990), it was held that the important date for 'occupation' is the date of completion and as the claimant was not in occupation at this date the claim failed.

(c) There must be an intention between the two parties that one party is holding the property on behalf of both of them. This intention could be express or, more commonly, implied, for example, by the spouse making a contribution to the purchase price and/or maintenance and/or mortgage repayments. The implied intent can be overcome by a specific contrary intention. However, in *Lloyds Bank plc* v *Rossett* (1990), it was held that the intent cannot be implied by the mere fact of marriage or co-habitation. Along with failure to comply with the above conditions, another association when an overriding interest cannot apply, was decided in *City of London Building Society* v *Flegg* (1987). In this case the property was held in the name of two parties, as joint tenants, on behalf of other members of their family. It was held, by the House of Lords, that where the property is jointly owned by two or more persons an overriding interest (in respect of other persons in occupation) cannot exist. It has been put forward that this could result in mortgagees insisting that all mortgaged properties are in joint names, possibly with the mortgagee. As yet there does not appear to be any great movement in this area and the main defence is described below.

Rights of occupation and unregistered land

One important point to note is that overriding interests as described above apply only to registered land and so the cases mentioned do not apply to unregistered land. However, a similar concept does exist with unregistered land known as a right of occupation; it is an equitable interest in the property and any one **with notice of its existence** is bound by it. The controversial point is deciding what is to be deemed as notice; the commonly accepted situation is that where the person claiming a right of occupation is not in physical occupation actual notice must exist, and where the mortgagor himself is in occupation enquiry must be made of any party who could possibly have a right of occupation. Where the mortgagor is not in occupation, then enquiries must be made on all parties in occupation.

However, a worrying case for mortgagees is *Kingsnorth Finance Co.* v *Tizard* (1986), where the court decided that the mortgagee had notice of the existence of a wife in occupation and should have questioned her as to her right of occupation. The basis of the decision was that the valuer appointed by the bank should not have made a prearranged appointment to visit the property and should have opened cupboards and drawers to check for evidence of the wife's possessions and thus of the wife's existence. In fact in this case the husband had arranged for the spouse to be conveniently absent when the valuer visited the property and had attempted to conceal her existence. It was held that the bank (via its agent – the valuer) should have been aware of the existence of the spouse and so had constructive notice of her existence. The bank's charge was therefore postponed behind the interest of the wife and was made effectively unenforceable.

Defences against overriding interests and rights of occupation

(i) Firstly the bank must ascertain if any person exists who could possibly have either an overriding interest or a right of occupation. It can do this by asking the legal title holder to list the occupiers of the property and complete a written questionnaire accordingly. The bank can also take the added precaution of inspecting the property and checking for other persons in occupation.

(ii) Secondly any persons discovered can be asked to sign a postponement of rights, postponing their interests behind those of the bank, or alternatively sign the legal charge form, effectively becoming a party to the charge itself, an obvious problem to overcome here would be undue influence.

Other problems in taking land/property as security

Forged signatures

In *First National Securities Ltd* v *Hegarty* (1985), it was held that where the signature of a joint mortgagor (in this case − the wife) has been forged, the charge is totally unenforceable against her interest in the property. However, in contrast to the *James Graham* v *Southgate Sands* case where a forgery on a guarantee rendered the guarantee totally unenforceable, the court decided that the document still created an equitable charge over the husband's interest in the property. This would appear to be a sensible decision as the bank would not have a power of sale or other rights associated with a legal charge, but should the property be sold, the bank would still be able to claim from the husband's share of the sale proceeds. This problem should be easily overcome by either insisting on identification from unknown mortgagors or insisting on the signatures being witnessed by an independent solicitor.

Lack of consent

Where an equitable charge is taken the intent of **all** legal title holders must be present. In *Thames Guaranty Ltd* v *Campbell* (1985), it was held that where the wife had not consented to the deposit of the title deeds as security she could insist on the return of the title deeds. The easy solution is obviously to insist on all title holders signing a memorandum of deposit, signifying their consent to the equitable charge.

Limited company mortgagors

Where the land/property is owned by a limited company, then additional formalities are necessary. These are discussed in full in the next chapter but are basically:

(a) **Inspection of memorandum and articles of association**. These are the rules of the company and the bank must ensure the company has the power to give the security and that the directors have the power to act on the company's behalf.

(b) **Passing of a resolution**. This is necessary as it indicates that the matter has been voted on and has been accepted by the company.

(c) **Registration at Companies House** within 21 days of creation, self explanatory.

(d) **All other formalities**, as described later in this chapter, need to be completed **in addition** to those above.

NB: It is important that you are familiar with the implications of Companies Act 1989 in respect of (a), (b), (c) above.

Land as security for a Consumer Credit Act 1974 regulated agreement

Where the security for a Consumer Credit Act regulated agreement is land, then the following procedures must be complied with:

(a) Each borrower must receive a borrower's withdrawal copy agreement, along with a specimen copy of the legal charge form.

(b) The borrower is then given a compulsory seven-day consideration period, during which no communication between the borrower and the bank, on this matter, is permitted.

(c) At the end of the consideration period the original agreement is forwarded, along with further specimen charge forms, for signature and return to the bank. At this stage the borrower is entitled to a further seven day period, which may be shortened by the borrower signing the agreement.

(d) Despite the agreement being signed off bank premises the agreement is non-cancellable.

(e)   If the security is third party the mortgagor must receive a copy of the agreement and charge form.

(f)   Agreement of the court is necessary before the bank can realise its security via its power of sale.

Law of Property (Miscellaneous Provisions) Act 1989

Under the above Act it has become necessary for any documentation relating to the disposition of an interest in land (eg, a charge) to be made in writing and signed by the creditor and all mortgagors. This is interpreted to include memorandum of deposits and many prudent bankers are also including legal charge form. Also, any verbal offers of facilities to be secured by land must be confirmed in writing, signed on behalf of the bank. However, such documents need not be executed under seal, merely refer to the document as a deed.

Fire insurance

Technically it is a requirement that each time an interest is taken in a property, for example a legal charge, a notice of interest should be expressed to the fire insurance company. However, as you can imagine, the paper work and the administration of such a system was becoming a large and non-profitable burden on the insurance companies. The British Insurers Association (BIA) has come to an agreement with the Confederation of London Clearing Banks (CLCB) that only in certain circumstances is it necessary for a mortgagee to express his interest to the insurance company. At present the times when notice is required are as follows:

(i)   Where the property is of a commercial nature (eg, shops, factories etc.)

(ii)   Where the property is of a residential nature it is necessary to give notice only when the cover exceeds £200,000.

Thus the incidence of notice being given has been substantially reduced and at all other times proof at the time of making a claim will be sufficient for the insurance company to forward the claim monies direct to the mortgagee.

Valuation

Where the property is residential it is now usual banking practice for the local manager to give a valuation of the property. However, should the property be unusual or of a commercial nature, or if the borrower is buying the property, then it is usual to obtain a professional valuation. Care needs to be taken with professional valuations in that:

(a)   They are addressed to the bank so that if any deficiencies are later discovered which could have a detrimental effect on the bank's security, the valuer will be responsible to the bank for breach of duty or negligence.

(b)   The valuer should be suitably qualified.

One advantage of obtaining a professional valuation is that should the valuer be negligent the bank will be able to reclaim damages from the valuer; *Swingastle Ltd* v *Gibson* (1990).

Local Land Charges Register

This is a list of entries against properties, the register held by the local authority. The entries that are typically registered here will include road widening schemes, slum clearance areas and compulsory purchase orders. The entries tend to affect the value of the property. You will need to remember which registers relate to each type of land; the easiest method of remembering the items revealed by a search of the Local Land Charges Register is that they will be local in their nature, and held at the local town hall.

Where the bank's charge is to be a second or subsequent charge it is not unusual for the bank to waive (ie, not insist on) the formality of such a search. This will usually be where the prior mortgagee is a reputable building society or bank, and their charge has been taken recently. Each bank tends to have its own interpretation of 'recently'; personally I feel two years is a reasonable time, after which I would expect a fresh search to be insisted on.

Second or subsequent charges

Due to the title deeds being held by the first mortgagee (unregistered land), or the land certificate being retained by the District Land Registry (registered land), a subsequent mortgagee needs to find the title details from an alternative source. This is done by sending a questionnaire, bearing the mortgagor's written consent, to the first mortgagee asking the following questions:

- the owners of the property;
- is the land unregistered or registered? If unregistered, the date of the last conveyance/ assignment and if registered the title number (these details are required to identify the property in the charge form, and the title number also permits other searches to be made);
- is the tenure freehold or leasehold and if leasehold the details of the lease;
- the fire insurance details (is notice necessary?);
- the details of the first mortgagee's advance (amount outstanding, and are further advances compulsory − known as tacking − power of consolidation − can other advances be covered by the charge − and are repayments up-to-date?) in order that the equity and hence value as security can be calculated.

∎ Method of taking the security

Due to the complexity of land, I will discuss each type of charge separately, and will assume that the earlier sections of the chapter have been read in depth and fully understood. If there are steps with which you are not familiar, I suggest that you re-read the earlier sections above.

Unregistered land legal charge

First legal charge unregistered freehold land

(a) Obtain the title deeds and ensure a good root of title exists (15 years). If not, forward to a solicitor for a report of title.

(b) Value the property. Remember a decision needs to be taken as to whether a professional or manager's valuation will be acceptable.

(c) Search at the Land Charges Department. The mortgagee will be looking for any entry that could affect the mortgagor's title to the property, or the bank's charge.

(d) Search at the Local Land Charges Registry and confirm the acceptability of the property as security.

(e) Ensure that no rights of occupation exist, by the completion of a questionnaire by the title holder, and/or a visit to the premises. If there is a possibility of such an interest the spouse should be asked to complete a separate declaration or become a party to the legal charge form.

(f) Ask the legal owners of the property to execute the legal charge form.

You now need to ask yourself the two questions **where**? and **why**? The answers are: in the presence of a solicitor, or senior bank official; to ensure the bank is not exposed to the risks of *non est factum*, forgery, undue influence (a typical plea on land where the security is third party in its nature), misapprehension and misrepresentation.

(g) Register the charge at the Land Charges Department if necessary (not necessary if the title deeds are held as here), Companies Registry if the mortgagor is a limited company and give notice to the fire insurance company if necessary.

(h) Search again at the Land Charges Department, to ensure no further entries have been made since the last search.

First legal charge unregistered leasehold land

The formalities are exactly the same as above except:

(i) The lease should be examined to ensure that no restrictive covenants are present.
(ii) The mortgagee must give notice to the lessor, or gain his consent, as necessary.
(iii) The latest ground rent receipt must be obtained to ensure that the ground rent is up-to-date.

Second legal charge unregistered freehold land

(a) Forward a prior mortgagee questionnaire to the first mortgagee; assuming all replies are satisfactory continue as below.

(b) Value the property.

(c) Search at the Land Charges Department. Remember that as registration by the first mortgagee is not necessary, his charge will not be revealed by the search.

(d) Search at the Local Land Charges Department, remembering that this search may be waived depending upon the standing of the first mortgagee and the date of the last search.

(e) Ensure that no rights of occupation exist, or if they do, ensure that a separate memorandum is signed by the occupiers or they are party to the charge.

(f) Execute the legal charge, remembering the two questions **where**? and **why**?

(g) Register the charge as a puisne charge at the Land Charges Department, give notice to the fire insurance company if necessary, and register at Companies House if the mortgagor is a limited company.

(h) Give notice to the first mortgagee. Section 94(1) Law of Property Act 1925 states that where notice is not given to a prior mortgagee, then the whole of his advance will rank in priority to that of the subsequent mortgagee, and not merely the amount outstanding at the date of creation of the subsequent charge or any other date. Giving of notice fixes the level of priority of the first mortgagee at the balance outstanding on the date of receipt of notice of the subsequent mortgagee: *Deeley* v *Lloyds Bank Ltd* (1912), and if the first mortgagee is lending on running overdraft and does not stop the account, *Clayton's case* will act to the detriment of the first mortgagee, and in favour of the second, by credits to the account reducing the amount claimable under the first charge and new debits creating a new debt ranking after that of the subsequent mortgagee.

(i) Search again at the Land Charges Department, remember the mnemonic SCENT, as discussed above.

Second legal charge unregistered leasehold land

The procedures are exactly as above, with the one exception that the lease details supplied by the first mortgagee need to be checked, for restrictive covenants, notice or consent, and ground rent receipt.

Registered land legal charges

First legal charge registered freehold land

(a) Obtain the land certificate, and make a note of the class of title (NB, absolute, good leasehold are the only ones usually accepted) and inspect for other details quoted such as overriding interests, charges etc.

(b) Update the land certificate, either by forwarding it to the District Land Registry, or by requesting office copies. Note that the registered owner's written consent will be necessary.

(c) Request an Official Search (on form 94A), and on receipt note the date of expiration of the protection period.

(d) Value the property.

(e) Search at the Local Land Charges Department (usually at the Town Hall).

(f) Ensure no overriding interests exist, by asking the registered owner to complete a questionnaire and asking any person disclosed to postpone their interests by a separate memorandum or by becoming party to the charge document.

(g) Ensure that the legal charge document is executed, remembering the two questions **where?** and **why?**

(h) Register the charge at the District Land Registry, within the protection period.

(i) Give notice to the fire insurance company if relevant.

(j) Receive the Charge Certificate from the District Land Registry, within the protection period.

Alternative method of taking first legal charge registered land

Note: (a), (d), (e), (f), (g) and (i) are identical to immediately above. However, (b), (c) and (h) are replaced by:

(i) Forward the Land Certificate to the District Land Registry along with a 'Notice of Deposit': land registry form 85A. The District Land Registry will register the bank's interest (as a caution) and undertake to inform the bank of any dealings on the title and will give the bank fourteen days' notice to take action deemed necessary, usually registering its legal charge. Registration of a Notice of Deposit as a caution (which gives the protection referred to above) is within rule 239 Land Registration Rules 1925, and its validity was confirmed in *Barclays Bank Ltd* v *Taylor* (1974).

(ii) The advantage of this procedure is that it is generally quicker and does not incur a registration fee (usually met by the customer).

(iii) The bank will receive back a Land Certificate with the notice of deposit recorded therein.

Many banks now adopt this procedure due to the advantages in (ii) above, and consider that this will give them an edge over their competitors in that the security will be perfected more quickly and funds will be released sooner.

First legal charge registered leasehold land

The procedures adopted are identical to the procedures above, plus an investigation of the lease details from the Land Certificate and sight of the latest ground rent receipt. Points to note will be:

● is notice to (or the permission of) the lessor necessary?
● is the ground rent up to date?
● are there any restrictive covenants?

Second legal charge registered freehold land

(a) Obtain the details of the first mortgagee, and forward the standard questionnaire as described in Initial Security Procedures above. Providing the details are acceptable, proceed as follows:

(b) Request office copies, and inspect their contents upon receipt.

(c) Submit an Official Search form to the District Land Registry, noting the expiry of the protection period.

(d) Ensure the lack of overriding interest.

(e) Search at the Local Land Charges Department (if not waived).

(f) Ensure that the legal charge form is executed, remembering the questions **where?** and **why?**

(g) Register the charge at the District Land Registry within protection period.

(h) Give notice to the first mortgagee, fixing the debt covered by the first charge (see *Deeley* v *Lloyds*) and receive confirmation of receipt.

(i) Give notice to the fire insurance company, if relevant.

(j) Receive back the Charge Certificate from the District Land Registry.

Second legal charge registered leasehold land

The procedure to be followed here is as immediately above, together with the procedure outlined under 'First legal charge registered leasehold land'.

Procedures for taking equitable charges

Generally

There are many methods of taking an equitable charge over land. Basically these include the mere retention of the title documents (deeds or land certificate) in contravention of Law of Property (Miscellaneous Provisions) Act 1989, or their retention plus the execution of a memorandum of deposit either under hand or under seal. The execution of a memorandum of deposit gives the mortgagee (the bank) the protection of the clauses contained in the document, such as continuing security, all monies etc. If the memorandum of deposit is executed under seal the mortgagee will also acquire a power of sale without the necessity of approaching either the mortgagor (owner) or the courts. The full advantages and disadvantages of an equitable charge are discussed in full in Chapter thirteen.

Unregistered land

The most common method of taking an equitable charge over unregistered land (freehold or leasehold) is to obtain the title deeds, supported by a memorandum of deposit under seal. As the bank will hold the deeds no registration at the Land Charges Department is necessary. However, if the title deeds are not held, a C(iv) General Equitable charge should be registered.

Registered land

The land certificate should be obtained, supported with a memorandum of deposit under seal. The bank will forward the land certificate to the District Land Registry along with a Notice of Deposit. If the land certificate is not available (for example, following the delay on a first registration) a Notice of Intended Deposit can be registered and the District Land Registry will forward the land certificate to the equitable mortgagee when available.

Priorities

Generally, for both registered and unregistered land, the first registered charge (be it equitable or legal) has priority, with the one notable exception of the possession of title deeds by the first mortgagee plus a clear Land Charges Department search in unregistered land giving that mortgagee absolute priority.

Therefore, if a prospective legal mortgagee becomes aware of the existence of an existing equitable mortgagee (usually by the absence of the title deeds or as a result of a search at either the Land Charges Department or District Land Registry), then it cannot overcome the equitable mortgage merely by registering a legal charge. If the legal mortgagee wants priority over the equitable interest, it must have the equitable interest postponed in its own favour.

▌ Release of charges on land

Basically, the theory that to release your charge all you need to do is reverse the steps you took in taking it, holds good with land. If the land is unregistered the charge document needs to be vacated, under seal by an agent appointed under a power of attorney, and stored with the deeds (ie, either returned to the mortgagor if a first charge or forwarded to the prior mortgagee if a subsequent charge, to be placed with the deeds). If the land is registered land a Form 53 needs to be sealed on behalf of the bank (again by an agent appointed under a power of attorney) and this form is then forwarded to the District Land

Registry. Following this, everyone that you made aware of the existence of your charge now needs to be informed of your lack of interest in the land/property.

Therefore, the procedure for the discharge of a charge over land is as follows:

If unregistered land

First charge

(a) Vacate the legal charge form and place this with the title deeds.

(b) Return the title deeds to the mortgagor and obtain a receipt from him.

(c) Inform the lessor, if leasehold and notice was necessary under the lease.

(d) Inform the fire insurance company, if notice had been given.

(e) If there is a subsequent mortgagee the bank must forward the title deeds and vacated legal charge to that mortgagee, as that mortgagee will now move up the order and become the first mortgagee.

Subsequent charge

You will need to follow stages (a) to (e) above plus:

(f) Inform the prior mortgagee and forward to him the vacated legal charge form for placement with the title deeds.

(g) The C(i) puisne charge will need to be removed from the Land Charges Department.

Equitable charge

Usually notice is not necessary as no notice/registration would have been effected. However, the memorandum of deposit will need to be stamped 'cancelled' and is usually retained by the bank. It is not placed with the deeds as it does not form part of the chain or root of title. The title deeds then need to be returned to the equitable mortgagor and a receipt obtained for them. Alternatively, if there is a subsequent mortgagee the title deeds must be forwarded to him.

If registered land

First charge, legal charge registered

(a) Submit completed Form 53 and the Charge Certificate to the District Land Registry. The bank will receive back the land certificate and this should be returned to the mortgagor and a receipt obtained from him.

(b) Inform the lessor, if leasehold and notice was necessary under the lease.

(c) Inform the fire insurance company, if notice had been given.

(d) If there is a subsequent charge, the bank must inform the subsequent mortgagee of the removal of its charge and naturally in those circumstances no land certificate will be issued.

First charge, notice of deposit registered, legal charge held unregistered

(a) The reverse of form 85A (notice of deposit) is completed and forwarded to the District Land Registry along with the land certificate. The bank will receive back the land certificate with its interest removed. The land certificate must be returned to the mortgagor, along with the vacated legal charge form. A receipt should be obtained from the mortgagor. The procedure then follows (b), (c) and (d) immediately above.

Subsequent mortgage

(a) Complete Form 53 and, along with the Charge Certificate, forward it to either the District Land Registry, or alternatively to the prior mortgagee along with a notice of release of charge. Technically, the former is the correct procedure, with the mortgagee being responsible for the removal of his charge. However, recently the latter has become more and more common. Either way the bank will not receive anything other than an acknowledgement from either party.

(b) If the Form 53 and Charge Certificate have been forwarded to the District Land Registry, as is correct, the bank must inform the prior mortgagee.

(c) Inform the lessor, if leasehold, and notice was necessary.

(d) Inform the fire insurance company if necessary.

Equitable charge

Obviously, procedures to remove the charge depend upon the steps taken when perfecting the charge. If a notice of deposit has been registered then this must be removed as described above, and if a memorandum of deposit has been taken, this should be stamped 'cancelled' and retained by the bank. The land certificate needs to be returned to the mortgagor and a receipt obtained from him. Alternatively, if there is a subsequent mortgagee the bank must notify him of the removal of the bank's charge and naturally a land certificate will not be issued.

▮ Land – summary

Without doubt land is the most complicated security you need to cover in the syllabus. However, if you get your 'foundations' solid, then it is amazing how simple it can become. You need basically to understand the differences between the following options:

- Registered and unregistered,
- Freehold and leasehold,
- Legal and equitable,
- First and second charge,
- Residential and commercial property

and be able to apply them in one sentence, for example, a first legal charge over unregistered freehold residential property.

Also, a good understanding of overriding interests and rights of occupation is essential as this is a favourite area for examination questions. Other popular areas for past examiners have been priorities (remember, the date of registration decides priority with the one exception of possession of the title deeds – if unregistered land) and the possible disadvantages of third party charges over land, the main disadvantage being undue influence, charges over the matrimonial home (forgery of signatures and charges registered under the Matrimonial Homes Act) and remedies of a legal mortgagee (remember the mnemonic FEAR and the importance of a surplus proceeds search).

All in all, it is a difficult but very interesting and relevant area of the syllabus and one which has featured on every examination paper for as long as I can remember. It is this fact which makes it an important area of study. Unfortunately many students approaching the examination and getting nervous look for areas to leave out and land tends to be a favourite area. However, this is self defeating for three reasons:

(i) You can almost guarantee a question on land — how many areas of the syllabus can you say that about?

(ii) It is one of the more relevant areas of the syllabus as most people with a progressive branch or administration orientated career will encounter land as security, be it as security for a loan or overdraft or at least as a mortgage advance. The customer will expect you to know and understand at least the fundamentals behind the taking of the security.

(iii) It recurs later in your studies, under what was previously known as Practice of Banking I and is now known as Branch Banking — Law and Practice.

This is an important area of the syllabus and one to be tackled seriously and with venom.

▌Advantages and disadvantages of land as security

Advantages

(a) In the past property values have tended to rise, although at the time of writing there is speculation that this trend is coming to an end.

(b) It tends to be the most popular type of asset held, especially since following the boom in the property-owning community, the majority of families in Britain own their home and coupled with (a) above this means that most will also have an equity in these properties.

Disadvantages

(a) It is difficult to obtain an accurate assessment of the market value (particularly when compared with stocks and shares and life policies).

(b) It is complicated to take and can take up to three months to complete.

(c) It is difficult to realise — there can be a long delay in between taking the decision to realise the security and receiving the proceeds.

(d) Problems can exist with overriding interests or rights of occupation.

(e) If the property is residential, the consent of the court is necessary before possession is possible, unless the mortgagor voluntarily vacates the property.

FACT SHEET

Land

1. Options
A. Legal estates — freehold or leasehold.
(i) freehold — fee, simple, absolute in possession.
(ii) leasehold — term of years absolute. Special considerations include restrictive covenants

(NB, bankruptcy clause), possibilities that lessor's consent to charge is necessary or notice must be given, ground rent must be up-to-date.

B. Title – registered or unregistered.

(i) unregistered – title evidenced by bundle of title deeds. Good root of title needed (15 yrs) or report on title.
- Land charges department – record of charges other than where deeds are held.
- Priorities – by holding deeds or date of registration of charge. SCENT.
- Loss of priority *Deeley* v *Lloyds* or release of deeds.

(ii) registered – title evidenced by land certificate. Class of title, state guarantee. Absolute or good leasehold accepted.
- District Land Registry – registers held. Protection period, other items registered (NB, caution – notice of deposit, restriction – by legal mortgagee preventing subsequent charge without its consent).
- Priorities decided by date of registration.

C. Charge – first or second. Why? and action to be taken on receipt of notice of a subsequent charge.

D. Charge – legal or equitable. Remedies, FEAR if legal, if equitable depends on whether memorandum of deposit is under hand or seal. If under seal mortgagee has a power of sale. Taking the charge, equitable tend to be quicker.

Initial security considerations

1. Charges under the Matrimonial Homes Act 1983. Treat as any other charge, can have complications if present when taking the security or if mortgagee receives notice, after monies have been released.
2. Overriding interests. Registered land. Very important, regular exam topic. Base case *Williams & Glyn's* v *Boland*, conditions now accepted as:
   (a) Must have contributed to property – *Winkworth* v *Edward Baron, Midland* v *Dobson*.
   (b) Must be in actual occupation – s.70 LRA 1925, *Lloyds* v *Rossett, Abbey National* v *Cann*.
   (c) Must be intent that land is held on behalf of other party – can be implied, for example, shared input, but cannot be implied by marriage or co-habitation; *Lloyds* v *Rossett*.
   Cannot exist where joint owners already exist, the claim must be against the owners from the sale proceeds; *City of London B.S.* v *Flegg*.
3. Rights of occupation. Unregistered land. The mortgagee must have notice. Notice can be constructive: *Kingsnorth Finance Co* v *Tizard*.
4. Defences against 2 and 3. Questionnaire completed by legal owners and possible inspection of the property. Rights postponed by separate memorandum or by becoming party to legal charge.
5. Other problems can include forged signatures: *First National Securities* v *Hegarty* and lack of consent of all parties to an equitable charge: *Thames Guaranty* v *Campbell*.
6. Limited company mortgagors – inspect memorandum and articles, resolution and register at Companies House within 21 days. Companies Act 1989
7. CCA complications. Where the agreement is regulated, consideration and cooling off periods. Court consent needed before power of sale can be exercised.
8. Law of Property (Miscellaneous Provisions) Act 1989
9. Fire insurance – details of the BIA/CLCB agreement should be known.
10. Valuations – when a manager's valuation is acceptable and if professional, must be addressed to bank and valuer must be qualified.

11. Local Land Charges Register – town hall, local matters disclosed. Sometimes waived if subsequent charge is being taken and prior mortgagee is reputable.
12. Second or subsequent charge. Questionnaire procedure.

Taking the charge
No need to repeat here.

Release of the charge
Reverse the procedure for taking the security and return title deeds/land certificate to the mortgagor or inform first mortgagee if subsequent charge. If first charge the deeds must be sent to subsequent chargee if one exists.

Question (October 1989)

Albert, a builder, needed a loan of £150,000 and an overdraft of £20,000 to finance the building of a bridge, because he would not be paid until the bridge was completed. His bank agreed to give him the overdraft facility against the deposit of the title deeds of Victoria Park, a freehold property with unregistered title which is owned by Albert. Albert signs a memorandum of deposit in favour of the bank to secure his current account.

Later three of Albert's friends, Tom, Dick and Harry, each lent him £50,000 against mortgages over Victoria Park. The three mortgages were all signed and dated on the same day and the £150,000 of loans were advanced to Albert on that day.

Tom has an equitable mortgage which he has not registered. Harry and Dick have legal charges. Harry's was registered two days before Dick's. Harry also wrote to Albert's bank giving it notice of his mortgage. Neither Dick nor Tom has given notice to the bank.

Albert's business has failed and his bank has made formal demand. Tom, Dick and Harry have also called in their loans, all of which remain outstanding.

Discuss the respective priorities of the four mortgages given to Albert's bank, Tom, Dick and Harry.

[20 marks]

Key words
overdraft £20,000.
deposit title deeds, freehold unregistered.
all signed and dated on same day
Tom equitable . . . not registered
Harry and Dick legal . . . Harry's registered two days before Dick's.
Harry wrote to bank giving notice.
neither Dick nor Tom given notice
Discuss respective priorities.

Answer

The bank's mortgage does not require registration at the Land Charges Department, because the bank holds the title deeds. The bank will have priority over all the subsequent mortgages for all advances it makes to Albert, except for subsequent current account debits which will rank behind Harry's mortgage.

The effect of the bank receiving notice of Harry's charge is to postpone behind Harry's charge (and any debt owed by Albert to Harry secured by that charge) all current account advances made by the bank to Albert after the date of receipt of that notice.

This would not apply if the bank was obliged to make further advances to Albert: s.94 Law of Property Act 1925, doctrine of tacking. This is extremely unlikely with an overdraft facility which is repayable on demand: *Hopkinson* v *Rolt* (1861).

The rule in *Clayton's Case* means that all subsequently received credits on Albert's current account will repay the earliest debits on that account, thus reducing the bank's priority over Harry's charge: *Deeley* v *Lloyds Bank Ltd* (1912). Any new debits to the account would create a new debt that would rank after Harry's charge.

Harry's charge will also have priority over Dick's charge, because Harry's charge was registered first (as a C(i) puisne mortgage). Date of registration, not date of creation governs priority over charges on unregistered land.

Dick's charge will also rank after all advances on Albert's current account with his bank, because Dick did not give notice of his charge to the bank. Registration at the Land Charges Registry is not sufficient to give notice to a prior mortgagee for the purpose of gaining priority over continuing advances on current account: s.94(2) Law of Property Act 1925. However, when disposing of the proceeds the bank is compelled to undertake a 'surplus proceeds' search at the Land Charges Registry to check for the existence of any subsequent mortgagee prior to the disposal of the funds to the mortgagor: s.198(1) Law of Property Act 1925. Thus, the charge would be effective but would mean that *Clayton's Case* would not operate against the bank.

Notwithstanding that Tom's charge is equitable it must still be registered (Tom could have registered a C(iii) general equitable charge at the Land Charges Registry). As it is, Tom's charge is void against purchasers for value, for example other mortgagees, a trustee in bankruptcy and a bona fide purchaser (the purchaser must give value): s.13(2) Law of Property Act 1925. However, it will still be valid against Albert and will therefore rank after Albert's bank, Harry and Dick, unless Albert goes into bankruptcy in which case Tom will be effectively unsecured.

Author's comment

This question helps to underline the rule that the longer the question, the easier the answer. Once the key words have been ascertained the question is a straightforward one on priorities of charges on unregistered land. One interesting point from the question is the Chief Examiner switching from mortgage to charge and back again throughout the question, showing that the two words are indeed interchangeable. Many candidates miss the relevance of *Clayton's Case* and of those that mention it, 90 per cent miss that because Dick has not given notice **all** of the bank's overdraft will rank before Dick's charge. All in all a reasonably easy question once the candidate has removed the 'padding' and got down to the bare facts of the question.

Question (Spring 1987)

(a) In the case of registered land, when is a wife's interest in the matrimonial home an 'overriding' interest, and how does a lender protect himself against this, or other, overriding interests?   (13 marks)

(b) In the case of unregistered land, if a customer with an unencumbered freehold title approaches the bank for a loan to be made at short notice, how may the bank take an equitable mortgage, and how safe is this?   (7 marks)

Key words

(a) registered land	*(b) unregistered land*
when?	*unencumbered freehold*
wife's	*loan*
'overriding' interest	*short notice*
protect himself?	*how?*
or other	*equitable mortgage*
	how safe?

Answer

Reasonably popular and reasonably well done, though with a marked 'practical' approach. There was a great deal of confusion, however. Many went on about undue influence, which seems unnecessary. There was gross misunderstanding about overriding interests, though most knew about the *Boland* decision. Practically no-one understood trusts for sale. Many thought the wife's Matrimonial Homes Act interest was *ipso facto* overriding. They did not understand the significance of financial contributions in establishing interests, or of occupation as the other half of the equation. They tended to assume the wife was in occupation. They all knew the practical point of seeking her consent, etc. On part (b), they generally knew how to take the charge, but were weak on the risks involved. Many thought that the charge had to be registered, though the bank had the deeds. In both parts there was confusion between registered and unregistered land.

Part (a). The wife's interest under the MHA 1983 is not, of course, an overriding interest. Apart from that there may be an overriding interest if the wife has an equitable interest and is in occupation. 'Occupation' can be problematical (eg, the wife on holiday, or just driven out by the husband). The equitable interest may come from an express contract, declaration of trust, or the making of a financial contribution with the intention that the wife take an interest in the land. Relevant cases: *Williams & Glyn's* v *Boland; City of London BS* v *Flegg; Winkworth* v *Baron*, etc.)

The bank protects itself by inspecting the property for occupation, (see *Tizard* for hazards in doing this) and by obtaining consents from anyone found in occupation (or by joining wife in the mortgage). After the *Flegg* decision, it is safe to deal with two trustees for sale (ie, with two persons who are legal owners) because they can give a good receipt for monies received (they can overreach the equitable title) and thus defeat any third parties, unless the bank knew of breach of trust.

Part (b). The question asks only about unregistered land. The first method is by deposit of title deeds. This can be oral, but should have Memorandum of Deposit. The advantages of the Memorandum are: (i) evidential, (ii) the undertaking to execute legal mortgage and other useful terms, (iii) if under deed s. 101 LPA applies and gives statutory power of sale enabling other mortgages to be discharged so as to give purchaser good clear title. The problems are: (i) possible postponement of priority, by estoppel (rare, as only applies if deeds given back to mortgagor); (ii) registration of charge, if given by company, and if not registered may be affected by s. 395 CA 1985, and no lien arises instead; (iii) defeat of mortgage, if bona fide purchaser of legal interest is given reasonable explanation for lack of deeds (absence then does not give him notice. It is impossible to protect by registration as land charge); (iv) if only deposited by one co-owner as in *Thames Guaranty Ltd* v *Campbell* where the spouse, who had not agreed to the charge, could insist on the return of the deeds.

The other methods of equitable mortgage (rarely undertaken by banks, as indeed are any equitable mortgages these days) are equitable charge, agreement to execute legal mortgage, conveyance of equitable estate with proviso for redemption.

Author's comment

This question was set in 1987, and so there are a number of cases either not included or which have been decided since the question was set, these include *Midland* v *Dobson* (payment towards family budget and redecorating not sufficient) and *Lloyds* v *Rossett* (daily cleaning visit to semi-derelict property was sufficient). When set the question was well met and this is an area of the syllabus which is growing all the time, with more and more cases being decided each year. This illustrates the point that students need to keep themselves up to date by reading *Banking World* each month and the Updating Notes provided each year by the Chartered Institute of Bankers. In (b) the main problem tends to be that students concentrate on the procedures in taking the charge and very little attention is given to the problem as to how safe the charge is. The simple solution is to underline the key words to the question and ensure that the answer actually relates to the question (remember UPRAY).

CHAPTER 16

Stocks and shares as security

Syllabus requirements
- The legal principles of taking, protecting, priority position, enforcement and realisation of, and the effect of insolvency on stocks and shares as security.

∎ Introduction

Many candidates find this topic one of the easiest in the syllabus due mainly to the fact that many of them have had some experience in shares, either as part of their profit-sharing package or from selling or buying shares for customers. For those of you who have not come across stocks and shares before and have no prior knowledge at all in this field, the contents of this chapter are structured with you in mind.

The first question must be, 'What is a share?' Basically, a share is indicated by the possession of a share certificate and denotes ownership by the person named on the share certificate of a proportion of the company issuing the certificate. A stock generally denotes ownership of a loan to the company; so, whereas the shareholder is a part owner of a company, a stockholder is its creditor.

The second type of security covered in this chapter is bearer bonds where the certificate is issued in the name of 'bearer', making the document a fully negotiable instrument (see Chapter ten) and title is transferred by mere delivery providing it is taken in good faith, for value and without notice of any defect in the title of the transferor.

∎ Types of stocks and shares covered

Registered stocks and shares

The first thing to note is that the register referred to is the register held by the issuing company of the shares issued by it. The register will hold details of the holder and number of shares held **plus** other sundry details. It is a record of ownership and is used for the distribution of dividends when due. The company issues a share certificate in the name of the registered owner, despite the fact that it may be held in trust for someone else and this is an area that we will come back to later.

The share certificate is issued in the name of the registered owner. It contains the number of shares held and is authenticated by the company's seal impressed on to the certificate.

The issuing of a share certificate is *prima facie* evidence of title to the shares: s.186 Companies Act 1985. However, it is important to remember that share certificates are not negotiable instruments and transfer of title (gift, charge or sale) is possible only by the completion of a form of transfer including the signature of the holder or his agent. This form when completed is submitted to the issuing company, along with the share certificate (normally via a stockbroker) and a new certificate will be issued in the name of the new owner.

Once a share certificate is issued, the company is estopped from denying the truth of any statement in it to a person who acted on it in good faith and suffered a loss: *Balkis Consolidated Co* v *Tomkinson* (1892). Thus if the certificate was issued as a result of a forgery, the company would need to compensate the new 'holder' either financially or by buying a similar number of shares on the open market to replace the forged ones.

Bearer securities

As previously mentioned, bearer securities are issued in the name of bearer and this has the effect of making them fully negotiable instruments. Hence transfer takes place by mere delivery (for example, handing the certificate to the transferee without endorsement or the support of any other documentation), providing the transaction takes place:

(a) **in good faith** – according to s.90 Bills of Exchange Act 1882 as 'something done honestly whether negligently or not',

(b) **for value** – not necessarily the face value, but in exchange for something with a monetary value, and

(c) **without notice of defect in the transferor's title** – for example, if the purchaser is aware that the instrument has been stolen, then he will not be able to obtain a legal title for himself but he may be able to pass on a legal title to someone who takes the instrument subject to the three criteria.

One problem with bearer securities is the issuing of a dividend, in that the issuing body does not hold a register of the owners. The dividend has to be claimed either in response to an advertisement (for example, in *The Financial Times*), or by submitting coupons attached to the certificate.

Bearer shares tend to be issued by government or large multi-national companies.

▌Initial security considerations

Type of issuing company

Registered shares can be issued by either a Public Limited Company (PLC) or a Private Limited Company (Private Company), but with the following differences:

TOPIC	PLC	PRIVATE COMPANY
Transferability	As a member of the stock exchange there can be no restrictions	Possible restrictions in articles of association, for example, to another company or outside the family.
Valuation	*Financial Times* or stockbroker.	Can be difficult and reference to balance sheet or similar-sized PLC is necessary.
Lien	A PLC cannot have a lien on its own shares	It is possible for a Private Company to have a lien on its own shares for monies owed to it by the registered owner (eg, partly paid shares)

TOPIC	PLC	PRIVATE COMPANY
Realisation	A ready market for the sale of quoted shares is present on the stock exchange.	It is possible that there will be a significantly smaller demand for shares in a Private Company, as the company may not be well known or may have restrictions in articles.

Partly paid shares

As you will see later, when a bank takes a legal charge over stocks and shares the bank actually becomes the legal owner. If the shares are only partly paid (as with many recent privatisations or flotations), the bank as the legal owner will be liable for any outstanding calls. The problem is intensified by the fact that if the issuing company should be wound up, it can approach any holder within the 12 months previous to the winding-up petition (or resolution) for payment of the subsequent call should the present holder fail to pay. Therefore the bank could have a potential liability for up to 12 months after releasing its charge.

Director's shareholding

If a banker is lending to a director of any limited company and is taking, as security, shares issued by that same company, then care must be exercised as it is possible that in order to qualify as a director he must hold a minimum number of shares and by giving a legal charge (transferring them into the bank's name) he may fall below this minimum and have to resign his directorship.

Forgery of transfer document

It was held in *Sheffield Corporation* v *Barclay* (1905), that if a forged transfer form has been passed to the issuing company by the bank in order to transfer title, then the bank must indemnify the issuing company against loss. In this particular case the bank had to re-imburse the issuing company for any loss suffered.

Duplicate certificates

If the bank takes an equitable charge it may well not notify the issuing company of its interest. If this is so then there is nothing preventing the owner from obtaining a duplicate certificate, selling his holding and leaving the bank with a worthless piece of paper. These are actually the facts in *Rainford* v *James Keith & Blackman Co Ltd* (1905), and therefore the risk is real and not merely theoretical.

Prior equitable interests

As previously mentioned, a share certificate is issued in the name of the registered owner and any equitable interest (eg, shares held in trust or subject to an equitable charge) that may exist will not be quoted. This is of little consequence to the bank if taking a legal charge providing they have no notice of the prior equitable interest. If the bank has notice of the prior equitable interest then this cannot be overcome by taking legal charge: *Coleman v London County & Westminster Bank* (1916). If the bank is taking an equitable charge and is not aware of the prior equitable interest, this will still automatically rank before its own equitable charge. The only method of overcoming this problem is to take legal charge before becoming aware of any equitable interests.

Rights and bonus (scrip) issues

Basically a rights issue is the issuing company giving its existing shareholders the right to buy further shares, made strictly in proportion to their existing shareholding, usually at a price below the current market price. It is used by the company as a vehicle to raise capital.

A bonus (or scrip) issue is the issuing of free shares by the company direct to existing shareholders in proportion to their shareholding. The usual reason for this is that the company is 'capitalising its reserves' and it is merely a bookkeeping entry to make its shares more marketable, because a capitalisation issue, like the rights issue, lowers the market price of the shares concerned.

Since both types of issues will usually have a detrimental effect on the market price of the share, it is important that the bank takes appropriate steps to protect itself (as it could find itself holding a lower value of security than prior to rights/bonus issue). If the bank has taken a legal charge then, as the legal owner, the original correspondence will come to the bank first (and must be passed on to the customer); this will give the bank the opportunity to insist that any further shares bought or received by the customer be deposited with the bank. If the bank holds an equitable charge, then it may have no notice of the dealings at all and, unless vigilant, will have to rely on the honesty of the customer, or on the clause in its memorandum of deposit insisting that any further shares received in this manner be deposited with the bank.

∎ Method of taking security

Legal charge

As we have already discussed, when taking legal charge over stocks and shares the bank actually becomes the legal owner. We will now see how this is so:

(a) The certificate will be deposited with the bank. This will enable transfer into the bank's name as the certificate must be sent to the issuing company (not with bearer shares); it will also help to defeat any prior equitable charge, taken by retention of the certificate (see 'equitable charge', below).

(b) A memorandum of deposit will be completed by the registered holder of the certificate (or the bearer of the bearer shares). This will have the effect of putting the mortgagor's intent beyond doubt and will also give the bank the protection of the clauses quoted within the memorandum of deposit, such as continuing security, whole debt clause etc. It is important to remember that the memorandum of deposit is signed by the holder, or bearer, as this person could differ from the customer if the security is third party.

(c) If the security is not made to bearer, then a stock transfer form is also signed by the holder. The bank must take care that the signature is genuine. Obviously if the holder is a customer, this should not prove to be a problem, but extra care is necessary if the holder is not a customer. The reason for this care has been discussed previously in this chapter, ie, the bank could be called upon to indemnify the issuing company should the signature on the transfer document be a forgery: *Sheffield Corporation* v *Barclay* (1905).

(d) Non-bearer shares are then forwarded to the issuing company along with the transfer document, and a new certificate will be issued in the name of the bank. The bank will be the legal holder of the shares.

(e) If the security is bearer security, it is merely retained with a completed memorandum of deposit and, providing the shares are taken in good faith (usually presumed in the case of banks), for value (eg, the granting of the facility) and without notice of a defect in the transferor's title (a matter of fact relating to each individual transaction), the bank will have an absolute legal title which will defeat any defect that a previous holder may have had.

(f) If the shares are issued by a Private Limited Company the bank will need to examine the articles of association for any restrictions on transfer, liens on shares etc.

Equitable

The procedure for taking an equitable charge depends upon the strength of the charge required.

(a) The weakest equitable charge is the mere deposit of the certificate. However, this is prone to claims by the holder that the certificates were not intended as security. It is common for bearer shares to be held by banks, on their customers' behalf, for the purpose of safe keeping and hence such a claim by the holder is not totally unfeasible.

(b) Banks, therefore, tend at the least to take the certificates and require the holder (or bearer) to execute a memorandum of deposit. The memorandum of deposit will give the bank the protection of its clauses as mentioned above under legal charge. However one other important clause is that the holder will undertake to forward any shares obtained under a rights or bonus issue. If the memorandum of deposit is executed under seal the bank will be able to enforce its security without the need to refer to a third party (either the courts or the holder), as it will contain a power of attorney clause, the mortgagor appointing the bank as his agent. The bank will then be able to sign the transfer form on behalf of the holder and sell or transfer the shares.

(c) Normally the bank will ask the holder to sign an undated stock transfer form (known as a blank transfer). This will enable the bank to sell or transfer the shares easily should the borrower default, without needing to approach a third party if the memorandum has been executed under seal. However, should the holder die, the bank transfer will be unforceable.

(d) The bank may serve a 'stop notice' on the issuing company. This has the dual purpose of:

    (i) limiting any lien that the issuing company may have (applicable only where the issuing company is a Private Limited Company) up to the amount outstanding at the time of receipt of the notice, and

    (ii) requesting the company to advise the bank of any movement in the shares, for example, the issue of a duplicate share certificate, to overcome the dangers discussed earlier in *Rainford* v *James, Keith, Blackman Co Ltd* (1905). It is possible, and indeed common, for the issuing company to refuse to accept the notice to avoid any legal liability, but it will normally informally make a note in the register and then inform the bank accordingly.

(e) Care needs to be taken with Private Limited Companies, as discussed above.

■ Priorities

As mentioned above, if the bank takes bearer shares as security then, provided they are taken in good faith, for value and without notice of a defect in the transferor's title, the bank becomes the absolute legal owner of the shares and its title cannot be defeated by any claims either subsequent or previous to its own.

If the bank is taking a charge over registered stocks and shares and becomes aware of a previous equitable interest, then this cannot be overcome by taking legal charge: *Coleman v London County and Westminster Bank* (1916). Other than this rule, if the bank takes legal charge, then as the shares are actually transferred into the name of the bank's nominee company, the bank is still the owner of the shares. If the bank is taking an equitable charge, then it will rank behind a prior equitable interest, even if it had no notice of such a charge.

Hence, by far the most secure form of taking shares as security is to take legal charge without notice of a prior interest, and due to the simplicity of taking such a charge this is the method usually adopted.

■ Realisation on borrower's default

Stocks and shares are one of the easiest forms of security to realise. If legal charge has been taken, then the bank merely needs to sell the shares on the market (on the stock market, if a PLC stocks and shares). If the shares are issued by a Private Limited Company, then the sale of the shares could be more difficult as the market is likely to be more restricted and indeed the articles of association could restrict the sale of the shares to another limited company or an individual outside 'the family'.

If the security is bearer security, the bank would merely need to sell them on the market.

However, if only an equitable charge is held, under hand, without a supporting blank transfer form, then the bank would have to rely on the goodwill of the registered holder or approach the courts for a court order.

■ Release of security

In general, to release any security, the bank merely needs to reverse the transaction when it took the security.

Legal charge

(a) The bank will transfer the shares back into the name of the mortgagor and obtain a new certificate in the mortgagor's name.
(b) It will return the certificate to the mortgagor and mark the memorandum of deposit 'cancelled'.
(c) If it is a bearer security, then the bank will merely return the certificate to the mortgagor.

Equitable charge

The procedure followed depends on the 'strength' of the charge. Assuming that the charge is the strongest possible, then:

(a) The bank will remove the stop notice with the issuing company.

(b) It will mark the memorandum of deposit cancelled.
(c) It will then destroy the blank transfer form.
(d) Finally, the bank will return the certificate to the mortgagor.

■ Summary

In a way similar to life policies, stocks and shares (and especially bearer security) are an excellent form of security, their main advantage being the absolute legal title available. The main disadvantage is the wide fluctuation in price that is possible (eg, in the crash on 19 October 1987). The other disadvantages are relatively obscure, rare and easily overcome.

■ Advantages/disadvantages of stocks and shares as security

Advantages

1. Absolute legal title available.
2. Easy and inexpensive to take.
3. Easy to realise (possible problems with Private Limited Company shares).
4. Notices of rights/bonus issues come direct to bank.

Thus, like life policies, equitable charges are unusual except when a large and active portfolio is held. If a legal charge was held in these circumstances, then every time the mortgagor wishes to sell or buy, the bank would need to be involved, releasing or taking its charge.

Disadvantages

1. Fluctuations in value.
2. There can be problems in realising the security if the security is issued by a Private Limited Company.
3. If a legal charge is taken, the following problems can arise:

   ● **Forgery:** *Sheffield Corporation* v *Barclay*
   ● **Possible claim of negligence** against the bank if it fails to pass on important documentation received (as legal owner) intended for the holder (eg, notice of rights/bonus issues)
   ● **Additional administrative expenses,** for example, passing on dividends
   ● **Responsibility for unpaid calls** on partly-paid shares
   ● **If the mortgagor is a director of the issuing company,** the shares could be part of a minimum share holding required by the articles and a transfer into the nominee company's name could result in the director giving up the position
   ● **If a large, active portfolio is held,** in these circumstances an equitable charge is usually taken, sometimes supported by an undertaking from the stockbroker handling the portfolio.

4. If an equitable charge is taken, the following problems can arise:

- It can be defeated by a prior equitable charge
- There is the possibility of the holder obtaining a duplicate certificate: *Rainford* v *James, Keith, Blackman*
- A bonus/rights issues can affect the value
- With a Private Limited Company, there could be restrictions in the articles or the lien.
- If a memorandum of deposit under hand plus a blank transfer form is taken, should the holder die, the blank transfer form is unforceable and the bank will need to approach the courts.

FACT SHEET

Stocks and shares

Types
Important to realise the difference between registered shares and bearer security.

Initial security considerations
  (i) A Private Limited Company or a PLC, and the effects of this on the security.
 (ii) If partly paid, problems if legal charge, NB, 12-month rule.
(iii) Director's shareholding – care if legal charge, equitable OK.
 (iv) Forgery – care if legal charge taken: *Sheffield Corporation* case.
  (v) Duplicate certificates – care needed if equitable: *Rainford* case.
 (vi) Prior equitable interests – notice decides priority: *Coleman* case.
(vii) Rights and bonus issues – care needed if equitable, problem overcome if legal.

Taking the security
1. Legal – by transferring into nominee company's name.
2. Equitable depends on the 'strength' required.
Both: memorandum of deposit is taken to protect bank.

Priorities
Absolute legal title cannot be defeated for bearer securities. If registered shares, then the transfer into nominee company is defeated only by knowledge of prior equitable interest.

Realisation
- If a PLC sells stocks and shares on the stock market.
- If a Private Limited Company, there can be problems.

Release
Simple: merely reverse the method of taking the charge.

Question (Spring 1987)

(a) In taking a legal charge over registered shares in a public company, what risks does a bank run?
            (12 marks)
(b) Would the risks be increased if the charge were equitable?   (6 marks)
(c) Would the risks be affected in any way if the shares were bearer shares?   (2 marks)
            (Total 20 marks)

Key words

(a) legal	(b) increased?	(c) affected in any way?
registered shares	equitable	bearer shares
public company		
risks?		

Answer

(a) The bank will not get good title by registration if it has actual or constructive notice of the existence of an equitable owner (*Colonial Bank* v *Cady and Williams* (1890), *Société Générale de Paris* v *Walker* (1885) etc. [including *Coleman* v *London County & Westminster Bank* (1916)]). Otherwise it will get good title but must (a) follow correct transfer method (forgeries ineffective; incomplete deeds ineffective – *Powell* v *London and Provincial Bank* (1893) etc.), and (b) seek registration of it's title with the company. The difference should be considered between (i) a share certificate issued to a thief by the company after theft and forgery of transfer where thief presents it to bank for mortgage (the company is estopped: *Balkis Consolidated Co* v *Tomkinson* (1892)); and (ii) share certificate stolen and presented to the bank with forged transfer and the bank seeks registration (the company is not estopped; true owner can rectify register and is entitled to any dividends; bank liable to any purchaser from the bank and to the company if it is used by someone who subsequently relies on a certificate issued by the company to the bank – *Sheffield Corporation* v *Barclay* (1905) and other cases). NB there is no risk from forgery of share certificate itself, since the company will say so.

Avoidance of problems: if signature unknown, require clear identification, signature in bank etc.

(b) Equitable title gives none of the advantages of legal title, so (i) a later legal title may defeat, (ii) an earlier unknown equitable title may take priority, (iii) bank has not same degree of control, including right to sell, and all share rights (bonuses, dividends, votes etc.). However, a signed but otherwise blank transfer form may be taken from the customer to enable sale, or an irrevocable power of attorney may be taken, or if by deed s.101 Law of Property Act 1925 applies (giving the bank a power of sale). Further, the possession of certificate is protection against later legal purchasers unless customer defrauds by obtaining new certificates. A 'Stop' notice might be served, but is expensive. There is no risk of lien for a public company (s.150 Companies Act 1985).

(c) Yes, bearer shares are negotiable instruments. No registration/certificate problems, bona fide purchaser for value without notice gets perfect title.

Author's comment

This is the type of question that makes the underlining of the key words an absolute necessity. I have seen too many students attempt this question and waste sheets of paper talking about equitable charges in (a), and shares in private companies (liens, restrictions of transfer in articles etc) in (a) and (b). There are many obvious points omitted from the answer above and these include in (a) liability for future calls on partly paid shares (up to 12 months following release of charge), possible liability for forwarding important correspondence, effect of rights/bonus issues. In (b) many students tend to concentrate on a definitive 'yes' or 'no' to the answer instead of discussing how they come to their decision.

All in all an easier type of question to the alert candidate who has done his preparation.

CHAPTER 17

Life policies as security

Syllabus requirements

● The legal principles of taking, protecting, priority over, enforcement and realisation of life policies as security and the effect of insolvency on life policies as security.

▌ Introduction

It is not necessary to know word perfect the legal definition of a life policy. However, it is important to realise that a life policy is a legal agreement between the insurance company and the proposer (NOTE not necessarily the person whose life is insured) that in return for the payment of regular premiums (these can be, for example, annually, monthly, weekly etc.) the insurance company will pay a sum in money to the proposer on the death of the life insured or on some other pre-agreed date (eg, maturity of policy or insured reaching 21).

For some of you this may be the first contact with a life policy. However, as banks continue to move more and more into the selling of life insurance products, many students will have experience of selling life policies and some others will have taken out some form of life insurance, possibly linked to their mortgage (endowment or mortgage protection) or in some other form. As many Law Relating to Banking Services students are in their early twenties or late teens, however, the proportion of them having some form of life insurance is likely to be lower than that of the adult public, where it is unusual not to have some form of life cover. It is this popularity which in itself makes life policies a common form of security to be offered and taken. Another factor is that if the bank should take a life policy as security for an advance, and the debtor should die, the bank will have the advantage of being able to settle the advance from the proceeds of the policy without having to approach the relatives of the deceased for repayment.

In many ways a life policy is an excellent form of security, but the degree of excellence depends upon the type of policy taken, and this makes a comparison of the different types of life policy an obvious starting point for a discussion of life policies as security.

▌ Types of policy

Endowment policy

This is a policy with two-fold objectives of:

(a) To provide a lump sum on maturity/encashment of the policy. Once the initial period has passed, each premium paid increases the value of the policy and it is possible to encash the policy and receive the policy value as it stands at that time. This value is known as the surrender value and it is this value which gives the policy its value as security. The fact that the surrender value progressively increases, providing of course that the premiums are paid, is one of the major advantages of an endowment policy as security.

(b) To pay a minimum amount upon death of the assured. Quite often this is the main reason for taking out a life policy, but this coupled with the surrender value gives the customer an opportunity to couple the death cover with an investment opportunity. The minimum amount payable on death is known as the sum assured, and in practice the insurance company undertakes to pay the higher of the sum assured or the surrender value at the time of death. So if the surrender value exceeds the sum assured (as is common with a policy that has been running for a number of years) then it is the surrender value that will be paid, and if not, then the beneficiary and next of kin of the assured will at least receive the sum assured.

These policies are common when connected to an endowment mortgage. In this case a sum is advanced to enable the borrower to purchase a property, and the policy is taken out to repay the advance from the value at the end of the term or death of the assured. As the popularity of endowment mortgages has increased and continues to increase it is probable that more and more customers and bank staff will become familiar with this type of policy.

Term life policy

This is a life policy taken out for a specific term and the insurance company will pay out only if the person whose life is insured should die during the term of the policy. There is no surrender value. Payment can be made either in one lump sum or monthly, over a pre-agreed number of years to the beneficiary or to the next of kin of the assured.

This type of policy is useful, either to those people who require a basic life cover but can afford only the much reduced premiums of a term life plan compared with those of an endowment policy, or to bankers or other lenders looking for life cover on the borrower during the term of the advance.

Whole life policy

Where this type of policy is taken out, the insurance company will pay out on the death of the life insured whenever that may occur, assuming of course that the policy has not been cancelled and is in force at the time of death. The surrender value is substantially lower than that of an endowment policy and so the premiums are lower. It is important to realise that whole life policies do attract a minimal surrender value and it is this characteristic, plus the life cover, that differentiates between them and term life policies.

Both whole life and endowment policies can be with or without profits and this phrase relates to the option of the value of a with profits policy increasing as the insurance company allocates a proportion of its profits to the policies issued by it. Naturally, the premiums of a with profits policy will be higher than those of a without profits policy.

Other sundry life insurance policies

Industrial policies

This type of policy typically has a very small value and is usually taken out to pay for, say, the funeral of the life insured. The policy is accompanied by a receipt book and the small (weekly, fortnightly or monthly) premiums are collected from the house and recorded in the receipt book. They tend not to be used as security due to the small value and the difficulty in ensuring that premiums are up to date; regular inspection of the receipt book would be necessary. (From my personal experience I have had two main problems with this type of policy. The first was that when I was a child I could always guarantee that the premium collector would call just as my parents would sit down for their meal on a Friday night, and this would put them in a bad mood on the very night that I had to ask for my pocket money. Secondly, when I was dealing with the funeral expenses at the death of a relative there were several of these small policies and yet still barely enough to pay for the funeral; for example, four such policies had a sum assured of less than £100).

Mortgage protection policies

These policies are taken out to ensure that a person taking on a repayment mortgage (a loan for house purchase not supported by an endowment or similar policy) it has sufficient life cover to settle the unpaid mortgage should death occur within the term of the advance. In the past, lenders have merely recommended that the policy be taken out, but more recently it has been my experience that lenders are insisting that these life policies should be taken out. These policies are similar to term life policies except that the sum assured falls as the policy ages. This is meant to reflect the fact that the amount outstanding on the mortgage (and hence the life cover required) progressively falls as repayments continue to be made.

Pension policies

Due to the deregulation of the pension industry it is likely that this type of policy will become more popular in the years to come. They are designed to give either a lump sum or regular income (or both) on retirement. It is important to realise that these policies are not assignable (the legal implications of this are discussed below) and basically this means that the bank cannot take a legal interest in the policy.

Unit linked insurance policies

The underlying principle of these policies is collective investment and diversifications, with some life cover for the policy holder and a guaranteed death payment. Units of these policies are bought at the prevailing offer price and sold at the current bid price. Unit trust funds, including unit-linked insurance policies, provide investors with simple, indirect access to the stock market and professional investment management. By purchasing units in a fund, investors pool their money, which is invested, and managed by professional fund managers. Typically the investment may be in a very wide selection of UK and overseas companies' shares, or in safe securities like British government stocks. The value of the units and therefore of one's investment, can go up or down according to the performance of the fund.

▋ Parties to a life insurance policy

The proposer

The proposer of a contract of life assurance is the person who wishes to take out the policy and completes the proposal form, and is usually also either the beneficiary or the life assured under the life policy.

The life assured

This is the person on whose life the policy is taken out. It is on his death that the policy monies will become payable.

The beneficiary

The beneficiary is the person receiving the monies upon the death of the life assured and is in effect the owner of the policy. It is the beneficiary (or beneficiaries) who must sign the legal charge form, known as the deed of assignment, and if the beneficiary is not a debtor, then the security is third party and the bank must be aware of the possibility of undue influence as discussed in previous chapters.

The beneficiary is usually named in the policy document but it is possible for the policy to be drawn under the Married Women's Property Act 1882, when the beneficiary would be described as 'my wife and children'. It was decided in *Re Browne's Policy* (1903), that this created a trust in favour of the wife and children of the life insured who are alive when the policy monies become due. In this case the monies had to be shared between the wife and children of the first marriage and the wife and children of the second marriage. Hence to be effective the assignment should have been signed by all these beneficiaries. This presents the following obvious problems for the banker looking to the beneficiary to sign the deed of assignment:

(a) The 'wife' who claims payment under the policy could well be a completely different person from the 'wife' at the time of taking the assignment by the bank, due to death or divorce and remarriage.
(b) The children could be minors (under the 'age of capacity' – 18 at present) and as such have no power to contract and so are unable to sign the deed of assignment.
(c) There could be children born after the date of assignment, who would not be party to the assignment.

Hence policies drawn under this statute, or indeed any other policy where the beneficiary is a minor, or is not clearly defined, are not acceptable forms of security.

■ Initial security considerations

The first step when taking a life policy as security is to obtain the actual policy. The obvious reason for this is to inspect its contents, but a more basic reason is that the non-production of the original policy by the customer (take care with policies marked 'duplicate') can be deemed to be constructive notice of a prior assignment, as per *Spencer* v *Clarke* (1878), and anyone with constructive notice of a prior charge cannot defeat that charge (ie, rank before it): *Dearle* v *Hall* (1828). Priorities are discussed fully later in this chapter. The main reason other than the above for obtaining the original policy is to check that the details are acceptable to the bank. The main details to be checked are:

Insurable interest

Under s.1 Life Assurance Act 1774, no valid contract of life assurance can be effected without the presence of insurable interest between the life assured and the beneficiary. The reason for this is to differentiate between a policy of insurance and a gambling contract, and the point of insurable interest can be satisfied by asking the question 'would the beneficiary suffer financially by the death of the insured?' If not, there is no insurable interest. There are eight accepted instances of insurable interest:

   (i) Any person with contractual capacity can insure his/her own life.

   (ii) A husband can insure his wife's life and vice versa.

   (iii) A creditor can insure the life of a debtor, but only to the limit of the debtor's liability: *Anderson* v *Edie* (1795), (this is of on-going importance to bankers).

   (iv) A guarantor can insure the life of the debtor, again to the extent of the guarantor's possible liability.

   (v) An employer can insure the life of a key employee: *Hebden* v *West* (1863), and vice versa; similarly a company can insure the life of a company director.

   (vi) A trustee may insure the life of a beneficiary or beneficiaries under the trust, unless the Trust Deed states otherwise: *Tidswell* v *Ankerstein* (1792).

   (vii) A litigant can insure the life of his judge.

   (viii) A parent can be insured for the benefit of a child who is a dependent: *Howard* v *Refugee Friendly Society* (1886).

Despite the above list, there are many instances where insurable interest does not exist, unless proved to the contrary (ie, by showing a financial/pecuniary interest), eg, a parent cannot insure the life of a child: *Halford* v *Kymer* (1830), or a woman the life of her sister: *Evanson* v *Crooks* (1911).

However, insurable interest is unlikely to affect the bank because:

(a) An assignee (the bank) does not need to have an insurable interest: *Ashley* v *Ashley* (1829).

(b) Insurable interest needs to be present only at the time of taking out the policy, not at any other time: *Dalby* v *India and London Life Assurance Co* (1854). Thus, if the employee should leave the employ of the beneficiary employer, or if the husband should divorce the beneficiary wife, the policy would not be invalidated and the insurance company would still meet the claim.

(c) It is unlikely in practice that a reputable insurance company would refuse to pay out to an assignee for value, on the grounds of a lack of insurable interest between the life assured and the beneficiary.

Hence, although insurable interest is an important concept when inspecting life policies, it is unlikely to be one of great concern to the bank as an assignee for value.

Uberrimae fidei

A contract of life assurance is a contract '*uberrimae fidei*', which literally translated means 'of the utmost good faith' and has the practical effect of making the contract voidable at the option of the injured party should all material facts not be disclosed. Thus if the medical history, or dangerous pastimes of the life assured (or any other fact which could be material to the risk covered by the insurance company) are not disclosed, or are misrepresented, then the insurance company (as the injured party) will be able to avoid the contract and refuse to make payment under it.

A material fact has been defined in s.18 Marine Insurance Act 1906, as one which 'would influence the judgement of a prudent insurer in fixing the premium, or determining whether he will take the risk'. Examples of non-disclosure have included:

● not informing the company of a criminal record when applying for household insurance: *Woolcott* v *Sun Alliance and London Insurance Ltd* (1978),

● failing to disclose doubts as to the mental health of the life assured (increasing the probability of a suicide),

● failing to disclose that the risks proposed had previously been declined by other insurers: *London Assurance* v *Mansel* (1879). It should be quite easy to relate the *Mansel* case to *uberrimae fidei* by imagining Nigel Mansell (note the different spelling) arranging life insurance without mentioning that he is a professional racing car driver, which would obviously leave the insurance company with a greater possibility of having to pay out than if he did not have this rather dangerous occupation. (Please note that this scenario is purely fictitious and only mentioned to help you remember the case. Do not quote it in answering a question, as one of my students did!)

It is also important to realise the following:

(a) Unless there is a specific statement to the contrary on the proposal form, it is not sufficient merely to answer the questions asked. The concept of *uberrimae fidei* places the onus to disclose on the person with the knowledge; the onus is not on the insurance company to ask the right questions. Therefore the proposer must disclose all facts relevant to the proposal, whether asked or not by the insurer.

(b) A contract of life insurance is not subject to the conditions of Unfair Contract Terms Act 1977, and does not have to pass the test of reasonableness referred to in Chapter one.

(c) A change in circumstances after the acceptance of the risk by the insurance company, which could be deemed as material (as defined in the Marine Insurance Act 1906), must be disclosed: *Canning* v *Farquhar* (1886).

(d) Even if the non-disclosed fact is not relevant to the claim (for example, the racing car driver not disclosing his occupation but dying from cancer), the insurance company can still avoid the policy.

Hence, it is important for banks taking a life policy as security to ensure that all material facts have been disclosed, and if the bank is aware of any facts which could be deemed to be material, then it would be prudent to check that these have been disclosed. Although there is no specific agreement between banks and insurance companies, it is thought unlikely that the insurance company would refuse to pay to an innocent assignee and thus the effect of *uberrimae fidei* is somewhat diluted. Until there is a formal agreement or statute, banks will still be aware of the implications of *uberrimae fidei* and will still check their records for compliance.

Age admitted

If the insurer has seen evidence of the age of the life assured, the policy will be marked 'age admitted', and if this is not present the bank will require evidence of age, to prevent future avoidance by the insurance company. Once the bank has obtained documentary confirmation (usually birth certificate, or birth certificate and marriage certificate of a married woman) it then has two options. It can either send certified copies to the insurance company and have the age admitted on the policy, or it can retain the copies itself for use should there be any future dispute.

Beneficiary

The bank would check that the beneficiary is named on the policy and, as discussed above, would pay particular attention to the possibilities of third party security, and to beneficiaries being minors or policies being drawn under the Married Women's Property Act 1882.

Murder, unlawful killing and suicide

No-one can benefit from his own unlawful act and so a murderer cannot claim under a life policy which may be held on the life of the victim: *Cleaver* v *Mutual Reserve Fund Life Association* (1892). (You should at least be able to recall the first name of this case on the topic of murder!) However, should the killing be other than murder, then the court has a measure of discretion: Forfeiture Act 1982.

Since the Suicide Act 1961, suicide is no longer a crime, but some insurance policies will still not be payable on the event of death of the life assured by suicide, especially if committed within a short time of the commencement of the policy, (say 6 to 12 months). It is necessary to inspect each policy for an express clause stating the position following suicide. Quite often the clause would state the exact position following the suicide of the life assured. Many policies contain an assignee for value clause, stating that payment would be paid to an assignee for value regardless of the suicide of the life assured.

Hence, it is not possible to give a definite answer to the question, 'what would happen to the policy monies, if the life assured should commit suicide?' the only accurate answer one could give would be to refer to the policy document.

Cooling-off period

All persons committing themselves to a contract of life assurance have a period of ten days to withdraw from the contract: ss.75–76 Insurance Companies Act 1982 (subject to a possible extension under the Financial Services Act 1986). Despite the presence of this cooling-off period, it should have little effect on lending bankers, as most policies taken as security are already in existence, but where the banker is taking charge over a new term life policy (taken as life cover for the advance), then the banker should take this period into consideration.

Non-payment of premiums

When taking a life policy as security one of the procedures to be followed is that the bank should check that premium payments are up to date, either by enquiring from the insurance company or by requesting sight of the latest premium receipt. However, the major problems with premiums occur once the policy has been taken out and then, for whatever reason, the premiums are not paid. It is not unusual for a bank to insist on the premiums being paid via an account with themselves, either by direct debit or standing order, thus giving the bank a degree of control and by marking their records it will be immediately apparent should problems occur.

Where the bank is aware (from whatever source) that premiums have not been paid it has a number of options:

(i) **Bring the premiums up to date and realise the security** (see below). This is viable only if the policy has a surrender value.

(ii) **Pay the premiums on the customer's behalf**, although if the bank is not careful this would only add to the debt and could result in a greater loss for the bank.

(iii) **Convert the policy to a fully paid-up policy**. This means that the policy value is frozen and no further premiums are payable. Not all policies have this option and therefore inspection of the policy for a clause permitting conversion to a fully paid-up policy is necessary.

The effect of non-payment of premiums depends upon the policy. Most policies allow a period of grace (usually 30 days), within which if the premiums are brought up-to-date the policy will not be affected in any way, and again inspection of the policy for details of the effects of non-payment will be necessary.

▌ Method of taking assignment

Obviously the method of taking the assignment depends on the type of assignment to be taken (ie, legal or equitable), and we shall discuss each separately.

Legal assignment

The method of taking a legal assignment is governed by the Policies of Assurance Act 1867, as follows:

(a) Obtain the original policy document; this is for three reasons:

    (i) to prevent a claim of constructive notice of earlier charge: *Spencer* v *Clarke* (1878).

    (ii) to allow a detailed inspection of the policy clauses and details (insurable interest, *uberrimae fidei*, age admitted, beneficiary, suicide, cooling-off period and non-payment of premiums), as discussed above.

    (iii) When the policy is produced the discharged assignment deeds of any previous assignees should also be seen, to prove a good chain of title.

(b) Proof of up-to-date payment of premiums should be obtained.

(c) The bank's standard deed of assignment is to be executed, by the beneficiary, in the presence of a senior bank official or solicitor (if you are not aware of the reasons of their being present, then refer to Chapter fifteen). Although there is strictly no necessity to use a deed of assignment, the bank would insist on the use of such a document due mainly to the protective clauses contained therein (continuing security, commitment to keep premiums up-to-date, realisation without referring to a third party − courts or beneficiary).

(d) Notice of the bank's assignment is given to the insurance company, requesting written acknowledgement by the company. The advantages of doing this are:

    (i) Priority of equal charges is decided by the date of receipt of the notice by the insurance company *Dearle* v *Hall* (1828) (see note on priorities, below).

    (ii) To give the bank the right to sue on the policy in its own name.

    (iii) The acknowledgement commits the insurance company to pay the policy monies only to the bank.

    (iv) To set the limit at which the insurance company can exercise set-off for any claims which it may have against the policy holder.

(e) The bank will hold the policy, the deed of assignment and the receipted notice of assignment.

Equitable assignment

The method of taking an equitable assignment depends upon the strength of the assignment required by the assignee (the bank). The most informal method of taking an equitable assignment would be by merely accepting the deposit of the policy. However, the most common method would involve:

(a) Obtaining the original document and checking its contents, as discussed above.

(b) Obtaining the necessary signature on a memorandum of deposit. This puts the intent of the assignor (the beneficiary) beyond doubt and also gives the bank the protection of the clauses in the memorandum of deposit (continuing security etc.).

(c) Giving notice of the assignment to the insurance company, although this could be returned as the insurance company is not obliged to recognise equitable interests.

(d) Retaining the policy along with the completed memorandum of deposit and acknowledged notice.

■ Priorities of assignments

Where there is more than one assignment over the same policy, then priority is decided by the date of receipt of notice of the assignment by the insurance company: *Dearle* v *Hall* (1828). However, if the assignee has notice of an earlier assignment, then that will automatically rank higher in priority. This notice could be actual or constructive; an example of constructive notice could be the inability to produce the original policy document, unless a satisfactory explanation is received and verified: *Spencer* v *Clarke* (1878). Hence, if no policy is produced or if the document is marked 'duplicate', then the bank should automatically be on its guard, and should seek alternative security from the borrower.

■ Realisation/remedies on borrower's default

If the borrower should default on the agreed borrowing, the bank will be able to enforce (or realise) its security. The method of doing this will depend on the type of security taken.

Legal assignment

Upon default and after the serving of statutory notices the bank will be in a position to exercise its power of sale, giving the bank the option to:

(i) arrange a loan from the insurance company on the strength of the policy, (unlikely);

(ii) sell the policy on what is now becoming a thriving market, transferring the title to the purchaser, (again unlikely, but more probable than (i) above); or

(iii) surrender the policy by completing the insurer's standard form of surrender and send the completed form plus the policy and 'non-vacated' (see below) form of assignment to the insurance company. It is important that the deed of assignment is not vacated at this stage; to vacate the deed of assignment releases the assignor from the commitment contained in the deed. Unfortunately I have experienced a situation where an inexperienced security clerk arranged to vacate deeds when the bank was enforcing its security and this resulted in a loss for the bank.

As you may imagine, the most common method of realising the bank's security is under (iii), above.

If the borrower and the beneficiary are the same person and that person dies, then the bank needs to submit the policy and a certified copy of the death certificate to the company in order to claim the policy monies.

Equitable mortgage

Normally, an equitable mortgagee has no power of sale and needs the consent of a third party in order to enforce its security. This third party can be either the customer (through his written consent) or the courts (via a court order). The one exception to this would be if the memorandum of deposit were executed under seal and contained a power of attorney clause, nominating the bank to act on the customer's behalf, effectively giving the bank a power of sale.

∎ Release of security

In general, to release its security the bank merely needs to reverse the procedures undertaken when taking its charge. Thus:

With legal assignment

(a) The bank must firstly vacate its deed of assignment, by executing a form of discharge, under seal, on the document. In the past I believe separate forms were used for this purpose, but at present the form of discharge tends to be incorporated in the original document.

(b) The bank will then return the policy and vacated deed of assignment to the customer, informing him of the need to keep the two of them together, so that should a claim be made the insurance company could well insist on production of the discharged deed before paying out.

(c) The bank will inform the company of its lack of further interest in the policy.

With equitable assignment

(a) The memorandum of deposit is stamped 'cancelled' and retained by the bank and the policy is returned to the customer.

(b) If notice was given to the insurance company this should now be removed.

∎ Summary

In many ways a life policy is an ideal form of security. Its main advantage is the fact that the value will usually continue to increase as time passes. It is also easy and cheap to take, plus extremely easy to realise. Once the inherent legal technicalities have been attended to (insurable interest and *uberrimae fidei*), there are very few difficulties. All in all, life policies are an excellent form of security, etc. with the one proviso that close examination of a policy is necessary to ensure that the right type of policy is being taken and that there are no detrimental clauses contained within the policy (suicide, assignees for value etc).

■ Advantages/disadvantages of life policies as security

Advantages

These are

1. Its increasing value.
2. It is easy and cheap to take.
3. It is easy to realise.

Due to these advantages, it is usual for a bank to take a legal charge, and equitable charges over life policies are rarely seen.

Disadvantages

1. The possible invalidation of the policy due to a lack of insurable interest, *uberrimae fidei* or non-payment of premiums.
2. The possible bad publicity if the policy was for the benefit of the deceased's widow and children.
3. A careful examination of the policy is necessary, which if not undertaken might mean that the bank could be under the misapprehension of being protected when it is not (for example, suicide, non-payment of premiums, fully paid up etc).

FACT SHEET

Life policies as security

Types of policy
- Endowment – surrender value as well as sum assured. Investment and life cover. The surrender value gives the security value.
- Term life – to provide death cover. Valid only for pre-agreed term.
- Whole life – a combination of the above with very low surrender value, payable until death, at any time policy is in force.
- Other types of policies – not important.

Parties
- Proposer.
- Life assured – on whose death the monies will be payable.
- Beneficiary – the person who signs the deed of assignment. Take care with third party implications (undue influence) and MWPA 1882.

Initial security considerations
- Insurable interest – must know the eight circumstances where presumed (eg, employer/employee: *Hebden v West* (1863) and debtor/creditor; *Anderson v Edie* (1795)) and when this needs to be proved. Needs to be present only at time of

acceptance: *Dalby v India and London Life Assurance Co (1854)*, and assignee does not need insurable, interest: *Ashley v Ashley* (1829).

● *Uberrimae fidei* – the onus is on the person with the knowledge to disclose all material facts and not on the insurance company to ask the right questions. The defin tion of material fact should be known (s.18 Marine Assurance Act 1906) and examples should be known (*London Assurance v Mansel* (1879, etc.).

● Murder and suicide – cannot benefit from an unlawful act (eg, murder: the *Cleaver* case), suicide no longer a crime, so reference to policy is necessary.

● Non-payment of premiums – consequences and options (pay, pay and realise, or convert)

● Others – cooling-off period, beneficiary, and age admitted.

Method of assignment
Examine policy, deed of assignment, or memorandum of deposit, to be signed by beneficiary (where and why?), notification to the insurance company (why?).

Priorities
Dearle v Hall (1828): first notice received by the company, unless notice of previous charge. Notice can be actual or constructive: *Spencer v Clarke* (1878).

Realisation
● If legal: loan from company, sell or surrender. Usually surrender, NOTE: send policy, completed company form and non-vacated assignment.
● If equitable: approach courts, beneficiary or rely on power of attorney clause.

Release
Reverse procedures for taking charge: ie, vacate assignment deed or cancel memorandum of deposit, return policy and vacated assignment deed (if taken). Notify company.

Question (Autumn 1987)

(a) In relation to the taking of a security over a policy of life assurance, what, in practice, are the advantages or disadvantages (if any) to the bank of a legal charge as against an equitable charge?
[10 marks]

(b)What are the priorities of different charges taken by different persons over the same policy?
[10 marks]
[Total for question – 20]

Key words
(a) advantages & disadvantages, in practice, **to the bank** *of a legal charge against equitable charge.*
(b) priorities of different charges over same policy.

Answer

(a) In practice, there are no great advantages from one or the other, although since legal assignments are so easy they are generally taken. Under the Policies of Assurance Act 1867, the legal charge requires signing and witnessing, while the equitable charges, even by deposit of the policy, may have a memorandum of deposit, and this is (to a lawyer) certainly advisable, even if not frequently done in practice. Both types of assignment require notification to the insurer as part (b) of the question should reveal. Both are subject to defences of set-off or counterclaim between the assured and insurer, though no new right may arise after notice to the insurer. In both cases, non-production of the policy gives constructive notice of prior rights. In a legal charge, the bank may surrender or sell the policy, because it is the legal owner. In an equitable assignment it cannot sell unless it has taken a promise in the memorandum to make a legal assignment if called on to do so, and the memorandum is under seal, and this then gives it a power of sale under s.101 Law of Property Act 1925. In addition it may be given an irrevocable power of attorney, enabling it to sell in the assignor's name. In practice, then, there is no real difference. In a legal assignment the bank can give a good discharge to the insurer for payment of monies, and in theory equitable assignments require the insurer to interplead to stay out of trouble, but in practice the terms in the memorandum mentioned above solve this problem also, and the bank can give good receipts. In practice, therefore, it is difficult to see any positive advantage of taking a legal charge, though since it is so easy to do, it might as well be done.

(*Note*: while the insurer has no duty to note equitable interests on his records, his failure to do so does not justify payment to anyone else, and seems to make no real difference. Some insurers may think they can ignore equitable interests; they are quite wrong).

(b) Whether a charge is legal or equitable, the priorities are the same, the basic rule being that in *Dearle* v *Hall* (1828). These rules are:

(i) If a second assignee has notice of a prior assignee, the prior assignee takes priority (even if equitable)

(ii) Notice for this purpose probably means notice at the time of making the contract (though possibly at the time of informing the insurer).

(iii) Notice may be actual or constructive (*Newman* v *Newman* (1885); *Re Weniger's Policy* (1910)) and constructive notice may be found as a fact where a bank has taken insufficient care to discover the facts. An obvious case is where the policy has not been produced: *Spencer* v *Clarke* (1878).

(iv) If the subsequent assignee has no notice (actual or constructive) of the prior assignment, then priorities, according to *Dearle* v *Hall*, are determined by the order in which the insurer is notified of the assignments. This is almost certainly so whether the assignment is legal or equitable, (though some would argue that *Dearle* v *Hall* was decided at a time when there were no legal assignments, and that the bona fide purchaser rule applies to a legal assignment. This seems to ignore s.136 Law of Property Act 1925 which specifically says that legal assignments are subject to prior equities.) Section 3 Policies of Assurance Act 1867 says that the insurer is bound to pay only on notice of an assignment and is discharged by earlier payment to another. As between assignments not notified to the insurer, priority depends upon normal rules (actual or constructive notice, and the bona fide legal purchaser rule.)

Author's comment
In (a) it is important to realise that the examiner specifically asks for the advantages and disadvantages 'in practice'. He does not ask for the different procedures necessary to effect each type of charge. Many candidates misread this question and lose many easy marks. In (b) you should instantly see the additional information required by the examiner in a 10 mark question as in the question above as opposed to a 5 mark question on the same topic. On a technical point in (b) (ii) the time of executing the charge would probably coincide with the giving of notice.

CHAPTER 18

Limited company securities

Syllabus requirements

- The legal principles of taking, protecting, priority over, enforcement and realisation of limited company security. Also, company security for director's liabilities and group guarantees.

■ Taking the charge

When taking security from a limited company there are a number of items that must be borne in mind. These are:

Powers of the company and its directors

As we have already discussed in Chapter eight, the rules by which a company operates are known as the memorandum and articles of association. Until recently any transaction that took place outside these rules was '*ultra vires*' and void, as in *Re Introductions* (1969).

However, s.108 Companies Act 1989 states that any act done by the company shall not be called into question by reason of anything in the memorandum. The one condition is that the third party must act in good faith, and knowledge of a lack of authority will not amount to bad faith.

The intention is to remove completely the danger to third parties of *ultra vires* and instead place the liability on the shoulders of the directors to ensure that they act within the powers laid down in the memorandum and articles of association.

Registration of charge

You will be aware that certain charges over assets need to be registered with various bodies, for example, a first legal charge over registered land must be registered at the District Land Registry, and that priority between charges on the same asset is decided by date of registration and not date of creation.

However, in addition to the normal registration procedures some securities given by limited companies must also be registered at Companies Registry. Section 93 Companies Act 1989 (updating s.396 Companies Act 1985), states that the following charges must be registered:

(a) a charge on land;
(b) a charge on goods or any interest in goods, other than a charge under which the chargee is entitled to possession either of the goods or of a document of title to them;
(c) a charge on intangible movable property (except money), of any of the following descriptions:
    (i) goodwill,

(ii) intellectual property (trade marks, copyrights etc),

(iii) book debts of the company,

(iv) uncalled share capital;

(d) a charge for securing an issue of debentures;

(e) a floating charge on the whole or part of the company's property.

There are a number of notable exceptions to this list. Charges that do **not** require registration include charges over life policies, stocks and shares and guarantees.

Charges requiring registration **must** be registered at Companies Registry within 21 days of creation: s.95 Companies Act 1989. In *Esberger and Son Ltd* v *Capital and Counties Bank* (1913), an undated charge form was held by the bank for nine months, the form was then dated and registered within 21 days of the date on the form. It was held that registration was outside the required period (ie, later than 21 days of creation).

If the particulars of the charge are not delivered within the 21 day period, the charge is void against an administrator or liquidator of the company or any person who for value acquires an interest in, or right over, property subject to the charge. It is important to realise that the unregistered charge will still be enforceable against other creditors (providing such creditors do not have an interest in the property) if the company is not insolvent; *Mace Builders (Glasgow) Ltd* v *Lunn* (1986).

Once the charge is registered the registrar will maintain the charges register, and any person may require that the registrar provide a certificate (signed and sealed by the registrar) stating the date on which the particulars of a charge were delivered to him: s.94(3) Companies Act 1989. Once issued the certificate will be conclusive evidence that the particulars were delivered to the registrar no later than the date stated in the certificate; s.94(5) Companies Act 1989. This supports the decision in *Re C.L. Nye Ltd* (1970), and is a great comfort to bankers, who are now safe in the knowledge that once the certificate is received the validity of their charge cannot be challenged.

It is the duty of the company to register the charge, although anyone interested in the charge may register. Thus the current practice of the bank (as chargee) of registering the charge will almost certainly continue, as it removes the possibility of non-registration (for whatever reason) by the company.

Late registration

In certain circumstances (vaguely referred to in the Act as 'prescribed particulars in the prescribed form') late registration of charges is permitted, without reference to the courts, (a prior condition under s.404 Companies Act 1985). The late registration will be subject to the conditions quoted in s.95 Companies Act 1989, in that if the company at the date of delivery (if outside the 21 day period) of the particulars is unable to pay its debts as per s.123 Insolvency Act 1986 in consequence of the transaction, or if insolvency proceedings begin within 'the relevant period' (see later) commencing with the date of the late delivery of the particulars, the charge is void against the liquidator or administrator. The 'relevant period' is defined as:

(i) two years in the case of a floating charge created in favour of a person connected with the company,

(ii) one year in the case of a floating charge created in favour of any other person (eg, a bank),

(iii) six months in any other case (eg, a charge over land).

Furthermore, if a purchaser for value or subsequent mortgagee effects the purchase or charge without notice of the late-registered charge, their purchase or charge will automatically have priority over the late-registered charge.

If the documentation delivered for registration purposes is incomplete or inaccurate, the charge registered is void against a liquidator, administrator or subsequent person who acquires an interest in the property. However, the court may order that the charge is effective, if the omission or error is not likely materially to have misled any unsecured creditor, or that no person became an unsecured creditor during the period that the registered particulars were incomplete or inaccurate, or if a person acquiring an interest in the charged asset did not rely on the registered particulars that were incomplete or inaccurate.

∎ Nature of a bank debenture form

Generally speaking a debenture is a written acknowledgement of a debt, issued by a company, usually under seal and secured against the assets of the company. You would have come across the term in Chapter sixteen, debentures sometimes being referred to as loan stock. The interest is paid regardless of the level of profits made and the capital is repaid in priority to the shareholders in the event of a winding-up.

A bank debenture is similar to the above, except that it will usually be drafted as an 'all-moneys debenture' which means that it will incorporate a fixed and a floating charge securing **all** the debts of the company to the bank.

Clauses included in a bank debenture form will typically include:

Fixed charge

A fixed charge attaches itself to the easily identifiable assets of the company. These are:

(i) the fixed assets, such as land and buildings, machinery;

(ii) the intangible assets, such as trade marks, copyrights and uncalled share capital;

(iii) future acquired fixed assets, such as plant and machinery and land and buildings acquired after the date of the debenture. NOTE, only an equitable charge is created in these circumstances;

(iv) the **future** (NB, not only present but future) book debts of the company. These are debts 'arising in due course of business . . . (which) would or could in the ordinary course of such a business be entered in the well kept books relating to that business'; *Independent Automatic Sales Ltd* v *Knowles and Foster* (1962). To avoid a dispute as to what debts are caught by the fixed charge, the bank will usually word the debenture to include all 'book debts and other debts'. The effect of a fixed charge over future book debts is that all the monies received from the business debts owed to the company should be paid into an account held by the fixed charge holder. Such a charge can obviously have serious consequences for a banker (bank A) opening an account for a company subject to such a charge, in that all book debts paid into the new account are caught by the charge and must therefore be paid into an account held with the debenture holder (bank B). As a result of this the account at bank A could have a balance of say £5,000, but have received credits to a total of say £50,000. It would be this latter figure of £50,000 which would have to be paid over by bank A to bank B, leaving bank A with an unsecured debt of £45,000.

The risk to bankers of an existing fixed charge over future book debts is very much a real one, with many banks having lost money under similar circumstances to the facts related above. The only method by which a bank can protect itself is to search at Companies Registry, and ensure the absence of such a charge, before accepting credits to a new account for any limited company.

The validity of a fixed charge over future book debts was confirmed in *Siebe Gorman and Co Ltd* v *Barclays Bank Ltd* (1979).

Floating charge

The nature of a floating charge was defined in *Re Yorkshire Woolcombers' Association* (1903), as:

(i) a charge over present and future assets;

(ii) the assets caught under the charge will change from time to time in the ordinary course of the company's business;

(iii) until the floating charge holder takes steps to enforce its security (known as 'crystallisation') the company will be free to carry on its ordinary business. Upon crystallisation the company will no longer be able to dispose of the asset without the specific consent of the floating charge holder.

One interpretation of the nature of the floating charge is that the charge floats over the liquid assets of the company, until crystallisation at which time it freezes over the assets held at that time, preventing them flowing away.

The floating charge will catch all future and present assets not subject to a fixed charge, but is aimed mainly at stock. Due to this fact the floating charge carries many inherent defects, making it a popular area for exam questions, usually referred to as the disadvantages of a floating charge. These are:

(a) The stock value is very difficult to assess. This will usually be the first item to suffer when the company is in difficulty and this is the one time the bank will be looking towards these very assets for repayment. The test for this defect is the successful shop compared with the unsuccessful shop. The successful shop will normally stock almost any item that you ask for, where as the unsuccessful shop will not have the available cash to replace stock as it is used, and will probably not stock the items requested. This in itself will have a knock-on effect on the poor trading performance. Obviously if the bankers of each shop hold a floating charge the bank holding the charge over the assets of the unsuccessful shop is far more likely to realise its security, and will probably discover that its charge is worth substantially less than anticipated. In *Re Borax Co* (1901), the transfer of assets covered by a floating charge into the name of another company was held to be a valid transfer and the bank's floating charge was worthless.

The bank can protect itself against this by requesting regular figures of current assets and liabilities (known as quick or short figures), or by building into the debenture form a 'debenture formula', whereby the company undertakes to maintain the assets caught at a certain proportion of the advance. If the assets caught should drop below this figure the bank will be able to crystallise the charge. As both of these protections rely upon the integrity of the company they are open to abuse by the company.

(b) Assets seized by judgment creditors. Where a company is experiencing trading difficulties it is not unusual for its assets to be claimed by court officials acting on behalf of judgment creditors. An example could be seizure of assets by bailiffs, following an unsatisfied order by the courts. Early crystallisation is the only protection available.

(c) Subsequent fixed charge. Where a creditor later takes a fixed charge over the assets covered by the floating charge, it is possible that the fixed charge will take priority over the floating charge, providing there was no restriction on the creation of subsequent charges or, if such a restriction did exist, the fixed charge holder did not know of its existence. To protect themselves banks include in the debenture form a 'negative pledge' clause, whereby the company undertakes not to create a subsequent charge on the assets covered by the floating charge, and the bank quotes the presence of this cause when registering its charge at Companies Registry. As such registration is deemed to be notice to the world it effectively prevents the possible occurrence of this problem.

(d) Preferential creditors. As you will be aware from Chapter nine, if a company is wound up a floating charge holder will receive repayment of its debt only after the preferential creditors have been repaid in full. Thus, if there are insufficient assets to meet the preferential creditors the floating charge holder will receive nothing.

(e) The hardening period. Under s.245 Insolvency Act 1986, a floating charge may be invalid. For the charge to be invalidated, both the following conditions must apply:

(i) The charge must be created within 12 months of the commencement of insolvent liquidation, or the presentation of a petition for an administration order. You should recall from chapter nine that corporate insolvency is deemed to commence at the date of the petition or resolution. this period is extended to 24 months where the creditor is an associate of the company (for example, a director, or another company that is a member of the same group). It is unlikely that a bank will be held to be an associate see *Re M C Bacon Ltd* (1989).
(ii) The company must be insolvent at the date of giving the charge, or become insolvent as a result of giving the charge.

If the above conditions apply the charge is invalid for any debts outstanding at the time of taking the charge. The charge is still valid for money advanced at or after the date of taking the charge. If the advance is only to be released after the taking of the charge, the whole of the advance will be secured against the charge, providing the above conditions do not appiy. If the bank is taking security to secure an existing advance the charge may not be valid, but if the existing advance is on overdraft the rule in *Clayton's Case* will work to the bank's advantage. This is because new credits to the account reduce the debits outstanding on the account from before the date of the charge and new debits to the account will create new debts covered by the charge. Thus on an active overdrawn account the whole balance on account may well be represented by monies advanced after the date of the charge and the whole of the advance will be covered by the valid floating charge as per *Re Yeovil Glove Co Ltd* (1965).

It is not possible for the bank to protect its advance by creating a new advance after the date of the charge, a condition of the new advance being that the advance outstanding at the date of the charge (and therefore not covered by the charge) be repaid by the new advance. Such an attempt failed in *Re G.T. White and Co Ltd* (1982), and is unlikely to succeed in the future.

(f) Retention of title clauses. As we have previously stated, the main asset covered by a floating charge is the stock held by the company. However, in the now famous case of *Aluminium Industrie Vaasseen B V* v *Romalpa Aluminium Ltd* (1976) (thankfully known and accepted as the *Romalpa Case*), it was held that the company supplying the stock can have a clause in its sale contract quoting that the purchaser does not become the owner of the stock until it has been paid for in full, and until that time is merely holding the stock in trust for the supplier. Also, any proceeds from the sale of the stock were likewise held on behalf of the supplier until paid over to him.

When first decided, this case had a great effect on bankers and traders alike, and although *Romalpa* has been accepted as the 'foundation' case, and would no doubt rank in any top ten of the most important cases affecting bankers, there have been many later cases testing and modifying the court's decision. The current position is as follows:

(i) The wording of the clause must not create a charge, as it would be void if not registered at Companies Registry within 21 days of creation (see above). Such a situation occurred in *Re Bond Worth Ltd* (1979), where the supplier attempted to claim back stock held by the purchasing company. It was held that the clause created a charge and the reservation of title clause failed. In *Re Peachdart Ltd* (1983), the clause contended was over the sale proceeds, but it was held that the agreement created a charge and again the claim failed due to non-registration.

(ii) The goods must still be easily identified. In *Borden (UK) Ltd* v *Scottish Timber Products Ltd* (1979), it was held that as the resin supplied had been 'mixed' with the other products to produce chip board, it was no longer easily identified and could not be separated and returned to the supplier. Thus the clause failed. The easy way to remember this case is by thinking of 'chip boarden UK' and this should remind you of both the name and principle of the case. Secondly, in *Hendy Lennox (Industrial Engines) Ltd* v *Grahame Puttick Ltd* (1984), although the engines supplied had been added to other components to create generators, the engines themselves were still easily identified and easily removed. Thus the clause succeeded.

(iii) In respect of reserving title to the proceeds of sale the position is accepted to be:

● the contract must state that the sale proceeds be held on a separate account, thus establishing the 'trust' relationship,
● if a bank holds a fixed charge over book debts, as per *Siebe Gorman and Co Ltd* v *Barclays Bank Ltd* (1979), this charge will automatically take precedence over the reservation of title clause.

The decisions in *Romalpa* and subsequent cases are obviously of great importance to bankers, because where they previously thought that they were secured by the floating charge over the stock, the bulk of this asset could in fact be reclaimed by the supplier leaving the bank with no security. The protections available to bankers are the inspection of sale contracts, if the stock is 'mixed' to produce the end product the clause will not be effective and if the bank holds a fixed charge over book debts the reservation of title over the sale proceeds will not be effective.

So if a floating charge has so many defects, why do banks take them? The answer is that a floating charge has the following advantages:

(i) The charge itself is easy to take, and allows the bank to take a charge over assets that are normally outside their reach (ie, stock and future acquired assets).

(ii) A floating charge holder can prevent the appointment of an administrator, under an administration order. Such an appointment would mean that the bank would be unable to realise its security without the consent of the administrator or the court and the administrator can act as the manager of the company, taking away this option from the bank. The bank will be informed of the forthcoming appointment of an administrator and will have seven days to block his appointment by appointing its own administrative receiver, and this is discussed in full later.

Other sundry clauses included in a bank's debenture form

We have discussed many of the clauses to be found in a bank's debenture form above including fixed and floating charge, production of quick figures, debenture formula, negative pledge, fixed charge over book debts and appointment of an administrative receiver. Other clauses will include assets to be adequately insured, debt repayable on demand, whole debt clause, etc. (see previous chapters).

■ Realisation of bank debenture

Crystallisation of floating charge

As mentioned above, a floating charge floats on the liquid assets of the company until crystallisation, at which time the charge freezes on the assets covered and the company is no longer free to deal with them. Crystallisation will occur when either:
(a) the debenture holder appoints an administrative receiver, see below, or
(b) winding up proceedings commence, or
(c) the company ceases to trade, or makes preparations to cease trading, or
(d) on the occurrence of some other event quoted in the debenture form: *Re Brightlife Ltd* (1986). This case also supported the bank's right to convert the floating charge to a specific charge upon crystallisation, thus defeating the usually prior claims of preferential creditors.

Appointment of administrative receiver

General

An administrative receiver is a licensed insolvency practitioner, appointed in writing by a floating charge holder, usually following default by the company or some other reason for crystallisation, as above. His appointment automatically prevents the appointment of an administrator under an administration order. Although the administrative receiver is appointed by the bank, he is in fact the agent of the company and not of the bank. This means that the bank is not liable for any contracts entered into by him, nor for his negligence. However, should the bank interfere with the administrative receiver, the bank will be liable as per *Standard Chartered Bank Ltd* v *Walker and Walker* (1982), where the bank pressurised for an early sale and as a direct result of this insufficient funds were received to clear the debt to the bank. The bank was held liable to the guarantors as it had interfered with the normal processes.

The powers and duties of an administrative receiver are as follows:

Duties

(i) Immediately to notify the company of his appointment.

(ii) Within three months he must prepare a report stating the events leading up to his appointment, the disposal or proposed disposal of assets and the funds available to each category of creditor.

(iii) To realise those assets caught under the debenture. Where a fixed and floating charge has been taken this will be the total assets of the company.

(iv) To distribute the proceeds received in the following order:
- his expenses,
- payment of the debt secured by the fixed charge (if one exists),
- payment of preferential creditors,
- payment of debt secured by floating charge,
- any surplus is paid to the company.

Powers

(i) To get in and realise the assets of the company, either by public auction or other method thought fit at that time. Where the assets are secured by a charge in favour of another creditor, the administrative receiver can approach the courts for their consent to sell or otherwise dispose of the asset. If an asset appears to belong to the company and is wrongly seized and disposed of, the administrative receiver will acquire no personal liability.

(ii) To bring or defend legal actions in the name of the company.

(iii) To use the company seal to execute contracts on the company's behalf.

(iv) To carry on the business of the company. This important power will enable the administrative receiver to sell the company, or part of it, as a going concern.

(v) To grant or accept leases or tenancies on the company's behalf.

(vi) to call up an uncalled capital.

Other remedies of a debenture holder

As with any other secured creditor the debenture holder will have the following powers in addition to the above, should the borrower default:

- to sue for default and/or prove in the winding up of the company,
- to apply to the court for a foreclosure order (unlikely to succeed as it removes the company's 'equity of redemption'),
- to exercise its power of sale under its legal charge.

∎ Discharge of the charge

In addition to the procedures necessary with the removal of any charge (eg, removal of charge at District Land Registry), the charge must also be removed at Companies Registry. This is done by written memorandum signed by both the company and the chargee, and both will receive written confirmation; s.98 Companies Act 1989.

∎ Other limited company security matters

Interested directors

As mentioned in Chapter eight, transactions whereby a director gains a personal benefit have caused problems for bankers in the past. An example of such a transaction would be the giving of direct director's guarantee, as in *Victors Ltd* v *Lingard and Others* (1927). However, as discussed in full in Chapter eight, this problem would appear to have been removed by s.108 Companies Act 1989 which states that if a person deals with a company in good faith the power of the directors to bind the company shall be deemed free from any limitations.

Group guarantees

These occur when a company is a member of a trading group of other companies, sometimes, but not always, with one main holding company at the 'top of the tree' which controls the composition or board of directors of the other companies in the group. If the bank is considering making an advance to the group as a whole or more likely to a member of the group, it is not unusual to ask for inter-company or cross guarantees. As with all transactions the memorandum and articles of association need to be checked (remember the effect of the Companies Act 1989), but the bank needs to pay special attention to the problem of commercial justification. In *Charterbridge Corporation Ltd* v *Lloyds Bank Ltd* (1969), it was held that each transaction entered into must be for the benefit of the company, and if the company itself was not gaining a benefit from the giving of the guarantee, then it was unenforceable. Indeed even the Companies Act 1989 states that where a company's memorandum states the company to be a general commercial company, it is free to do all such things as are incidental or conducive to the carrying on of any trade or profession by it. This would appear to indicate that commercial justification is still a requirement and bankers need to be aware of the implications of its absence.

Company security for director's liabilities

Again this is discussed in full in Chapter eight and that section must be re-read in full. Basically, certain transactions are prohibited and these include the giving of a guarantee or other security in respect of the borrowing by a director. Hence banks need to be very careful when making an advance to directors where the security offered is to be a guarantee from the company of which he is a director. The conditions and exceptions are discussed in full in Chapter eight.

▌ Summary

This has been a favourite area for past examination questions and will no doubt be so in the future. The main areas are the advantages and disadvantages of a floating charge as security and the effect of outside transactions on that security (eg, reservation of title clauses, appointment of an administrator). As you progress through your career many of you will encounter limited company borrowing and hence limited company security. The whole aim of this chapter is to make you aware of the problems that you may (or may not) encounter and the possible methods of overcoming them.

FACT SHEET

Limited company securities

Taking the charge

1. Powers of the company: Memorandum and articles of association, s.108 Companies Act 1989.
2. Registration of charge: What charges need to be registered, within 21 days of creation (*Esberger* case), if not registered within 21 day period charge is void against liquidator, administrator or other purchaser, mortgagor for value; *Mace Builders (Glasgow) Ltd v Lunn* (1986). Conclusivity of registrar's certificate; s.94(5) Companies Act 1989.
3. Late registration: permissible without approach to court, but can have detrimental effect (these effects should be known). Effect of incomplete or irregular registration.

Nature of bank debenture form

1. Fixed charge:
   covers fixed assets (land, plant and machinery), intangible assets, equitable charge over future acquired assets and a fixed charge over future book debts (the validity and consequences of which should be known),
2. Floating charge:
   (a) Definition from *Re Yorkshire Woolcombers* is important and must be known, as should the practical implications of such a charge.
   (b) Disadvantages – difficult to value, run down of assets (*Re Borax Co*), judgment creditors, subsequent fixed charge (negative pledge), preferential creditors, hardening period (s.245 Insolvency Act 1985), *Clayton's case* working to bank's advantage, *Re Yeovil Glove* and *Re G.T. White and Co Ltd* (1982)), and retention clauses on stock (*Romalpa Case*, can be defeated if creates an unregistered charge; *Re Bond Worth* or if goods mixed: *Borden (UK) Ltd v Scottish Timber Products*) or retention clause on sale proceeds.
   (c) Advantages – easy to take and the bank will be able to prevent the appointment of an administrator, thus preserving the bank's ability to make its own decisions concerning its security.
3. Other clauses: adequate insurance, repayable on demand and whole debt.

Realisation of bank's debenture

1. Crystallisation of floating charge; when it occurs and consequences.
2. Appointment of an administrative receiver:
   (a) General – a licensed insolvency practitioner, appointed by floating charge holder following default, but is held to be an agent of the customer not the bank, unless the bank should interfere. His appointment prevents an administrator being appointed.
   (b) Duties – mainly to realise the assets covered by the floating charge and distribute the proceeds in the laid down order.
   (c) Powers – 'to get in and realise the assets' including approaching the courts for consent to dispose of assets charged by other secured creditors.
3. Other remedies:
   Sue, foreclose, exercise power of sale.

Discharge of registered charge

By written memorandum signed by both mortgagee and mortgagor.

Other company security matters

1. Interested directors; problems largely removed by s.108 Companies Act 1989

2. Group guarantees; the nature of a group guarantee and the necessity for the presence of 'commercial justification', *Charterbridge Corporation Ltd* v *Lloyds Bank Ltd* (1969).
3. Company security for directors liabilities; prohibited subject to conditions covered in Chapter eight.

Question (Autumn 1989)

Toolco Limited makes spanners. It obtains steel from Ironworks Limited on terms stating that Toolco Limited will not have legal ownership of a consignment of steel until it has paid Ironworks Limited the full purchase price of that consignment.

Toolco Limited has an overdraft facility with Traders Bank, but only pays Ironworks Limited in full for a consignment of steel when the spanners made from that steel are sold to, and paid for by, Toolco's wholesaler (who receives title on payment). Toolco Limited has given Traders Bank a floating charge over all its assets. Toolco has become insolvent and a receiver appointed by Traders Bank under the floating charge enters Toolco's factory and finds the following:

(i) some sheets of steel delivered by Ironworks Limited;
(ii) some half-made spanners on a shelf; and
(iii) a box of finished spanners, with a label on the box marked 'sold to wholesaler and paid for'.

(a) Which, if any, of the items in (i), (ii) and (iii) can the receiver take under the floating charge, and why? [13]

(b) How would your answer to (a) differ if the spanners were made from an alloy of steel and another metal in equal parts, the other metal being supplied to Toolco Limited by a company other than Ironworks Limited? [7]

[Total marks for question − 20]

Key words
not have legal ownership of steel until full purchase price paid
overdraft
made from that steel
floating charge
become insolvent
(i) sheets of steel
(ii) half-made spanners
(iii) finished spanners . . . 'sold to wholesaler and paid for'
(a) which items can the receiver take? . . . why?
(b) how . . . differ . . . alloy of steel and another metal
supplied by other than Ironworks Limited

Answer

Many candidates knew *Romalpa* and the basic points about identity of original goods and mixing. However, there was a lack of depth to their knowledge.

(a) If the seller of goods expressly retains title until payment, then this is enforceable so long as the goods remain in the same form as originally delivered: *Romalpa Case* (1976).

The goods do not therefore become owned by the purchaser until payment. The purchaser cannot therefore charge the goods to the seller, nor can they fall into the purchaser's floating charge: *Clough Mill Limited* v *Martin* (1985).

The receiver, as the purchaser's agent cannot deal with them under the floating charge or otherwise.

Without the clearest wording, goods which are mixed with other goods are unlikely to be successfully caught by a 'ROT' (Reservation of title) clause: *Borden (UK) Ltd* v *Scottish Timber Products Ltd* (1979).

Any agreement by the seller to accept payment by instalments is likely to invalidate a ROT clause: *Hendy Lennox (Industrial Engines) Ltd* v *Grahame Puttick Ltd* (1984) and *Re Andrabell* (1984).

(i) Sheets of steel remain in ownership of Ironworks Limited and cannot be dealt with by Toolco Ltd's receiver.

(ii) The same applies to the half-made spanners.

(iii) The finished spanners have been sold, and title transferred to the wholesaler, so that they no longer belong to Toolco. The receiver cannot deal with them. As they have been fully paid for, Ironworks Limited has no claim to them either.

(b) If goods subject to a ROT clause are mixed with other goods to create a finished product, it is possible to provide that title to the finished product vests in the seller who has the benefit of the ROT clause, but careful wording is necessary.

If mixed goods are separable or can be converted to their original states a reservation of title clause can still be effective: *Hendy Lennox (Industrial Engines) Ltd* v *Grahame Puttick Ltd* (1984).

It would seem that the buyer will not have title to the finished product, and cannot therefore (i) create a charge in the seller's favour, or (ii) pass title to a sub-purchaser: *Clough Mill Ltd* v *Martin* (1985).

A trust or joint ownership are unlikely.

A charge allows the seller to recover only what he is owed.

A charge allows a sub-purchaser to take good title subject to the charge or with the seller's interest being transferred to the sale proceeds, if the latter is agreed by the seller.

One problem with a charge is that it could be void against other creditors and a liquidator of the purchaser (Toolco Ltd) if not registered at the company's registry.

Author's comment

The length of the question appeared to be one reason for many candidates not attempting this question. However, candidates should realise that unnecessary facts are rarely quoted in examination questions, with all disclosed material being included for some reason. The more facts disclosed, the more information given, meaning (theoretically) the easier the answer. Also, many candidates failed to spot the main words of 'why' in (a) and 'alloy' in (b), along with the fact that (a) was worth approximately twice as many marks as (b) which meant that approximately twice as much time (and pen pushing) should have been spent on (a).

Question (Spring 1989)

(a) Describe the main differences between a fixed and a floating charge, and the advantages and disadvantages of each. (15)

(b) Can a bank take a fixed charge over a future book debt, and if so, how? (5)

[Total 20 marks]

Key words

(a) main differences	*(b) Can*
advantages	*fixed charge*
disadvantages	*future book debt*
	how?

Answer

This was very popular and usually very well done, especially in part a). Many candidates, however, are unsure about the effect of the appointment of an administrator.

(a) *Definition.* A fixed charge means that the property charged is encumbered, and cannot be dealt with except with the consent of the debenture holder. This may be inconvenient with many types of assets, where stock is bought in for sale, or for manufacture and sale. A floating charge means that the debtor can continue to deal with the assets in question, until the charge becomes fixed (crystallises) by reason of some term in it, or by the company ceasing business, or by the appointment of a receiver, or by the start of liquidation. See *Re Yorkshire Woolcombers' Assn*. This enables changing stock to be easily secured.

Types of assets. Fixed charges relate to specific assets named in the charge documents, and this may be cumbersome, and sometimes impossible, with changing assets. Floating charges may relate to a class of assets, or all a company's assets, and may include its whole undertaking (ie, its whole business, and goodwill, thus enabling the sale of the business, possibly a hived off part, as a going concern).

Who can give? Fixed charges can be given by individuals or companies. Floating charges can be given only by companies.

Administrators. Floating charges enable the debenture-holder to veto the appointment of an administrator. Fixed charges do not. If an administrator is appointed, he can sell floating charge assets (though the debenture-holder is still secured on the proceeds). The administrator cannot sell fixed charge assets except with the court's consent, and then he must get the best market price.

Payment priorities. Fixed charges have first priority in liquidation or receivership, while floating charges rank behind preferential creditors.

Charge priorities. Floating charges, being equitable, may be defeated by later legal charges, even if the later mortgagee knows of the floating charge, unless the floating charge has a prohibition against later charges, and the later mortgagee has actual notice of this.

12-months rule. Fixed charges are not subject to the 12-months rule. Floating charges are.

These were the main points, but others might be mentioned, and were rewarded. For example, a fixed charge on stocks and shares is not registered, but a floating charge is. A fixed charge on land is registered but a floating charge is not (except in the companies register).

(b) Yes, the type clause is called *Siebe Gorman* clause after the case in which they were held possible. The clause provided that the bank will have a fixed charge on the future book debts when they come into existence. It is vital to the success of the clause that the clause provides for payment of funds to the bank, and imposes a restriction on their free use (ie, the bank must consent to withdrawals: *Siebe Gorman* v *Barclays Bank; Re Brightlife*).

Author's comment

The above answer is far from exhaustive and other items that could be mentioned would include *Romalpa* clauses and the possible methods of overcoming them, judgment creditors, run down of assets (*Re Borax*) etc. All in all a general type of question on an area of the syllabus with which many candidates find difficulties. However, many candidates fail to achieve the maximum marks on (b) due to their lack of appreciation of the fact that under the fixed charge **all** debtor's money received must be paid to the floating charge holder's account, with the bank being able to reclaim any monies deposited elsewhere.

CHAPTER 19

Insolvency and securities

Syllabus requirements
● The effect of insolvency on securities.

■ Effect of insolvency on securities

Effect of insolvency of principal debtor on third party securities

Early repayment by principal debtor

If the principal debtor should clear the indebtedness, without pressure being brought to bear on him by the bank, there is a danger that the transaction could be reclaimed by the trustee/liquidator as a preference. The conditions for a preference being reclaimed are:

(i) the payment must be made voluntarily by the debtor (the bank would usually protect itself by the serving of formal demand, thus removing the interpretation that the payment was made voluntarily), and

(ii) at the time of the payment the debtor must have been insolvent or became insolvent as a result of the transaction, and

(iii) the transaction must have taken place within six months of the commencement of the insolvency (the order for individual insolvency and the petition/resolution for corporate insolvency), or 24 months if the party preferred is an associate or connected person, for example, if the guarantor is a director of the company debtor (*Re F P & C H Matthews* (1982)), or if the guarantor is the spouse of the debtor.

The result of the transaction being recalled as a preference is that, if the bank has released the guarantor from his liability, the bank could be left with an unsecured debt.

As you may or may not recall from Chapter fourteen, banks will include a clause in the guarantee document (or indeed any third party security document) stating that the guarantor/surety will not be released from liability until six (or 24 if an associate is involved) months have passed. The reason for the inclusion of such a clause should now be clear.

The realisation of third party security, the debtor being involved in insolvency proceedings

To all intents and purposes third party security can be ignored when proving in the insolvency of the principal debtor, in that the creditor does not have to inform the trustee/liquidator of its existence. Upon the realisation of third party security, the bank has the right to apply the funds to a suspense account and not directly to the account of the principal debtor. The bank has the right to do this due to the 'whole debt clause' included in its third party security document, and it will leave the bank free to claim for the full indebtedness in the estate of the debtor: *Re Sass* (1896).

Perhaps a numerical illustration would be of benefit. If we assume the following:

the bank debt is £20,000,
the bank recoups £10,000 from the guarantor,
a dividend of 50p per pound is declared (ie, the debtor can meet only half of his debts).

Option one: the bank places the money received to the debtor's account:

Debt	£20,000
less, amount received from guarantor	£10,000
Amount claimed in debtor's bankruptcy	£10,000
less, amount received from bankruptcy proceedings (dividend 50p in £)	£5,000
Loss	£5,000

Option two: bank places money received to a suspense account:

Debt	£20,000
amount claimed in debtor's bankruptcy	£20,000
less, amount received from bankruptcy proceedings (dividend 50p in £)	£10,000
less, amount received from guarantor (previously held in suspense account)	£10,000
Loss	Nil

The reasons for the placing of the amount received from the guarantor to a suspense account should now be clear.

Effect of insolvency of guarantor/surety

If the guarantor or surety should be involved in insolvency proceedings this will be grounds for serving formal demand on the principal debtor and enforcing the security. This will protect the position of the bank and will allow the bank to prove in the bankruptcy of the guarantor/surety.

Effect of insolvency of principal debtor on direct security

Options of a secured creditor

When a secured creditor becomes aware of the insolvency of the debtor he has four choices:

(i) Release the security and not prove in the insolvency. This is an unlikely course of action to follow.

(ii) Rely on the security and not prove at all. Although this would at first appear to be an attractive option it is not realistic for two reasons:
   (a) There may be a problem with the security that the bank would not be aware of until the security is released, for example, non-registration. It is unlikely that the bank would expose itself to this risk, when the option to prove is easily achievable.
   (b) The trustee/liquidator may object. This would be likely to occur where the security has a value considerably higher than the debt, whereby the trustee/liquidator may

insist that the asset be realised with the excess being used for the benefit of all the creditors.

(iii) Value the security and prove for the shortfall (must be at least £750). This option will normally be exercised where the security is not easily realisable, eg, land. Where there is a discrepancy between the value placed on the asset by the creditor and the trustee/liquidator the sale of the asset can be insisted upon.

(iv) Realise the security and prove for the shortfall (must be at least £750). Usually used where the security is easily realisable, such as stocks and shares or life policies. If the realisation should produce in excess of the debt the excess must be passed onto the trustee/liquidator and not to the debtor.

Order of distribution

As we discussed in Chapter nine, secured creditors rank in priority to all others in respect of the distribution of the bankrupt's funds. However, this is true only to the extent of the secured element of their debt; they will have to prove as unsecured creditors for the balance. It is important therefore to realise that one creditor can appear as both a secured creditor and an unsecured creditor and possibly even in a third position if part of the unsecured element is preferential (for example, a wages account).

Appropriation of security proceeds

Once the security has been realised, the bank has a choice as to which debts the proceeds can be credited to. Obviously, if the bank has a preferential and a non-preferential debt, the bank would prefer to credit the monies to the non-preferential element, leaving the preferential debt intact. The other creditors would obviously prefer the proceeds to be applied to the preferential element, leaving a greater amount available for the unsecured creditors. In *Re William Hall (Contractors) Ltd* (1967), it was held that the bank had the right of appropriation and that it was permissible to credit the whole of the monies received to the non-preferential debt, leaving the preferential debt intact.

This ruling is in contrast with the ruling on combination on insolvency, illustrated by *Re Unit 2 Windows Ltd* (1985), in that any accounts combined must be combined on a proportionate basis. An account in credit will therefore be combined with a preferential and non-preferential debt in strict proportion with the level of debt in each account.

Direct security and preferences

Where a bank takes direct security from the debtor there is always a possibility that either the giving of the security is a preference or the debtor obtained the asset offered as security via a preference. The possibilities of either occurring are thought to be remote, the bank being able to take comfort from *Re F.L.E. Holdings Ltd* (1967). In this case the execution of a legal charge in favour of the bank was held not to be a preference as the only intention by the creditor was to remain on good terms with the bank, not actually to prefer it. Thus as there was no intention voluntarily to prefer the bank the claim failed.

Section 342 Insolvency Act 1986 states that the court may agree to reinstate the security providing the bank acquired its interest (the charge) in the property in good faith, for value and without any notice of the relevant circumstances.

Floating charge and insolvency

As discussed in the previous chapter, a floating charge created within the twelve months prior to the commencement (the date of petition/resolution) of the winding up of a company may be declared invalid and unenforceable: s.245 Insolvency Act 1986. The company must be insolvent at the time of giving the charge or giving the charge must have resulted in the company becoming insolvent. However, the floating charge is invalid only for monies outstanding at the time of the charge and is valid for new monies lent. Therefore *Clayton's Case* applies in the bank's favour. For a full discussion, including case references, see Chapter eighteen.

Legal charge over partly paid shares

You may or may not recall that one of the major disadvantages of partly paid shares as security is that the bank (as legal owner) may be called upon to meet any subsequent calls on the shares should the issuing company be wound up, and that this liability may be present not only during the term of the bank holding the shares as security but also for up to twelve months later. Again this has been fully discussed in Chapter sixteen and if the mechanics of this ruling are not fully understood, then the section on partly paid shares as security should be re-read.

▌ Summary

The effect of insolvency on securities is an important area and at least one former chief examiner felt that the relationship was extremely important because 'insolvency dictates why the banks have adopted the procedures as they have'. By this he was passing comment on such things as the whole debt clause, the retention of third party security, the appropriation of the proceeds of realised security etc. It is for this reason that it has been included in its own separate (although small) chapter to give it the importance it merits.

FACT SHEET
***

Insolvency and securities

1. Insolvency of principal debtor and third party security
(a) Early settlement by principal debtor. Possible preference, conditions need to be known, bank can protect itself by serving formal demand or by retaining the guarantee.
(b) Realisation of third party security. Place funds received to suspense account, prove for full amount of debt; *Re Sass* (1896).

2. Insolvency of guarantor/surety
Call in debt, prove in insolvency of guarantor.

3. Insolvency of principal debtor and direct security
(a) Options. The four options need to be known and when each is used.
(b) Order of distribution. Secured creditors receive their share first, but only to limit of the security held. Can prove as unsecured creditor for any shortfall.

(c) Appropriation of realisation proceeds. *Re William Hall (Contractors) Ltd* (1967), funds received placed to non-preferentials debt, leaving preferential debt intact.

(d) Preference. Rarely affect bank in this situation, *Re F.L.E. Holdings Ltd* (1967), and s.342 Insolvency Act 1986.

(e) Floating charge and insolvency. 'Hardening period'; s.245 Insolvency Act 1986, invalid if company is wound up within 12 months of creation of floating charge, conditions must be known.

(f) Partly paid shares. If bank takes a legal charge it could be liable for any future calls.

As this chapter is merely a collection of relevant material, no direct question has (as yet) been set, but it is an important area for bankers and questions solely on this area of the syllabus are not unexpected.

Index